Baptism as an Event of Taking Responsibility

A New Reading of Romans 5:12–6:23

Pontien Ndagijimana Batibuka

© 2022 Pontien Ndagijimana Batibuka

Published 2022 by Langham Monographs
An imprint of Langham Publishing
www.langhampublishing.org

Langham Publishing and its imprints are a ministry of Langham Partnership

Langham Partnership
PO Box 296, Carlisle, Cumbria, CA3 9WZ, UK
www.langham.org

ISBNs:
978-1-83973-234-8 Print
978-1-83973-752-7 ePub
978-1-83973-753-4 Mobi
978-1-83973-754-1 PDF

Pontien Ndagijimana Batibuka has asserted his right under the Copyright, Designs and Patents Act, 1988 to be identified as the Author of this work.

All rights reserved. No part of this publication may be reproduced, stored in a retrieval system or transmitted, in any form or by any means, electronic, mechanical, photocopying, recording or otherwise, without the prior written permission of the publisher or the Copyright Licensing Agency.

Requests to reuse content from Langham Publishing are processed through PLSclear. Please visit www.plsclear.com to complete your request.

Scripture quotations marked (NIV) are taken from the Holy Bible, New International Version®, NIV®. Copyright © 1973, 1978, 1984, 2011 by Biblica, Inc.™ Used by permission of Zondervan.

Scripture quotations marked (NJB) are taken from *The New Jerusalem Bible*, published and copyright 1985 by Darton, Longman & Todd Ltd and *Les Editions du Cerf*, and used by permission of the publishers.

Scripture quotations marked (NRSV) are from the New Revised Standard Version Bible, copyright © 1989 National Council of the Churches of Christ in the United States of America. Used by permission. All rights reserved.

Scripture quotations marked (RSV) are from Revised Standard Version of the Bible, copyright © 1946, 1952, and 1971 National Council of the Churches of Christ in the United States of America. Used by permission. All rights reserved.

British Library Cataloguing-in-Publication Data
A catalogue record for this book is available from the British Library

ISBN: 978-1-83973-234-8

Cover & Book Design: projectluz.com

Langham Partnership actively supports theological dialogue and an author's right to publish but does not necessarily endorse the views and opinions set forth here or in works referenced within this publication, nor can we guarantee technical and grammatical correctness. Langham Partnership does not accept any responsibility or liability to persons or property as a consequence of the reading, use or interpretation of its published content.

Contents

Abstract ix

Abbreviations xi

Foreword xvii

Chapter One 1
Baptism in Romans 6 and the Idea of Taking Action
   1.1. The Research Question 1
   1.2. On Methodology 4
      1.2.1. Action is Not Always Physical: "Speech-Act Theory" 5
      1.2.2. Socio-Religious Approach to Romans 5:12–6:23 8
   1.3. Structure 16
   1.4. Two Presuppositions on Romans 5:12–6:23 17
      1.4.1. Romans 5:12–6:23: A Pericope on
           Transition and Action 17
      1.4.2. Baptism in Romans 6: Initiation as the Meaning 20
   1.5. Literature Survey: Action in Baptism, an Overlooked Aspect 25
      1.5.1. The Baptismal Candidate Considered as Passive 26
      1.5.2. Hints at Baptism as a Time of Action 36
   1.6. Conclusion 49

Chapter Two 51
The Four Stages of Entry into the New Life in Paul's Time
   2.1. Introduction 51
      2.1.1. Ethnic Origin of Believers in Rome 52
      2.1.2. Relevant Religious Settings and Structure of
           Chapter Two 55
   2.2. The Four Stages and the Mysteries 58
   2.3. The Four Stages and State Religions 71
      2.3.1. Initiation to Adulthood 72
      2.3.2. Entry into Marriage 76
   2.4. The Four Stages in Jewish Context 79
      2.4.1. Proselytes' Entry in Second Temple and Rabbinic
           Judaism 79
      2.4.2. Entry into the Qumran Community 91
   2.5. Summary 98

Chapter Three 101
Paul's Conversion and the Four Stages of Entry
   3.1. Introduction 101
   3.2. Methodological Issues in Connection with
       Paul's Conversion 102
   3.3. God's Light and Glory Given to Paul (Stage One) 109
   3.4. Blind But Fasting and Praying (Stage Two) 124
   3.5. Sealing Attachment to the New Way: Baptism
       (Stage Three) 131
   3.6. The After-Entry Life Anticipated in the Entry Process
       (Stage Four) 133
   3.7. Summary 137

Chapter Four 139
The Four Stages and Action in Romans 5:12–6:23
   4.1. Introduction 139
   4.2. Divine Action at the First Stage: ἡ χάρις τοῦ θεοῦ καὶ
       ἡ δωρεὰ ἐν χάριτι . . . Ἰησοῦ Χριστοῦ εἰς τοὺς πολλοὺς
       ἐπερίσσευσεν (5:15) 142
   4.3. Second Stage Action: Death to the Old Way of Life
       (ἀπεθάνομεν τῇ ἁμαρτίᾳ, 6:1–2) 147
       4.3.1. Stating the Issue 147
       4.3.2. Death to Sin and the Initiatory Act of Breaking
             with the Old Way 150
   4.4. Third Stage Action: The Ritual of Baptism, Sealing the
       Rejection of the Old and the Bond with the New (6:3–4) 162
   4.5. Fourth Stage: The After-Entry Life Embraced in the
       Transition Process 176
       4.5.1. βασιλεύσουσιν (5:17) and Initiatory Future in
             Romans 5:12–6:23 177
       4.5.2. Διὰ δικαιοσύνης (5:21): Forensic, or the Initiate's
             Righteous Life? 184
       4.5.3. Walking in the New Existence (ἐν καινότητι ζωῆς
             περιπατήσωμεν, 6:4–5) 192
       4.5.4. Serving the New Existence: The Slave Motif
             (6:6, 13–22) 199
   4.6. Summary 206

Chapter Five 207
   Conclusion
      5.1 Summary of Findings 208
           5.1.1. The Rite that Seals Entry, a Time for Action:
           Chapters Two and Three 208
           5.1.2. Baptism in Romans 6: A Time for Action 209
      5.2. Suggestions for Further Research 216
      5. 3. Achievement 222

Bibliography 225
   1. Books and Articles 225
   2. Intertestamental, Greco-Roman, Rabbinic and Early
      Christian Writings 245
   3. Reference Books 248

Abstract

This study offers a new understanding of ἐβαπτίσθημεν, "we were baptized" (Rom 6:3), setting it within the wider section of Romans 5:12–6:23, which is about the transition from one system of existence to another – from sin's rule to the reign of grace (cf. 5:21).

My study is that Paul's view of the believer's transition and baptism in this pericope encompasses both divine intervention and human action. As the literature review outlines, Romans 5–6 has usually been read with christological lenses. As a result, the agency of the initiand has been underestimated. Applying a socio-religious approach, this study argues that Paul's understanding of baptism involves the initiand in taking active responsibility, as implied by the initiation process. In line with the older view (associated with the *Religionsgeschichtliche Schule*) that Paul's understanding of baptism grew out of contemporary views of initiation in Greco-Roman society, this study suggests that initiation entailed four stages in which both divine and human action was taken, and that this may have influenced Paul's thinking. In particular, the study argues that the deliberate action of the believer, rather than the action of Christ, is the focus in key expressions like "we died to sin" (6:2), "we were baptized" (6:3), "we were buried with him" (6:4) and "will reign" (5:17). En route, our study also offers a new perspective on the old debate about whether the Damascus Road event is best seen as a conversion or a call.

To demonstrate this, the study is structured in five chapters. After an introduction outlining the methodology and literature survey, the second chapter proposes the four stages of initiation and the divine and human action that they imply, drawing upon both secular and religious initiation texts and processes at the time of Paul. In the third chapter, a similar inquiry is applied to Paul's own transition. Insights from Paul's world and experience in relation to divine and human agency in one's entry to a new life are considered as the fourth chapter examines whether these have influenced Paul's thinking in Romans 5:12–6:23. The fifth chapter is the conclusion.

Abbreviations

AB: The Anchor Bible
ABD: The Anchor Bible Dictionary
AC: Alcuin Club
ACCS/NT: Ancient Christian Commentary on Scripture: New Testament
ACW: Ancient Christian Writers
AE: Anthropology and Ethnology
Ag. Ap.: Against Apion (Josephus)
AGRL: Aspects of Greek and Roman Life
ANE: Ancient Near East
ANTC: Abingdon New Testament Commentaries
AOT: The Apocryphal Old Testament
Apoc. Zeph.: Apocalypse of Zephaniah
Ar. Rhet.: Art of Rhetoric (Aristotle)
Asc. Isa.: Ascension of Isaiah
b. Abod. Zar.: Abodah Zarah in *The Babylonian Talmud*
BDSS: *The Bible and the Dead Sea Scrolls*
BECNT: Baker Exegetical Commentary on the New Testament
BFC: La Bible en Français Courant
Bib: Biblica
Bibel/ES: Die Bibel / Einheitsübersetzung
Bibel/EÜ: Die Bibel / Elberfelder Übersetzung
Bibel/NDUMLuthers: Die Bibel / Nach der Deutschen Übersetzung Martin Luthers
Bib Int: Biblical Interpretation: A Journal of Contemporary Approaches
b. Ker.: Kerithoth in *The Babylonian Talmud*
BL: The Bampton Lectures

BLG: Biblical Languages: Greek
BNTC: Black's New Testament Commentaries
b. Pesah.: Pesahim in *The Babylonian Talmud*
BQ: *Baptist Quarterly*
BSac: *Bibliotheca Sacra*
BTB: *Biblical Theology Bulletin*
BTS: Biblical and Theological Studies
b. Yeb.: Yebamoth in *The Babylonian Talmud*
CBAA: The Catholic Biblical Association of America
CBQ/MS: The Catholic Biblical Quarterly Monograph Series
CCC: The Crossway Classic Commentaries
CCo: Cascade Companions
CEA: *Companion Encyclopedia of Anthropology*
CGD: *Collins German Dictionary*
CLCEGNT: *A Critical Lexicon and Concordance to the English and Greek New Testament*
Col.: column
Cons. Ap.: Consolatio Ad Apolllonium = A Letter of Condolence to Apollonius (Plutarch)
CRJNT: Compendia Rerum Judaicarum ad Novum Testamentum
CUP: Cambridge University Press
DA: *Dictionnaire de l'antiquité*
DEA: *Dictionnaire de l'ethnologie et de l'anthropologie*
DECA: *Dictionnaire encyclopédique du christianisme ancient*
Defec. Or.: De Defectu Oraculorum, The Obsolescence of Oracles (Plutarch)
Dir.: Director
DJG: *Dictionary of Jesus and the Gospels*
DNTB: *Dictionary of New Testament Background*
DPL: *Dictionary of Paul and His Letters*
DSS: The Dead Sea Scrolls
DSS/ HAGTET: *The Dead Scrolls: Hebrew, Aramaic, and Greek Texts with English Translations*
EB: Etudes bibliques
EC: *The Encyclopedia of Christianity*
EDNT: *Exegetical Dictionary of the New*

Testament
EDSS: Encyclopedia of the Dead Sea Scrolls
EKKNT: Evangelisch-Katholischer Kommentar zum Neuen Testament
EL: Entrée Libre
EQ: Evangelical Quarterly
ETR: Etudes théologiques et religieuses
ExpT: Expository Times
Fn.: Footnote
FC/NT: The Fathers of the Church: A New Translation
FRLANT: Forschungen zur Religion und Literatur des Alten und Neuen Testaments
GECNT: The Greek English Concordance to the New Testament
GEL: A Greek-English Lexicon
GELNT-OECL: A Greek-English Lexicon of the New Testament and Other Early Christian Literature
GGBB: Greek Grammar Beyond the Basics: An Exegetical Syntax of the New Testament with Scripture
GL/EU: The Gifford Lectures for 1909–1910
Her. Mal.: De Herodoti Malignitate, On the Malice of Herodotus (Plutarch)
Hist. Pel. War: History of the Peloponnesian War (Thucydides)
HL: The Hibbert Lectures
Hmn: Hermeneia
HTR: Harvard Theological Review
HUL: Hutchinson's University Library
HUP: Harvard University Press
IAI: Institut Africain International,
IBI: Introduction to Biblical Interpretation
ICC: The International Critical Commentary
IGNT: Idioms of the Greek New Testament
IHGEB: The Interlinear Hebrew/Greek English Bible
IM: Innovations in Mission
Int: Interpretation
IntBCTP: Interpretation: A Bible Commentary for Teaching and Preaching
ITG: Introduction to Theological German
IVP: InterVarsity Press

IVPNTS: IVP New Testament Series
J. Ant.: The Jewish Antiquities (Josephus)
JBL: Journal of Biblical Literature
Jos. As.: Joseph and Asenath
Ju.: Judith
KEKNT: Kritisch-exegetischer Kommentar über das Neue Testament
LCC: Library of Christian Classics
LCL: The Loeb Classical Library
LD: Lection Divina
LJPPSTT: The Literature of the Jewish People in the Period of the Second Temple and the Talmud
LNTS: Library of New Testament Studies
LXX: Greek Septuagint
MEA: Monographies ethnologiques africaines
m. Ed.: Eduyoth in *The Mishnah*
MFC: Message of the Fathers of the Church
m. hag.: Hagiga in *The Mishnah*
MJP: Messianic Jewish Publishers
MLO: Martin Luther: Oeuvres
m. Pesah.: Pesahim in *The Mishnah*
MUP: Manchester University Press
NAB: The New American Bible
NDT: New Dictionary of Theology
NEB: New English Bible
NIBC: New International Biblical Commentary
Nic. Et.: Nicomachean Ethics (Aristotle)
NIDB: The New Interpreter's Dictionary of the Bible
NIDNTT: The New International Dictionary of New Testament Theology
NIGTC: New International Greek Testament Commentary
NIV: The New International Version
NIV/IHEOT: NIV Interlinear Hebrew-English Old Testament
NJB: The New Jerusalem Bible
Neot: Neotestamentica
NovT: Novum Testamentum
NRSV: The New Revised Standard Version
NSBT: New Studies in Biblical Theology

NTCom: New Testament Commentary
NTD: Das Neue Testament Deutsch
NTIGF: Nouveau Testament Interlinéaire Grec/Français
NTL: New Testament Library
NTS: New Testament Studies
NTT: New Testament Theology
OCD: Oxford Classical Dictionary
ODJR: The Oxford Dictionary of the Jewish Religion
OTM: Oxford Theological Monographs
OTP: The Old Testament Pseudepigrapha
OUP: Oxford University Press
PCNT: Paideia Commentaries on the New Testament
PGL: A Patristic Greek Lexicon
PMI: Probe Ministries International
PSJCO: Princeton Symposium on Judaism and Christian Origins
PTMS: Pittsburgh Theological Monograph Series
PUF: Presses universitaires de France
Quaest. Exod.: Quaestiones et Solutiones in Exodum, Questions and Answers on Exodus (Philo)
Quaest. Gen.: Quaestiones et Solutiones in Genesin, Questions and Answers on Genesis (Philo)
RB: Revue Biblique
RD/IPC: The Road from Damascus: The Impact of Paul's Conversion on His Life, Thought, and Ministry
ref.: Reference
RSG: Regent's Study Guides
RSV: The Revised Standard Version
RV: The Revised Version
SAP: Sheffield Academic Press
SBib: Sources Bibliques
SB/LS: La Sainte Bible, Traduite d'après les textes originaux hébreu et grec, par
Louis Segond
SBS: Stuttgarter Bibelstudien
SBT: Studies in Biblical Theology

Sept: Septuaginta
SJT: *Scottish Journal of Theology*
SNT: Supplements Novum Testamentum
SNTIW: Studies of the NT and its World, ed. John Riches
SNTSMS: Society for New Testament Studies Monograph Series
SPB: Studia Post-Biblica
SPS: Sacra Pagina Series
SSE: *The Social Science Encyclopedia*
TDNT: *Theological Dictionary of the New Testament*
THNT: Theologischer Handkommentar zum Neuen Testament
TNTC: Tyndale New Testament Commentaries
TOB: La Traduction oecuménique de la Bible
t. Pesah.: *Pesahim* in *The Tosefta*
TPI: Trinity Press International
TPINTC: TPI New Testament Commentaries
Trans.: Translated by
TynB: *Tyndale Bulletin*
UPA: University Press of America
VE: *Vox Evangelica*
VGT: *The Vocabulary of the Greek Testament: Illustrated from the Papyri and Other Non-Literary Sources*
WBC: Word Biblical Commentary
WEC: The Wycliffe Exegetical Commentary
Wis.: *Wisdom of Solomon*
WJKP: Westminster John Knox Press
WJL: The William James Lectures, delivered at Harvard University in 1955.
WTJ: *Westminster Theological Journal*
WUNT: Wissenschaftliche Untersuchungen zum Neuen Testament
YUP: Yale University Press
ZGRS: Zondervan Greek Reference Series

Foreword

It gives me great pleasure to write the foreword to this book by Dr. Pontien Batibuka. I first met him when he arrived in London in September 2007 to begin his PhD work at London School of Theology – and needed immediately to be assisted with warmer clothes to cope with the British autumnal temperatures! Then began over four years of painstaking work that resulted in the book in your hands – a remarkable tour de force, when one considers that Pontien was working and writing in what was then his third language (English), on a project which required him to acquire a fourth (German). It was my privilege to accompany him through this work as his doctoral supervisor.

A glance at any of the pages will reveal the extent to which, and care with which, Pontien Batibuka engages with the necessary dialogue-partners in any PhD project, both the primary first-century sources and the contemporary scholarly evaluations of them. The result is a study that holds its head up high among contemporary readings of Paul, and of Romans 6 and the Pauline doctrine of baptism in particular.

From the start I remember that Pontien's concern was pastoral. He was concerned by what he saw among some converts to Christianity in his native Congo, namely a tendency to treat baptism as a social rite of passage undertaken without a deep-rooted sense of radical spiritual and behavioural reorientation. He felt instinctively that this was wrong, and that there must be solid grounds for making the case from within the New Testament that baptism betokens and entails radical change. But at the same time, he was concerned that some interpretations of Romans 6 actually reinforced this "passivity" among converts by emphasizing the "sacramental" nature of baptism as an action of God within which we are simply passive recipients of grace. He felt sure that this was wrong, and that Paul wanted the Romans to believe that baptism changed everything for them and that they had committed themselves to this change by being baptized. The problem, he thought, was that the passive verb "be baptized" sounds like we have something done to us, just as "dying to sin" (Rom 6:2) definitely does not sound like something involving decisive action!

So this may look like a "pure" piece of New Testament research, but it actually has powerful pastoral roots – and implications. As Pontien sought to develop the rather counter-intuitive case that "to die to sin" is to take decisive action, gradually his thesis about the "four stages" of initiation emerged. He then developed an argument to test this approach to the interpretation of Romans 6 by looking broadly at initiation in a wide variety of forms in the first-century Mediterranean world. He thought – and I agree – that a helpful approach to the interpretation of a passage like Romans 6 is to ask what would have been the instinctive assumptions of Paul's readers about baptism as the Christian initiation, since they (like Paul himself) were already familiar with other forms of initiation in their world. And since Paul himself had been through a dramatic "initiation" into Christian faith, it makes sense also to ask what would have been the theological residue of that, passed over into Paul's general view of Christian initiation.

His thesis is a brilliant illustration of the truth that context is everything, in biblical interpretation as much as elsewhere. The words that we speak, and the words that we hear, are laden, freighted with ideas and associations from within the cultures and contexts that surround us. And this is as true for the words of the Bible as it is for any other words! We are creatures rooted in particularity, and in the contexts of our lives we are all challenged to take action – to die to sin and to walk with Christ in the new life he opens up for us.

Supervisors do not have to agree with the work of the students whom they seek to support through to successful examination. I have certainly supervised successful theses with which I did not agree. But in Dr. Batibuka's case I am convinced: to die to sin is to take decisive action in breaking with our old life, and that action may be helpfully thought of as the second stage of a four-stage initiation process, anticipating the ongoing commitment to Christ, which is supremely expressed in our baptism and then shapes our whole existence.

I feel very privileged to have worked with Pontien on this project and am delighted now that it is "seeing the light of day" in this published form, so that the sacrifice of those London years, spent away from his family in that cold, very non-African climate, can bear further fruit within Pontien's ministry.

Steve Motyer
Watford, UK, September 2020

CHAPTER ONE

Baptism in Romans 6 and the Idea of Taking Action

1.1. The Research Question

S. Heald identifies various approaches for understanding the meaning of initiation in primitive societies; one approach is "looking to the subjective effects of ritual and the concepts of personhood mediated by the ritual process."[1] The subjective effect of baptism, in Romans 6, still requires attention. What do the clauses ἀπεθάνομεν τῇ ἁμαρτίᾳ, "we died to sin" (Rom 6:2) and ἐβαπτίσθημεν, "we were baptized" (v. 3) really mean? In these utterances, it looks like the baptizand is completely passive in "dying" and "being baptized" (cf. the passive form of the verbs). But these utterances do not necessarily refer to a passive state. What did the transition to Christian life mean to Paul and first-century Christians? By stating that in the process of becoming a Christian, the person "dies to sin" and "is baptized," does Paul mean the person is simply passive, or is he implying by these words that the person takes a serious responsibility to never again ἐπιμένω τῇ ἁμαρτίᾳ, "remain in sin" (6:1–2)?

The purpose of this study is to understand the full import of Romans 6, concerning the initiand's agency in baptism.[2] The ways in which the balance between divine and human agency in the Christian's transition and baptism

---

1. Heald, "Rites of Passage," 748–49; a Komo who undergoes circumcision proves he has power for fathering and takes this responsibility, W. de Mahieu, *Structures et symboles*, 26.

2. Thus, a biblical study on baptism; other ways include focusing on the history, or the doctrine of baptism, cf. Fisher, *Christian Initiation*, xii.

1

(which touches on the debate over "synergism"[3]) is understood by Pauline scholarship motivates us to consider whether in Romans 6 Paul shows baptism to be a time for action, or passivity. Some recognize that Paul's words in Romans 6:1–4 imply that the person takes action in baptism. This is Morris's idea when he states, "The aorist in the verb *died* points to an action rather than a state . . . Becoming a Christian is a decisive step."[4] Also focusing on the person concerned by baptism, Hodge states, "We died does not mean 'are dead,' nor 'have died,' but 'died.' It refers to a specific act . . ."[5] What Morris and Hodge do not show is how Paul and his readers should have understood baptism as implying taking such action.

Other scholars simply reject any idea that in Paul's thinking the believer takes action in baptism. For example, speaking of baptism in Romans 6 Käsemann states that "the activity of believers recedes completely behind what is done to them."[6] Also the view of Cuvillier is that "Le baptême tel qu'on peut le comprendre chez Paul n'est . . . pas d'abord lié à une décision de l'homme. Plus précisément, le baptême n'appartient pas à la sphère de la volonté humaine . . ."[7] Cuvillier insists on this when he reiterates, "Le baptême appartient à l'ordre de ce qui a été reçu comme don de Dieu. La volonté humaine n'est pas prise en compte."[8] The overall idea of Cuvillier is that the person is just passive in baptism. This is especially clear when he stresses, "Dans l'énoncé paulinien, c'est au contraire le statut passif du croyant qui est

---

3. In this study, often statements are made touching on the debate over "synergism," which is not our focus. The object of this debate is stated by P. Helm:
> How the divine will in its savingly gracious operations harmonizes with the human will is a special case . . . Even if it is said that such divine grace constitutes a *rescue*, it is still nevertheless a rescue which does not violate the distinctive powers of human nature but rather restores and redirects them. Such radical conclusions have been disputed by adopting less radical views of human need and of divine provision (Helm, "Will," 722 col. 2 [italics his]).

For more on synergism, see Helm's article and bibliography; Neuner, "synergism," 271–73 and bibliography; Nygren, *Romans*, 70–71.

4. Morris, *Romans*, 245 [italics his].
5. Hodge, *Romans*, 175.
6. Käsemann, *Romans*, 164.
7. Cuvillier, "Baptême chrétien," 168. Translation: Baptism, as it may be understood in Paul, is . . . not primarily attached to a decision of a human being. More precisely, baptism does not belong to the sphere of human will . . .
8. Cuvillier, 164. Translation: Baptism belongs to the nature of things that have been received as a gift of God. Human will is not taken into account.

souligné."⁹ Keck's view is no different when he states (on 6:5), "One is united with Christ by the rite of baptism, not by an act of will."¹⁰

It is clear from these views that the passive voice that Paul uses is the focus. This is evident when Beasley-Murray makes reference to the Lutheran view and states:

> The Lutherans are quite right in calling attention to the fact that the characteristic voice in Rom 6:1ff is *the passive*: we were baptized, we were buried, we have become planted with the likeness of Christ's death, we were crucified with Christ – these are all acts of grace and power so surely as our resurrection with Christ is an act of grace and power, deeds which we can simulate but never produce by our own efforts.¹¹

This shows that the focus is on the passive ἐβαπτίσθημεν, "we were baptized" (6:3), συνετάφημεν, "we were buried with" (v. 4) and συνεσταυρώθη, "[it] was crucified with" (v. 6). In this way, the agency of God (and his minister)¹² is the main focus. This study will show that these words imply more than the passivity of the believer. The passive form can hide an active sense. As Vanhoozer points out, communication involves more than grammar.¹³ This applies to events (including baptism) which Vanhoozer considers as "institutional facts."¹⁴ As Searle points out, institutional facts "mean or symbolize something beyond themselves"¹⁵ implying that they "involve a variety of physical movements, states, and raw feels [sic]."¹⁶ In other words, institutional

---

9. Cuvillier, 163. Translation: In Paul's idea, on the contrary what is underlined is the passive state of the believer.

10. Keck, *Romans*, 161.

11. Beasley-Murray, *Baptism*, 142 [italics mine].

12. This study considers that the priest acts on behalf of God; so e.g. T. F. Torrance's idea that Christ himself is the one baptising, cf. Torrence, *Theology in Reconciliation*, 83, 87. Dunn: "the baptizer saw himself acting as a representative of . . . Jesus," cf. Dunn, *Unity and Diversity*, 155.

13. Vanhoozer, *Is There Meaning*, 217; for a similar idea, Searle, *Speech Acts*, 16, 17.

14. Among such facts he mentions baptising, marrying, and commissioning, cf. Vanhoozer, 245. More on action of utterances linked to institutional facts, cf. Briggs, *Words in Action*, 210–211; Evans, *Logic of Self-Involvement*, 12, 66–68.

15. Searle, cited by Vanhoozer, *Is There Meaning*, 276 fn. 217; so also Bott, "Psychoanalysis and Ceremony," 217, 223–25.

16. Searle, *Speech Acts*, 51.

facts are more than passivity. As we will see this concerns the initiand, not only the initiator.

As will be outlined in the literature survey (with more in chapter 4), in general ἀπεθάνομεν τῇ ἁμαρτίᾳ ("we died to sin") has commonly been understood as meaning that Paul speaks of the death and action of Christ on the cross on behalf of believers. In this study, the intention is to see whether what Paul implies is an act of the believer, namely, an act of death which is different from Christ's action on the cross.

This study seeks to demonstrate that in Romans 5 and 6 Paul has in mind a baptismal process in which God takes action (cf. 5:15–18) and the convert also takes action. The study will seek to show how "to die to sin" (cf. ἀπεθάνομεν τῇ ἁμαρτίᾳ, "we died to sin," 6:2) and to ratify this death by a ritual (cf. ἐβαπτίσθημεν, "we were baptized," v. 3) are actions taken by the new convert during the process of his or her *passage* from sin to God. This balance of God's action and the believer's action during the person's transition from sin to God is the focus of this study. The study intends to examine whether divine and human agency in initiation shapes Paul's thinking about baptism in Romans 5–6 (see especially chapter 4). In order to understand this, one element which is considered in the study (see chapter 2) is whether this balance of divine and human action during the person's *passage* from one way of existence to another is present in the cultural reality of Paul and his readers. Also, since Paul speaks of a baptismal process that he has experienced himself (cf. "we," e.g. in 6:2–3), another aspect considered important in this study (see chapter 3) is how much this idea of divine and human agency is present in Paul's own transition to Christian existence. The methodology and structure adopted in this study will be now considered in order to explain further the importance of these parts and their connection.

1.2. On Methodology

To understand whether "to die to sin" (6:2) and to ratify this death by a ritual (6:3) are actions taken by the believer in his or her transition from sin to the Christian life, two elements are used. One element is speech-act theory according to which words (e.g. promises, oaths) imply serious action. In this thesis the role of this theory is limited to an ideological role of reminding us that words are deeds. Speech-act theory is referred to because it allows us in the analysis to bear in mind that such an expression as "we died to sin" can imply action, even if it does not denote effort. Also, the idea that the passive utterance "we were baptized" can imply action is explained by speech-act theory.

Another element of methodology that is used is the socio-religious approach to Paul's thinking about Christian initiation in Romans 5 and 6. Engberg-Pedersen suggests that one way of understanding Paul is a focus not on (just) theology but also "the ancient ethical tradition."[17] In this study, it is considered that "we died to sin" and "we were baptized" mean action (cf. speech-act theory) based on the idea of baptism as an initiation rite observed in the first century. The socio-religious element is more significant in this study because the framework of the whole study is based on this aspect.

The approach we adopt then is to read baptism in Paul against the Greco-Roman background; it is a Greco-Roman socio-religious reading. There are social methods for examining baptism which are distinctively "Christian" and theological, especially approaches that emphasise the Old Testament background to baptism, and the background in the ministries of Jesus and John the Baptist. This study has not sought to explore what these other approaches could show about the idea of taking action in baptism. As we will propose later, that might be a topic for further study.

On examination of the socio-religious life of Paul's time, a pattern of four stages of initiation and action emerges which is the means that is used to show whether in Paul's thinking baptism is about action or passivity. In this study, evidence is provided that these four stages can be discerned (with variation) in all sorts of initiation, both religious and secular, Graeco-Roman, Jewish and Christian. For more clarity, the two methodological elements and their importance for this study are explained.

1.2.1. Action is Not Always Physical: "Speech-Act Theory"

Actions need not be strongly physical to imply that a serious responsibility is taken. This idea is implied when A. Kuen reflects on baptism and states:

> Si nous comparons nos gestes symboliques à nos gestes efficaces, nous constatons que les premiers nous engagent bien plus que

---

17. Engberg–Pedersen, *Paul and Stoics*, 1.

les seconds. Car nous exprimons par eux nos options fondamentales et existentielles: signer un acte a une portée bien plus grande qu'écrire notre nom sur un papier, prononcer un seul mot devant le maire au moment du mariage lie davantage que toutes les déclarations passionnées des amoureux.[18]

There is a link between this idea of Kuen and Paul's words in Romans 6. Ἀπεθάνομεν, "we died" (6:2), denotes event or state rather than action *per se*. Also, ἐβαπτίσθημεν, "we were baptized" (6:3), is in the passive. Does Paul mean by these that action is taken by the baptizand, or does he mean just passivity? This study is intended to demonstrate that despite their grammatical form these verbs imply that the believer takes action. To show this we rely on speech-act theory which is in line with Kuen's idea. As Evans shows, according to this theory, "any language can involve a speaker logically in something more than a mere assent to a fact."[19] When the words "we were baptized" are considered in this way, Paul's utterance implies action. Evans shows a parallel to this when he speaks of "*institutional* action."[20] The example is when one says, "The Queen has appointed me as her steward."[21] Even though in the actual appointment the steward is passive, the appointment implies a process of application, deliberation, planning and acceptance in which the potential steward is far from passive. He or she was involved in taking a serious responsibility when the Queen was entrusting him or her with the task. We should note that the sense of the sentence is the same in the passive "I was appointed" just as in the passive "we were baptized."

Thus, the words "I was appointed" imply action. It is more than just recognizing a fact. As Evans states, by making this utterance the person is saying, "I commit myself to future conduct in accordance with the status and role"[22]

---

18. Kuen, *Baptême hier*, 17. Translation:
    If we compare our symbolic gestures to our effective gestures, we find that the former engage us much more than the latter. Because through them we express our fundamental and existential options: signing an act has a far greater significance than writing our name on a piece of paper, pronouncing a single word in front of the mayor at the time of marriage binds more than all the passionate declarations of lovers.
19. Evans, *Logic of Self-Involvement*, 11.
20. Evans, 12 [italics his].
21. Evans, 12.
22. Evans, 12.

which are related to this appointing. Our study focuses on the transition of a person to the new status and considers it as the time when the idea "I commit myself" takes effect.

To say that "we died to sin" and "we were baptized" mean action, we are assuming that action takes place even when physical movement and effort is not used. Speech-act theory recognizes this idea and serves as a guide. The examples from Evans belong to this theory. Austin, the founder of speech-act theory, provides more on how words stand for action.

Austin shows that it is commonly understood that "doing an action must come down to the making of physical movements with parts of the body."[23] His view is that an action can be made by words, and sometimes words, too, do not show action in a direct manner, because "to utter the sentence . . . is not to *describe* my doing of what I should be said in so uttering to be doing."[24] This shows that words may imply an action even though they may not "describe" it clearly. This is clearly demonstrated in more detail when Austin speaks of "performance utterances" stating,

> . . . if a person makes an utterance of this sort we should say that he is *doing* something rather than merely *saying* something. Suppose, for example, that in the course of a marriage ceremony I say, as people will, "I do" – (sc. take this woman to be my lawful wedded wife). Or again, suppose that I tread on your toe and say "I apologize". Or suppose I say "I bet you sixpence it will rain tomorrow". In all these cases it would be absurd to regard the thing that I say as a report of the performance of the action that which is undoubtedly done – the action of betting, or christening, or apologizing. We should say rather that, in saying what I do, I actually perform that action when I say "I do" (sc. take this woman to be my lawful wedded wife), I am not reporting on a marriage, I am indulging in it.[25]

---

23. Austin, *Philosophical Papers*, 178–79; cf. Austin, *How to Do Things*, 4–11.
24. Austin, *How to Do Things*, WJL, 6 [italics his].
25. Austin, *Philosophical Papers*, 235; cf. also Austin, *How to Do Things*, 4–11.

What Austin says applies to baptism and to initiation. Strong and life-binding utterances were a key aspect of transition to new life in antiquity. One example is the proselyte's pledge as showed in these words:

> One who comes to be made a proselyte in the present time is to be asked: "why dost thou come to be made a proselyte? Dost thou not know that at this time Israel is afflicted, buffeted, humiliated and harried, and that sufferings and sore trials come upon them?" If he answers: "I know this, and am not worthy," they are to accept him immediately.[26]

This shows a pledge to attach to Israel's life and honour it despite any cost that this would mean. A serious responsibility is taken, signifying action. This way of taking on responsibility characterizes initiation into mysteries, state religions and Judaism as the second chapter will show.

In the words quoted from Austin, he uses the expression "what verbs, as used on what occasions." These words are part of his idea that events or occasions can make a word to mean action even if commonly that word does not show action. The verb "to die," that Paul uses in Romans 6:2, is such a word. "To die" has different connotations, depending on when it occurs. In Romans 7:2 this verb is in its usual meaning denoting a state. However in 6:2 to die means to take action against sin (cf. also "to die to the Law": Rom 7:4, Gal 2:19; "die to sins": 1 Peter 2:24, Col 2:20; Gal 6:14). In this way "to die" becomes a "new idiom," in Austin's words.[27] In this case as Austin says, it has been moved from "ordinary language" and "semantic conventions,"[28] to a position of an "extraordinary case."[29]

1.2.2. Socio-Religious Approach to Romans 5:12–6:23

As Mead speaks of the method of the *Religionsgeschichtliche Schule* of the late nineteenth century he recognizes that this method could still "lead to greater understanding of the Bible's religious beliefs and practices and the ways they

---

26. *b. Yeb.* 47a–b (if not indicated otherwise, all references to *b. Yeb.* are translations from I. W. Slotki (trans. and ed.), 'Yebamoth,' *b. Seder Nashim*, vol. 1, ed. by I. Epstein, London: Soncino Press, 1936); this utterance as action, e.g. Barrett, *New Testament Background*, 165.
27. Austin, *Philosophical Papers*, 69.
28. Austin, 68.
29. Austin, 68.

should form and inform theological interpretation."[30] As this study will show (especially the literature survey and chapter 4), Romans 5:12–6:23 is about the socio-religious idea of moving from one religious existence to another. Hence, we concur with Mead that a socio-religious reading is necessary to understand what Paul says in this pericope. This religious approach is necessary to demonstrate whether Paul means action when he says "we died to sin" and "we were baptized."

As Gorman recognizes, "Paul is a religious figure."[31] The person's transition from one existence to another, as Romans 5:12–6:23 shows, is also a religious idea (more on this in the second chapter). This pericope has essentially been interpreted with a focus on Christ and his deed. This is Ponsot's understanding, who considers Romans 6:1–11 to be "christocentrique."[32] Schreiner also shares this view when he speaks of the connection between dying to sin, baptism, and burial with Christ (6:2–4). He points out that the "emphasis" is on "the historic and definitive death and resurrection of Christ," not on "baptism" as an event.[33] This focus on Christ is adopted even when it is recognized that Paul thinks of initiation. Carlson shows this when he states,

> an appreciation of what initiation entailed in the ancient world is significant. It helps us to understand how Paul interprets the common rite of Christian initiation in relationship to the sacred story of the Christ-event and to the reality that the Christ-event negates, inaugurates, and anticipates as the center of God's plan of salvation.[34]

These elements show that the interpretation of the pericope has been focusing on what Paul says about Christ.

This thesis focuses on the person undergoing the transition to a new existence, as what Romans 5:12–6:23 is about. As this chapter will show, the transition from living under sin to the Christian life is the idea in Romans 5:12–6:23. Paul's focus is on this change to a new religious existence and on

---

30. Mead, *Biblical Theology*, 39.
31. Gorman, *Reading Paul*, 1.
32. Ponsot, *Romains*, 109. Translation: Christocentric.
33. Schreiner, *Romans*, 310.
34. Carlson, "Role of Baptism," 257.

the person involved in this transition. In other words, the pericope shows a socio-religious reality.[35]

Some scholars have recognized this, Wedderburn being one of them; he states that what Paul is showing concerning baptism is that "its effect is rather upon the meaning of a person's life both to that person and to those around him or her; its meaning is pastoral and social (or ecclesiological) rather than theological, controlling how that individual sees himself or herself and how his or her fellow-Christians and non-Christians regard that person."[36] Carlson also acknowledges that what we have here is "existential (and social) transformation, negation and incorporation, obliterated and newly established boundaries . . ."[37] The socio-religious reality of baptism is also recognized by Gisel, when he states, "le baptême renvoie à des dimensions anthropologiques plus larges. Se condensent du coup en lui les données d'un *rite de passage* aux facettes multiples, existentielles, communautaires, sociales."[38] In the light of this, Gisel suggests that "une prise en compte des réalités anthropologiques . . . peut nous délivrer d'une focalisation . . . sur le seul moment du salut."[39]

This sociological and religious meaning of baptism is very much present in the early Church. For example, Finn notes that the baptismal process and the acts that this process included "had important social function,"[40] because they marked the "passage from a hostile society with powerful institutions of social control (Rome) to a new community."[41] Also the process had "religious significance,"[42] because it meant that believers came out of the rule of Satan to living God's way. They understood that "the power of their old way of life, lived under Satan's rule, had to be broken gradually by religious" acts, which included "instruction, exorcism, renouncing Satan and his (Roman)

---

35. Ponsot's view is that only in 6:15–23 Paul's approach is "plus anthropologique," cf. *Romains*, 109.

36. Wedderburn, *Baptism and Resurrection*, 370.

37. Carlson, "Role of Baptism," 257.

38. Gisel, *Pourquoi baptiser*, 8 [italics his]; also R. Gounelle speaks of "la fonction sociale du baptême," cf. "Le baptême aux temps patristiques," 184–85, cf. 68–78 for detail. Translation: Baptism refers to more wide anthropological dimensions. In that case, in it come together the data of a *rite of passage* with facets that are multiple, existential, communal, and social.

39. Gisel, *Pourquoi baptiser*, 72. Translation: "To take into account anthropological realities . . . could release us from focalising . . . on the only one moment of salvation."

40. Finn, *Early Christian Baptism and the Catechumenate: Italy*, 45.

41. Finn, 45.

42. Finn, 45.

legions, professing new allegiance to the Trinity, to the Church and to the resurrected life."[43]

In the light of these aspects, we adopt a socio-religious approach. Our reference is especially Malina's "social context approach," which consists of identifying the social "domain of reference or scene referred to by the text" and "then using the identified domain of reference as the larger frame within which to situate the meanings proposed in the text as far as this is possible."[44] The social domain of reference that is discerned in Romans 5:12–6:23 is the *passage* from one way of existence to another. To be more precise, this historical approach is the key to our study of what Paul's idea about baptism is in Romans 5:12–6:23. However, since the study is dealing with the meaning of words, literary elements will be associated with the historical aspect, as Barton suggests.[45]

Hence to understand whether the action of the initiand is implied in "death to sin" (6:2) and the ritual that seals this death (6:3), attention is given to how initiation worked in Paul's time. From Paul's cultural world, four stages (features)[46] of action in initiation are detected and are used to grasp what he means in Romans 5:12–6:23. The idea of stages in initiation has been applied, but we are suggesting a different view not only about their number, but also a new way of defining these stages.[47] The way they are designated in this study is intended to demonstrate whether initiation consisted of the action of both

---

43. Finn, 45.
44. Malina, *Christian Origins*, 4.
45. Barton, "Social-Scientific Approaches," 892 col. 1.
46. Is "stages" the right word here? J. Ferguson speaks of "features," cf. *Religions of Roman Empire*, 99. R. Reitzenstein calls them "actions," cf. *Hellenistic Mystery-Religions*, 196. E. Hatch says "stages or acts," cf. *Influence of Greek Ideas*, 284, fn. 3. The word "stages" is chosen because the divine action generally stands as the basis for the rest (so stage 1) and the new life is the purpose for the process (thus stage 4).
47. The stages are often seen as three. Van Gennep speaks of "separation, transition, and incorporation," cf. *Rites of Passage*, 93–95. Ferguson speaks of three: "purification, communion with gods, promise of life beyond the grave," cf. *Religions of Roman Empire*, 99; Reitzenstein also three: "baptism, transformation of the temple, banquet," cf. *Hellenistic Mystery-Religions*, 196; and Sorel, "Mystères d'Eleusis," 1486 col. 2. Hatch shows five: κάθαρσις – purification, σύστασις – rites and sacrifices, τελετή or μύησις – prior initiation, ἐποπττεία – the higher initiation, and this leading to παράδοσις τῶν ἱερῶν – the holiest act, cf. *Influence of Greek Ideas*, 284 fn. 3. Tertullian shows three: acquaintance with God, breaking with sin, and undergoing the water ritual, cf. *On Penance* 6, in Tertullian, *Treatises on Penance*, 25–26.

the deity and of the initiand. The four stages of action that are detected in religious initiation in antiquity are as follows:

(1) The first stage is the encounter with the deity and the salvation that takes place. Tertullian speaks of this as "the first baptism of the catechumen" and he means the time when the catechumen has come "in contact with the Lord."[48] At this stage the action is divine; the candidate is rather passive. As the fourth chapter of this study will show, in our pericope a clear parallel to this is God's justification of sinners (5:12–18). But as G. E. Wright states, "Man alone among the creatures of earth is able to receive and act upon God's visitation."[49] The divine act enables (but does not remove) what the candidate does in his or her entry process. Stages two to four focus more on the candidate.

(2) The second stage is the liminal state of standing in a sort of vacuum between the past and the new. This is done by the seclusion of the initiand, which was a practice in ancient Greece[50] as it is still today in the communities that continue to live by primitive standards.[51] In Greco-Roman life, initiation meant a "seclusion of the initiands from everyday life to a marginal existence."[52] This was the "interstitial status" for the initiand, as Burkert puts it.[53] The purpose for this vacuum between two existences is to experience a death to one's old way of life. The characteristics of this stage show this idea of death, as is evident from anthropological reflections, such as Obelitala's statement:

> Parler de l'initiation, c'est d'abord envisager les épreuves, souvent très pénibles, qui aguerrissent et préparent à la vie sociale. Cet aspect de l'initiation est sinon le plus important, en tout cas le plus difficile pour le novice qui doit endurer de violentes agressions tant physiques que morales.[54]

---

48. Tertullian, *On Penance* 6, 26.
49. Wright, *God Who Acts*, 88.
50. Obelitala, *Initiation en Afrique noire*, 36.
51. Turner, *Forest of Symbols*, 93–111; Batulukisi, "Ngindi and Mukanda," 86; Gennep, *Rites of Passage*, 81; Lembezat, *Populations païennes du Nord-Cameroun*, 183; Wei, *Paradis tabou*, 94.
52. Burkert, *Greek Religion*, 260.
53. Burkert, 260.
54. Obelitala, *Initiation en Afrique noire*, 79, cf. 49, 57 on death; also Gennep, *Rites of Passage*, 81; Lembezat, *Populations païennes*, 183; Lewis, "Magic, Religion and Rationality," 583. Translation:
> Talking about initiation means first of all considering the often very painful

As Zahniser describes, at the *liminal* phase the candidate experiences a sort of "chaotic limbo condition of transition."[55] The person experiences a "state of non-being in order to be reborn into a new and unknown reality."[56] For this state of non-being to imply a serious sense of death, it often includes very threatening experiences. In the patristic period, the time to renounce Satan was conceived as a moment where "everything . . . is frightening and terrible" and one had to "stand in fear."[57] There were other hard things to experience, as the second chapter of this study explains.

Hence, the initiation death was not just a metaphor; the initiand endured some hardship that symbolized it. Furthermore, to die did not mean to do something to the initiand while he or she was passive, rather it meant a personal act. The liminal phase between the old and the new is not just a passive state. As Zahniser recognizes (citing V. Turner), the limbo state is intended to stir up "creativity,"[58] because it is a state in which one's previous "social roles" are "abolished"[59] and "little is taken for granted."[60]

So action is the core of this stage. As Jeffers notes, in the Greco-Roman religious life the goal is that the candidate will "*achieve* union" with both deity and fellow adherents.[61] Due to the fact of being between the old and the new, sometimes the liminal stage is described as a confinement, but this is no passivity. As Reitzenstein shows, in the mysteries the word for this episode is κατοχή.[62] This word means "detention,"[63] "to hold fast, keep, possess."[64] So the

---

trials that harden and prepare for social life. This aspect of initiation is if not the most important, in any case the most difficult for the novice who has to endure violent attacks, both physical and moral.

55. Zahniser, *Symbols*, 93.
56. Zahniser, 94.
57. Ordo of Constantinople, cf. Finn, *Early Christian Baptism and the Catechumenate: West and East Syria*, 99.
58. Zahniser, *Symbols*, 95.
59. Zahniser, 93.
60. Zahniser, 95.
61. Jeffers, *Greco-Roman World*, 96 [italics mine].
62. Its word group includes κατέχειν / κατοχος, cf. Reitzenstein, *Hellenistic Mystery-Religions*, 245–48. The verb κατέχω which means "to hold back, to detain, to retain, to possess," see https://www.blueletterbible.org/lexicon/g2722/kjv/tr/0-1/. The word κατοχή means "possession, occupation," see https://en.bab.la/dictionary/greek-english/κατοχή
63. *PGL*, s.v. 'κατοχή.'
64. *PGL*, s.v. 'κατέχω.'

initiand is in a sort of "confinement, imprisonment."⁶⁵ Yet this is more than being just a prisoner: the initiand takes action. As Reitzenstein notices, the purpose is to dedicate oneself "to serve and honor" the deity.⁶⁶ The κατοχή of the initiand of the cult of Sarapis is such that the person gives "himself to the deity (Sarapis)..., worships the goddess (Astarte), and for eighteen years guards her temple."⁶⁷ As the second chapter of this study will show in detail, the goal of this episode is a radical break with the old way (thus the idea of dying to something) and being strongly attached to the new.

(3) The third stage is the ritual (e.g. the water baptism itself) that seals the entry. The fact of submitting oneself to the ritual ratifies and seals the decisions made in stage two. The ritual is undergone in the presence of the gods and fellow members. This makes it a serious act of responsibility. In fact, by undergoing such a ritual, the initiand pledges to the god(s) and the community that the new status that he or she has embraced will be seriously observed. As Gounelle notes, the baptismal process shows this feature of initiation that may be described as "l'aspect collectif" (the collective aspect).⁶⁸ In the early church, the ritual of water baptism implied this agency of the baptizand. Basil and Origen make that point.⁶⁹

(4) The fourth stage consists of the new life itself. This is the way the person is to lead his or her life when he or she has become an initiate member of this new community. This new way of living begins in initiation. It is embraced and practised from the time of the transition. As the Ordo of Constantinople shows, the bishop says to the catechumen,

> See that you guard yourselves. You have renounced the devil, hate him until the end. You have submitted yourselves to Christ, confess him until your last breath. Die in this orthodox confession, and do not be shipwrecked in the faith. I have hesitated to say these hard things to you. Henceforth, you will know how to

---

65. Reitzenstein, *Hellenistic Mystery-Religions*, 246.
66. Reitzenstein, 247.
67. Reitzenstein, 247.
68. Gounelle (referring to *Apostolic Tradition* 21), cf. "Baptême aux temps patristiques," 184, for more 184–85.
69. Basil speaks of "concluding an agreement" by baptism, cf. Basil, *Baptism*, cited by Ferguson, *Baptism*, 585. Origen shows this in his "I" covenant idea, cf. Translation from von Balthasar, *Origen*, 187, section 457.

take care of yourselves . . . I have told you these awe-inspiring things in advance that the sword may not cut into this people and carry off one soul.[70]

This shows that the new life starts at the initiation. The bishop says that they have renounced the devil, that they already hate him, and have submitted to Christ. They have started the new life, which then the church minister seriously commands them to keep until death. More detail on this idea that the new existence begins at the initiation is given in the second chapter. As we will see in chapter 4, the effect of this on the meaning of Romans 5:12–6:23 is that the parenesis in 6:11–23 should be understood as referring not to a life that just begins after one's baptism, but to the responsibility that the Christian has taken during his or her baptismal initiation. In the same line of thought, the future that Paul uses in the pericope is the future of initiation (a present future), rather than eschatological. As we will see in chapters 2 and 4, these aspects link with what in Paul's time initiation (its fourth stage) appears to show.

It is difficult to ascertain how much Paul's thinking about the Christian transition and baptism in Romans 5–6 was influenced by cultural initiation patterns. Paul may have turned against the "worldly" pattern in his understanding of baptism, or radically modified it.[71] On the other hand, as E. Dassmann points out, "Paul, qui a voulu se faire "tout à tous". . . écrivait aux Grecs et aux Romains en s'adaptant à leurs caractères différents."[72] (Paul, who wanted to be 'everything to all' . . . wrote to the Greeks and Romans, adapting to their different characters). We are not presuming the presence of the four stages in Paul (echoes are outlined at the third chapter) just as in his contemporary society, but trying out what an exegesis of Romans 5–6 looks like, when read against the background of the presumptions about initiation that Paul's readers would have had.

---

70. The Ordo of Constantinople, cited by Finn, *Early Christian Baptism: Syria*, 100.

71. E.g. Cuvillier, "Evangile et traditions," 7–8; Viard, *Saint Paul: Romains*, 141; A. Schweitzer sees a difference between the "receiving" in Paul and the mysteries, cf. *Mysticism of Paul*, 374.

72. Cf. Loi, Dassmann, *et al.* "Paul," 1940 col. 1, referring to 1 Cor 9:22.

1.3. Structure

In the light of these stages of initiation, to understand whether in Romans 5:12–6:23 the believer's move from sin to the realm of Christ shows divine and human agency, this study is structured in five chapters. After this first and introductory chapter, the next chapters will be as follows:

The second chapter is an inquiry into the way initiation or entry to a new existence worked in the religious setting of Paul's time. We take into account Judaism and Gentile (mystery and state) religions, because of Paul's contact with both worlds, and as we shall see his readers in Rome likely had initially been attached to these religions before their conversion. The purpose is to find how much Paul's social *milieu* informs us about the religious transition. As we will see, despite some differences from the various religious contexts which are considered in this study, there is evidence that initiation comprised the four stages that have been outlined earlier and these stages comprise the agency of both the god and the initiand.

In the third chapter we examine whether the four stages of initiation are present in Paul's own move from being a Pharisee to Christianity. As we will see, there is evidence that the agency of both God and Saul characterizes Paul's transition as well. When Paul says "I am compelled to preach the Gospel" (1 Cor 9:16), it appears that this expresses his accountability not only to God who changed him and commissioned him, but also to the responsibility he personally endorsed. In this section that is about Paul's transition, we consider Paul's own account of it in his letters, but we also consider the Acts accounts because of the whole progression of the Damascus Road event that Luke provides. The four stages are more evident in Acts where Luke tells the story. More detail is given in the third chapter.

The fourth chapter is an analysis of Romans 5:12–6:23. In this part the purpose is to show what impact the elements found in chapters 2 and 3 have on Romans 5:12–6:23, where Paul deals with the transition from a life under sin to a life under the rule of God.

The fifth chapter is the conclusion. This part consists of three sections. The first section gives a summary of our findings. For further research, the second section proposes some ideas that were touched upon in this study, but not expanded upon. The third section summarises what we consider to be the achievement attained.

Before we come to these chapters, a survey of the scholars' understanding of the balance of the divine and the human agency in baptism is considered. Also, two presuppositions are made about Romans 5:12–6:23. These presuppositions, which are to be examined in the study, are important because they are essential to demonstrating how the four stages shape Romans 5:12–6:23.

1.4. Two Presuppositions on Romans 5:12–6:23

1.4.1. Romans 5:12–6:23: A Pericope on Transition and Action

For understanding whether the four stages of initiation are present in Romans 5:12–6:23, two presuppositions are considered. The first is that in this pericope the transition from sin to God is the idea which is on Paul's mind. The focus in this section is on showing how the believer's transition of which baptism is a part covers this pericope, and how this is essential for explaining whether to die to sin (6:2) and to undergo the ritual of water (6:3) show the baptizand's action.

As will be shown in this part, it is generally recognized that the idea of a transition to new life emerges in Romans 5–6. This idea is considered here with a focus on how this unit of Romans fits with the hypothesis of the four stages of initiation.

Very often only some aspects of 5:12–6:23 are considered when approaching the issue of the transition from sin's rule to living the Christian way. This is reflected in the views concerning the text that baptism covers. Some scholars' view is that only Romans 6:2–5 is about baptism.[73] Others recognize that Romans 6:1–11 (or 14) deals with baptism.[74] Still others think that the

---

[73]. E.g. Tannehill, *Dying and Rising*, 9; Moo, *Romans 1–8*, 371, 380; Dunn, *Baptism*, 139–140; also Dunn, *Romans 1–8*, 308; Flemington, *New Testament Doctrine*, 61; Osborne, *Romans*, 149.

[74]. E.g. Käsemann, *Romans*, 159; Bruce, *Epistle of Paul*, 128; Fitzmyer, *Romans*, 430; Schlier, *Der Römerbrief*, 190.

entire chapter covers the subject of baptism,[75] or it is with reference to Paul's theme of the change of reign from sin to God that Romans 6 is considered.[76]

This study considers 5:12–6:23 as the unit that deals with the transition from sin to God.[77] Baptism then (6:1-4) is part of the subject of the transition from sin to God that spans 5:12 to 6:23. Thus this transition provides the framework in which the meaning of to die to sin (6:2) and to undergo the water ritual (vv. 3-4) will be considered, particularly whether they imply passivity or action.

The importance of Romans 5:12–6:23 as the unit for understanding what "we were baptized" implies rests on the fact that in this pericope Paul structures his thought in a way which shows that during the believer's transition there is both divine action and the person's agency. The detail on this will be given in the fourth chapter of this study which is the exegetical analysis of this pericope, but this balance of divine and human agency in Paul's thinking on Christian initiation in this text is briefly outlined here. The pericope begins with a stress on God's act of saving people (stage one). As we will see, this is stressed in Romans 5, especially in 5:15-18.

However, Paul appears to show that grace is active not only with God but also with people who receive it (οἱ . . . λαμβάνοντες, "those . . . receiving," 5:17). The grace that makes God to act overflows to people (cf. ἐπερίσσευσεν, "abounded"; τὴν περισσείαν, "the abundance," 5:15, 17). As will be shown in chapter 4, God's grace makes people take action in their transition (cf.

---

75. E.g. P. F. Esler's title for chapter 6 is "Romans 6: Baptism and Sin," cf. *Conflict and Identity*, 202; Wedderburn's view is that "many of Paul's statements in Romans 6 echo" the fact of being "united with Christ in baptism," cf. *Baptism and Resurrection*, 67. Also Furnish, *Theology and Ethics*, 171–72; G. Wagner sees chapter 6 as "instructive with regard to the Pauline view of baptism," cf. *Pauline Baptism*, 1; also Hultgren, *Romans*, 241.

76. E.g. P. Stuhlmacher's heading of 6:1–14 as "The change of Lordship," cf. *Romans*, 89, cf. 100; Osborne speaks of "entering a new realm of existence," cf. *Romans*, 149, cf. 147; J. Ziesler speaks of "transition from the rule of Adam/sin to the rule of Christ," cf. *Romans*, 153; Käsemann: "the break between two aeons," cf. *Romans*, 158; Schlier: "Die Befreiung von der Sündenmacht," cf. *Der Römerbrief*, 190.

77. E.g. S. Westerholm considers 5:12–6:23 as a unit, cf. *Preface to Study*, 69. Cuvillier: "6,1-14 est en continuité directe avec 5,12-21" (6:1-14 is in direct continuity with 5:12-21), cf. "Evangile et traditions," 5. Moo speaks of 5:21 and various passages of chapter 6 and states, "Paul presents the Christian as one who has moved from 'the reign' of sin and death to that of righteousness and life," cf. *Romans 1-8*, 369. Esler: "The New Identity in Christ: Origin and Entry (Romans 5–6)," cf. *Conflict and Identity*, 195.

stages two, three and four). Paul mentions several actions which should be understood in relation to this move from sin to God.

One act that will be explained in this study is the candidate's act of death as the feature of the "liminal" stage or the second stage of initiation (cf. ἀπεθάνομεν τῇ ἁμαρτίᾳ, "we died to sin," 6:2). Another action of those involved in the transition from sin to God is the third stage act of undergoing the ritual that seals the process. As it will be explained, this is expressed with ἐβαπτίσθημεν, "we were baptized" (6:3-4).

As we will see, these acts mean to take responsibility in initiation, and this is better understood when another act of responsibility is also considered, that is, the fact that the new life is decided in initiation and starts there (cf. the fourth stage outlined earlier). Paul shows that the new life is part of the process and that it is not to be regarded as something that comes after initiation. As the study will demonstrate, in the process of change from sin to God believers are to acknowledge the fact that they are to reign (cf. οἱ . . . λαμβάνοντες . . . βασιλεύσουσιν, "those who . . . receive . . . shall reign," 5:17, also v. 21).[78] This means that βασιλεύσουσιν (shall reign) does not point to something eschatological; it is considered in this study as an act that begins in initiation and continues into the future, when the candidate lives as an initiate (i.e. the present future). The detail on this is given in the second and fourth chapters when the future linked to initiation will be explained. As we will see, the awareness that God is to reign (cf. ἡ χάρις βασιλεύσῃ, "grace might reign," 5:21) is an element of the process of the change from sin to God, but this reign is through those who move from sin to God (cf. οἱ . . . λαμβάνοντες . . . βασιλεύσουσιν, "those who . . . receive . . . reign"[79] – 5:17; also "through their δικαιοσύνης, righteousness," 5:21). In other words, in their transition believers are appointed to manifest God's reign. This appointment by one's Lord implies that a serious action is taken, as speech-act theory has illustrated earlier.

Further evidence in support of the fact that the person embraces the new life during the time of the transition can be found in the concepts δικαιοσύνη, "righteousness" / δίκαιος, "righteous" (e.g. 5:19, 21) and ἐν καινότητι ζωῆς

---

78. In 5:21, the subject of βασιλεύσῃ, "might reign" is χάρις, "grace." But as we will see (cf. chap 4), Paul implies believers (i.e. χάρις, "grace," stands for those who receive the grace, cf. v. 17).

79. The NIV, for example, translates βασιλεύσουσιν in the present: "[they] reign."

περιπατήσωμεν, "in newness of life we may walk [live]" (6:4). More on all these elements is given in the exegesis of Romans 5:12–6:23 (cf. the fourth chapter of this study).

The focus in this section was on 5:12–6:23 and on how it is considered in this study as the unit which covers the idea of the Christian's transition and baptism. The point was to show how important this pericope is to this study. The importance is that this unit shows how the transition from sin to God consists of four stages of action and that in these stages the agency of both God and the believer emerges. In the next section the second presupposition is expressed. This is the presupposition that when in Romans 5:12–6:23 Paul speaks of the believer's transition and baptism, initiation is the idea on his mind. This next part deals with Paul's approach to the subject of initiation which constitutes an essential element for understanding that "to die to sin" (6:2) and to take part in the water ritual (6:3) mean action, not passivity.

1.4.2. Baptism in Romans 6: Initiation as the Meaning

In antiquity initiation consisted of four stages of action; it is against this background that we examine whether the agency of both God and the believer is present in baptism. Thus, the second assumption is as follows: the hypothesis that dying to sin and entering the water of baptism imply action is explicable based on the assumption that when in Romans 5:12–6:23 Paul speaks of the believer's transition and baptism, he thinks of how initiation works. The point in this section is whether it is reasonable to consider that initiation is the idea in Romans 5:12–6:23. The evidence for this consists of two elements which are the focus in this part: 1) the wide recognition that baptism was initiation; 2) some internal evidence from Romans 5:12–6:23 showing how initiation is Paul's idea in this pericope.

1) There is a wide consensus that baptism functioned as the rite of "initiation" (or "entry to a new way of life"[80]) of the early church. This is recognized by biblical interpreters of various traditions and by anthropologists. This is

---

80. In this study we use interchangeably the words initiation, transition, entry, and *passage* to new way of life. They are seen as synonymous: e.g. Gennep speaks of initiation, transition and *passage* synonymously when rites of *initiation* are described as *transitional* rites and that these latter are one category of rites of passage; cf. *Rites of Passage*, 11; also Walsh, *Sacraments of Initiation*, 70. Elsas, about initiation and entry, cf. "Initiation Rites, 1: Religious," 703.

Calvin's view.⁸¹ Also Ingham makes a strong case for it when he thinks that baptism is practised as initiation in John the Baptist, is alluded to in the language of Jesus to Nicodemus, in Peter's instruction on Pentecost and in "every subsequent reference to baptism in Holy Writ."⁸² Beasley-Murray also recognizes that "the consciousness of baptism as a passage from the unbelieving world (or unbelieving Israel) to the believing people of the Messiah seems to have existed from the beginning of the Church."⁸³ A similar view is shown by M. Quesnel when he states, "le baptême devint rite d'initiation" and "il dut prendre le caractère de signe d'appartenance dans les années 50, celles qui suivirent immédiatement l'Assemblée de Jérusalem où il avait été décidé de ne pas imposer la circoncision aux chrétiens non juifs."⁸⁴ There are many who support this view; they range from the Church Fathers to modern scholars.⁸⁵

This idea that baptism assumed the role of initiation in early Christianity is also common in anthropological thinking. For example, Gennep's view is that in the first century baptism had the characteristics of any initiation: separation, transition, and incorporation.⁸⁶ With this anthropological lens, Dunn also understands that baptism "constituted almost literally a 'rite of passage.'"⁸⁷ A similarity between the Christian rite of baptism and initiation in other settings is also perceived by Walsh when he states,

> One can get a feel for the rite of baptism not only from its own history but also from the way it matches the general patterns of human behaviour that are revealed by anthropological studies,

---

81. *Calvin: Institutes*, vol. 2, LCC 21, 1303.

82. Ingham, *Handbook on Christian Baptism*, 8–10.

83. Beasley-Murray, *Baptism*, 103.

84. Quesnel, *Petite bible du baptême*, 87–88, also 91. Translation: "baptism became a rite of initiation" and "it must have taken on the character of a sign of *belonging to* in the years 50, the time immediately following the Jerusalem Assembly, during which it was decided not to impose circumcision on non-Jewish Christians."

85. e.g. Ambrose of Milan, *On the Sacraments* 1.12, 64; Betz, "Transferring a Ritual," in Engberg-Pedersen, 86; Wedderburn, *Baptism and Resurrection*, 357–360, 372, 381–82, 389–90, 393; Wagner, *Pauline Baptism*, 5; Flemington, *New Testament Doctrine*, 29–30; Moo, *Romans 1–8*, 376; Grayston, *Romans*, 43; Stendahl, *Meanings*, 179; Morris, *Romans*, 247; Maccoby, *Paul and Hellenism*, 127; McRay, *Paul, His Life*, 401; McKnight, "Proselytism and Godfearers," 845, col. 2; Schreiner, *Romans*, 307; Carlson, "Role of Baptism," 26; Gisel, *Pourquoi baptiser*, 8, 35, 37–38, 47. As means of entry into the church, cf. Kreider, "Worship and Evangelicalism," 17; and Gounelle, "Baptême aux temps patristiques," 184, 188.

86. Gennep, *Rites of Passage*, 93–95; also Quesnel, *Petite bible du baptême*, 109–112.

87. Dunn, *Theology of Paul*, 447.

especially in the domain of religion. Baptism can be classed as an initiation rite.[88]

In brief, it is widely accepted that baptism functioned as initiation in the early church. It is reasonable to assume that Paul thinks of initiation when he speaks of baptism. It is also reasonable to assume that his readers had the same idea, since this rite was practised by the church in general. As Barrett notes Paul "is . . . able to assume [baptism] as a rite familiar to all his readers."[89]

2) Apart from this wide recognition that baptism assumed the role of the rite of initiation, Romans 5–6 provides internal evidence that initiation is the idea on Paul's mind in this pericope. He thinks of what initiation implies when he speaks of baptism, especially to die to sin and to undergo the ritual. Beasley-Murray hints at the idea that this pericope shows aspects of initiation when he states that "Paul's language in Rom 6:1ff . . . implies that baptism is an initiation into life in Christ and the Church."[90] But he does not expound on how initiation is present in this text. The pericope features several elements of initiation. At this stage, the intention is to simply reference them. In the fourth chapter more detail will be given concerning their meaning and how, in the light of the four stages and action of the person's transition to a new life, this affects the reading of Romans 5:12–6:23.

As mentioned earlier, when Paul begins to speak of the transition from the rule of Adam (sin) to the reign of God, the emphasis is on the fact that God delivers people from their old way of life (5:15–18). As the second chapter will show, in antiquity this divine deliverance is an important aspect of initiation in any religious context. Apart from this divine act (cf. stage one), features of initiation continue in chapter 6. Not only does the term baptism (cf. 6:3–4) itself denote initiation, as showed earlier, but there is the idea of "dying" to one's past way of existence (v. 2) as the person attaches himself or herself to a new system. To die to one's system of existence is characteristic of initiation in Paul's world, as the second chapter will show when the second stage of initiation is explained.

Another idea which shows that initiation is on Paul's mind is "in [the name of] Jesus Christ" (v. 3) and its connotation of belonging to the new way of life.

---

88. Walsh, *Sacraments of Initiation*, 70.
89. Barrett, *Romans*, 121.
90. Beasley-Murray, *Baptism*, 95.

As Karecki recognizes, rites of initiation are intended to make people "experience a sense of belonging to their cultural and/or religious community."[91] In antiquity, this characterizes initiation, and all the religious settings show it as a common feature.[92] This will be clearer when in the second chapter the third stage is described.

The contract idea of initiation is seen in the fact that God saves from sin and the person offers himself or herself to God (e.g. 6:13). In antiquity, such a contract between the deity and the initiand is a pattern of initiation. It is obvious in Lucius' entry into the Isis cult,[93] and is a characteristic of initiation in Greco-Roman religions in general.[94] Another feature of initiation is the idea of dedication that emerges in the sharp command "sin never to begin to reign" (cf. Μὴ . . . βασιλευέτω ἡ ἁμαρτία, "let not sin reign," v. 12). There is also the slave motif with its idea of loyal service (cf. v. 6, 13–22). Initiation is also echoed by the idea of promotion or elevation and the fact that it entails responsibility (vv. 18, 22), and the fact of moving to "new life" and being bound to it (cf. ἐν καινότητι ζωῆς περιπατήσωμεν, "in newness of life we may walk [live]," v. 4). Each one of these elements is in connection with one of the four stages and action of initiation. This will show up when these stages of initiation are explained in the next chapters.

In the light of this assumption that the idea of initiation is on Paul's mind when he writes Romans 5:12–6:23, two ideas necessary to this study are deduced.

(1) This thesis will consider that Paul's words "we were baptized" are more a reference to the actual water ritual[95] than just to baptism as a metaphor.[96] E. Schweizer, for example, recognizes that "Rom vi.4–8 . . . clearly describes

---

91. Karecki, "Discovering the Roots," 172.

92. E.g. 1QS vi.18–20 (except when indicated otherwise, all references to the *DSS* are from F. G. Martinez, *The Dead Sea Scrolls Translated: The Qumran Texts in English*, 2nd ed., trans. W. G. E. Watson); *b. Yeb.* 47b; Philo, *Quaest. Exod.* ii.51; *Golden Ass* 11.5 (all ref. to the *The Golden Ass* is from Apuleius, *The Golden Ass*, LCL, trans. W. Addlington); Jeffers, *Greco-Roman World*, 77.

93. E.g. *Golden Ass*, 11.15–16, 30.

94. E.g. concerning Greco-Roman religions in general, cf. Jeffers, *Greco-Roman World*, 90; e.g. Mithraism, cf. Reitzenstein, *Hellenistic Mystery-Religions*, 10.

95. So Morris, *Romans*, 246; Légasse, "Etre baptisé," 553. Godet, *Commentaire*, 17; Schreiner, *Romans*, 306–07; Moo, *Romans 1–8*, 376, 382.

96. E.g. Dunn, *Baptism in Holy Spirit*, 139–40; also Dunn, *Romans 1–8*, 311; also Moule, *Birth of New Testament*, 38.

baptism."[97] The features just outlined make a strong case that Paul has on his mind the socio-religious process instead of just an inner spiritual experience. As chapter 4 will make clear, in Romans 6:3 Paul speaks of the water ritual and the responsibility implied by this public ritual of initiation. Albert Schweitzer downplays this when he suggests that in Paul's teaching and ministry, "baptism is no longer an act in itself."[98]

(2) The idea of Hamman, Dassmann and De Simone is here relevant, which about baptism states, "Par métonymie, le terme finit par exprimer tout le processus sacramental par lequel le catéchumène rompt avec le péché et les séductions du démon, entre dans un rapport nouveau par la foi avec le Dieu-trine et s'agrège au peuple de la nouvelle Alliance."[99] As the elements of Romans 5–6 show that Paul thinks of the various steps of the process of the Christian entry, when he says "we were baptized" he implies more than just the water ritual. By "we were baptized" he thinks of the whole time of initiation and what its different stages mean. This will be clearer when we expound on the different stages of initiation that emerge in 5:12–6:23.

As a conclusion to this section, initiation and the way it works is the frame of reference for understanding whether Paul implies the agency of God and the initiand when in Romans 5:12–6:23 he speaks of the believer's transition and baptism. The next chapter tests whether this balance between divine action and the initiand's action is present in the religious initiatory contexts of Paul's time. Before we move to this step, a survey of literature is done in order to have a better understanding of how scholarship has understood the balance of divine and human agency in connection with baptism.

---

97. Schweitzer, "Dying and Rising," 3.

98. Schweitzer, *Mysticism of Paul*, 263; Wedderburn thinks that "probably Paul never contemplated" the effect of baptism as a ritual, cf. *Baptism and Resurrection*, 370–71.

99. Hamman, Dassmann and de Simone, "Baptême," 332 col. 2– 333 col. 1. Translation: By metonymy, the term [baptism] ends up expressing the whole sacramental process by which the catechumen breaks with sin and the seductions of the devil, enters into a new relationship by faith with the Triune God and is aggregated with the people of the new Covenant.

1.5. Literature Survey: Action in Baptism, an Overlooked Aspect

This survey is intended to be more than a review; it critically considers some major contributions as to whether in Romans 5:12–6:23 Paul shows a balance between the action of God and the action of the Christian initiand in his or her transition and baptism.

The works on Romans 5–6 and baptism are many. In this review, we only consider some of those whose views are found to significantly touch on the balance between divine and human agency in relation to baptism. The ideas on what Paul says about baptism may be arranged in different groups.[100] Some offer a mystical interpretation.[101] The interpretation of others is sacramental.[102] There are some who present a sociological view.[103] The position of other scholars, such as Flemington, is rather a balance between the sacramental and the sociological views.[104] This survey could be organised after these strands, but these varied interpretations of Paul's teaching on baptism largely coincide in their interpretation of the role of the candidate in baptism. Hence the survey is structured as follows: 1) the views that clearly stress the passivity of the candidate, and 2) the views of some who have recognized that the baptizand takes action in this process of change from sin to God. The purpose is to show what is missing in each of the two strands of interpretation.

---

100. L. J. Kreitzer identifies four strands: "the eschatological framework," a focus on "the relationship between grace, faith and baptism," "the Trinitarian argument," and "the mystical interpretation," cf. "Baptism in the Pauline Epistles," 76–78.

101. That is, in baptism union with Christ takes place with the result that one's personality is replaced by Christ's; e.g. Schweitzer, *Mysticism of Paul*, 19, 125, 261–62. S. G. F. Brandon: baptism was conceived as "a ritual of mystical assimilation," cf. *History, Time and Deity*, 26–27.

102. That is, baptism as part of the salvation process. It operates in fellowship with Christ; the ceremony is thought of as having effectual powers; e.g. Carlson, "Role of Baptism," 258; J. Schreider, "ὅμοιος, ὁμοιότης" in *TDNT*, vol. 5, 195; G. Hunsinger, "The Dimension of Depth," 160, 163. More on the sacramental view, cf. Schweitzer, *Mysticism of Paul*, 228–29.

103. That is, as a means of entering the Church as one's new community; e.g. *Calvin: Institutes*, vol. 2, 1303; Wedderburn, *Baptism and Resurrection*, 58–59; R. Bultmann, *Theology of the NT*, 311; Rawlinson, "Corpus Christi," in Bell and Deissmann, *Mysterium Christi*, 232–33.

104. Flemington, *New Testament Doctrine*, 24, 29–30 (sociological view) and 84 (sacramental view).

1.5.1. The Baptismal Candidate Considered as Passive
Albert Schweitzer
Concerning Paul, his view is that baptism is a ceremony that unites the believer and Christ in "one corporeity."[105] Schweitzer thus emphasises the mystical quality of the action. In terms of action, Schweitzer's focus is on what God does. In fact, he states that baptism "works supernaturally."[106] Thus all action in this process is divine. This is clear when he says that what counts for Paul is the "sacred" in this ceremony.[107]

For Schweitzer, the baptizand takes no action in this process. As Schweitzer's statement concerning the baptizand makes clear, he "loses his creatively individual existence and his natural personality."[108] His view is that even faith is not something that works during this transition, because "The idea that it is only through a believing self-surrender to absorption in Christ that the Elect can *bring* about the mystical fellowship with Him is quite outside of Paul's horizon."[109]

These elements show that, for Schweitzer, only God takes action in baptism. The idea that the candidate's natural personality is inactive during the process overlooks the action of the initiand conveyed in such words as ἀπεθάνομεν τῇ ἁμαρτίᾳ, "we died to sin" (6:2).[110] Another clause of this type is for example ὑπηκούσατε δὲ ἐκ καρδίας τύπον διδαχῆς, "but you obeyed heartedly to the form of teaching" (6:17). Baptism is the context of this clause too. Hultgren, for instance, recognizes that this is the "wholehearted assent" to the teaching, and thinks that it is a reference to "the catechesis," which Paul's readers had taken.[111] Schweitzer disregards such an assent when he separates baptism and the exercise of faith, as mentioned earlier. Faith is a feature in this believer's transition and baptism. Apart from the idea of faith in 6:17, faith is also expressed in 5:17, where Paul speaks of "receiving" God's grace. In terms of passivity or taking action, what does this assent mean in the person's

---

105. Schweitzer, *Mysticism of Paul*, 19; also Morris, *Romans*, 247; Kim, *Origin of Paul's Gospel*, 301.
106. Schweitzer, 233.
107. Schweitzer, 20.
108. Schweitzer, 125.
109. Schweitzer, 19.
110. In addition to some mentioned earlier, so also Hultgren, *Romans*, 243.
111. Hultgren, *Romans*, 262.

transition from sin to God? As the analysis of 5:15–18 will show (cf. fourth chapter), receiving God's grace and salvation means taking responsibility. It is more than just passivity.

James D. G. Dunn

Dunn sees that Paul speaks of initiation in Romans 6. He states that "baptism was already well established prior to Paul's conversion" and that in 6:4 (also mentioning other texts) "he simply takes it for granted."[112] Dunn sees here an act of initiation because his view is that very early baptism "became established as the rite of entry into the community" and an "expression of the initiate's commitment to that community."[113] This idea of initiation is linked with 6:2 when about this verse Dunn states, "at conversion-initiation the convert died to sin."[114] Is this dying the convert's agency? Dunn's view is that this is "the initial identification with Christ in his death and life so that his death and life may work themselves out in the believer."[115] The issue is whether Paul and his readers will have understood their initiatory death as (just) identification with the death of Christ.

Also the issue appears with the separation which Dunn makes between verses 3 and 4. He considers "baptised into Christ" (v. 3) and thinks that this "should not be taken as an abbreviation of . . . 'baptised into the name of Christ.'"[116] The difference that Dunn sees is that "the latter is a . . . reference to the baptismal act"[117] and the shorter phrase is "a *metaphor*, rather than . . . the ritual act,"[118] the sense of the metaphor being that what Paul implies in 6:3 is to be "baptised in Christ in the Spirit."[119] Thus Dunn sees two types of baptism in verses 3 and 4 because, as mentioned earlier, he recognizes that Paul implies the rite of baptism in 6:4. This study expects to show that the

---

112. Dunn, *Unity and Diversity*, 154–55.

113. Dunn, *Jesus and Spirit*, 183. Also Dunn: "Paul recognized that Christian groups (like all groups) have a ritual boundary (baptism in the name of Jesus – 1 Cor 1.13)," cf. *Parting of Ways*, 103, and 315 fn. 40.

114. Dunn, *Jesus and Spirit*, 335.

115. Dunn, 335.

116. Dunn, *Unity and Diversity*, 158.

117. Dunn, 158.

118. Dunn, 159 [italics his]; also *Baptism in Spirit*, 140.

119. Dunn, *Christology in Making*, 183; and "to be baptised in Christ" is "to be baptised in Spirit," cf. Dunn, "Birth of Metaphor," 175.

water ritual is Paul's focus in both verses and that the emphasis is on the pledge that this ritual implies. As we will see, Paul structures his idea so that in 6:1–2 he speaks of dying to (breaking up with) the old way of life (cf. stage two of initiation), and in 6:3–4 about the ritual and the pledge implied by undergoing such a ritual (stage three).

Concerning the initiand's agency, one element that this thesis will focus on is the "we" of ἀπεθάνομεν τῇ ἁμαρτίᾳ, "we died to sin" (6:2) and ἐβαπτίσθημεν, "we were baptized" (v. 3). Dunn's idea on this is considered. His view is that βαπτίζεσθαι (to be baptized) is here used metaphorically; "what it describes is the spiritual mystical reality of union with Christ effected by God."[120] His focus is on what God does to the person. However, apart from God's deed, in 6:1–3 Paul points out what his readers in Rome personally did in their transition to Christian life: they personally died to sin and underwent the water ritual.

Attention to this initiand's agency is missing when Dunn speaks of 6:2. He notes that this verse is the key when he states, "Too many commentators speak as though v. 2 was not there. On the contrary, v. 2 is the key without which the meaning of the passage cannot be unlocked and opened up . . ."[121] What he is stressing about this verse is that "we died to sin" (v. 2) means a death such as "the sinful act is no longer possible" and that "what Paul had in mind is a death which puts the individual beyond the power of sin."[122] This shows a focus on Jesus's action because only Christ's act of death defeats sin. Dunn is not the only one to focus on (just) Christ's act when interpreting this verse.[123] Indeed as Paul speaks of the transition from sin to God, Christ's act that defeats adamic sin is stressed (5:12–21; cf. Rom 7:24–25; Col 1:13). There is a reference to this death of Christ in 6:3. But the focus in 6:1–4 is more on the action that believers as initiands take in their transition and baptism.

Thomas F. Torrance

As baptism is also a subject of theological debate, the view of a theologian on the issue of divine and human agency is considered important to this study. Torrance's idea serves our purpose although he is not commenting on

---

120. Dunn, *Baptism in Spirit*, 141.

121. Dunn, 140.

122. Dunn, *Romans 1–8*, 307.

123. E.g. J. R. Edwards asks, "what is the meaning of *we died to sin*?" and the answer is a "reference to Christ's death," cf. *Romans*, 159 [italics his].

Romans 6 as such. Torrance focuses on God's saving action when he states that baptism "must be interpreted in coherence with the whole Gospel of the Incarnation, *in a dimension of depth* going back to the saving work of God in Jesus Christ, and as grounded so objectively in that work that it has no content, reality or power apart from it."[124]

Indeed, baptism is grounded in Christ's saving work and so must be also any power that baptism as an event brings about. However, Torrance's view downplays the idea that any power or ability to take action is implied by baptism when he states that "baptism sets forth not what we do . . . but what God has already done in Christ, and through his Spirit continues to do in and to us. Our part is only to receive it, for we cannot add anything to Christ's finished work."[125] This idea is repeated when he states, "Baptism is . . . not a sacrament of what we do but of what God has done for us in Jesus Christ, in whom he has bound himself to us and bound us to himself, before ever we could respond to him."[126] From this focus on Christ's saving action, Torrance's view is that "this precludes us from regarding baptism . . . as an event in itself, either as a ritual act that has its meaning in and with its performance, or as an ethical act that has its meaning in the response of man to what God has already done."[127] So baptism is only about God's agency. Torrance's view is that Christ is "himself both its [our baptism's] material content and its active agent."[128] Still the initiand's agency is not in view when Torrance advances, "Its meaning does not lie in the rite itself and its performance, nor in the attitude of the baptised and his obedience of faith"; "by its nature" it is "a passive act."[129]

This shows that Torrance's focus is just on God's act. The rite itself and its performance are downplayed. Paul's words "we were baptized" (6:3) appear to refer to the performance. This study intends to focus on what the performance of a ritual that seals entry to new life means for Paul and the first-century Christians to whom he writes. Did such a ritual focus only on divine action?

Torrance seems to find an idea of initiation to be inappropriate as he understands that also the early church tried to avoid any idea that would

---

124. Torrance, *Theology in Reconciliation*, 82–83 [italics his].
125. Torrance, 87–88.
126. Torrance, 103.
127. Torrance, 83.
128. Torrance, 84.
129. Torrance, 103.

make baptism appear as any "rite of religious ablution."[130] This danger of misunderstanding baptism is also in Gunther's view that the use of βαπτισμός in Colossians 2:12 is Paul's response to his opponents' idea that "Christian baptism is the new counterpart of the ceremonial washing of cups, pots and vessels."[131] While the danger of seeing baptism as identical to any ritual of initiation was real, the water ritual and the pledge that it entails is an important idea in Romans 6, as we will see.

Herman Ridderbos

Ridderbos states, "For however much baptism derives its character from the fact that it is administered to believers and that the baptismal act can be described in terms of believers "submitting themselves to baptism," the subject is not faith, but God."[132] Ridderbos highlights this personal act of "submitting themselves." Then he proceeds to stress the divine agency. In fact, his view is that "the passive pronouncements point to this."[133] It all leads to a conclusion that "Baptism is the means in God's hand, the place where he speaks and acts."[134] There is evidence that in Romans 5–6 the baptismal transition is also a means in the believer's hand, the place where he or she acts. The water ritual is Ridderbos' focus because he speaks of "administering" baptism. This thesis intends to show (cf. the exegesis of 6:3) how this time of the water ritual is the third stage of initiation and that this comprises the role of God and his community (their presence) and the act of the initiand of swearing his or her attachment to the new system of life.

Still Ridderbos downplays the candidate's agency in baptism when he states, "Baptism and faith are both means to the appropriation of the gospel. However, while faith according to its nature is an act of man, baptism according to its nature is an activity of God and on the part of God."[135] It is not clear that baptism is only "an activity of God" and yet Ridderbos recognizes that baptism, like faith, is the "means of appropriation of the gospel" of God. Certainly, this appropriation denotes an act of believers. "Appropriation" is

---

130. Torrance, 84.
131. Gunther, *St Paul's Opponents*, 134.
132. Ridderbos, *Paul*, 411.
133. Ridderbos, 411.
134. Ridderbos, 411.
135. Ridderbos, 412.

the goal of it all. As the study intends to show, what all these stages and actions stand for is a serious appropriation of the new way of life (cf. stage four).

R. David Kaylor

Concerning the agency of the Christian initiand in the baptismal process, faith has been an important aspect. Ridderbos has just been referred to on this aspect. Earlier Schweitzer's idea that the act of faith should not be thought of as a part of the baptismal process was referred to. Kaylor also recognizes the connection of faith and baptism, but he describes the act of faith as a negation of one's human power to achieve something. For instance, he states:

> Baptism is a burial, an ending, before it is a resurrection, a new beginning. Just as Jesus' death is God's "no" to human pride, *achievement*, wisdom, and *power*, so baptism is the "no" of faith to the merely human. Baptism symbolizes faith, that moment of *passivity* in which one allows God to be God in one's life and accepts that reality as an end to one's own idolatrous self-assertion.[136]

The stage of the encounter with God (Rom 5:15) will be considered; it will be shown that indeed this is a step when the believer just receives (v. 17) what God's grace does to him or her. For Kaylor, this idea of just receiving means a "no" to human achievement and power. As this quotation indicates, his view is that human achievement and God being God in one's life are two things which are mutually exclusive.

But as we shall see, Paul considers that these two things comprise the Christian's transition and baptism. People are saved from sin by God, but this does not suggest they are unable to achieve things. Paul shows that the process begins with the stage in which God's act is received and allowed to work on the person's life as Kaylor notes. As we said earlier, Paul stresses this in Romans 5:15–18 and a recapitulation is made in chapter 6 (e.g. vv. 3, 5–6). In the present study, this divine act is referred to as the first stage action of the process.

However, human power to act is also an aspect of this process of initiation according to Paul. In Romans 6:1–3 Paul reminds his readers of the

---

136. Kaylor, *Paul's Covenant Community*, 122 [italics mine].

responsibility they have taken. He says they can no longer continue in sin since they died to sin (6:2). By undergoing the ritual (v. 3) they made a serious pledge. There are other actions that are part of the process. These elements show that human power to take action is part of baptism. In fact, Kaylor recognizes this power to act when he states:

> Baptism is intended to result . . . not in a mystical experience but rather in a conscious self-determination by which the baptized must consider themselves "dead to sin and alive to righteousness." What takes place in baptism is to take place in human consciousness. Baptism is not merely a sacrament that happens to a person; it is a personal happening as one knowingly and willingly sets aside one mode of existence and takes up another within a new community of faith.[137]

The idea that the baptizand takes action is recognized in stating that the person "sets aside one mode of existence and takes up another" and thus "baptism is intended to result . . . in a conscious self-determination by which the baptised must consider themselves 'dead to sin and alive to righteousness.'" This is a focus on the after-initiation life (fourth stage).

A. J. M. Wedderburn

As Wedderburn speaks of "death to sin" (6:2), the believer is given a passive role. "Death" implies Christ's act, as it is made evident by this statement:

> There is one final point to be considered which also arises out of our treatment of Romans 6, the evaluation of the rite of baptism as a dying. For it has often been argued that this is a point which baptism has in common with the initiation rites of the Greco-Roman mystery-cults. Does this rite in fact fit into a pattern common to all initiatory rites, including those of the mysteries? But, in looking for such patterns we shall at the same time also have to bear in mind that *this dying is not just the individual's death, but that he shares in Christ's death*, and we shall have to ask whether this aspect of Paul's thought does not distinguish

---

137. Kaylor, 123–24.

his view from all other common patterns of initiation rites and rites of passage.[138]

We are particularly drawn to the words "this dying is not just the individual's death." The issue is when the sense of it as "individual death" is juxtaposed with the idea that in this death "he shares in Christ's death." These are two different things. As our fourth chapter will show, often interpreters of Romans 6 have not distinguished the two ideas.

In terms of action, "to die to sin" loses its sense of being the act of the baptizand if it is "the dying that he shares in Christ's death." Initiation or entry to new life involved both divine action and the person's own death to his or her past way of life. As our study seeks to demonstrate, this is also what Paul shows in Romans 5:12–6:23. This is overlooked when Wedderburn states, "Even when speaking of the initiatory death in baptism Paul is . . . speaking not so much of the baptised person dying himself or repeating Christ's experience for himself, but rather of the Christian acknowledging an experience already previously undergone by Christ on his behalf."[139] Here Wedderburn recognizes this death to be an "initiatory death." What is exactly overlooked is the fact that in antiquity, as we shall see, initiatory death is more than just acknowledging the experience of another person or deity. This lack of distinction between God's deed and the action of the initiand makes the baptizand passive.

Richard P. Carlson

Carlson concurs with the idea that baptism is initiation. However, some of his ideas overlook what Paul seems to mean concerning this rite. Referring to Eliade, Leach and Meeks, Carlson recognizes that "initiation included a negation of the old reality with its peculiar boundaries."[140] This is the initiatory action of breaking with one's past. However, as Carlson applies this to baptism, his view is that this negation is not an action taken by the convert who undergoes the rite. While he recognizes that "to negate sin" is Paul's concern in 6:1–3,[141] his view is that this negation of sin is Christ's action. This is clear

---

138. Wedderburn, *Baptism and Resurrection*, 69.
139. Wedderburn, 389.
140. Carlson, "Role of Baptism," 257.
141. Carlson, 258.

when he states, "For Paul, Christ's death, not our baptism negates sin,"[142] and also in his statement that the "Christ-event negates" sin.[143]

This thesis will argue that this overlooks the idea of the initiand dying to his or her old way of existence during his or her move to a new existence. The firm stand against sin in 6:1–3 underlines the responsibility that the believers have since the time they personally broke with sin in their baptismal transition. As evidence, the following are some of the elements that will be expanded on. It is noted that this responsibility permeates Romans 6, mainly referring to an event that meant a break with sin. In 6:2, Paul says that the people to whom he is writing died to sin, and the responsibility that this entailed is such that it is inappropriate for them to serve sin any longer. They are reminded to count themselves dead to sin but alive to God (6:11; also vv. 12–13). These appear to be not just the consequences of God having acted on one's behalf, but a reference to the responsibility taken during one's transition to Christian life. This is downplayed if the idea of negation of sin in 6:2 is seen as just the negation of sin that happened in Christ's act on the cross.

In fact, Carlson concurs with the idea that "something was thought to have happened in the rite. The rite itself effects the transition from the old state to the new."[144] But his focus is only on the divine agency because his view is that it is all "the work of the Spirit rather than the work of individual Christians."[145]

Carlson's approach is the sacramental approach, which sees baptism as a means by which God operates salvation. This indeed focuses on what God does, but as this study will show, the divine action is just stage one of initiation. The sacramental view is implied when he states that in Paul's thought baptism "is a baptism into the salvific event of Christ's death."[146] Putting it in other words, he says that the role of baptism "is to incorporate us into the salvific event of Christ's death."[147] Since only God is able to incorporate a person into salvation, the stress is on what God does. The candidate is rather passively being changed, as Carlson states:

---

142. Carlson, 258.
143. Carlson. 257.
144. Carlson, 257.
145. Carlson, 260.
146. Carlson, 258.
147. Carlson, 258.

> Paul's reason for using baptism at the juncture of his argument [meaning when moving from chapter 5 to 6] is to show how all Christians are transformed by God . . . from the dominion of sin and death to the dominion of Christ. Baptism in Christ's death is how this transformation occurs.[148]

As we will see in the second chapter of this thesis, initiation was more than a passive state in which only the deity worked. In fact, Carlson consistently keeps the idea that transition (so initiation) is in Paul's thinking when he speaks of baptism. This is clear when in this quotation Carlson speaks of the move "from the dominion of sin . . . to the dominion of Christ." He recognizes that Paul places baptism at the centre of the transition from sin to God. Even the word "alteration" is used,[149] which is a reference to such a change of existence. In his view there is nothing the believer does in this change of his or her life. Rather Carlson thinks that it is all the "inauguration entailed" by the fact that the person is "incorporated into the cross of Christ."[150] As his other words show, it is all about the fact that the "inclusion into the once-for-all death of Christ involves a passage . . . from the old dominion to the new dominion."[151]

The question is whether Paul really means that without any active role the baptizand is just incorporated into Christ's death and a new existence that this death meant. This suggests that baptism is about a transition that has already happened with Christ and that by baptism the person is just symbolically incorporated into the move to a new way which Christ's death meant. As this thesis intends to show, the believer's transition and baptism is about Christ's death and the *passage* that it inaugurated, but Paul's attention is also on the move to a new existence that the convert personally undertakes. As evidence for that, Paul speaks of Christ's death "with" the believer (6:4–6),

---

148. Carlson, 258.

149. Carlson, 263.

150. Carlson, 263; this meaning of "incorporation into Christ" (or synonyms: participation in, inclusion into, corporate destiny with) is used by many, e.g. Tannehill, *Dying and Rising*, 10–12; Kim, *Origin of Paul's Gospel*, 301; Kim, *Paul and New Perspective*, 50, 212; Beasley-Murray, *Baptism*, 142–44, 286–87; Moo, *Romans 1 – 8*, 371; Ridderbos, *Paul*, 412–13; Wagner, *Pauline Baptism*, 292–93.

151. Carlson, "Role of Baptism," 263.

which indeed means a move to a new realm (vv. 18, 22; cf. also Col 1:13; 1 Thess 2:12; Gal 5:1).

This act of Christ has a connection with the believer's move from sin to the new way, but apart from this, Paul reminds his readers of the fact that they can recall an event in their life and the actions that they took in its process. As we will see, during the time of this move (stage one), they encountered God's saving action and embraced it (cf. 5:15–17; 6:17). As another step of this time of their initiation (stage two), they renounced their past way of life and died to it (6:2, 11). They underwent the water ritual (cf. 6:3) to show publicly the seriousness of their decision (stage three) and took other actions which showed that they embraced the new life and started to live it out in the time of their transition (stage four).

In other words, in the pericope of 5:12–6:23, Paul takes into account Christ's deed for believers, and he also considers what they personally did in the process of their transition from being under sin to being Christians. How the two harmonize without contradicting each other is what this study intends to show.

1.5.2. Hints at Baptism as a Time of Action

Some hints have been made at the idea that the believer takes action during his or her baptismal process. This section considers the views of some scholars who present this aspect, especially when they speak of "we died to sin." The purpose is to show what is missing, when action is linked with baptism in Romans 6. Some of the scholars, whose statements have been discussed in the last section, are also considered here. The idea is to show that there are cases where the same interpreter makes statements that seriously disregard the action of the baptizand and, on the other hand, expresses words that hint at action in baptism. This clash is deliberately brought into the discussion in order to show that the action that baptism implies is still something that requires clarification.

Tertullian

In the Patristic period, the baptismal process is conceived as a time of action. For example, this is stressed in the Ordo of Constantinople.[152] Also Tertullian's words show that the catechumens are to take action against sin in the time they prepare for baptism:

> When we are baptized, then, I fancy, will be time enough to be free from fault. By no means! Rather we should rid ourselves of sin when pardon is in abeyance and punishment in prospect; when we do not yet merit deliverance, so that we may be able to merit it; when God threatens, not when He pardons.[153]

It appears that here Tertullian denounces the belief of some who may have thought that baptism rids of sin. He shows that the catechumens "themselves" must break with sin before they take the ritual of baptism. Tertullian sees the catechumen's preparation as a time in which the person has to separate himself or herself from sin before the water ritual itself. This believer's agency which is also described as "to cease with sin" is again expressed when he states, "We are not baptised so that we may cease committing sin but because we have ceased, since we are already clean of heart."[154]

Tertullian sees it all as a process that shows the stages of initiation that this thesis uses as a theory of explaining whether the baptizand's agency is a feature of baptism. As mentioned earlier, Tertullian's view is that the water ceremony of baptism must follow the separation from sin. This act against sin also comes next to the moment the believer "makes His [God's] acquaintance."[155] With this, Tertullian recognizes that the person encounters God, breaks with sin, and then undergoes the water ritual. What he does not show is what these actions imply to a contemporary who is involved in a religious transition from one way of existence to another.

---

152. For more on what the Ordo of Constantinople says on this, cf. Finn, *Early Christian Baptism: Syria*, 98–101.
153. Tertullian, *On Penance* 6, in Tertullian, *Treatises on Penance*, 25.
154. Tertullian, 26.
155. Tertullian, 26.

John Calvin

One point that this study intends to prove is how in Paul's thought the water ritual (cf. 6:3) implies the initiand's act, a pledge in the presence of God and God's people that he or she takes the responsibility of belonging to the new community. Calvin recognizes this, when he defines a sacrament as an event in which "we . . . attest our piety toward him [God] in the presence of the Lord and of his angels and before men."[156] The sacrament that Calvin is speaking about is baptism.[157] It is evident with the words "we attest" that Calvin acknowledges the candidate's agency during the water ritual.

Also, Calvin hints at action in connection with "death to sin" (6:2). Speaking of Romans 6:3–4, he states, "we are admonished through baptism to die to our desires."[158] It is clear that Calvin understands "dying to sin" to imply the agency of the believer. But Calvin does not show how all this applies to Romans 5–6. He does not show why to Paul and his contemporaries, baptism should mean such acts of the baptizand. Calvin admits that baptism was the rite of "initiation" by which people entered "into the society of the church."[159] Any connection between this idea of initiation and what the person is and does in baptism is not dealt with by Calvin.

Karl Barth, G. R. Beasley-Murray

Karl Barth and Beasley-Murray show very similar views concerning baptism and action. On this issue Barth states, "Neither by exegesis nor from the nature of the case can it be established that the baptized person can be a merely passive instrument (*Behandelter*, one being treated). Rather it may be shown, by exegesis and from the nature of the case, that . . . the baptized is an active partner (*Handelnder*, a doer)."[160] It is clear here that for Barth baptism encompasses divine and human agency. This idea is also present when he comments on ὅσοι ἐβαπτίσθημεν εἰς Χριστὸν Ἰησοῦν, "we all who were baptised into Christ Jesus" (Rom 6:3): "as human faith is enclosed invisibly by the faithfulness of God; so also the *human act* of baptism is enclosed by that

---

156. *Calvin: Institutes*, 1277.
157. *Calvin*, 1304.
158. *Calvin*, 1307.
159. *Calvin*, 1303.
160. Barth, *Teaching of the Church*, 41.

action of God on behalf of men which it [baptism] declares."[161] This view of divine and human action in relation to baptism is linked with Barth's thought of baptism "as a rite of initiation,"[162] and this is in connection with the religious role of baptism: "baptism is an occurrence belonging to the concrete world of religion."[163] The question is why a first-century person could understand that baptism, as a time of transition from one religious existence to another, means to take action. This is not answered by Barth.

Very much in the same line of thought as Barth, Beasley-Murray also agrees that baptism is about action, when he states:

> The penitent sinner who knows that his Representative has died for him, that by the judgment and mercy of God he died in Him on Golgotha, who by faith accepts God's judgment on his sin and in Christ finds life from the dead, *in that very act of turning to God* renounces his sinful life, condemns it to the grave of baptism and by grace begins the life of discipleship to the praise of God.[164]

The issue is in which sense for the first-century person the rite of baptism meant renunciation of his or her previous life and how this agrees with a baptismal pericope such as Romans 5:12–6:23. Beasley-Murray does not really show this.

In the view of Beasley-Murray the water ceremony encapsulates the entire theological connotation implied by the process. As the quotation shows, Beasley-Murray suggests that the very time of turning to God is also the time of renouncing sin, condemning it to the grave of baptism and beginning the new life. He sees it all happening at "the grave of baptism" and it is clear that his focus is on "when baptism is administered."[165] As we will see, Romans 5–6 shows that all these acts are part of the person's transition from sin's rule to living the life that God's grace brings about. They are each different from the water ceremony. Paul sees them as stages of a process, and these stages

---

161. Barth, *Romans*, 192 [italics mine].

162. Barth, 192.

163. Barth, 192.

164. Beasley-Murray, *Baptism*, 143 [italics his], also 144–145 concerning "they crucified the flesh (Gal 5:24)."

165. Beasley-Murray, *Baptism*, 103.

are a sequence between God's saving act (5:15–18) and the believer's act of undergoing the ritual of water (6:3). What theological point Paul is making out of this?

Hermann W. Beyer, Paul Althaus

The idea that baptism is about action is very much recognized by Beyer and Althaus. In their view on Galatians 5:24, but also speaking of Romans 6, Beyer and Althaus state:

> Das Geschehen bei der Taufe ist nicht naturhaft, sondern ganz personhaft. Was der Taufakt an ihnen vollzog, dazu bekannten sie sich selbst und machten es zu ihrem eigenen Akte. So kann das, was Röm 6, 2ff. als Widerfahrnis, das der Mensch in der Taufe erleidet, zu stehen kommt, hier als sein persönlicher Akt bezeichnet werden: er hat den altern Menschen mit seinen Leidenschaften und Begierden gekreuzigt, ihm abgesagt – eine grundsätzliche Entscheidung ein für allemal, die dann freilich . . . zugleich die immer neue Aufgabe für das ganze Leben des Christen stellt.[166]

Beyer and Althaus understand that Christ's action against sin is at work in baptism. This is clear when they state that in this event there is what believers profess to and make their own act. Their emphasis however is that what the person "endures" (erleidet) is to be seen as a "personal act" (sein persönlicher Akt). The person crucifies and renounces (hat . . . gekreuzigt, abgesagt) the old way. For Beyer and Althaus, Luther's translation – which emphasises passivity as referred to earlier – misses this agency of the baptizand, this "once for all decision" (Entscheidung ein für allemal) that baptism implies. What is not shown is what this action of the baptizand against his or her old way of life

---

166. Beyer and Althaus, "Der Brief," 49. Translation:
>What happens at baptism is not natural, but very personal. What the act of baptism did to them, they confessed to themselves and made it their own act . . . So things in Rom 6:2ff., as an experience that a person suffers in baptism, are referred to here as a person's act: he crucified the old person with its passions and desires, refused it – a fundamental decision [taken] once and for all, which of course . . . at the same time represents the ever new task for the whole life of the Christian.

really is. Also it is unclear why to Paul and his contemporaries baptism and the transition to new life should have meant to take such action.

James D. G. Dunn

Earlier in this survey, some of Dunn's statements in which human action in baptism is underestimated have been considered. Here we consider some examples where he hints at the baptizand's agency. As indicated earlier, this sort of clash of ideas shows that the issue of human agency in baptism has not been clarified.

The agency of the baptizand is indicated when Dunn speaks of being "baptized in the name of Christ" and states that one meaning of this is that baptism was "*an act whereby the baptizand handed himself over to be the property or disciple of the named.*"[167] He also concurs with the idea that baptism meant "repentance."[168] On "dead to sin" in 6:11, Dunn also states that "the believer . . . is not a merely passive object played upon and manipulated by transcendent forces."[169] Earlier it was noted that about "we died to sin" (6:2) Dunn stresses Christ as the agent instead of "we." But still on 6:2 (an idea that does not reappear in his later commentary on Romans), Dunn states, "Baptism is best seen here . . . as the means and step of commitment to Christ which results in new life. Without renunciation of the old life and commitment to the new there is no death and no life."[170] The initiatory death as a personal act does not emerge clearly. Here, however, Dunn makes a connection between baptism and such acts as to make a commitment to Christ and to renounce the old way of life. To the question why baptism means this, Dunn replies that

> as the initiate surrenders himself to the baptizer, giving him control of his body so that the plunging beneath the surface of the water is wholly in his hands, so he surrenders himself to God for God to put to death and bury his old self.[171]

The issue is that Romans 6:1–3 appears to point to a personal death, not God putting the person to death. In antiquity and particularly in a religious

---

167. Dunn, *Unity and Diversity*, 158–59 [italics his].
168. Dunn, *Jesus and Spirit*, 183; and *Unity and Diversity*, 155.
169. Dunn, *Romans 1 – 8*, 324.
170. Dunn, *Baptism in Spirit*, 145.
171. Dunn, 145.

setting, the idea of death in initiation is a personal act and as we will see this is what Paul asserts in Romans 6.

Leon Morris

Morris writes on "we died to sin" and its connection with baptism in Romans 6:2–3. As a reference given earlier shows, he recognizes the human agency in baptism when he states, "The aorist in the verb *died* points to an action rather than a state: "we who died" rather than "we are dead". . . Becoming a Christian is a decisive step . . ."[172] Morris notes that Paul then "turns to baptism" and that he "emphatically" shows to his readers that if they "do not understand what it means to die to sin, they do not understand what baptism means, and baptism comes right at the beginning of the Christian life."[173]

Morris' view is that, for Paul, baptism as an event of change to a new life is a serious act of decision. Like others who recognize that baptism entails action, Morris does not really elucidate why, to Paul and his readers, baptism is an event that should mean a decisive action, which is the point we seek to illuminate. Apart from this, we may point out at least two other issues arising from his opinion.

First, he recognizes action, but only in connection with "to die to sin" (6:2). When he speaks of water (6:3), the serious pledge that the water ritual implies, as we shall see, is overlooked. The water ritual is used to explain the idea of death that Paul speaks about in verse 2.[174] In the fourth chapter of this study it will be shown how the fact of undergoing the water ritual is also seen by the apostle as implying action. Both the act of dying and the pledge implied by undergoing the water ritual make stronger the responsibility of which Paul is reminding his baptized readers. This will be clear as the study develops.

Another issue concerns the presence of both the agency of God and that of the baptizand. Morris recognizes that Christ's death is the "ground" of what the believer does and experiences: "It is the death of Christ that makes anyone

---

172. Morris, *Romans*, 245. Similar idea of "death to sin" as radical choice: Walsh, *Sacraments of Initiation*, 91; Sanday and Headlam, *Romans*, 154.

173. Morris, *Romans*, 246.

174. The fact that Christian initiation implies a serious act of "dying" is drawn by Morris from an etymological survey of baptism, cf. *Romans*, 246–47; also Stacey, *Groundwork of Biblical Studies*, 327.

a Christian, and apart from that death baptism is meaningless."[175] This is stated when he is dealing with Romans 6:3. But Morris does not examine in depth how this works in Paul's argument. More specifically, he does not show how Christ's action is the ground of the action that the believer takes in his or her initiation. This study seeks to understand whether there is evidence of such a relationship between the agency of Christ and the baptizand.

This is important because, as was outlined earlier, the pericope shows what the believer does but is also very much about Christ and what he did. As far as what Paul says is concerned, how do Christ's agency and the believer's agency meet in the process of baptism in such a way that the first is the ground for the second? In which way does Christ's deed play a part in the believer's initiation? This study tries to answer these questions that have often been touched upon but left unclear.

John A. Ziesler

Ziesler shows that "to die to sin" is action, but it is difficult to discern whether he speaks of the believer or Christ. This is evident in his statement, "'*To sin*' may indicate possession, so 'died to sin' means release from possession by sin. In any case there is complete separation."[176] The words "release" and "complete separation" denote action. The issue is whose action it is. If "release" and "separate" are in the reflexive sense (i.e. the believer releases himself or herself), the believer is involved in the action. But if the passive is the meaning (i.e. the believer is separated from sin), what is thought of is Christ's deed. In terms of action, some words are not very clear.

Ziesler appears to consider the believer to be the actor, when he says, "belonging to Christ involves dying, not in the meantime a physical dying, but a dying to all that has controlled the old self and in particular sin."[177] But then Christ is made the actor when Ziesler attributes all to Christ's death. For instance, he suggests that "death to sin" in verses 6–8 is a share in the *liberating* death of Christ. He states,

> The transition from the rule of Adam/sin to the rule of Christ is not a smooth one. It requires a death, especially to sin. Since

---

175. Morris, *Romans*, 247.
176. Ziesler, 153 [italics his].
177. Ziesler, 157.

the crucifixion of Christ, cf. 5:6–8, death has taken on a new nuance. It no longer stands simply for the result of condemnation, but now constitutes the gateway to life. When *shared in* by the believer, *Christ's death is liberating*.[178]

It is clear that the release referred to earlier is the act of Christ, because his death is *liberating*. The believer's act is seen just as sharing in what Christ has done. But as this study will try to prove, what Paul means in 6:2 is more than just the believer's state in Christ.

In sum, the ideas of Ziesler reveal the difficulty. It is unclear when on the one hand Ziesler's words show that "we died to sin" is an act of the believer and on the other hand he makes it to be Christ's act. This shows that agency in baptism still requires clarification. Our study tries to show that in line with what initiation is in Paul's world, the apostle speaks of what the deity does, but also of the responsibility that the candidate assumes in his or her entry to new existence.

Douglas J. Moo

Moo notices the act of dedication to righteousness in Romans 6.[179] This study also considers whether in Romans 5–6 this is another aspect that shows the baptizand's agency in his or her transition from life under sin to a Christian existence. This study (cf. the exegesis of 5:19, 21) will seek to throw light on whether righteousness (i.e. taking the responsibility to live a righteous life) is one of the actions that Paul ascribes to a person's transition from sin to God (cf. 5:19, 21). Moo hints at the personal responsibility to live righteously, when he states:

> Both paragraphs, vv. 1–14 and 15–23, look at the Christian's transfer from the realm of sin to that of righteousness. But the first focuses on the negative *release* from sin and the second on the positive *dedication to righteousness*.[180]

---

178. Ziesler, 153–54 [italics mine].
179. Moo, *Romans 1–8*, 368.
180. Moo, 368 [italics mine].

As these words show, verses 1–14 are about God's act of "release." In his view, the believer's dedication to righteousness is in verses 15–23, because it is "a consequence"[181] of God's release.

This study will argue that Paul's thought on the Christian transition and baptism and on the divine and human agency which this transition features begins from 5:12 and continues to 6:23. Concerning dedication to righteousness, which is the focus here, the intention in this study is to show that in Paul's argument this aspect comes even earlier than 6:15 (cf. 5:19, 21). This will be explained when we consider how the idea of attaching to the new life (stage four) works in Romans 5–6.

As this study seeks to argue, the new life is the reason for initiation and change from one system of existence to another, and righteous life is the reason for the transition to new life that Romans 5:12–6:23 is about. A dedication to live the new life, as we will see, is at the core of the process. This dedication is linked to each stage of the process of the believer's transition. This dedication is taking place when the person rejects sin (6:2) and when he or she undergoes the water ceremony and pledges to God and to the community (6:3). This dedication to and attachment to the new way of life is even linked with the first stage of encountering God, as we will see. This study seeks to show how in Romans 5–6, in relation to the idea of transition and baptism, dedication to new life is more significant than Moo suggests.

The "Apocalyptic Paul" Movement

Some interpreters of Paul argue that the apocalyptic ideas of Second Temple Judaism have much influenced the apostle's writings. The representatives of this group are, just to name a few, J. Louis Martyn, Martinus C. de Boer, Beverly Gaventa and Douglas Campbell.[182] Does interpreting Paul as an apocalyptic thinker consider baptism and transition from sin to God's way of life as a time of action? Or to pose the question in a direct link with the topic of the present work, does that transition feature just God's action or does it show also that people who are involved in that change are not just passive? Reflections that have a connection with these questions have been made. For example, Martyn thinks that the believers are "enlisted in their baptism

---

181. Moo, 368.
182. See Davies, *Paul Among Apocalypses*, 211.

as combatants in the cosmic struggle of the Spirit against the Flesh and the elements of the old cosmos . . ."[183] The question is whether baptism is a time of being passively enlisted by other people, or a time of taking personally full responsibility of waging the war against sin and evil powers.

The apocalyptic approach is much concerned with the believers' change from one realm to another, and this presupposes a time of transition. This can be seen in the scholars' debate on Paul's apocalyptic ideas. For example, there is a change of realms when Paul claims, as noted by D. A. Campbell, that God has resurrected and located him within a new creation,[184] a new existence.[185] And N. T. Wright, commenting on apocalyptic ideas in Galatians, finds that Paul's argument is that "in fulfilment of the divine purpose, Jesus gave himself for our sins to rescue us from the present evil age"[186] so that we may "share in God's new world."[187] This shows a move from one way of life to another, i.e. from living as the "slaves" of sin to living as God's "children and heirs."[188] In other words, it is the "new exodus-narrative"[189] that Paul seems to have in mind. Importantly for our study, as Wright notes, at the heart of this exodus lies a transitional time or event: "the slaves are set free by coming through the water."[190] Does this transition imply the believer's action?

In the approach to Paul's apocalyptic ideas, hints at action are made by scholars. They link action especially with God. For example, in his commentary on *The Acts of Paul*, Blackwell notes that "One primary element in apocalyptic writings is the activity of God in rectifying the problem of evil in the world . . ."[191] Because of that intense activity of God against evil powers, the interpreteraters of Pauline apocalyptic thoughts depict God as involved in a battle, a war, or an invasion. For example, speaking of Pauline soteriology, Martyn describes God's salvation as a battle; Christ's work is construed as

---

183. J. L. Martyn, cited by Davies, *Paul among the Apocalypses?* 159.
184. D. A. Campbell, "Apocalyptic Epistemology," 1383.
185. Campbell, 1387.
186. Wright, "Apocalyptic," 2428–2433.
187. Wright, 2441.
188. Wright, 2443.
189. Wright, 2505.
190. Wright says this with reference to Romans 6; see "Apocalyptic," 2505.
191. Blackwell, "Second-Century Perspectives," 3550.

"the apocalyptic battle of the end-time."[192] In the same line of thought, M. C. de Boer understands the eschatology of Paul as a time of a war between Christ and evil powers (including sin).[193] The question is whether action is taken by God only, while the believer remains passive in this battle for his or her liberation.

Since biblical apocalypticism points to a change which is so drastic that it can only be initiated by a divine force, the tendency has been to emphasise God's action to the detriment of what the believer is supposed to do in that process of moving to the new realm. In fact, in some scholars' views, human action appears as something that has no place when God saves his world from being enslaved by evil powers and sin. For exemple, as De Boer thinks about the OT prophetic eschatology, he realises that "The new Jerusalem will replace the old Jerusalem" and "the new order of reality will replace the old order of reality."[194] His view is that "This act of replacement will be initiated and brought about by God and God alone, which is to say that it cannot be initiated by human beings or effected by them."[195] Clearly, divine action is at the fore. This view is reiterated in De Boer's reflection. Drawing on what Weiss wrote concerning Jesus's proclamation of the Kingdom of God, he writes,

> By force and insurrection men might establish a Davidic monarch . . . but God will establish the Kingdom of God without human hands, horse or rider, with only his angels and celestial powers; God himself must come and make everything new; the actualization of the Kingdom of God is not a matter for human initiative, but entirely a matter of God's initiative.[196]

The incapacity of humans is again emphasised when De Boer states later that "human beings are not capable of putting an end to the old order of reality ("this age") and replacing it with a new one ("the age to come")."[197] He continues to argue that "It is only God who can bring life out of death,

---

192. J. L. Martyn's idea, summarised by Davies, *Paul Among Apocalypses*, 159.
193. M. C. de Boer's view, summarised by Davies, 161; see also M. C. de Boer, "Apocalyptic," 1037, 1069.
194. De Boer, 927.
195. De Boer, 927.
196. De Boer, 935.
197. De Boer, 977.

something out of nothing . . . and for that reason, there is no remedy for the human plight apart from God's own intervention."[198]

There is truth in these arguments. However, too much focus on what God does in the salvation process risks overlooking the person's action which is also meant in any transition to his or her new life. As the present work seeks to demonstrate, in Greco-Roman social and religious settings, any *passage* from one way of life to another seems to show not only divine action but also the action of the person involved in that change. Paul's teaching, as we will see, seems to show also that in the believer's change from sin to the Christian way of life, action is taken by God *and* the believer. Of course, God plays the major role. He is the main actor. All starts with his mighty intervention. Divine action stands at the first step in a person's transition to new life. As Martyn has noted, "Since humans are fundamentally slaves, the drama in which wrong is set right does not begin with action on their part. It begins with God's militant action against all the powers that hold human beings in bondage."[199] However the idea that comes next to these words is not convincing, when Martyn adds, "Thus, that action of God, instead of consisting at its center of a call for the slaves to repent and seek forgiveness, proves to be the deed by which God frees human beings."[200]

Martyn suggests that God's deed does not consist "at its center of a call for slaves to repent and seek forgiveness". The question is whether we can really separate the intervention of God from the moment he calls the person to repent. When the person is still in bondage, of course there is nothing he or she can do. But, when the bondage is dealt with by God, the freed person now has the ability to act. He or she can repent and ask forgiveness. In fact, Martyn's opinion, as we have just quoted, raises the following questions: For which purpose does God act to break the bondage of human beings? In other words, is the person set free to stay passive, or is he or she delivered in order to take active part in "the battle" (cf. Eph 6:10–18)[201] against the powers that

---

198. De Boer, 977–981.

199. J. L. Martyn, cited by Shaw, '"Then I Proceeded,'" 603–7.

200. Martyn, cited by Shaw, 607.

201. Ephesians 6:10–18 supports well the idea that the believer is very active in God's eschatological salvation. Here N. T. Wright's suggestion is noteworthy: "if we are serious about the 'apocalyptic Paul,' there is no excuse for not bringing 2 Thessalonians and even Ephesians in from the cold. Ephesians is explicit about the divine plan hidden for ages but now revealed,

have been enslaving the person? Loren T. Stuckenbruck notes that apocalyptic thought, in the Second Temple Period, has "an understanding of the faithful as those who . . . share in the divine triumph over evil" because they are people who are endowed with "the possibility of combating evil"[202].

It appears that apocalyptic thinking understands the saving act of God as one that is intended to cause or empower humans to take action. This causality is noted by Campbell, for example, when he states that "Paul's own account of his location [in Christ] *attributes its principal causality to divine action.*"[203] What he leaves unanswered is the question whether Paul is passive as to when his location in Christ takes place. Campbell does not show whether God's action enabled Paul to do anything during the time of his entry into Christ. Our purpose in the present work is to fill this gap in attempting a new explanation of Paul's teaching on baptism.

1.6. Conclusion

This chapter has presented what this study is about, namely, the idea that a balance between divine action and the initiand's role in baptism is still something which requires attention, and has proposed a socio-religious approach based on the four stages as a means for understanding whether this balance has a connection with Paul's thinking in Romans 6. Now that we have explored the scholarly landscape in relation to this balance of divine and human agency in baptism, we may proceed. This next step is a consideration of whether such a balance is a pattern of religious initiation in Greco-Roman life, and whether this balance is something that Paul also experienced in his own transition to Christian life. How this impacts the reading of Romans 5–6 will then follow.

---

and about ongoing warfare with the 'powers'"; see his "Apocalyptic and Sudden Fulfillment," 2517–21.

202. Stuckenbruck, "Some Reflections," 2748–51.
203. Campbell, "Apocalyptic Epistemology," 1390 [brackets and italics his].

CHAPTER TWO

The Four Stages of Entry into the New Life in Paul's Time

2.1. Introduction

In the early church, the teaching of converts evidences the stages of initiation. The *Didachè* features an instruction that exposed the believer to the "two Ways", that is, "the Way of Life" and "The Way of Death" (cf. its chs. I-VI).[1] This reflects the liminal second stage, where the person is in the state between the old and the new. Coming next to this is baptism (cf. its ch. VII), as these words state, "Having first taught all these things, baptize ye."[2] This is the ritual that seals entry (stage three). What the convert becomes and must do is embraced in this process of change (stage four); the new way of living is expressed as the liminal aspect of breaking with sin presented in chapters I to VI of the document.

This second chapter focuses on the socio-religious life of Paul's time, in order to understand what view concerning initiation both Paul and the Christians in Rome had before they became Christians, so that we can then test in the fourth chapter whether this had an impact on Paul's understanding of baptism in Romans 6. The focus is on whether in this social background both the deity and the initiand take action in initiation. To understand this,

---

1. Translation from Schaff, *Teaching of Twelve Apostles*, 162–184.
2. Trans. Schaff, 184.

the chapter explores how much the four stages of initiation and the idea of action connected to these stages are present in religious life in antiquity.

The first thing is to consider the ethnic origin of believers in Rome; this will then enable us to specify the settings of social life which are most relevant to this study and set a structure for this chapter.

2.1.1. Ethnic Origin of Believers in Rome

In order to understand the initiation assumptions that the readers of Romans could have, their cultural origin is considered here. Scholars have found that an important colony of Jews lived in Rome since 63 BCE;[3] in connection with this, it is very much believed that "Christianity in Rome originated among the Jews."[4] In fact the view of Mark Nanos is that Christ-followers to whom Paul writes are to be understood as Jews and Gentiles who lived and practised in "Jewish communal context"[5]; they were a "subgroup of the Jewish communities that believed Jesus represented the dawning of the awaited age."[6] This suggests that Judaism is one of the social settings to focus on if we want to comprehend the initiation ideas these believers had before they became Christians. But one must think of more than one ethnic-religious background for the group of Christians in Rome.

There have been different views as to which group is the audience that Paul has in mind when he writes Romans. Ferdinand C. Baur thought of "the addressees [of Romans] to be Jewish-Christians."[7] Other scholars emphasize the Gentiles as the addressees. For example, W. Campbell's view is that "Paul

---

3. It is believed that when Pompeius conquered Palestine in 63 BCE, he brought Jews as prisoners to Rome, see e.g. Edmundson, *Church in Rome*, 4; Brändle and Stegemann, "Formation," 119–20. The church in Rome was mainly made of Jewish Christians. One evidence is the expulsion of the Jews from Rome in AD 49 AD by Emperor Claudius. It is believed that this happened because of disturbances among Jews, and that these disturbances were probably caused by the objections of Jewish community to preachings by early Jewish Christians in the synagogues (http://www.owlapps.net/owlapps_apps/articles?id=38210052&lang=en, accessed 28 July 2021). As Dunn suggests, these were disturbances among Jews concerning Jesus, that is, disagreements between Jews who had accepted Jesus as Messiah (Jewish Christians) and Jews who rejected the Christian claims (Dunn, *Romans 1–8*, xlviii–xlix). For more detail on the hypothesis that the Christian groups in Rome emerged from within the Jewish Community that lived in Rome, see Dunn, *Romans 1–8*, xlvi–xlix."

4. Clarke, "Jew and Greek," 110.

5. Nanos, *Romans*, see the whole article (esp. 17–19); cf. also Nanos, "Jewish Context, 284.

6. Nanos, *Romans*, 20–23; cf. also Nanos, "Paul and Jewish Tradition," 65.

7. F. C. Baur's view, summarized by Wiefel, "Jewish Community," 85.

addresses the gentiles almost if not completely exclusively."[8] Also A. Das states that "Romans is ostensibly addressed to Gentiles,"[9] although his focus is on showing that "Jewish concerns dominate throughout."[10] Another strand of scholars simply considers that Paul writes to the two groups. For example, Edmundson thinks that the letter is sent to "a body of Jewish Christians" and "a larger body of converted Gentiles."[11] A detailed study of who is the main addressee of Paul is not our purpose. As our aim is rather to understand the original ethnic and religious background of the readers, we want to focus on what these different views have in common: i.e. that both Jews and Gentiles were members in the Church of Rome.

Drawing from Romans (esp. chapters 1, 2, 7, 9–11, and 15–16) and from external evidence, in general scholars agree that the Church of Rome comprised Jews and Gentiles[12] and that the Gentiles formed the majority.[13] Thus, as Clarke points out, it is recognized that "there was ethnic diversity within the Christian community" in Rome.[14]

What backgrounds are to be considered in this chapter in order to understand these believers' assumptions about initiation?

Judaism (i.e. what initiation meant in this setting) will be explored, because Jewish believers are a part of Paul's audience. This Jewish setting encompasses Jews and God-fearers.[15] As mentioned earlier, there is a wide consensus that those who started the church in Rome were Jews and Gentile

---

8. Campbell, "Addressees of Paul's Letter," 12.

9. Das, *Solving the Romans Debate*, 70; cf. 149.

10. Das, 70.

11. Edmundson adds a third group: "the mass of unbelieving Jews" (*Church in Rome*, 17); also P. Carrington's attention to "to all those in Rome who are loved by God and called to be saints" (*Early Christian Church*, 148, cf. 149–150, 170).

12. Lampe, "Roman Christians," 224–25; Watson, "Two Roman Congregations," 204; Clarke, "Jew and Greek," 110; Fitzmyer, *Romans*, 27–29; Dunn, *Romans 1–8*, xlv; Esler, *Conflict and Identity*, e.g. 12, 135, 137; Jewett, *Romans*, 61.

13. Stressing this, e.g. Campbell, "Addressees of Romans," 10–12; Lampe, "Roman Christians," 225; Brändle and Stegemann, "Formation of First," 124; Wiefel, "Jewish Community in Rome," 96.

14. Clarke, "Jew and Greek," 108.

15. E.g. Das: "His [Paul's] audience consisted of Gentiles – but rather atypical gentiles . . . [who] were familiar with the Jewish Scriptures, Israel's heritage, and the customs necessary for respectful behaviour in the presence of Jews" (*Solving Romans Debate*, 149, cf. 70).

God-fearers emerging from a Jewish *milieux*.[16] Judaism was their religion before they became Christians; initiation in this religion will be considered in order to understand initiation assumptions of Christians originating from this background.

But the Gentiles of the church in Rome presuppose a more diverse religious origin. As Edmundson points out, "a study of the names" has led to "the conclusion that the Roman Christians mainly belonged to the class of Greek-speaking freedmen and slaves,"[17] and these "would consist of people of every nationality, but among those converted to Christianity probably a large proportion were Orientals by race."[18] Thus other religions are a possible background. It should be noted that among those who immigrated to Rome were "the preachers and teachers of many philosophies, cults, and modes of worship, Greek, Egyptian, and Phrygian."[19] People had been observing their original religions before they became Christians. These could be oriental religions,[20] but other foreign populations could be worshippers of state deities.[21] In view of this, we may now specify the settings of social life that are most relevant to this study and set a structure for this chapter.

---

16. Focusing on this, e.g. Nanos, "Jewish Context," 284; Lampe, "Roman Christians," 225; Brändle and Stegemann, "Formation of First," 118.

17. Edmundson, *Church in Rome*, 25; so also Lampe, "Roman Christians," 228.

18. Edmundson, 25 fn. 1; cf. Lampe, "Roman Christians," 219, 226–27.

19. Edmundson, 4.

20. E.g. Wiefel, "Jewish Community," 86, 88.

21. The foreign populations were not only slaves; there were even officials, as Edmundson notes: "The legionaries were recruited in all parts of the empire; the Pretorian camp contained contingents drawn from distant frontier tribes" (Edmundson, *Church in Rome*, 4).

2.1.2. Relevant Religious Settings and Structure of Chapter Two

Initiation was much known and practised. Evidence for this is the language of initiation (especially τελετή[22] and μύησις[23])[24] which is widely used by classic thinkers, though sometimes metaphorically.[25] The widespread use of this

---

22. τελετή means "a ceremony, a ritual with religious significance, an official gathering to celebrate, an official or social occasion / function," https://www.bsarkari.com/teleth/meaning-english-greek/9927, accessed 28 July 2021. The meaning that is more in the sense of initiation is this: "a ceremonial by which a person attains or accomplishes a certain moral state, or attains purity or holiness," https://www.jstor.org/stable/700976, accessed 28 July 2021.

23. The lexicons and dictionaries provide the following meanings for the word μύησις: "Initiation" (ref. to LSJ), 'initiation aux préceptes d'une religion,' in English 'initiation to the precepts of a religion' (ref. to Bailly abrégé), see https://lsj.gr/wiki/μύησις (accessed 28 July 2021). In the Eleusinian Mysteries, especially in the cult of Demeter and Persephone, μύησις refers to the first stage of initiation, during which a sacred account and special symbols were revealed to the mystes, that is, the person who was undergoing initiation, https://thenamesdictionary.com/name-meanings/myesi/name-meaning-of-myesi, accessed 28 July 2021.

24. For more about the difference between τελετή and μύησις, e.g. Burkert, *Greek Religion*, 276.

25. E.g. Philo (first century AD) speaks of Moses initiating people into his mysteries (μυσταγωγῶν), cf. *On the Virtues* 178; also that people will see God "if worthily initiated (ἐὰν δ' ἀξίας τελεσθῇς τελετάς)," cf. *Quaest. Exod.* ii.51; also *Quaest. Gen.* iv.8. Philo and Plutarch see that philosophy takes people "through . . . stages of μύησις – initiation" (cf. G. Bornkamm, 'μυστήριον, μυέω', *TDNT*, vol. 4, 809). Dio Chrysostom (AD 40–110) says, in mysteries (ἐν τοῖς μυστηρίοις) things to do are shown to those being initiated (τοῖς μυουμένοις), cf. *Discourses* 17.5. Epictetus (mid-first to second century AD) speaks of the mysteries (τὰ μυστήρια) of Eleusis, cf. *Discourses* iii.21.13–17. Nock points out Seneca (first century AD) who sees in philosophy like in initiation the "seeing" (*epopteia*), cf. Nock, *Conversion*, 82. Lucian (second century AD) speaks of moving to higher mysteries (μετὰ τὰ μυστήρια), cf. *Hermotimus* 4. Plutarch (before AD 50 to after AD 120) speaks of "to sojourn in Eleusis during the Mysteries," μυστηρίοις ἐν Ἐλευσῖνι (*On Exile* 604c); he denounces those who mimicked the rites as they tried to "make" their party "a Telesterion," τελεστήριον ἐποίησαν (cf. *Table-Talk* i.4.621c); he recommends not listening those who say that "there are religious ceremonies and mystic rites disregarded by the gods," τελετὰς καὶ ὀργιασμοὺς ἀμελουμένους ὑπὸ θεῶν (cf. *Defec. Or.* 417a); also *Defec. Or.* 417b; *Her. Mal.* 857c; and metaphorically in *Cons. Ap.* 107e. Quoting Aristotle, Synesius (AD 370–413) shows that "initiates into mysteries do not learn anything . . . but rather have an experience . . . and are put in a certain state of mind," cf. Meyer, *Ancient Mysteries*, 12.

The initiation of Paul's time came down from more ancient Greek society. As Burkert states, initiation "is older than the developed *polis* system" and that it "could also lead beyond it" (*Greek Religion*, 278; and Hatch, *Influence of Greek Ideas*, 283; Pellegrino, "Culture classique et Christianisme," in *DECA* vol. 1, 597 col. 2 – 598 col. 1; Epictetus: "all these things were established by men of old time," cf. *Discourses* iii.21.15). Thus, initiatory ideas antedating Paul can be noted here. Lycophron (third century BCE) speaks of brave acts of the initiate (μύστη), cf. *Alexandra* 1325–29. Aristotle (384–322 BCE) speaks of the secrecy of mysteries (τὰ μυστικά), cf. *Nic. Et.* iii.1.17; and the mysteries (τὰ μυστήρια) as the most honoured of all festivals (πασῶν τιμιωτάτη τελετή), cf. *Ar. Rhet.* ii.24.2. Demosthenes (384–322 BCE) speaks of τελούση (cf. *De Corona* 259). Plato (429–347 BCE) speaks of being initiated into perfect mysteries (τελέους ἀεὶ τελετὰς τελούμενος), cf. *Phaedrus* 249c.; having been initiated (μεμύησαι), cf. *Gorgias* 497c; Plato speaks of Diotima's wish for Socrates to be initiated (σὺ μυηθείς), cf. Plato, *Symposium* 210a;

language leads one to the conclusion that Paul and his readers were very familiar with the idea of initiation and what was involved in undergoing such a transition to a new way of life.

Among the various settings in which initiation appears, this practice was chiefly connected with cults, especially mysteries. As Bornkamm points out, these cults were such that "those who wish to take part in their celebration must undergo initiation."[26] Other religious *milieux* initiated new adherents too. As Carlson recognizes, "in the life and self-understanding of ancient religions be they Christian, Jewish, Isian, mystery, Gnostic, or whatever, an initiation rite was a standard element or pattern."[27] Beside religions, as Wedderburn notes, initiation was so "widespread" that there were "rites of passage in other settings and other ages."[28] Some of these settings in which an entry process was a key element were "voluntary clubs," the *collegia*.[29] People entered these associations in response to the economic and social conditions of the era.[30] The importance of *collegia* in Greco-Roman time[31] is another element which shows that Paul and his readers had a strong idea of what a process of initiation meant.

Apart from the voluntary initiation of cults and the *collegia*, the category of initiation which Zempléni calls "les initiations obligatoires" (obligatory initiations)[32] also featured in the Greco-Roman world. In this category are

---

see 208–211. Thucydides (fifth century BCE) denounces the fact that mysteries (τὰ μυστήρια) of Hermes were being performed in private houses in mockery (cf. *Hist. Pel. War* vi.28.1). For more, see Meyer, *Ancient Mysteries*; also Jaeger, *Paideia*, vols. 1, 2 and 3 (e.g. vol. 1, 177).

26. Bornkamm, "μυστήριον," 803; Wedderburn, *Baptism and Resurrection*, 394.

27. Carlson, "Role of Baptism," 257; M. Eliade, *Rites and Symbols*, 116.

28. Wedderburn, *Baptism and Resurrection*, 394.

29. Tidball, "Social Setting," 888 col. 1; Tod and Hornblower, "Clubs, Greek," 352–53; Jeffers, *Greco-Roman World*, 72, 73.

30. Rose, *Ancient Roman Religion*, 50; Jeffers, *Greco-Roman World*, 73.

31. The *collegia* comprised 4 types: 1) of professions and trade, 2) religious, 3) of burial, 4) of households, cf. Jeffers, *Greco-Roman World*, 74–77. In fact, ἑταίρα/ ἑταιρια, which means "association or brotherhood," suggests more because this word-group includes not only the "collegia" sort, but also clubs and political unions (cf. *GEL*, s.v. "ἑταίρα") and "fellow-membership of disciples of a school of philosophy" (*GEL*, s.v. "ἑταῖρος").

32. A. Zempléni shows that ethnology distinguishes 3 categories: 1) "les initiations religieuses" (religious initiations), 2) "les initiations facultatives et volontaires" (optional and voluntary initiations), 3) "les initiations tribales obligatoires" (compulsory tribal initiations), see Zempléni, "Initiation," in *DEA*, 375.

found the *passage* to adulthood (e.g. the *toga virilis* for Roman boys)[33] and the entry of a bride into her husband's family.

Hence, Greco-Roman life shows several settings which one may explore in order to understand in which sense in antiquity a transition from one way of life to another entailed either action or passivity. Since Romans 5:12–6:23 is about this kind of transition, it is appropriate to give attention to the religious circles. In fact, the *collegia* were all connected with a deity, even those which were not primarily formed for religious purposes.[34]

As Fitzmyer recognizes, history shows that "many persons with foreign names" were in Rome and "foreign cults too were brought there: that of Mithras . . ., Isis and Osiris, of Dea Syria . . ., of Judaism, and of Christianity."[35] To understand whether in Paul's thinking, and in particular in the assumptions of his readership, the transition to a new religious life implies divine agency and the agency of the initiand, this chapter is divided into three sections which explore three main streams of religion to which Christians in Rome may be assumed to have been linked before their conversion to Christianity:

1) The first section focuses on the mystery cults and seeks to understand whether these acts that underline the agency of the candidate in his or her entry to new life are present in mystery worship. The mysteries are important because, as Dunn shows, scholars suspect that Paul was influenced by mysteries, especially concerning initiation.[36] Schweitzer and others argue that Paul draws on mystical language but uses it with very different meanings compared to general ideas linked to initiation in the cults.[37] In this study, the intention is not another discussion of whether Paul was influenced by mysteries or not. Rather, our purpose is to find what assumptions about initiation

---

33. Cf. Harrill, "Coming of Age," 252–77. For explanation of *toga virilis*, see the section "The Four Stages and State Religions," particularly at its sub-sction "Initiation to Adulthood" which begins on p. 61 of the present work.

34. Rose, *Ancient Roman Religion*, 50; Highet and Lintott, "Clubs," 352 col. 2; Tidball, "Social Setting," 888 col. 1.

35. Fitzmyer, *Romans*, 26–27.

36. Dunn, *Romans 1–8*, 308; more on this: 308–311.

37. Schweitzer, *Mysticism of Paul*, 14, 125, 374; Wagner, *Pauline Baptism*, 43; Wedderburn, *Baptism and Resurrection*, 2–3, 5, 69; Bultmann, *Theology of New Testament*, 312; Ferguson, *Backgrounds of Early Christianity*, 239; Davies, *Paul and Rabbinic Judaism*, 98; Oepke, ἐγείρω," in *TDNT*, vol. 2, 336; Edwards, *Romans*, 160.

the Christians in Rome, who might have formerly been members of mystery cults, could have had.

2) The second section focuses on initiation into state religions. This is to examine whether a Christian who had undergone an initiation into state religious life would have experienced the four stages and the action that they imply.

3) Another aspect is what presumptions about entry to new life Paul as a Jew, and the Jews among his Roman readers, could have. Thus, in the third section we consider what the process of entry into Judaism is like.

This chapter will demonstrate that entry to a new religious life in Paul's society was such that the divine saving action was the first stage of this transition to a new way of life. Other stages (stages two, three and four) also were present, and these were about the initiand's action. Breaking with one's old way of life or dying to that life was the second stage of action in this transition process. It will also be demonstrated that the third stage action shows up in the public ritual which usually featured in the process of such a transition. As this third stage will show, to undergo such a ritual was a pledge to the new community and to their deity that the break with the old (in stage two) was serious. Another element that will be shown to be a feature in Paul's time is that the new life begins in the transition. This consideration of the context of Paul regarding the four stages of a transition to new life is significant to this thesis. These insights will illumine the third chapter (which is about Paul's own transition and baptism) and the fourth chapter (which explores the believer's transition and baptism in Romans 5:12–6:23).

2.2. The Four Stages and the Mysteries

First, initiation or entry into the mysteries is considered. The focus is on whether initiation in these cults evidences the four stages, and on what kind of action is involved in these stages. This is done by combining insights from the different cults (despite their differences).[38] This approach is necessitated by 1) their number and 2) by their secrecy, which makes information about

---

38. E.g. Nash, *Christianity*, 122.

them scanty.[39] First, mystery cults were so many[40] that, as Nash observes, "Each region of the Mediterranean seems to have produced its own mystery religion."[41] To deal with each of them separately would be beyond the scope of this study. Second, besides the large number, they were secret religions.[42] This means we only have fragmentary information on their processes of initiation.[43] When these fragments are put together they show enough evidence of how the transition to a new religious life entailed, not only a saving act of the deity, but also the initiand's act of breaking with the previous way of life and the other stages of action that have been outlined in the first chapter.

We need to be precise about the use of sources here. This section builds upon the exploration of the original material on initiation into the mysteries, which has been fully undertaken already. Thus, secondary reviews of mystery religions are widely drawn upon in this part, especially when we consider that the material they contain is quite uncontroversial. In addition, in a few places we go back to the original primary sources such as Apuleius's *The Golden Ass*. That initiation was a feature of the mysteries is itself not a controversial issue. What has not been done is an analysis of this initiation into the four stages. This new analysis is the focus in this section. The same approach is also applied in the section about state religion and Judaism.

The second aspect is that in this section about mysteries and the next two sections, the numbers one to four are used to show where each of the four stages is dealt with. Another point concerns the third-person pronoun. Religious groups in the ancient world differed from each other, in offering initiation to men, or women, or both genders. The proselyte in Jewish tractates is especially referred to as "he." Some mystery religions were especially for women (that of Dionysus for instance – at least in places), while others were

---

39. Broneer, "Paul and Pagan Cults," 170.

40. Cf. Reitzenstein, *Hellenistic Mystery-Religions*, 240; Walsh, *Sacraments of Initiation*, 24; Broneer, "Paul and Pagan Cults," 170.

41. Nash, *Christianity and Hellenistic World*, 116; although H. Rahner thinks initiation was "confined to certain areas," cf. *Greek Myths and Christian Mystery*, 18.

42. E.g. Nash, *Christianity and Hellenistic World*, 122; Ferguson, *Religions of Roman Empire*, 111; Meyer, *Ancient Mysteries*, 4.

43. Dunn, "Mystery," 185 col. 2; Broneer, "Paul and Pagan Cults," 170; Wedderburn, "Soteriology of Mysteries," 62; Meyer, "Mysteries," 721 col. 1. Meyer points out some texts as giving detail, i.e Aristophanes' *Frogs*, the Rule of the Andanian Mysteries, Arnobius' *The Case against the Pagans*, Apuleius' *The Golden Ass* xi, cf. Meyer, *Ancient Mysteries*, 9. But it is really Apuleius's *The Golden Ass*, xi, that shows the process of transition *per se*.

for men only (e.g. Mithraism). For convenience, in this chapter the initiand is referred to as "he," except when it will be a transition that is specifically about a woman.

1) The first stage is the candidate's encounter with the deity which the new community worships. The important element is that the person is delivered at this stage. The stress is on the action of the deity. This element features in the mysteries.

As Meyer recognizes, "an immediate or mystical encounter with the divine" is a prevalent feature in mysteries.[44] For some mystery cults this encounter begins the process, and for others it is stressed at the end. But in both situations the rest of the process is motivated by the divine encounter. For example, it occurs at the beginning in the Isis mystery. In *The Golden Ass* (AD 180),[45] Lucius' first step into Isis' realm is when the goddess appears to him.[46] Also in the Dionysus cult, "presiding over the whole scene are the figures of Dionysus and Ariadne."[47] The intention is to stress the presence of the god through the entire event, even though the candidate meets the deity at the very beginning. Like Lucius, the experience of Aelius Aristides in connection with the Asclepius mysteries begins with his encounter with the "Saviour god" in a vision.[48] In other mysteries the encounter with the deity concludes the transition, but with the same sense that it motivates the rest of the process. For example, with the Cabeiri "seeing the spectacle," which includes meeting god, is the closing scene. It is connected with reaching the status of *epoptae*, bringing the initiates to a "higher grade."[49] Also a "vision of knowledge of god" lies at the end in the mysteries of Hermes Trismegistos.[50]

Whether the encounter is placed at the very beginning as propelling the person into initiation, or whether it is highlighted at the end as the goal of the whole process, the meaning is the same: that to meet the gods, or as Wedderburn puts it "approaching the gods" and being "close to them" in

---

44. E.g. Meyer, *Ancient Mysteries*, 8.

45. A later source (around AD 180), see Salmon, "Apuleius," 74, but important for the Isis initiation.

46. Apuleius, *Golden Ass*, xi.5.

47. Ferguson, *Religions of Roman Empire*, 103.

48. Ferguson, 111.

49. Ferguson, 123.

50. Ferguson, 109.

"communion with them,"[51] is the basis of initiation. At this stage the action is divine, and it motivates the rest of the actions which the candidate makes at stages two to four. We may now focus on this divine action.

The deliverance which the deity performs for the initiand is the focus of the action at this stage. For example, Isis appears to Lucius and offers to save him as these words show: "Behold I am come to take pity of thy fortune and tribulation; behold I am present to favour and aid thee; leave off thy weeping and lamentation, put away all thy sorrow . . ."[52] Isis says it is a favour. Later in the process the priest makes a connection with this divine benevolence by drawing Lucius's attention to the fact that the altar he is reaching out to is but "the altar of mercy" which "not [his] birth, or his position [as a lawyer],[53] or even [his] fine education" could provide him.[54] In fact, Lucius himself recognizes that "salvation was obtained by favour."[55]

Lucius had "washed" and "prayed" before Isis came to restore his life.[56] But at this stage the focus is really on what the goddess does rather than on the act of Lucius. His prayer and purification prove not to be a condition fulfilled to merit the god's action. Hatch interprets Lucius' prayer as a condition for his deliverance,[57] but such a sense hardly applies in reality. His prayer and purification reveal his dependence and need of grace.[58] One must note that it is laced with "weeping" for aid.[59] A similar kind of repentance in the need for grace appears in the cult of Hermes Trismegistos[60] and the cult of Dionysus.[61]

Around this episode of deliverance, the initiand appears to take some action when Lucius is to go and get "the roses" (of deliverance)[62] from the

---

51. Wedderburn, "Soteriology of Mysteries," 59; Badke, "Baptized into Moses," 99.
52. *Golden Ass*, xi. 5.
53. *Golden Ass*, xi. 30.
54. *Golden Ass*, xi. 15.
55. *Golden Ass*, xi. 21.
56. *Golden Ass*, xi. 1–2.
57. Hatch suggests that self-purification was the 1st stage and condition to "approach God" (cf. *Influence of Greek Ideas*, 285).
58. A hint from Wedderburn, "Soteriology of Mysteries," 59.
59. *Golden Ass*, xi. 1.
60. Ferguson, *Religions of Roman Empire*, 109.
61. Ferguson, 103.
62. He eats the roses and is restored, cf. *Golden Ass*, xi. 13.

priest's hand.⁶³ But still the focus is on divine deliverance. What Lucius does, shows the receiving and an obedient heart which goes hand in hand with the god's saving act (compare Paul's words in Rom 5:17). Isis exhorts Lucius to get the roses, but not because she is imposing a condition for deliverance. In fact, when she exhorts him to undertake that action, she also re-assures him that her "good will" to save him stands.⁶⁴

So concerning action, the encounter with the deity stresses the divine saving act. The obedience of opening one's heart to receive the god's favour is far from being an act *per se* because the initiand is not accountable for doing so. The action that really means responsibility is connected with stages two to four. We may now consider stage two.

2) The second or liminal stage in the transition process is when the candidate is between the old and the new, breaks with the way in which he was living and decisively attaches to the new life. Although Paul's expression "to die to" something is not used directly in the mysteries, the idea is still present. In order to have a deep sense of dying to the old and passing through a sort of no-life, various means are used in the mysteries, including difficult experiences. As Burkert recognizes, "trial" is one of the three things that shape the process of initiation.⁶⁵ To ponder, in order to engage seriously with the new way is the touchstone of this phase.

Many elements in the mysteries reveal this second stage. For example, Lucius went through a time in which he "learned" about "the obligations" of the cult and "pondered these matters again and again."⁶⁶ It should be noted that what he ponders are "obligations." Clearly, the idea is to take action. In the mysteries of Hermes, the initiand experiences a time of "contemplation" that goes together with a test of asceticism.⁶⁷ The contemplation involves wonder at the new and all its differences from the old. This reflects the action of the person who is between the old and the new.

---

63. *Golden Ass,* xi. 6.

64. *Golden Ass,* xi. 6.

65. Apart from "trial," there are "preparation" and "investiture" cf. Burkert, *Greek Religion,* 262, also page 277 on "suffering" and initiation.

66. *Golden Ass,* xi. 19; Reitzenstein: the demand of the Isis cult caused "many to shrink from it" (cf. *Hellenistic Mystery-Religions,* 20).

67. Ferguson, *Religions of Roman Empire,* 109.

The act of dying to the old is symbolized by the hard experience which is the key characteristic of this liminal phase. The mysteries show such trials. For instance, the frescoes from the Dionysus' cult show that a "long rod" is being "wielded" and the candidate's "bared back" is made ready "for the blows."[68] The ordeal for the worshippers of Mithras consists of branding, ordeals by heat and cold, fasting, scourging, and journeying.[69] In the Cybele cult even "self-castration" was practised.[70] What the healing god Asclepius commands in his healing scheme includes "walking barefoot" and "taking cold baths."[71] Sometimes the hardship is less physical but highly significant in breaking with the old. For example, the worshipper of Hermes undergoes "asceticism," "moral purity," and the ability to "control the senses."[72] In the Isis' cult, Lucius has to endure "ten days of abstention and continence" and show "religious zeal."[73] The reason is that he has to show a "triumphant step" before he "joins the procession of the saviour."[74] So entry into mysteries includes serious episodes. Plutarch's words summarize what they generally consisted of: "wandering, wearisome roaming, and fearful travelling through darkness with no end to be found. Then, just before the consummation (*telos*), there is every sort of terror, shuddering and trembling, and perspiring, and being alarmed."[75] This illustrates "the state of non-being" of the liminal phase, as referred to earlier.

What does this hard experience mean? Ferguson suggests that the aim is to "test the endurance."[76] Indeed those who enter the new life should prove that they are able to endure its requirements. However, these severe experiences mean more than to test endurance alone. The primary purpose is the person's break with the old way of life, in two respects: (i) the idea is to die

---

68. Ferguson, 103–104.
69. Ferguson, 112. Mithraism had 7 levels of initiation (cf. Reitzenstein, *Hellenistic Mystery-Religions*, 10; Walsh, *Sacraments*, 24), which means 7 testing times, cf. Jeffers, *Greco-Roman World*, 97–98.
70. E.g. Wedderburn, "Soteriology of Mysteries," 70.
71. Ferguson, *Religions of Roman Empire*, 111.
72. Ferguson, 109.
73. Apuleius, *Golden Ass*, xi. 28
74. Apuleius, xi. 15.
75. Plutarch's fragment in Stobaeus, *Anthology,* cited by Meyer, *Ancient Mysteries,* 9.
76. Cf. Ferguson, *Religions of Roman Empire,* 104, 112.

to something, a separation from it; (ii) this death means action because it implies personal choice, and that this choice entails accountability.

(i) First the idea with the ordeal is to die. The hard condition that is part of initiation rests on the idea that new life springs out of death. As Ritzenstein recognizes, the hard test symbolizes "a passing away."[77] In other words, as Meyer states, initiation is "the place of death."[78] This experience was more than to meditate on the day when one's physical death would occur. For example, Burkert speaks of the mysteries and recognizes that their initiation includes death when he states that "Deadly terror provoked and dispelled in ritual can be experienced and interpreted as anticipation and overcoming of death."[79] The initiation episodes that we have just illustrated meant more than to deal with the fear concerning one's physical death. The primary idea was that the initiand experienced a death and died to the old way of life. This sense is required by the fact that the person was in the context of transition from the old life to a new way. Ferguson notes that the flagellation of the worshippers of Dionysus rests on the idea that "a death must precede resurrection."[80] In fact this idea of dying has been noted in mysteries in general.[81]

(ii) This death is chosen personally.[82] This element shows strongly that it is an act. Skemp notes Synesius's statement (himself quoting from Aristotle[83]) that "The initiates went not to learn something but to have something done to them."[84] In fact it was more than to "have things done to" the initiand. As this second phase shows, the initiand himself did serious acts that meant his death to the old. Earlier we mentioned the "self-castration" of the initiands

---

77. Reitzenstein, *Hellenistic Mystery-Religions*, 211.
78. Meyer, *Ancient Mysteries*, 9; Plutarch's comparison of "to be initiated" and "dying," cited by Meyer, "Mysteries," 721 col. 1.
79. Burkert, *Greek Religion*, 277.
80. Ferguson, *Religions of Empire*, 104.
81. Meyer, *Ancient Mysteries*, 8; also Reitzenstein, *Hellenistic Mystery-Religions*, 211–212.
82. Meyer, *Ancient Mysteries*, 4, and Meyer, "Mysteries," 720 col. 2.
83. Meyer, "Mysteries," 721 col. 2.
84. Skemp, *The Greeks and the Gospel*, London: Carey Kingsgate Press, 1964, 71.

of the cult of Cybele. Lucius speaks of this death as "a voluntary death,"[85] the *voluntaria mors* as Reitzenstein puts it.[86] This is also the view of Philo.[87]

The idea of voluntary death appears in several accounts. Another example is the *taurobolium* of the Cybele worship, though it is dated much later than Paul's time.[88] It consists of descending into a pit, which in Reitzenstein's view has the meaning of "a grave."[89] The act symbolizes the person's death to the old way because the meaning is that by this act the person separates from "everything that is earthly."[90] It must be noted that this was a personal action. Not only did the initiand descend into "the grave" by himself, he also catches the blood and fills all his senses (mouth, eyes, nose and ears) with it.[91] It is a personal death.

The Dionysus mysteries also show that the candidate takes it deliberately. Before the ordeal takes place, the neophyte girl has presented offerings. The thing to note is that the offering is received by another girl, a maidservant.[92] The fact that the girl is welcomed by another girl suggests a deliberate act. In such a formal context, and in primitive society, to depose the offering into the hands of an elderly official would have suggested the idea of an obligation. Earlier we noted that the Hermes mysteries considered asceticism and other things to be indispensable. For these too, "the initiate [initiand] was expected himself to take the initiative."[93] The action was his. He had to break with the old way as this exhortation to the devotees of Hermes shows clearly:

---

85. *Golden Ass*, xi. 21, cf. also xi. 15.

86. Reitzenstein, *Hellenistic Mystery-Religions*, 212 [italics his].

87. Philo means the process of life, not just the transition, but speaks of voluntary death, τῶν ἀνόθως φιλοσοφησάντων, ἐξ ἀρχῆς ἄχρι τέλους μελετῶσαι τὸν μετὰ σωμάτων ἀποθνῄσκειν βίον, "of those who have *given themselves* to genuine philosophy, who from first to last study *to die to the life in the body*" (cf. *On the Giants*, 14) [as opposed to those who] "*have abandoned themselves* to the unstable things of chance," τυχηροῖς πράγμασιν ἑαυτούς (*On the Giants*, 15 [italics mine]).

88. Nash thinks initially it was to sacrifice the bull and then after AD 300 "it evolved into the blood bath." Cf. *Christianity and Hellenistic World*, 155.

89. Reitzenstein understands the pit is a "grave" (cf. *Hellenistic Mystery-Religions*, 45).

90. Reitzenstein, 45.

91. Cf. Prudentius' account on *Taurobolium*, cited by Ferguson, *Religions of Empire*, 104–105; also Reitzenstein, *Hellenistic Mystery-Religions*, 45.

92. Ferguson, *Religions of Empire*, 103.

93. Ferguson, 109.

"rid yourselves of darkness and grasp light; forsake corruption and partake of immortality."[94] Similarly, in Mithraism the ordeal is intertwined with renunciation. As Ferguson shows, "The soldier was offered a crown across a sword; this he had to win and then *renounce* with the words, 'Mittras is my crown.'"[95] To cross a sword conveys a strong sense of dying. We may note that the death to the old way is associated with renouncing. This element of renouncing or making oaths was in fact customary.[96] It suggests another action. The third stage reveals further what constitutes this action in the mysteries.

3) The third stage is the aspect of initiation that consists of a public ceremony by which the initiand recognizes his or her rejection of the old way. By this act the attachment with the new system is sealed. As Burkert states, the person becomes "sacred" because "the boundary which separated the sacred from the profane" is crossed.[97] This phase is mainly represented by a ritual (or a series of rituals) undergone before an "audience of witnesses."[98] The presence of witnesses is a common feature.[99] This is another element showing action; the idea is to swear to other members that the new status is seriously embraced and will be honoured.

The examples of this public act are many in the mysteries. In the Lucius account, this is demonstrated by the act of enrolling. His enrolment is a

---

94. Ferguson, 109.

95. Ferguson, 112.

96. E.g. Isis cult (*Golden Ass*, xi. 15); Andanian mysteries, Meyer, *Ancient Mysteries*, 52–53; for other mysteries, cf. Reitzenstein, *Hellenistic Mystery-Religions*, 237–60; Qumran community's idea of "covenant," from Hebrew *berith*, which is "acceptance *upon oath*" (cf. White, *Biblical Doctrine of Initiation*, 19); oath in DSS, e.g. 1QS i.7; 1QS v.7–11; CD xv.5; 1QS i.20 – ii.12; more on this, Josephus, *Jewish War* ii. 137–42; D. Hill, "On Suffering and Baptism," 188; Schiffman, "Oaths and Vows," 621.

97. Burkert, *Greek Religion*, 77–78.

98. Meyer just hints at this, cf. *Ancient Mysteries*, 11–12, also 9–10.

99. The "confession" of the Cabeiri presupposes witnesses (cf. Ferguson, *Religions of Empire*, 123); the Andanian mysteries, the oath is before "the priest and the sacred men"; cf. Meyer, *Ancient Mysteries*, 52–53; the person undergoing *taurobolium* is awaited by people (cf. Nock, *Conversion*, 69), the same as in the Isis cult (cf. Ferguson, *Religions of Roman Empire*, 108). In the Dionysus mysteries, witnesses are gods and people. It is not only gods pictured at every step, the devotees' watching is noteworthy: the guiding matron, the maiden who receives the neophyte's offerings, the priestess and her attendants, the woman in the corner "staring in terror" apparently telling the neophyte that "the road to bliss lies through suffering," the kneeling woman with a phallus, and the woman who holds "in her lap" the neophyte and "comforts her" (cf. Ferguson, *Religions of Roman Empire*, 103–104).

personal act. In fact, the priest says: "make thyself one of this holy order."[100] There is action also in the fact that his enrolment means that he "dedicates [his] mind to obeying" the cult.[101] In other words, he takes responsibility. Another ritual in this respect is Lucius' baptism,[102] a practice which is also found in many mysteries.[103] The author links this washing with the idea of "demanding pardon of the gods" and "purification of body."[104] Thus Ferguson interprets this to mean "remission of sins."[105] But the act means more than this. It "solemnly proclaims"[106] that the attachment is decisive, and that full responsibility is taken.[107] First, evidence of this is its public aspect because he is "accompanied with all the religious, *religiosa cohorte*."[108] Even the gods are considered as witnesses.[109] Second, Lucius' baptism is connected with his acts of "taking residence in the temple"[110] and "diligent service" (worship) to Isis.[111]

In the Cabeiri mysteries, the ritual that actively indicates the solemnity of the decision consists in the acts of "wearing a crown" and then "an iron ring and a purple scarf."[112] In this also action is noted. To don a crown shows elevation and responsibility. The fact of taking it is itself a pledge to honour one's new status, especially because these rituals are performed in the presence of fellow members and the gods.

The meaning of the ritual that seals initiation is centred on the relation between the initiand and these witnesses to whom the pledge is made. Enemy

---

100. Apuleius, *Golden Ass*, xi. 15.

101. Apuleius, xi. 15.

102. Apuleius, xi.23; cf. Ferguson, *Religions of Empire*, 108; Reitzenstein, *Hellenistic Mystery-Religions*, 20–21.

103. Reitzenstein, *Hellenistic Mystery-Religions*, 196; Burkert, *Greek Religion*, 78; Nock, "Early Gentile Christianity," 112–14.

104. *Golden Ass*, xi. 23.

105. Ferguson, *Religions of Empire*, 108.

106. Reitzenstein, *Hellenistic Mystery-Religions*, 21 (from 20).

107. Cf. Nock's view of the Church baptism and its "character of finality, such as . . . with entry on the monastic life" (cf. Nock, *Conversion*, 261).

108. *Golden Ass*, xi. 23; also Nock, *Conversion*, 145; the intention is that initiates and non-initiates will all look at the act, cf. Golden Ass xi. 15–16. Especially the presence of dignitaries, cf. Meyer (ed.), *Ancient Mysteries*, 9–10.

109. Apuleius, *Golden Ass*, xi. 23; the *taurobolium* was to be "sanctioned" by the gods (cf. Nock, *Conversion*, 70).

110. *Golden Ass*, xi. 19.

111. *Golden Ass*, xi. 19, 21; Ferguson, *Religions of Empire*, 108.

112. Ferguson, 123.

spirits appear to be the primary concern when (in Ferguson's view, for example) the iron ring and the purple scarf are "talismans against danger."[113] These signs are closely linked to the protective gods. That is, these objects are a sign of a covenant with good gods. To wear them is itself a declaration of belonging to these gods, and thus a pledge to live a life that honours them. This means that the action that takes place in fact concerns the new life also. The relation between the action of the initiand and the new life is the fourth stage.

4) The fourth stage concerns the new life for which the person undergoes initiation. Our aim here is to show that (i) in the mysteries, initiation is more about the earthly life than the afterlife; and (ii) that the action taken in initiation concerning this life is evidence of what is said in (i). That is, the candidate assumes the responsibility to live in a certain way, and he begins to do so in the event itself. These two aspects are also evident in state religions and in Judaism, as we will show when we deal with these settings. This idea that in antiquity initiation focuses on the candidate's earthly life is important when we interpret what Paul's use of the future tense really means, when he speaks of the new life in connection with the believer's transition from sin to God.

(i) Initiation is about new life. This is evident in the mysteries, especially with the idea of "rebirth" which features in most of these cults.[114] It is believed that in the process, the old way stops and the new takes place. For example, about the mysteries of Mithras, as Reitzenstein recognizes, "*The man in him* [the initiand] must pass away when the deity is born or he is born as the deity."[115] The focus is on the new way, and on the idea that in the event the initiand starts to live it.

Indeed, mysteries were also concerned with life in the other world. As Hatch notes, "The initiated were by virtue of their initiation made partakers of a life to come."[116] For example, Rahner shows that in relation to the Cybele/Attis cult "the Roman Sextilius Agesilaus Aeddesius records the various

---

113. Ferguson, 123.

114. Meyer, *Ancient Mysteries*, 8; Ferguson, *Religions of Empire*, 105 (esp. on the *Taurobolium*), also page 100 about Eleusinian mysteries, 107 on Isis cult, 109 about Hermes Trismegistos, 121–122 on Mithras.

115. Reitzenstein, cf. *Hellenistic Mystery-Religions*, 211 [italics his].

116. Hatch, *Influence of Greek*, 290.

mysteries which had promised him 'everlasting rebirth.'"[117] However, despite such concern for future life, the focus is on how one lives after initiation. A wholly new future now begins: "the special status attained through initiation is claimed to be valid even beyond death: the orgiastic festival of the *mystai* (secrets) continues to be held in the afterlife."[118]

The rebirth which was meant to happen through initiation was a new life That began at the moment of initiation and then to go on "hereafter."[119] Initiation addressed the issue of what the person would be in the other world, but it primarily concerned life on earth. As many recognize, it provided "the hopes for the next life" but especially it answered the issue of what happens in "this life."[120] As Hatch states, "The effect of it was conceived to be a change both of character and of relation to the gods."[121] In other words, it was about what from that moment the person becomes. This is recognized when Hatch notes that "They were bound to make their life on earth correspond to their initiation."[122]

This is supported by much evidence in the mysteries. In the Dionysus ceremonies, when the ordeal is finished, the candidate girl dons "the scarf" and this is "the same scarf which swirls over the head of the sea-queen."[123] Obviously, this means a change of status and life, and such a change takes place from that moment. It does not wait for the future. In fact, "the scarf lay ready under her arms during the flagellation."[124] A similar symbolism of donning the new way through a piece of clothing (a common feature)[125] is noted in the Isis mysteries. After the ritual of death, the candidate "emerges wearing twelve stoles, a linen shirt and a 'cloak of Olympus.'"[126] This is

---

117. Rahner, *Greek Myths*, 23. The idea of "immortality" is common to the mysteries, cf. Ferguson, *Religions of Empire*, 109 (esp. on Hermes cult: being in company with gods and thus immortal), and 108 (on Isis cult: being one with gods); also Meyer, *Ancient Mysteries*, 8 (on Mithras).

118. Burkert, *Greek Religion*, 277.

119. Nock, *Conversion*, 12.

120. Meyer, *Ancient Mysteries*, 9; Wedderburn, "Soteriology of Mysteries," 59, 63; Nock, *Conversion*, 12.

121. Hatch, *Influence of Greek*, 290.

122. Hatch, 290, fn.3.

123. Ferguson, *Religions of Empire*, 104.

124. Ferguson, 104.

125. Also, the Cabeiri (cf. Ferguson, *Religions of Empire*, 123).

126. Ferguson, 108.

communion with the god and means that living in the way of this god starts. The *taurobolium*[127] also shows that the new life begins at the ceremony, symbolised by the act of filling one's senses with blood. Reitzenstein notes that "Hellenistic theology later thinks that the descending divine spirit *seals* the sense-organs against everything that is earthly."[128] This shows that the person becomes the property of the deity, and the implication is that he begins to live the life which is in the ways of this divinity.

(ii) During initiation, action is taken concerning this new life. The person takes responsibility to live the new life and starts it. For example, when Meyer points out that candidates "come to life in a liturgical drama" we may note that in the drama they are not passive but they "play the roles . . . to re-enact" what the gods have experienced and through this "they are borne . . ." into the new life.[129] This is noteworthy because it shows that the new life was not something they just learned about. Rather, as Meyer notes (drawing on Aristotle), they "tasted" it[130] during the transition time and continued with it when living as initiates.

The idea of service further reveals this. As Reitzenstein notes, in the mysteries "initiation was connected with the word *sacramentum*" and this meant "the *service* of the initiate generally regarded as military *service* for his deity."[131] This service was connected with initiation. Not only is the decision to "serve" taken in initiation, but also the service starts. For example, Lucius's act of "enlisting" was the beginning of living in the way required by Isis, because the priest made clear to him that to enlist meant to "take upon thee a voluntary yoke of ministry."[132] And the meaning of this, as the priest specifies to him, is "you begin to serve and honour the goddess."[133] Clearly the stress is on the fact that the responsibility is taken to live the new way and that the initiand starts to live so. When the future tense is used, the context is of telling Lucius

---

127. This is "a ceremony in the cult of certain Mediterranean deities (as Cybele and Mithras) in which worshipers were baptised with the blood of a sacrificed bull," https://www.merriam-webster.com/dictionary/taurobolium, accessed on 5 August 2021.

128. Reitzenstein, *Hellenistic Mystery-Religions*, 45 [italics his].

129. Meyer, *Ancient Mysteries*, 11–12.

130. Meyer, 12–13.

131. Reitzenstein, *Hellenistic Mystery-Religions*, 240 [italics mine].

132. *Golden Ass*, xi. 15.

133. *Golden Ass*, xi. 15.

that the "pledge" he makes concerns his "life until the hour of death."[134] In other words, the future tense is used because the new existence applies seriously all the time, when he lives as an initiate.

This section considered what entry into the mysteries is like, with a focus on action that is taken during the event. The four stages show that initiation was about action. Apart from what the deity does in the first stage, there is much that the initiand does in stages two to four. He dies to the old way, and this means to break seriously with it and to attach himself to the new. In the mysteries this idea of death consisted of very hard experiences. The initiand felt something of a death. This death was understood to be his or her personal act. The main idea was that he or she chose and deliberately underwent the ordeal.

The mysteries show that what the initiand does in initiation is a series of interconnected actions. The act of dying to the old and breaking with it (stage 2) is connected with other actions. Through a public ritual (stage 3), the initiand swears in the presence of other members that the death to the old and separation from it is seriously made. But the break with the old and the public oath really mean that the initiand takes the responsibility to start living the new life (stage 4). In brief, the mysteries show that the initiand takes action in initiation. As Nock recognizes, much is done "by him" [or her].[135] The focus now is on whether the four stages and action are present in state religions.

2.3. The Four Stages and State Religions

In this section consideration is given to whether the act of dying to one's old life and the other actions taken in connection with it are a feature in the context of state religions. First, it is necessary to understand in which sense this setting illuminates Romans 6. As mentioned earlier, people who joined Christianity were either coming from mysteries or from the *polis* religion. People were very religious, both in Greek and Roman society. In Greek society, as Sourvinou-Inwood notes, "all relationships and bonds, including social

---

134. *Golden Ass*, xi. 6.
135. Nock, "Early Gentile Christianity," 57.

and political ones, were expressed, and so defined, through cult."¹³⁶ Roman society was no different. As Rose states, in Roman life "once past babyhood" the child became "something . . . sacred" and was involved in active religious roles: "the boy was an acolyte . . . to his father" (and the girl to her mother) in fulfilling religious rites and duties.¹³⁷ The fact that religion was such an integral part of life suggests that virtually all who became Christians had been worshippers of mystery gods or of the state gods. For this reason, it is also important to examine what in the *polis* religion the process of admission says on this issue of passivity versus action. What presumptions about initiation might the new Christian convert from a state religion have? Are the four stages of entry and the action entailed by each stage a feature of this setting?

A structure is also important for this part. In institutionalized religious life, initiation was connected with different circumstances. For example, as Fowler shows, at infanthood there was admission of the child into "the family and its sacra."¹³⁸ The child does not take any responsibility. Other events of initiation, however, happened when people were more mature and accountable for their acts. These are for example initiation to adulthood and the bride's entry into marriage. These events meant respectively a change in physical and matrimonial respect, but in fact they were occasions whereby the person was "introduced to the cults of the *polis*."¹³⁹ They meant admission into religious concerns, the area of our study we mentioned earlier. We want to see what the four stages and the action that they mean were like, by considering 1) initiation into adulthood and 2) the bride's entry into marriage.

2.3.1. Initiation to Adulthood

First, we examine the *passage* from childhood to adulthood. Sourvinou-Inwood hints at a resemblance between mysteries and state religion when she states that "cult activities which in culturally determined terms would

---

136. C. Sourvinou-Inwood, "What is *Polis* Religion," 27.

137. Rose, *Ancient Roman Religion*, 42. On how religious the Roman society was, e.g. Jeffers, *Greco-Roman World*, 92–98.

138. Fowler, *Religious Experience*, 84.

139. Burkert, *Greek Religion*, 263; "those appointed days [of initiation] are festivals of the gods" (261); also Harrill, "Coming of Age," 258.

appear to pertain to "personal" religion are in fact also part of *polis* religion."[140] This section examines in which sense what we have already noted of mysteries works in state religion. Does this setting show that in initiation the initiand dies personally and takes other actions related to this death? To answer this question, some examples of initiation from Greco-Roman society will be considered. There is the ceremony of *Toga virilis* for Roman boys.[141] Also, as Burkert shows, there are accounts of puberty initiation from Dorian Crete, from Sparta, and "the naked boys" in connection with Apollo.[142]

1) The idea of an encounter with the deity as part of initiation appears in the fact that the process of donning the *toga* includes the episode whereby the boy "stands within the sacred precinct offering sacrifice . . . at the temple of Jupiter . . . that also housed the small shrine of Juventas, goddess of youth."[143] At Sparta, the initiand boys were brought to "the altar of Artemis Ortheia."[144] The girls also underwent a "consecration to Artemis."[145] The process for the "naked boys," the *epheboi*, included a similar moment of "consecration to a god."[146] These episodes echo the encounter with a deity.

In terms of the divine action that takes place at this stage, it is not made plain, as in the mysteries, that the god delivers. However, the notion of consecration is clearly present. This hints at the fact that the god does something to the initiand. But much focus rests also on what the initiand was doing in the event. This is clear as we consider stages two to four.

2) The second stage, namely, the episode whereby the person is between the old and the new, and dies to the old, appears in the transitional process that the youth undergo. About the *Toga*, Harrill recognizes that the boy's arrival at the temple marks the "threshold of manhood."[147] In other words,

---

140. Sourvinou-Inwood, "Further Aspects of *Polis* Religion," in Buxton, *Oxford Readings*, 54. The example is "a personal dedication to an oecist" (hero founder), cf. 54; and the "Eleusinian cult was intimately intertwined with the other central *polis* cults," "What is *Polis* Religion," 27; Burkert: "mysteries do not constitute a separate religion outside the public one" (*Greek Religion*, 277).

141. Details on *Toga virilis*, cf. Harrill, "Coming of Age," 252–277.

142. Burkert, *Greek Religion*, 261–263.

143. Harrill, "Coming of Age," 258.

144. Burkert, *Greek Religion*, 262.

145. Burkert, 263.

146. Burkert, 263.

147. Harrill, "Coming of Age," 258.

he is on the point of entering the new status. He is at the end of the episode whereby he was neither child nor adult, thus a sort of vacuum of identity. This state of non-identity begins when at home the boy dons the *toga virilis* "assuming the outward appearance of an adult male."[148] A state of non-identity is entered. It stops at the moment "the character and qualities" of an adult are reckoned, and this is when he comes to the gods and makes a sacrifice.[149] This kind of period in which the person is neither child nor recognized adult also features (generally as seclusion) in initiation at Sparta[150] and at Dorian Crete.[151]

Does this phase show action? The death to the old that characterizes this stage is a personal act and decision. In this initiation of the Greco-Roman youth, the fact of deciding the act personally does not apply, simply because this is the category of "les initiations obligatoires" as we mentioned earlier. But the idea that the person undergoes a death experience is taken seriously. As Burkert shows, at Sparta the boys were "whipped at the altar of Artemis" so seriously that "blood was to drop on the altar." In fact, during this ordeal "fatal injuries were not unknown."[152] Also at a certain time, these boys were to "lead a life of robbery, feeding themselves by theft."[153] At Dorian Crete, "for two months" the boy was taken by a man "to some place in the countryside" into what is believed to be a "homosexual relationship."[154] There is a sense that these abuses imparted a sense of dying to childhood.

3) After the ordeals there were rituals intended to show that the *passage* to the new life was sealed. The presence of community members and gods as witnesses meant that the responsibility to live as an initiate was serious. At Sparta where the purpose of initiation was militaristic, the ritual that sealed initiation was itself a hard experience. It consisted of "a contest in the endurance of pain."[155] This is a third-stage element because it is a public "spectacle."[156]

---

148. Harrill, 259.

149. Harrill, 259.

150. At Sparta this lasted 23 years: the boy was secluded from the family at 7 years only to enter manhood at 30 years, cf. Burkert, *Greek Religion*, 262.

151. At Dorian Crete, at least 2 months, cf. Burkert, *Greek Religion*, 261.

152. Burkert, 262.

153. Burkert, 262.

154. Burkert, 261.

155. Burkert, 262.

156. Burkert, 262.

In this ceremony the idea of action is evident. First, there is action because the candidates are involved in a contest. Second, the presence of witnesses means that they are taking responsibility. Not only is the spectacle performed in the presence of the priestess of Artemis; she also holds the "image of the goddess."[157] Hence the goddess herself is believed to be a witness.

At Dorian Crete, after the two-month ordeal the man who had been with the initiand boy in seclusion "had to present the boy with a warrior's robe, an ox, and a wine cup" and then he was "dismissed."[158] The boys are not just passive during this time of sealing their initiation. In fact, as Burkert states, they "strip off" to show "their sporting nakedness."[159] As for the meaning of the act, Burkert's view is that the purpose is to "prove their manly nature."[160] But what it really means is more than to show off. The meaning is rather to claim they are able to carry out the service of men with which the community would entrust them, and it is an oath to the community that they will honour their new status. This appears to be the sense, because initially the community, including the boys' own "relatives," ridicule and "mock" them at the time of entering the two-month ordeal.[161]

With the *Toga* initiation, a series of rituals publicly marks the boy's change. There is the donning of the cloth of manhood, the *toga*, and also the offer of a sacrifice which is the final act that ratifies the boy's new status as an adult. In these rituals the boy acted; he was not passive. First, he took responsibility before men and the gods and became accountable to them. As Harrill shows, the donning of the toga was before the family. Then a "public procession" followed for the community to witness. Finally, a sacrifice was offered, before the priests and the gods.[162] To be before these different groups was to take responsibility to honour the new status.

This responsibility was strengthened by the fact that before these witnesses the candidate personally took action concerning his change. The boy "laid aside" anything that represented his childhood (i.e. the amulet and

---

157. Burkert, 262.
158. Burkert, 261.
159. Burkert, 261.
160. Burkert, 261.
161. Burkert, 261.
162. Harrill, "Coming of Age," 255.

his childhood *toga*) and "donned the "toga of manhood.""¹⁶³ Fowler's view, focusing especially on the removal of the amulet, is that the boy does this because as a youth "he is endued with new powers."¹⁶⁴ However, the meaning is more than this. The fact that he removes them in this specific event of change to manhood and before the witnesses means that he publicly breaks with childhood. He gives a pledge to the community that he begins his status of manhood and that they may count on his ability and determination to secure the protection both of himself and of others. The idea that he begins his new way of life (i.e. the life of manhood) leads us to stage four.

4) The boy adopts his new status in the initiation itself. As Burkert notes, initiation "concentrates on the introduction of adolescents into the world of adults."¹⁶⁵ When they die to the old in initiation, the new begins. As we mentioned earlier, in the *toga* ritual, one of the steps the young man takes is to stand at the altar and to sacrifice to the gods. This marks the start of what becomes his life and activity. To sacrifice to the gods will be one of his roles as an adult.

Initiation of Greco-Roman youth included their preparation for military service. But this service was undertaken when the boys were still initiands. As Burkert notes, the "naked boys" could be found "guarding frontiers."¹⁶⁶ At Dorian Crete, when the boy is given a warrior's robe and an ox it meant he was "now famous."¹⁶⁷ He was a warrior and one able to serve his community. It already started in initiation; it was not something for the future. In fact, before this step of being declared "famous," he had been "hunting," and with other boys they had been "performing services" at the men's hall.¹⁶⁸ Thus actions of service, which would characterize their new life, began in initiation.

2.3.2. Entry into Marriage

As mentioned previously, the bride's entry into her husband's household is another initiation event in the context of *polis* religion. This is because 1) the bride was entering a new household and, as Fowler shows, any family dwelling

---

163. Harrill, 255.
164. Fowler, *Religious Experience*, 91 fn. 51.
165. Burkert, *Greek Religion*, 263.
166. Burkert, 263.
167. Burkert, 261.
168. Burkert, 261.

"was a sacred place . . . and the abode of the household spirits."[169] So her entry was in fact a religious event. 2) The bride's entry took place in connection with state religion because, as Sourvinou-Inwood points out, the "*oikos* cult was perceived to be part of the *polis* religious system from which it derived its forms."[170] We may now consider whether the four stages and the action that they entail are a feature in the entry of the bride.

1) The event includes the encounter with the divine. Speaking of Roman religious life, Rose notices that at the main door of the house there were "two presiding deities, Limentinus and Lima, the god and goddess of the threshold (*limen*)."[171] So the first phase in her entry was to meet the gods. The action which is taken at this stage is normally divine. There is a hint at this in the fact that this encounter means that the bride gains "the favour of the entire doorway."[172] Apart from what the gods do to her at the doorway, the bride's death to the old way and other actions related to this death show up as we consider stages two to four.

2) The second stage includes serious experiences which sometimes amounted to terror. In this way a sense of death is strongly attained. There is a connection with this in what takes place at the doorway. The *passage* over the threshold of the house was seen to be "dangerous."[173] There is here an idea of terror; it means the bride has to die to her old attachment. By a personal act she must seriously break with her old way of life at this point. This is the meaning of her act of "smearing the doorposts with wolf's oil and fat."[174] Fowler's view is that "The real reason was, no doubt, that it was a charm against evil spirits."[175] The idea of protection might be implied. But the evil spirits are not as much the primary focus as "the friendly spirits of household life."[176] What is at the fore is the breaking with the old gods and attachment with the new ones. Evidence of this is the "holiness" which is meant by the elements she uses. As Rose states, "the wolf . . . is a holy beast

---

169. Fowler, *Religious Experience*, 83.
170. Sourvinou-Inwood, "Further Aspects of *Polis* Religion," 53, for detail: 51–54.
171. Rose, *Ancient Roman Religion*, 32.
172. Rose, 32; so also Fowler, *Religious Experience*, 83.
173. So Fowler, *Religious Experience*, 83.
174. Rose, *Ancient Roman Religion*, 32; Fowler, *Religious Experience*, 83.
175. Fowler, 90 fn. 48.
176. Cf. Fowler, 84.

in Roman tradition."[177] By this act with oil and fat, she takes the "holy" state and establishes a holy relationship with the gods. She bonds with them and dies to her previous gods.

3 & 4) The entry of the bride shows elements of stage three and four as well. There was a final ritual in which she "was received by her husband into communion of fire and water, symbolic of her acceptance as materfamilias both by man and deities."[178] This episode features elements of the third and fourth stages. Whatever the meaning of fire and water, by this ritual she becomes a member. It seals her entry (stage three). The presence of "men and gods" who witness the entry is another element of the third stage. Also in the event, her new life takes place (stage four). This is revealed in the fact that she gains her new status as "mother of the family". When in her entry she is accepted as member, her status also changes.

Concerning action, she may be the person who lit the fire or who brought the water, but this is not specified. However, the simple fact of getting married is an active thing. What is also clear is that the ritual takes place in the presence of the community and deities. This means accountability. The ritual implies that a responsibility to live and honour the new status is taken.

To sum up, the examples of initiation to adulthood and entry into marriage show us that in the *polis*, the religious context of this initiation includes divine action (stage one). The deity consecrates the initiand and grants him or her divine favour. There is also much that is performed by the initiand (stages two to four). There is an act of dying to childhood in the *passage* to adulthood. Also, as the bride enters her marriage, she dies to the gods and other things to which she was attached in her previous life. To make real this idea of death, trials and terror were experienced. The change to adulthood and marriage shows that breaking with the old life goes together with the act of ratifying this change through a public pledge and beginning to live the new life.

The mysteries and the state religions reveal to us the underlying assumptions concerning the process of entry to new life which a Christian in Rome, with this religious background, could have had when he or she was reading Romans 5:12–6:23. Consideration will now be given to whether Judaism, too, gives evidence of understanding initiation in these four stages.

---

177. Rose, *Ancient Roman Religion*, 32.
178. Fowler, *Religious Experience*, 83.

2.4. The Four Stages in Jewish Context

Earlier we mentioned Wedderburn's observation that the patterns that the mysteries reveal were in fact widespread in other settings as well. This section seeks to examine whether in the Jewish setting the four stages of entry are present. The purpose is to note what kind of presumptions about initiation Paul himself and his Jewish readers could have had. When reading Romans 5:12–6:23, what sense could a Christian Jew have made of the personal death of an initiand to his or her old way of life and the other actions linked to this death? This requires us to examine what entry to new life meant in a Jewish *milieu*.

This section is divided into two parts. Judaism was operating in the mainstream. There were also sectarian groups. For a more representative picture of what in a Jewish *milieu* the initiand was supposed to be doing in the transitional process, we consider what the four stages were like 1) in second-temple and Rabbinic Judaism, and 2) in the Qumran community, as one of the major sectarian groups.[179]

2.4.1. Proselytes' Entry in Second Temple and Rabbinic Judaism

Our intention is not to suggest that the readers of Romans might have been influenced directly by this Rabbinic, latter stream. But if the same broad ideas are in evidence across such widely differing streams of Jewish as well as Gentile society, it is all the more likely that the readers of Romans would have brought these presumptions about initiation to their reading of Romans, and Paul would have been aware of this.

Some recognize that entry into Judaism shows stages. There is a difference however when the focus is on the action that the process entails. The book of *Judith* (second century BC) lists our four stages as it describes the conversion of Achior: "And when Achior had seen (ἰδών) all that the God of Israel had done, he believed in God greatly (σφόδρα), and circumcised the flesh of his foreskin, and was joined to the house of Israel . . ."[180] From this example of joining the people of Yahweh, Cohen discerns three aspects "of conversion

---

179. The reason this group is chosen will be given at the section where it is considered.
180. *Ju.* 14:10 (unless indicated otherwise, the apocrypha are from *The Septuagint with Apocrypha: Greek and English*, Peabody: Hendrickson, 2009).

to Judaism: belief in God, circumcision, and joining the house of Israel."[181] (Philo too speaks of three stages.)[182] Cohen makes them three because what he suggests as the first thing is the "*belief in God (and denial of other gods)*."[183] For us this is the second stage. The stage of encounter with God appears in the idea of "seeing" God. The divine encounter takes place as God impresses Achior's heart. As Cohen recognizes, Achior was "impressed by the might of the God of Israel."[184] This shows the encounter with God and the divine action that is normally connected with it. Based on what God does, Achior then takes action. The belief in God and denial of idols is Achior's action. It shows Achior's break with his old way. Instead of being the first thing in the process, it is rather a second-stage element.

The meaning of the initiand's action is better grasped when we consider the relationship of the series of actions which are involved in initiation. In this section we attempt to analyse the four stages of proselyte entry into Judaism. The focus is on the proselyte's act of dying to the old life and how this relates to the responsibility that the proselyte takes for the process.

1) First, we consider the encounter with God. Sanders notes that Palestinian Judaism shows a "covenantal soteriology" which "covers both native-born Israelites and proselytes."[185] Focusing on the proselytes, he states, "*accepting* the covenant both requires and is evidenced by *obeying* the commandments. Proselytes accept the covenant and bring sacrifices (for example) just as do native-born Israelites."[186] The actions mentioned (i.e. accepting the covenant, obeying the commandments) are what the proselyte does. They fall into stages two and four. Sanders is speaking of soteriology, which means primarily God's action toward the proselyte, but this divine action is not fully considered.

The encounter with God that prompts the proselyte to act is considered in this part. Since the Exodus transition, this aspect must have some consideration in Jewish thinking. As the book of Exodus shows, the words "the

---

181. Cohen, *From Maccabees to Mishnah*, 52.

182. As Philo speaks of the process of change of Abraham, he sees that it consists of 1) to discover God, 2) to be heaven-born (as he "searches into the nature of the ethereal region"), 3) becoming the man of God. Cf. Borgen, "Philo of Alexandria," 272.

183. Cohen, *From Maccabees to Mishnah*, 52 [italics his].

184. Cohen, 52.

185. Sanders, *Paul and Palestinian Judaism*, 206.

186. Sanders, 206 [italics his].

God of the Hebrews has met with us" (NIV) set the basis for the transition to Canaan (Exod 3:18; 5:3; cf. 3:2). As we will see, enabled by this act of God, Israel was to exercise their agency and action that a person's change to new life required.

In their initiation to Judaism, the proselytes experience an encounter with God. Philo recognizes this idea though he speaks of initiation metaphorically. He sees Abraham as "the prototype of proselytes" and shows that "to discover the One God" was the first experience of this patriarch.[187] Also in the myth of *Joseph and Asenath* (first century BC to second century AD), the conversion of Asenath[188] begins by an encounter with God through the agency of Joseph. He refused her kiss by telling her that "it is not fitting for a man who worships God, who will bless with his mouth the living God . . . to kiss a strange woman who will bless with her mouth dead and dumb idols" (*Jos. As.* viii.5). The effect of his words was that "she was cut to the heart strongly" and wept (viii.8–9). Joseph prayed to God to meet her and save her (viii.10–11). Through Joseph's words and prayer, Asenath is touched by God. The story says that she was "formed anew and made alive again."[189] This is God's work. It happens from that point when God is made known to her.

The *Talmud* also shows that encountering God is part of the process and that by this contact God forgives the person. This is especially in connection with the idea that in the process the proselyte becomes a "child newly born."[190] One possible meaning of this is that "all his previous sins are forgiven."[191] This refers to God's saving act, which is often linked with people's transition to serving God.[192] The idea of "gaining God's protection"[193] also hints at coming into contact with his action.

---

187. Philo, cited by Borgen, "Philo of Alexandria," 272. Also, to "see God" is stressed when in initiatory language Philo speaks of sanctification, cf. *Quaest. Exod.* ii. 51.

188. The spelling is "Asenath" in the MT and the LXX spell it "Aseneth," cf. Nickelsburg, "Stories of Biblical," in Stone, *Jewish Writings*, 65, fn. 173.

189. *Jos. As.* xv.5.

190. *b. Yeb.* 22a, 48b, 62a; *Bekoroth* 47a, Trans. from Miller and Simon, "Bekoroth," *b. Seder Kodashim*, vol. 3. Philo applies the idea of "heaven-born" to Abraham's transition from his polytheistic old life, cf. Borgen, "Philo of Alexandria," 272.

191. Cf. comment of I. W. Slotki, "Yebamoth," *b. Seder Nashim*, vol. 1, 320, fn. 6.

192. E.g. Philo speaks of God as "saviour" in the passage we just mentioned, i.e. *Quaest. Exod.* ii.51.

193. Paying attention to this, e.g. White, *Biblical Doctrine of Initiation*, 71.

Apart from this act of God toward the proselyte, in Judaism the proselyte's death to the old life is also stressed. The proselyte's public act of ratifying this separation and his act of proving this separation to be real by living the new life from the time of initiation are also present. This will become clear as we examine stages two, three and four.

2) The main idea of the second stage is the personal act of dying to the old life. The person is between the old and the new, decides for the new and breaks seriously with the old. The fact that the person is neither in the old nor in the new sometimes results in him being in a state of confusion, of no-life and no-identity. Hardship is also used for the person to have a sense that he or she dies to the old way.

The entry of the proselytes shows these elements. This is clear in the section that follows Asenath's encounter with the truth of God; she enters that state between the old and the new, a state in which she experiences a mixture of feelings. This is the episode which shows that she feels "the exceeding joy" of having been blessed by Joseph's words and yet she is also "disturbed, frightened, and sweating" due to the truth about God (ix.1–2).[194] She is happy to know God and is attracted to attaching to him and his people. Yet, she is "trembling of fear" (x.1). This gripping fear is caused by the fact that the decision to attach to God means to deny the gods that have been part of her life, the gods of her nation (ix.2). This episode shows the mixed feelings that characterize the state of being between the old and the new. Burchard recognizes this when he entitles this part of Asenath's story as "retire in confusion."[195]

Note the stress on Asenath's personal action. The intention of the author is to show that this phase is serious. In fact, the author calls the seven days of this episode "seven days of humiliation."[196] But she is herself responsible for what she is experiencing. The episode is her act of "repentance" (ix.2). This includes a series of actions. She fasts (x.1) and secludes herself from enjoying the company of even her maidservants (x.3–8). She decisively breaks with all that had been meaningful to her old life: she throws away the gods (x.12); she puts off ornaments and royal robes and puts on her mourning costume (x.8–11), which illustrates the idea of death very powerfully. The idea of death

---

194. *Jos. As.* ix.1–2, insights from both the Translations of Burchard, "Joseph and Aseneth."
195. Burchard, "Joseph and Aseneth," 217.
196. *Jos. As.* x.17; xi.2; xiii.1.

also emerges when her conversion is seen as coming "from death to life."[197] These actions show that the intention of the author is to stress that her break with the old is a personal act.

Rabbinic writings show this personal death and action. The idea is reflected in writings from the school of Hillel, which state that a person "who separates from the uncircumcised is one who separates from the grave."[198] Some scholars think that this implies impurity, like one who has touched the dead.[199] Although next to these words it is said that the person needs extra purification,[200] what the Hillelites mean is surely more than a comparison with one who only touched the dead. As the context here is one of initiation (entry), the Hillelites meant that the proselyte was in a state of death himself and that he has now dissociated from the old. The *Tosefta* expresses this when for "separate" it says "he takes his leave."[201] This shows a movement out of something with which one was seriously entangled.

How important is it to take action and die to one's old way of life as a phase of initiation? Flemington, for example, notes that to undergo initiation "was demanded by the Jews."[202] But he does not explain why. There is much evidence to show that the reason was to decide seriously and with a great sense of responsibility. The fact that the person had to undergo a "period of instruction"[203] was certainly in line with this purpose. Such instruction is important because of the dilemma of this phase of decision.

Personal choice and decision were at the fore. The conversion of the Idumeans and the Itureans (second century BC) is thought of as a "forced conversion," but as Feldmann shows one cannot be certain.[204] Many elements show that personal choice and strong decision were crucial in the proselyte

---

197. *Jos. As.* viii.10 (in fact viii.5, 10–11); giving attention to this, e.g. Nickelsburg, "Stories of Biblical," 68.

198. *Eduyoth* 5.2, Trans. From Blackman, "Eduyoth" (we use *m. Ed.* for other reference to this text); and *Pesachim* 8.8, Trans. From Blackman, "Pesachim," *Mishnayoth* (we use *m. Pesah.* for other reference to this text).

199. Sanders, *Judaism*, 74; Levison, "Proselyte in Biblical," 50.

200. *m. Ed.* 5.2; also *m. Pesah.* 8.8; and *Pesahim* 92a, Trans. from Freedman, "Pesahim," (we use *b. Pesah.* for other ref. to this text); *Pisha* 7.14, Trans. from Neusner, "Pisha (Pesahim)," (for other ref. to this we use *t. Pesah.*).

201. *t. Pesah.* 7.14.

202. Flemington, *New Testament Doctrine*, 11.

203. Ariel, "Proselyte," 550 col. 2.

204. Feldmann, "Jewish Proselytism," 374–75.

process. The Talmud says clearly that the proselyte was not "to be persuaded or dissuaded too much."[205] The emphasis was that he was to "come"[206] personally. When Philo speaks of Abraham as a model for proselytes, he emphasises that Abraham "left his native country and its polytheism."[207] This was serious action. As Feldmann points out, this meant "not merely denying one's ancestral gods but also one's native land and family."[208] This shows that the action is serious, and the personal aspect is emphasized.

In fact, the word "proselyte" itself expresses that connotation. As Levison points out, one meaning of "*pros-elthein* is to come near."[209] There is a personal act in this. As Hirsch notes, the LXX mainly uses προσήλυτος to translate the Hebrew גר [*ger* has normally a *patah*] which means a person who had come to Palestine and "who had put himself under the protection of the people among whom he had taken up his abode."[210] This shows a focus on the choice made. It also shows the personal responsibility of putting oneself under the protection of Israel (and their God). As an example of this, the Rabbis refer to the deliberate choice and responsibility which were taken by Ruth.[211] Her coming under the wings of God (cf. Ruth 2:12) is used as example of one who "hurried,"[212] which clearly shows action.

Taking responsibility was central. In fact, the proselyte process was to carry on only "if he had accepted."[213] This acceptance is more than just assent because it meant accepting "harassment and afflictions" together with Israel, and the possibility of being punished (including stoning) for sins.[214] Thus, the time of entry, becoming a servant of Yahweh, meant to take a serious

---

205. *b. Yeb.* 47b.

206. Cf. the words "if he comes," e.g. *b. Yeb.* 46b, 47a.

207. Borgen, "Philo of Alexandria," 272. On this action of Abraham who "abandons" the old way, cf. Philo, *On the Virtues* 219. More on this act of rejection of old way, cf. Philo, *On the Virtues* 102.

208. Feldmann, "Jewish Proselytism," 372.

209. Levison, "Proselyte," 45; literally, προσήλυτος means "one that has come to" (*VGT*, s.v. 'προσήλυτος).

210. Hirsch, "Proselyte," 220 col. 1.

211. *b. Yeb.* 47b.

212. *b. Yeb.* 48b.

213. *b. Yeb.* 47b.

214. *b. Yeb.* 47a.

responsibility. As White recognizes, it meant "entrance through repentance and acceptance of God's will."[215]

Some elements show why a serious break with the old was the core of the proselytes' transition. There was much doubt over their sincerity.[216] Israel believed that as a nation they suffered because of the uniqueness of their laws. This is clear when Josephus speaks of "our endurance under persecution on behalf of our laws."[217] To endure persecution just for the love of God's law was a serious thing. As Josephus shows, some proselytes had "lacked the necessary endurance."[218] This shows that initiation focused on a strong decision.

Another concern was that people could enter without having seriously dropped their "idolatry."[219] The consequence of this was believed to be a problem as "hard as a sore" for Israel.[220] This seems to be a reference to God's anger and punishment (Ariel thinks of the Roman use of proselytes to spy on the Jews[221]). Aspects of Israel's life were attractive to the Gentiles, such as gleaning and tithing, which showed concern for the poor.[222] Another attractive thing was the prosperity which was expected to take place when Israel's Messiah would come.[223] Jews were inclined to believe that people would enter just for these favours, without a real change. This shows that they took seriously the

---

215. White, *Biblical Doctrine of Initiation*, 71.

216. For more on this, e.g. Feldmann, *Jew and Gentile*, 339–40.

217. Josephus, *Against Apion* ii.283; *Josephus I: The Life* and *Against Apion* (other ref. to this source are abbreviated *Ag. Ap.*).

218. Josephus, *Ag. Ap.* ii.123.

219. *Abodah Zarah* 57a; Trans. from Mishcon and Cohen, "Abodah Zarah," *b. Seder Nezikin* (for other ref. to this text we use *b. Abod. Zar.*); on idolatry and other heathen inclinations, cf. *Sanhedrin* 56a–58b; Trans. from Schachter and Freedman, "Sanhedrin," *b. Seder Nezikin*. As Cohen shows, a gentile associated with the Jews in seven different ways: 1) admiring some aspect of Judaism, 2) acknowledging the power of the God of the Jews, 3) benefitting the Jews or being conspicuously friendly to Jews, 4) practising some or many of the rituals of the Jews, 5) venerating the God of the Jews and denying or ignoring the pagan gods, 6) joining the Jewish community, 7) converting to Judaism and becoming a Jew. Only a few of these meant real break with idolatry; for detail, cf. Cohen, "Crossing the Boundary," 14–30. Josephus shows this suspicion when he sees the Greeks as incorporating just "in some manner" (τρόπῳ τινὶ), cf. *J. War* vii.45. Serious abandonment of idolatry is the subject in *Jos. As.*, cf. Nickelsburg, "Stories of Biblical," 69–70.

220. *b. Yeb.* 47b.

221. Ariel thinks that this refers to "bitter historical experiences" that the Jews were suffering from Romans because "spies, under the guise of proselytes, were planted among the Jews by the Romans" (cf. Ariel, "Proselyte," 550 col. 2).

222. *b. Yeb.* 47a.

223. *b. Yeb.* 24b.

idea that the proselyte had to die to the old life. In fact, the rule was that in the process "if he desire to withdraw let him do so."²²⁴

When the person dies to his old way of life and seriously rejects it, he has to make a clear act of ratifying this death. This means a public ritual by which he recognizes in the presence of the community as witnesses that he belongs to the new way and pledges to live for its honour. This is the third stage, to which we now turn.

3) As the *Talmud* shows, entry into Judaism was sealed by the ritual of circumcision and baptism.²²⁵ By these two acts and "the sprinkling of the blood"²²⁶ the proselyte fully "entered into the Covenant"²²⁷ (cf. Exod 24:8).

One thing to note is that in Judaism this ritual shows clearly the sequence of the stages. For example, in the story of Isates's conversion,²²⁸ Josephus shows that circumcision and baptism happen when the person has been forgiven by God (stage 1) and when he or she has repented and attached to God's way (stage 2). Isates "converted himself" to Judaism and he changed seriously to become a worshipper of God.²²⁹ Then later he was to be circumcised.²³⁰ Also Josephus' view is that John's baptism²³¹ meant that the person came to it when the "soul was already thoroughly cleansed" (τῆς ψυχῆς δικαιοσύνῃ προεκκεκαθαρμένης).²³² In his view, baptism meant "not to gain forgiveness of

---

224. *b. Yeb.* 47b.

225. *b. Yeb.* 47b; *b. Abod. Zar.* 57a.

226. Before the destruction of the Temple, cf. *b. Ker.* 9a; Ariel recognizes this, cf. Ariel, "Proselyte," 550 co. 2.

227. *b. Ker.* 9a; also Cohen, *From Maccabees to Mishnah*, 53; in fact, the offer of sacrifice "qualifies him to enter into the congregation," cf. *b. Ker.* 8b.

228. Neusner shows that the conversion of this king is around AD 60, so contemporary to Paul, cf. Neusner, "The Conversion of Adiabene to Judaism," 60.

229. Josephus, *J. Ant.* xx.38, 41.

230. Josephus, *J. Ant.* xx.39–40.

231. Here is an example that shows that the four stages of transition to new life in the ancient world can be detected also in John's baptism. In fact, this work could have included an overview of baptism in Biblical material and tradition (the Gospels, Acts, the Epistles and Revelation). That could help to see clearly whether the four stages can be demonstrated from that context, and that could help to address the issue of a kind of discontinuity which some scholars raise between the biblical tradition and the initiation rituals of the cults. But this is an area already sufficiently covered by other scholars. For example, for an interesting discussion of the biblical tradition of baptism, see Ferguson, *Baptism in Early Church*, 99–198.

232. Josephus, *J. Ant.* xviii.117.

sins" (μὴ ἐπί τινων ἁμαρτάδων παραιτήσει) because this was already obtained.[233] He believes the ritual was rather a pledge for a life of chastity, awe and service to God (ἀλλ᾽ ἐφ᾽ ἁγνείᾳ).[234]

Another thing to note is that the episode of the ritual also involves the candidate's personal will and action. This is clear in the conversion of Isates. His circumcision is a subject of serious dilemma. As Josephus shows, Isates is a king, and his subjects would be unhappy to find that he was "devoted to rites that were strange and foreign to themselves."[235] This required a serious decision, and his decision shows a serious action. In fact, the ritual is described as something that "he had to do" (πράττειν[236] ἦν ἕτοιμος).[237] He finally underwent circumcision.[238] Also concerning baptism, the same personal will and action is showed when the *Mishnah* says that the proselytes "immersed themselves" (טוֹבְלִין).[239]

In the third phase, witnesses are another aspect which shows action. As we said earlier, it is because of this aspect that the candidate must have a sense that he is taking a serious responsibility. The role of witnesses is stressed on entry into Judaism. The *Talmud* says that when a man is baptized, "two learned men must stand by his side."[240] In fact, from the beginning of the person's initiation, the process had to involve the presence of "three men,"[241] who had to be Israelites[242] and none of them a close relative of the proselyte.[243] In addition, the entry process was invalid if it was conducted without the

---

233. See e.g. Gundry when he states that "acceptance" of God and his covenant "preceded" circumcision and baptism; Gundry, "Faith, Works," 11.

234. Josephus, *J. Ant.* xviii.117. The translator puts "consecration" for ἁγνεία. Used in connection with baptism, there is the idea of a pledge to live and serve because in fact ἁγνεία means "chastity" and is of the group of ἁγνός which means "full of religious awe, chaste," cf. *GEL*, s.v. "ἁγνεία, ἁγνός."

235. Josephus, *J. Ant.* xx.39–40.

236. One meaning of πράττειν or πράσσω is "to have to do," cf. *GEL*, s.v. "πράσσω."

237. Josephus, *J. Ant.* xx.38.

238. Josephus, *J. Ant.* xx.46.

239. *Mikevaoth* 1.7 (also 7:7), Trans. from Blackman, "Mikevaoth." Also a strong idea of action when Neusner translates, "one presses down, even with bundles of wood," cf. *Miqvaot* 7:7, Trans. from Neusner, *Mishnah*.

240. *b. Yeb.* 47b.

241. *b. Yeb.* 46b.

242. *Kiddushin* 62a, Trans. from Freedman, "Keddushin," *b. Seder Nashim.*

243. *b. Yeb.* 22a.

presence of the "Beth din."²⁴⁴ This expression means "literally 'house of law or judgment,' a gathering of three or more learned men acting as a Jewish court of law."²⁴⁵ This shows that any proselyte's entry was seriously judicial.²⁴⁶ The fact that the proselyte made his entry before a judicial body shows strongly that this new member knew that what he was doing by undergoing the ritual was a serious act. It was a pledge that he would live according to the new way; in other words, the action taken in the ritual concerns the new life itself. The fourth stage reveals this.

4) With the fourth stage, attention is given to the new life for which the person is initiated. The intention is to show that the action meant in stages two and three is related to the new life, but this embrace of new life is here treated as a separate stage to fully show what it holds. In the transition, action is taken to live the new life, which means that the new life starts during initiation. Josephus states that the proselytes come to "live" (ζῆν) the laws.²⁴⁷

The idea that the new life is embraced and people begin to live it already during their transition is actually present in Israel's transition from Egypt to Canaan. It is worth noting that in the transition to the new life the divine act is meant to enable the human act. In other words, after the divine initiative the human agency is supposed to follow. This is an important aspect which will be referred to in the next chapters. God reminds Israel of his action in Egypt and says, "I enabled you to walk (NIV for the Hiphil וָאוֹלֵךְ ²⁴⁸) as my people" (Lev 26:12–13). The idea of "walk" or "conduct" is crucial in second-temple Judaism, especially in the DSS, as the section on life at Qumran will show.²⁴⁹ When the people of Israel are still on the move, they are reminded that the purpose God delivered them for (stage one) was that, following this divine action, they should take action and "walk" in the ways of Yahweh's people. The new life is embraced in the transition, not after it.

Rabbinic Judaism shows that in initiation action is taken concerning the new life that the proselyte is going to live. As we mentioned earlier

---

244. *b. Yeb.* 47a.

245. Slotki, *Index Volume Soncino Talmud*, s.v. "Beth Din."

246. Giving attention to this, e.g. Torrance, "Proselyte Baptism," 151.

247. Josephus, *Ag. Ap.* ii.210.

248. "Enable" because of the "causal" meaning of the Hiphil; cf. trans. of *IHGEB*, s.v. Lev 26:13.

249. See Charlesworth and Claussen, "Halakah A: 4Q251," 271.

(ref. *b. Yeb.* 47a-b), during the process the proselyte had to know what the new life was about. This included suffering because of God's law, serious punishment for sin, and because God rewards righteousness. The candidate was to "accept" the law and then the process could continue.

When reference is made to Ruth's story, her situation shows strongly that the responsibility to live Israel's life is accepted during the transition. This appears in this conversation between Ruth and Naomi:

> "We are forbidden," she (i.e. Naomi) told her, "[to move on the Sabbath beyond the] Sabbath boundaries"! – "Whither thou goest" [the other replied] "I will go." "We are forbidden private meeting between man and woman!" – "Where thou lodgest, I will lodge." "We have been commanded six hundred and thirteen commandments"! – "Thy people shall be my people." "We are forbidden idolatry"! – "And thy God my God." "Four modes of death (in note: penalties of offences) were entrusted to Beth din"! – "Where thou diest, will I die." "Two graveyards were placed at the disposal of the Beth din"! – "And there will I be buried." Presently *she saw that she was steadfastly minded etc.*[sic].[250]

Clearly what Ruth is expressing is an oath. She takes action to move into the life that she is attaching to.

Ruth begins to live Israel's life when she is still on her way to Israel's land. Because the responsibility to live the new life is taken in the transition, the new life begins at that moment, but it continues after the initiation time. As Philo states, the initiand "takes a journey."[251] The fact that life begins in transition, and continues after it, appears clearly in what Ruth says in the quotation above. About the Sabbath, for example, she says "where you go I will go." One may note this interconnected present and future. In future she will do what Naomi will do about the Sabbath. But at the moment she is making her pledge, she is with Naomi; she is already obeying what Naomi obeys. The same applies to the other statements that she makes.

As we will find also in Romans 6, Jewish literature uses the future when the context is about the proselyte's transition. The future is used not to mean

---

250. *b. Yeb.* 47b [italics are from the source; brackets not mine; parentheses mine].
251. Philo, *On the Virtues*, 102.

something that is still to come but the continuation in future of something that has already begun at initiation. We find another example of this in the case of Asenath. The angel says to her, "From today, you will be renewed."[252] The renewal has actually happened. What the angel means is that her new status will not cease: "I have given you today to Joseph for a bride, and he himself will be your bridegroom for ever and ever" (xv.6).

There are more examples which show that life begins during the transition, because the action that is taken is the responsibility to live the new way. To undergo circumcision means not only that entry is accomplished, but also that the new way has begun. As Josephus shows, when Isates underwent his circumcision, he became "genuinely a Jew" (βεβάως Ἰουδαῖος).[253] This means not simply to be known as a Jew but to live the way expected of a Jew. This is what the Rabbis mean when they speak of the proselyte in his transition: "he is now an Israelite."[254] In fact, by entering the covenant (through circumcision, baptism, and sacrifice) the proselyte embraced the same obligations as the Jew (cf. Exod 12:19, 48–49; Lev 16:29; Ezek 14:7) and rights (Deut 1:16; 16:11–14; Ezek 31:12; 47:22–23). Thus, from the time the covenant was entered, the Rabbis could say, he "is included regarding the offerings"[255] and other commandments as well. He was "susceptible to uncleanness" like any other Israelite.[256] From then on, the Rabbis could say to their community: "he is compared to you."[257]

To be able to understand the initiation which both Paul and his readers had before they became Christians, this part has considered whether the four stages of entry to the new life and the action that they represent are present

---

252. *Jos. As.* xv.5.

253. Josephus, *J. Ant.* xx.38.

254. *b. Pesah.* 92a. This integration is object of debate. Cohen's view is that some Jews regarded the convert gentile as one who had "become not a Jew but a proselyte"; for detail on this, cf. "Crossing the Boundary," 29–30. But there is a strong sense of integration in elements as these that Ariel draws from Rabbinic tradition:

> He or she is considered like "a new-born child," and all former family ties are regarded as terminated. He or she is now called 'son/daughter of Abraham,' who is seen as the father of converts, and takes a Hebrew name (Abraham and Ruth – herself seen as the paragon of conversion – are favored). Cf. Ariel, "Proselyte," 550 col. 2.

255. *b. Ker.* 8b.

256. *b. Pesah.* 92a.

257. *b. Ker.* 9a.

in mainstream Judaism. Apart from this mainstream, in the time of Paul, Judaism had many sectarian groups.[258] One of these, the Qumran community, is very relevant to this study, because of "striking affinities" between this group and "the first Christians, in organisation, ritual, and spirit."[259] For this reason, this group is considered in addition to what was noted about the mainstream. This is expected to give us a better apprehension of what presumptions on entry to new religious life Judaism passed on to early Christians.

2.4.2. Entry into the Qumran Community

Admission to the Qumran community (or the Essenes),[260] as especially found in CD xv.5–xvi.6 and 1QS vi.13–23,[261] was also a staged process. This is recognized by Martinez when he states, "joining was regulated by a process with separate stages, at each of which a progressively higher level had to be reached, with its appropriate rites of passage."[262] This process meant effort and action, i.e. the agency of the initiand. Martinez hints at this when he writes that "at each one of these stages the candidate must give proof of his progress in the knowledge and perfect observance of all the precepts."[263] This is far from passivity! The focus in this section is on whether these covenanters' action at Qumran follows the pattern of the four stages in which both divine and human agency is involved. If we find initiation at Qumran patterned into the same four stages, the case will be stronger that this pattern crossed religious and cultural boundaries in the New Testament period and formed part of the cultural horizon of Paul and his readers.

1) An encounter with God (stage one) was a vital feature. As Charlesworth points out, the Qumran covenanters believed that they came into the desert

---

258. These groups were many (e.g. Driver, *Judaean Scrolls*, 51–125), including those in the diaspora. In Palestine the main ones were four (the Sadducees, the Pharisees, the Zealots and the Essenes), for more on this, e.g. M. Simon (drawing from Josephus), *Jewish Sects*, 2–3, 47; Stone, *Scriptures, Sects*, 71–72.

259. Simon, *Jewish Sects*, 55.

260. For a discussion on whether the Essenes and Qumran sect are the same group, cf. Deasley, *Shape of Qumran Theology*, 3–6.

261. Giving attention to this, e.g. Knibb, "Community Organization," 137.

262. Martinez, "Men of Dead Sea," 36; also Martinez, "Dead Sea Scrolls," 11. G. R. Driver notes that it was a process of two years, a practice of the Pharisees as well, cf. *Judaean Scrolls*, 111.

263. Martinez, "Men of Dead Sea," 36.

because there was a Voice calling for people to separate from "men of deceit."[264] They sought to meet God. In fact the covenanters perceived themselves to be "the Community of God."[265] They believed they were people who walked in God's sight,[266] a community among which God and his angels lived.[267] They thought of their community as the place where one was to "receive light," because they were a community of "the sons of light."[268] Evidence of this is when the scrolls say that they enter "in God's presence" (פני אל).[269] As Fitzmyer notes, many elements show their belief that God is among them actively purging them by his truth and his Spirit.[270] In other words, the covenanters understood that to join their community was to have a contact and relationship with God. A contact with God and the salvation that this entails emerge in these words:

> When they enter the covenant, the priests and the Levites shall bless the God of salvation and all the works of his faithfulness and all those who enter the covenant shall repeat after them: Amen, Amen. The priests shall recite the just deeds of God in his mighty works, and they shall proclaim all his merciful favours towards Israel.[271]

As this statement shows, when the person entered the covenant, a blessing was pronounced upon God because he was a Saviour. The idea is that the person enters the covenant because God has saved him, or the entry itself coincides with the fact that God saves him. In both cases, the person encounters God and God works in the lives of those who volunteer to be part of this community. This is an aspect of his "deeds" and "mighty works" which the group praises. In connection with this, we may note also that God

---

264. Charlesworth (ref. to 1QS 8.13–14; cf. Isa 40:3), cf. "John the Baptizer," 6–7.
265. 1QS i.12.
266. 1QS i.8.
267. Cf. CD xv.17.
268. Martinez, "Men of Dead Sea," 37. G. J. Brooke: they believed that "they were living at the time of the fulfilment of God's promises, that his blessings were theirs," which simply is to live with God, cf. Brooke, *Dead Sea Scrolls*, 51.
269. 1QS i.16; from the trans. of Brownlee, quoted by M. Black, *Scrolls and Christian Origins*, 94.
270. Fitzmyer, referring to 1QS 4:20–21; cf. Fitzmyer, *Dead Sea Scrolls*, 20.
271. 1QS i.18–22.

is thanked for showing his "merciful favour," which is clearly connected with his forgiveness.[272] As the DSS show, this divine act of forgiveness is believed to be done especially to "those who enter" this community.[273]

So, the DSS show that God's action is part of the entry of a new candidate. As in other settings considered earlier, God's act on the new covenanter enables this person's agency to be exercised. The Qumran covenanter is "freed"[274] and "saved"[275] "so that he can walk"[276] and "can take his place with the host of the holy one"[277] and so "that he praises the holy name and tell the wonders [of God]."[278] Hence, for the covenanters, God saves in order to make these actions possible. The focus is now on whether such actions, which show the agency of the initiand, are part of the entry process of the new covenanter. To understand this, stages two, three and four are considered.

2) Initiation into the Qumran community features the second stage, in which the initiand is between two systems, dies to the old and decisively attaches to the new life. To join this community is to be "introduced in the covenant," a covenant which in fact means to attach to the truth and "shun all sin."[279] As Black points out, it was a "Covenant of Repentance."[280] This means a serious separation from sin as these words show: "Cursed by the idols which his heart reveres whoever enters this covenant leaving his guilty obstacle in front of himself to fall over it."[281]

As we have noted with other settings, this second phase was characterized by trials which were intended to impart the idea of dying to the old life. Entry into the Qumran community entailed serious tests. Josephus says that the candidate spent one year in a test of self-control (ἐγκρατείας) and endurance, then he was sent back, then two years of test of character again, after which

---

272. 1QS ii.1 in connection with i.25–26.
273. 1QS i.16, 20.
274. E.g. 1QH xi.10.
275. 1QH xi.19.
276. 1QH xi.20.
277. 1QH xi.21–22.
278. 1QH xi.23; as J. Shulam puts it, to make "God's glory," cf. Shulam, *Jewish Roots of Romans*, 207, fn.44.
279. 1QS vi.14–15.
280. Attention to this, Black, *Scrolls and Christian Origins*, 92.
281. 1QS ii.11–12.

he then had his final enrolment.[282] As Thiering recognizes, it is clear that "to test the character" was at the fore.[283] To undergo all this, the scrolls show us that the purpose was "so that he can revert to the truth and shun all sin."[284] So the aim was to achieve breaking with sin.

What makes this action important is that to revert to the truth during the transition concerned both his "spirit and deeds."[285] The change was focused not only on knowledge; it was also about the person's way of life. Like the mysteries, the process at Qumran included both to know and to do things. As the scrolls show, the person had to be convinced concerning "insights, deeds and duties."[286] This shows that the intention was to make the candidate work on his transition from sin to God. To prove that the break with sin was serious, the person had to recognize it in the presence of the community. This is the third stage.

3) This community had various rituals to complete the process. At the end of each year of test, "a lot" was cast[287] by which the person was "enrolled in the society."[288] This entailed a ritual that meant admission. The person also had to undergo an immersion. As Charlesworth recognizes, it was especially this ritual which really meant "the end of a process."[289] Fitzmyer concurs that it was by this ritual that the new covenanter "became a member."[290] Immersion was an important feature. As Badia shows, there has been doubt over whether baptism was practised as an initiatory rite prior to the destruction of the Temple in AD 70.[291] Immersion was an important ceremony for this group, but there was another ritual. As Black notes, "the central rite of the sect" at this stage of concluding the process was "the act of 'entering into the covenant.'"[292] Immersion and entering the covenant are both important.

---

282. Josephus, *J. War* ii.137–42.

283. Thiering, "Qumran Initiation," 621; also Charlesworth, "Community Organization," 135.

284. 1QS vi.15.

285. 1QS vi.17.

286. 1QS vi.14, 16, 18.

287. In fact, at the end of each one of the two last years, cf. 1QS vi.18, 22.

288. Josephus, *J. War* ii.138; 1QS vi.22.

289. Charlesworth, "John the Baptizer," 8; so also Black, *Scrolls and Christian Origins*, 94, 96–97.

290. Fitzmyer, *Dead Sea Scrolls*, 20.

291. Giving attention to this, e.g. Badia, *Qumran Baptism*, 12.

292. Black, *Scrolls and Christian Origins*, 92.

One should note that the ritual that seals entry comes after God's action toward the person. As Charlesworth recognizes, the idea in 1QS v.13 is that the person "must not enter the water if he is impure."[293] This purification that takes place prior to entering the waters is the action of the Spirit of God: "it is by the Holy Spirit of the Community in his (God's) truth" that the covenanter "is cleansed from all his iniquities."[294]

The idea of taking action, which is the focus of this study, is especially seen in connection with the act of entering into the covenant.[295] Action appears in that this is the ceremony at which the person has to "swear tremendous oaths."[296] As Weinfeld notes, "swearing an oath" of commitment at the time of admission was common to associations of the Hellenistic era.[297] Admission at Qumran was no different, and this oath meant taking a serious action. The oath was a "covenant with God" in which the person pledged to "revert to the law of Moses with the whole heart and . . . soul."[298] The elements of the oath itself show a serious act. An oath in Jewish thinking entails great responsibility. Philo expresses this when he states that an oath "is no small thing" because "an oath is an appeal to God as a witness."[299]

The fact that young children were not permitted to make this oath[300] shows the seriousness of this responsibility. There is a stress on the fact that it was an act that each member should take personally.[301] As Schiffman notes, twenty years was the age required for the son of a member to swear his entry.[302] The

---

293. Charlesworth, "John the Baptizer," 8; recognized by Badia, *Qumran Baptism*, 13–14.

294. 1QS iii.7, also 6; Trans. from Charlesworth, *Dead Sea Scrolls*, 13.

295. Black, *Scrolls and Christian Origins*, 92; the concept of entry was particularly linked with the idea of "covenant" making, cf. Alexander, "Rules," 800; and Knibb, "Rule of Community," 793.

296. For more on the substance and meaning of these oaths, cf. Josephus, *J. War* ii.139–42.

297. Weinfeld, *Organizational Pattern*, 22.

298. CD xv. 7–10 [brackets and insertions are the editor's]. VanderKam sees here the concept of "agreement between God and a person," which is common to Israel's tradition and to religious life in general, cf. VanderKam, "Covenant," 151.

299. Philo, *Decalogue*, 85–86.

300. CD xv.1–2. The reason is that "If he swears and transgresses, he would profane the name [of God]," cf. CD xv.3. This fear that the too young may not take serious responsibility seems to be also the cause of refusing oaths for the "deranged." In fact, the "under-age boy" is placed in the same list with the "feeble-minded," cf. CD xv.15–17.

301. E.g. it was not automatically inherited. As Charlesworth notes, "one could not be born into the community," cf. "John the Baptizer," 10.

302. Schiffman, "Oaths and Vows," 621.

reason is that he is able personally to "talk to the Inspector of the Many."[303] This shows personal responsibility in that 1) at this age the person is able to "impose upon himself to return to the Law"[304] and in that 2) at this age he is liable for his sins and deserves severe punishment for misdeeds.[305]

The aspect of witness that reinforces the idea of responsibility at this stage is noted. 1QS v.8–10 shows that the oath to keep the law is to be "taken in public," as Weinfeld notes.[306] Moreover, some covenanters were appointed to oversee the life of the new member and to report at the examination session.[307] Also, as Black recognizes, "Entry into the new covenant took place at a solemn assembly or convocation of the sect."[308] The scrolls state, "Whoever enters the council of the community enters the covenant of God in the presence of all who freely volunteer."[309] This appears to reveal that it was to the whole council that this man had "to swear with a binding oath" that he would keep the Law of Moses and would "be segregated from all the men of sin."[310] There is a strong sense of taking responsibility. It is important to note that he swears 1) that his separation from the old way is serious, but also 2) that he would keep the laws. This shows that the new life starts at this point because it is itself the object of the responsibility and action which is taken. The fourth stage shows this link between the new life and the action that takes place.

4) In initiation, the person dies to the old way because he or she begins with the new life. The purpose of initiation is to begin the new life.

For the Qumran community perfection in the observance of the law was the foremost goal. Action was taken in initiation in connection with this idea. As Deasley notes, in relation to the idea of perfection the words "to walk" and

---

303. CD xv.7–8.

304. CD xv.12.

305. CD xv.13. Punishment included capital sentence. E.g. blasphemy incurred death, as Josephus shows (cf. *J. War* ii.145). But an under-age boy is in the status of innocence and cannot be condemned with such a sentence (cf. CD xv.4–5). Hence, he is not fit to enter.

306. Weinfeld, *Organizational Pattern*, 23.

307. The Many are questioned over the candidate, Cf. 1QS vi.15–16, 18.

308. Black, *Scrolls and Christian Origins*, 92, also 95–96.

309. 1QS v.7–8; also 1QS vi.15.

310. 1QS v.8–10.

The Four Stages of Entry into the New Life in Paul's Time 97

the "way" are recurrent in the scrolls.[311] This "walk" begins in the transitional period. The person was "taught the precepts of the community"[312] in order to make these precepts his norm of thought and action, which was to start in initiation. His ability to do so was examined at the end of each level.[313] In fact, when the new covenanter's conduct was satisfactory at the end of one year, when he was still to continue for two more years, they brought him closer to their δίαιτα,[314] which means their "way of life."[315]

It is clear from the scrolls that initiation was actually the time for the new life to begin (1QS viii.10–11). When the candidate showed his desire to join, "they prescribed for him their own rule of life" and required him to practise for one year.[316] Also at the early stage of the process the person was given their "white garment."[317] The new member already began to live in the new way. In fact, as mentioned earlier, his final enrolment was based on how he had proved to be capable of living the precepts of the community.

Also, his change of status took place in the middle of the process. By the time of his enrolment, the new member is already a "brother" to the other covenanters.[318] This meant he had the same rights and obligations "to which he bound himself."[319] This has to do with their way of life because the obligations consisted of obeying the law, observing purity, and placing his possessions in the common fund.[320] This meant "being included" in their way[321] (εἰς τὰς συμβιώσεις as Josephus puts it[322]). As Beall recognizes, this shows that

---

311. Deasley takes into account such passages as 1QS i.7–8; ii.2; iii.9–10; viii.1, 18, 20–26; iv.22; ix.2, 5–6, 19; cf. Deasley, *Shape of Qumran Theology*, 214–215; cf. also "not to *walk* in stubbornness of one's heart" (1QS ii. 13–14).

312. 1QS vi.15.

313. 1QS vi.14–18, 21.

314. Josephus, *J. War* ii.138.

315. Beall, *Josephus' Description*, 73. Thus Liddell and Scott: δίαιτα, "a way of living, mode of life," cf. *GEL*, s.v. "δίαιτα."

316. Josephus, *J. War* ii.137.

317. Josephus, *J. War* ii.138.

318. 1QS vi.22.

319. So Black, *Scrolls and Christian Origins*, 94.

320. 1QS vi.22, also 19–20.

321. 1QS vi.19.

322. Josephus, *J. War* ii.138.

during initiation "the common way of living" of the community becomes the life of the new member.[323]

Taking action in initiation connects with this. Life begins at initiation because taking the responsibility of living the new way is the key to the event. When the new covenanter is told that the idols which his "heart reveres" are an "obstacle in front of himself,"[324] clearly the concern is to clear the way for his life. He must act because he is told not to "leave" them "in front of himself."[325]

2.5. Summary

This chapter has considered the society of Paul's time, particularly examining what the four stages of entry to new life are like in religious circles. The purpose was to examine how the initiand's death to his previous life, and the ritual of recognizing this death publicly entailed action and was by no means a passive experience. These were actions of the second and third stage. They were taken in response to what God did to the initiand (stage one). Further, initiation involved these actions because the new life was itself something for which responsibility must be taken in initiation (stage four). What the Greco-Roman life shows in each of these stages, and the interconnection of the action they entail, is summarized as follows.

In all the settings examined, there is an encounter with the deity (stage one). In this encounter a divine action in the initiand's life takes place. The settings show different ways of emphasising the idea of encountering the deity. This act is placed either at the beginning of the transition process, or at the end. Or the presence of the deity dominates the event so that the entire process is about seeing the god. In this stage the deity acts to deliver, to save, or to forgive (cf. mysteries, Judaism) and to impart favours such as protection (cf. state religions). Then, as a response to the act of the deity, the initiand acts in turn.

His encounter with the reality of the deity and his deliverance led the initiand to the point of deciding seriously between the old and the new. All the

---

323. Beall, *Josephus' Description*, 74.
324. 1QS ii.11–12, and 14–18.
325. 1QS ii.12.

settings examined stress this aspect. The rejection of the old way amounted to dying to one's past life (stage two). Very challenging experiences were used to create a sense of death. In it all, the personal involvement and commitment of the initiand came to the fore.

In the presence of the new community and the gods (stage three), the initiand had to recognize that his break with the old way was serious. This public pledge to live the new way features in all the settings that we examined.

The last aspect, the new life (stage four), is the reason why action is taken. All the settings show that initiation prepares the person to live a new way and that this life begins within the initiation process itself. It is not something the initiand waits to find in the days to come. The death to one's past and the serious fact of swearing to the community and to the gods entail one's responsibility to live in the new way already embraced in the transition.

These aspects of the religious life of Paul's society give us the basis for our examination, in the fourth chapter, whether the baptizand's death to sin (Rom 6:2) and baptism (vv. 3–4) constitute personal and responsible actions. Before that step, the third chapter examines whether these insights from Greco-Roman life about divine and human agency in initiation are present in Paul's own transition from being a Pharisee to being a follower of Jesus.

CHAPTER THREE

Paul's Conversion and the Four Stages of Entry

3.1. Introduction

This thesis focuses on the idea that in antiquity the *passage* from one religious way of existence to another consists of four stages in which action is not only taken by the deity but the agency of the initiand is also involved. The purpose is to explore (in chapter four) whether "to die to sin" (ἀπεθάνομεν τῇ ἁμαρτίᾳ, Rom 6:2) and to ratify this death by a ritual ("being baptized," v. 3) are actions of the second and third stages of the believer's transition from sin to a life that is pleasing to God. The second chapter has outlined four stages of initiation and the action that they entail by considering the first-century religious contexts. This third chapter considers whether these four stages are present in Paul's own *passage* to new life.

This step is important for this study. In the first chapter it was outlined that Paul's idea in Romans 5:12–6:23 is the *passage* from sin to God and that baptism is a part of this process. Paul is speaking of a transition that he has also undergone. In 6:3, Cuvillier sees "une tradition baptismale" and his view is that "Paul fait appel à une tradition qu'il a en commun avec ses auditeurs."[1] The words ὅσοι ἐβαπτίσθημεν εἰς Χριστὸν . . . εἰς τὸν θάνατον αὐτοῦ ἐβαπτίσθημεν – we all who were baptized into Christ . . . into his death

---

1. Cuvillier, "Evangile et traditions," 9. Translation : Cuvilier sees "a baptismal trandition" and his view is that "Paul appeals to a tradition that he has in common with his listeners."

we were baptized (Rom 6:3) show clearly that baptism is an event that the readers of Romans and Paul himself have experienced.[2] Therefore to understand what in Romans 5 and 6 Paul sees to be the stages of initiation and the action that they imply, considering Paul's own "entry point into the Christian faith," as G. Fee describes it,[3] is the focus in this third chapter.

The importance of this is that Paul's conversion, broadly speaking, has not been read in this way. However, not only are these stages present in his own *passage* to Christianity, but also his experience of these stages has a connection to Romans 5:12–6:23, where he speaks of the transition of any believer. This will be made clear in this chapter and the next. This is of particular significance in relation to the issue of Paul's conversion, and the view of some (e.g. Nygren, Stendahl and Sanders) that it was not a conversion of the same kind as experienced by the readers of Romans. Did Paul experience the first stage of entry? In the light of our working theory of four stages of initiation in antiquity, this study will bring new arguments supporting the view that Paul's transition shows God's saving act. This is in fact essential to understanding his argument about the Christian's transition and baptism in Romans 5 and 6.

Structurally, we begin with the methodological issues connected with the study of Paul's Damascus Road experience. The key aspect here is to show why to conflate the elements of Acts and the letters' accounts is the approach that is taken, although some have been critical of this approach. After this methodological concern, in the light of what the second chapter outlines, the four stages of moving to a new religious life and the action that they imply are examined in connection with Paul's conversion.

3.2. Methodological Issues in Connection with Paul's Conversion

There are two methodological aspects regarding this event: (1) the study of this event has raised a debate about whether the accounts of Acts can be used or whether only evidence from the letters should be the source. As mentioned earlier, in this study conflating elements of both sources is the approach that is considered. This part gives the reason for this choice. (2) Another debate

---

2. E.g. Hendriksen, *Romans*, vol. 1:1–8, 195.
3. Fee, "Paul's Conversion," in *RD/IPC*, 166.

concerning this event is whether "conversion" is the term that defines what Paul underwent. This is also of interest to this study because at the forefront is whether Paul actually moved from one religious life to another, even if it is much recognized that Paul kept his Jewish identity.[4] In relation to this debate, considering the idea of the four stages of entry to a new existence helps our study forward.

1) On whether Acts can be used as a source for understanding Paul's life, the difficulty has been the historicity of Luke's accounts, which has been questioned.[5] However, for the reason given here, Acts is an important biblical source for explaining the four stages of the Damascus Road event and the action that is taken by God and Paul in these phases.

This event is found both in Acts and the letters. In Acts, Luke[6] mentions the story three times (Luke's narrative in 9:1–22, and Paul's own speech[7] in 22:3–16 and 26:9–20). In the letters, Paul speaks of this experience in Galatians 1:11–17 and Philippians 3:4–11 (in the disputed letters, cf. 1 Tim 1:12–17). Reference is also made to specific aspects of the event, such as his persecution activity (1 Cor 15:9) and Christ's appearance (1 Cor 9:1; 15:8–9). Some scholars think that the seventh chapter of Romans[8] and 2 Corinthians 4:6[9] are also about Paul's conversion.

For a better grasp of what the four stages and action represent in Paul's transition, in this study the two sources are conflated. There is a reason for this. Since Paul himself recounts his experience in the letters, any scholar would concur with F. F. Bruce that "Paul's letters are our primary source for

---

4. E.g. Nanos, "Paul and Jewish Tradition," 65.

5. Because of Luke's "apologetic stance," the historicity of Acts accounts has been questioned; for more on this, see Everts, "Conversion and Call," 159 col. 1.

6. This study considers Luke as the author of Acts; as Porter shows, the tradition holds this view, though Acts (like Luke) is "formally anonymous, and so certainty regarding authorship cannot be established"; Porter, *Paul of Acts*, 99, cf. 7; also Kümmel, *Introduction*, 147, detail 147–50.

7. Stressing this, see e.g. Blomberg, *From Pentecost to Patmos*, 40. It is Paul's own speech in Acts 22 and 26; so more than Longenecker's view of the three narratives in Acts as just "an account 'about' Paul," Longenecker, "Realized Hope," 18; on this, see Everts, "Conversion and Call," 159 col. 1.

8. Everts, 157 col. 1; Blomberg, *From Pentecost*, 41.

9. Bruce, *Paul*, 74; Kim, *Origin of Paul's Gospel*, 5, more in fn. 4, same page; Gaventa, *From Darkness to Light*, 2; Peace, *Conversion*, 33.

his life and work."[10] In fact, many recognize this to be the approach for any study regarding the Damascus Road event.[11] The strength of this view is that in fact Paul's letters contain elements related to this experience.

Elements are also found relating to the four stages, especially in Galatians 1–2. The divine encounter and action (the first stage) are seen when Paul speaks of the fact that God "called" him (1:15, cf. 1:6). God's "calling" denotes not only an idea of encountering God and his word, but also shows his action. As Burton recognizes, this verb denotes "the divine initiative of the Christian life (1 Cor 7:17–22), by which God summons men into the fellowship of his Son Jesus Christ (1 Cor 1:9)."[12] Paul speaks of his "rescue" by God (Gal 1:3–4) and juxtaposes the two ideas when he states that God calls and justifies (cf. Rom 8:30).[13]

The liminal time (i.e. the second stage) is also present in Galatians 1. Paul speaks of the time when he learned the gospel (Gal 1:12, cf. also v. 16: "he revealed his Son in me").[14] The mode that God used was revelation (ἀποκάλυψις). As Burton recognizes, this word denotes a learning activity,[15] which is a feature of the second stage, as it was outlined in the second chapter. The second chapter has also demonstrated that the liminal phase is the time between the old and the new, which is reflected by the three years in Arabia and Damascus (Gal 1:17–18), before his official integration into the church (Gal 1:22). The third stage, where the person becomes a full member of the community, is echoed by his official recognition and integration by Peter and James, the representatives of the church (Gal 1:18–19; 2:2, 9). Galatians 2:7 also reports the task and responsibility which Paul has taken from the Lord in his transition (πεπίστευμαι τὸ εὐαγγέλιον τῆς ἀκροβυστίας, "the gospel of uncircumcision was committed unto me"), which reflects the fourth stage.

---

10. Bruce, *Paul*, 16.

11. On valuing the letters' accounts over Acts narratives, e.g. Longenecker, "Realized Hope," 18; Gaventa, *From Darkness*, 17–18; for more on this, see Everts, "Conversion and Call," 157 col. 1.

12. Burton, *Galatians*, 20, 49.

13. Giving attention to this, e.g. Burton, 20.

14. For various meanings because of 'in me,' e.g. Burton, 49–50.

15. As Burton notes, other uses of ἀποκάλυπτω in Paul are about not just "which takes place in the mind of the individual" but show "actual perception" that "results in knowledge," cf. Burton, *Galatians*, 433.

From these elements, one may argue that the four stages of Paul's move are reflected in the letters. However, what the letters provide does not serve the purpose of our study, whose task is to consider descriptively the different stages of the transition.[16] This requires a descriptive account of Paul's transition, which is absent in the letters.[17] As Räisänen points out, the letters "do not directly describe Paul's call experience."[18] Hence Luke's descriptive story will be essential to this study. But Paul's account will also be used because, as Gaventa notices, it is important to consider "what Paul himself says concerning his move from persecutor to apostle."[19] Thus, we rely primarily on Acts' narratives, but we also draw on the letters for more evidence. Synthesizing insights from the two sources is the approach adopted here.

Conflating elements from Luke and Paul is possible. "To synthesize the two sources" is an approach that Gaventa refutes.[20] On the other hand, some have used this approach:

> Les lettres de la main de Paul adressées aux communautés qu'il avait fondées . . . constituent la première source pour la connaissance de sa personnalité et de son œuvre évangélisatrice. Mais, malgré les souvenirs autobiographiques qu'elles contiennent . . . les lettres n'offrent pas d'éléments suffisants pour établir une biographie complète. Pour ce faire, et malgré les problèmes inhérents à l'authenticité des *Actes des Apôtres* en quoi l'on voit une œuvre historique composée par Luc, disciple de Paul, les historiens du N. T. ont coutume d'utiliser les éléments narratifs des Actes, où Paul occupe la place de protagoniste pendant

---

16. A different approach that must be based on the letters is that which focuses primarily on the theological meaning of Paul's conversion. Thus e.g. Dunn applies "the reading of . . . Paul's theological rethinking" of it in his letters; Dunn, "Paul and Justification," 87.

17. As H. Räisänen points out, the letters "interpret" Paul's experience "in the light of his 'knowledge of Christ,'" see "Paul's Conversion," 408.

18. Räisänen speaking of Phil 3:8–11 ("Paul's Conversion," 408); others who recognize this, e.g. Porter, *Paul of Acts*, 98; Gaventa, *From Darkness*, 17; Everts, "Conversion and Call," 158 col. 2.

19. Gaventa, *From Darkness*, 18.

20. Gaventa denounces "synthesizing the two sources," see *From Darkness*, 18.

les trois quarts de l'œuvre, pour situer les données des épitres pauliniennes.²¹

As mentioned earlier, the issue has been doubt over the historicity of Luke's narratives in Acts. Some scholars affirm this historicity. For example, Bruce states that "the Paul of Acts is the historical Paul."²² Bruce's conclusion is that, for study of any aspect of Paul's life, Acts "is our principal secondary source."²³ This is very much recognized by other scholars, especially due to the strong agreement between Acts and the letters. Wenham, for example, notes that "it is clear that Acts and the Pauline letters do very frequently intersect" on this issue and his conclusion is that "the author of Acts is not vaguely familiar with the story of Paul."²⁴ Kim has a similar view. Pointing a finger at "the tendency to give little historical value to the speeches in Acts," he states that "the similarities between the accounts in Acts themselves, and between them and those in Paul's letters, lead us to think that all three accounts in Acts go back to Paul."²⁵

In the light of these elements, in this chapter Acts and the letters are considered. Even if Luke reports this event not exactly as Paul speaks of it, what is essential for our focus in this chapter is that Luke reflects the four stages in his telling of the story, and thus illustrates our contention that these four stages provided the basic shape for understanding any initiatory process.

2) As mentioned earlier, another element of debate has been whether Paul's experience is "a conversion." This is another methodological issue for a study that is about Paul's move to Christian existence.

---

21. Loi, "Paul," 1937 col. 1. Translation:
    The letters of the hand of Paul addressed to the communities which he had founded . . . constitute the first source for the knowledge of his personality and his evangelizing work. But, despite the autobiographical memories they contain . . . the letters do not offer sufficient evidence for establishing a full biography. To do this, and despite the problems inherent in the authenticity of the *Acts of the Apostles* in which we see a historical work composed by Luke, a disciple of Paul, NT historians are accustomed to using the narrative elements of Acts, where Paul occupies the place of protagonist in three quarters of the work, to situate the data of the Pauline epistles.

22. Bruce, *Paul*, 17; also Porter, *Paul of Acts*, 2, 5–6; for more on Acts historicity, see Lohfink, *Conversion of St. Paul*, especially the conclusion at 101.

23. Bruce, *Paul*, 16.

24. Wenham, "Acts and Pauline Corpus," 256, also 258.

25. Kim, *Origin of Paul's Gospel*, 30–31; Lohfink, *Conversion of Paul*, 23.

Paul's Conversion and the Four Stages of Entry

The accounts in Acts and the letters agree on the fact that Paul moved from one "*way* of life" (τὴν ἐμὴν ἀναστροφήν[26] ποτε ἐν τῷ Ἰουδαϊσμῷ, "my former conduct [behaviour or life] in Judaism", Gal 1:13–14; Acts 22:3) and joined the other "*way*" (τὴν ὁδὸν[27], Acts 22:4). A strongly zealous Jew left his pharisaic community for a community that worshipped Yahweh together with Gentiles indiscriminately.[28] As Everts points out, this is a "complete break" and "a radical reorientation of his life and his religious values."[29] Saul's experience is a real *passage* from one system of life to another, and many find the word "conversion" (ἐπιστροφή) to be very appropriate.[30] Du Toit, for example, is among the scholars who have adopted strongly the idea that Saul's change was a conversion. For Du Toit, "Paul underwent a fundamental change of identity and status."[31] He finds this especially in Philippians 3:7–9. Also, as he gives attention to the σάρξ-πνεῦμα (flesh-Spirit) dichotomy that is recurrent in Paul's writings, Du Toit argues that this "points to two ways of existence" in the life of Paul and of any other person (Jew or Gentile) who believes in Christ and chooses to follow Christ's way."[32] On the basis of these elements, and many others, Du Toit (in line with many scholars to whom he refers, e.g. Longenecker, Segal, Dunn, Fee, De Boer, Moo, Das, DeSilva) comes to a conclusion that "Paul's change of identity indeed points to a conversion."[33]

Conversion as the meaning of Saul's move to Christianity is a disputed matter indeed, and the issue is whether Paul's experience is a "conversion," "transformation," "alternation," or "call."[34] It is important to specify how this

---

26. Concerning ἀναστροφή as "mode of life," see *ALGNT*, s.v. "ἀναστροφή." This word means "way of life" in the Pauline corpus and Second Temple sources, see Gaventa, *From Darkness*, 24. Paul does not apply it (see Longenecker, "Realized Hope," 25), but uses a word of its group (ἐπιστρεφω) in his defence (Acts 26:18, 20) and there is echo in 2 Cor 4:6; 6:14–17.

27. Conzelmann's view is that ὁδός, "way" here "denotes Christian teaching as well as Christians as a group" (*Acts*, 71; for Haenchen, it denotes more "community" than "teaching" (*Acts*, 320 fn. 1).

28. So Everts, "Conversion and Call," 160 col. 2.

29. Everts, 'Conversion and Call,' 161 col. 1; also Segal, *Paul the Convert*, 18–19.

30. Bultmann, *Theology*, 188; Peace, *Conversion*, 85; Segal, *Paul the Convert*, 6–7, cf. 72; Blomberg recognizes conversion as "an appropriate label," *From Pentecost*, 40 fn. 102; also Longenecker, "Realized Hope," 24, cf. 27–28; for G. W. Hansen, Paul uses "in Judaism" "only to describe his life before his encounter with Christ" ("Paul's Conversion," 216).

31. Du Toit, "Was Paul a Christian?," 16.

32. Du Toit, 24.

33. Du Toit, 24.

34. For more, see *RD/IPC*, xiii.

study relates to the above discussion. The primary thing is the sense of these different ideas. Gaventa addresses this in her survey of the different theories on the conversion phenomenon.[35] This survey lists three ways in which a "personal change" to a new existence can be described: (1) as an *alternation*, i.e. "a relatively limited form of change that develops from one's previous behaviour (e.g. a person who moves from a Presbyterian to a Methodist church)," (2) as a *conversion*, namely, "a radical change in which past affiliations are rejected for some new commitment and identity," and (3) as a *transformation*, that is, "also a radical change, but one in which an altered perception reinterprets both present and past."[36] These three are applied to Paul's change. The fourth idea, used to define what Paul experienced on the Damascus Road, is a "*call.*" This is especially defended by Stendahl, the core of his argument being that Paul's event is a *call* instead of a *conversion*, because his situation is "not a change of 'religion.'"[37] Other scholars have found this view to be hardly convincing.[38]

Where does this study stand? It follows the line of scholars who understand that Paul's experience simply takes on these different meanings (conversion, transformation, alternation and call).[39] The idea of four stages shows that in fact each of these definitions has put a stress on one of the stages of transition.[40] There are three categories to which each of these definitions belongs. As Everts shows, there is first a "traditional view" that mainly emphasizes the

---

35. Gaventa explores the Lofland-Stark and the Berger-Luckmann models and the definitions of W. James, A. D. Nock and R. Travisano; for detail see Gaventa, *From Darkness*, 4–9.

36. For more on the three concepts, Gaventa, *From Darkness*, 8–12; also Longenecker, "Realized Hope," 27–28.

37. Stendahl, *Paul among the Jews*, 7, 11; for more supporters of this view, Dunn, "Paul and Justification," 86.

38. On those disputing this opinion, e.g. Everts, "Conversion and Call," 161 col.1; for Segal, "conversion is a decisive . . . change in religious community, even when the convert . . . affirms the same religion" (*Paul the Convert*, 7, cf. 30–32); also Peace, *Conversion*, 27–28.

39. E.g. Longenecker, "Realized Hope," 27–28 (alternation, transformation and conversion) and page 26 ("call" meaning "conversion"); so also Hansen, "Paul's Conversion," 213; Gaventa: "These distinctions are not hard and fast" (*From Darkness*, 12). In the letters, she notes a "transformation" (40, cf. 33), but also a "conversion" (28). For Everts, both "conversion" and "call" describe the event ("Conversion and Call," 162 col. 1, cf. 159 col. 1); so also Marshall, "New Understanding," 53; Peace, *Conversion*, 29; Segal, *Paul the Convert*, 6–7.

40. A danger can be defining a transition with a focus on one aspect. A transition is a complex whole. Thus, Marshall draws attention to "not just the . . . experience outside Damascus but also the associated complex of events and intense personal reorientation that filled the . . . ensuing period" ("New Understanding," 45).

dimension of justification for Paul.[41] This focuses on the divine act, which will be clear when we examine stage one. A second line has been a sociological understanding of seeing in Paul's transition, particularly the "conscious choice to socialize to a new group."[42] As we will see, this choice and decision shows a focus on the actions of stages two and three. The third view emphasizes that the event is "a call" to serve as an apostle to the Gentiles.[43] This focuses on Paul's after-entry life, which is explained at stage four.

In brief, our study lines up with the idea that Paul's experience encompasses all these senses and thus offers a new explanation as we examine the four stages and explore how Paul takes action in his transition to the Christian life.

3.3. God's Light and Glory Given to Paul (Stage One)

The idea of the divine act is important, because the clarity of what the believer does depends on how distinct the role of God is made. As the second chapter has outlined, the transition to a new religious life consists of both the divine saving act and the candidate's consequent action (breaking with his or her previous existence, through a ritual making an oath of belonging to the new system and adopting the new way of life as one's personal responsibility). The "call" interpretation of the Damascus Road event essentially suggests that salvation was not necessary for Paul. This touches upon the first stage of a transition to a new religious way of life in antiquity. In the light of how the "divine action" stage was seen in Paul's time (cf. chapter two), this section argues that Paul was a "sinner" who needed to be saved, as the context of his transition from a Pharisee to being a member of the Jesus community seems to imply. According to Saint Ambrose, Paul believed "the law of the flesh [leads] into the bonds of sin that he himself in the stress of human frailty believed that help could be rendered him through Christ."[44]

---

41. Idea of Paul's change "from a sense of failure to being right as he discovers Christ's justification," for more on this and on the three views, Everts, "Conversion and Call," 156–162; also Corley, "Interpreting Paul's Conversion," 1–3.

42. See Everts, "Conversion and Call," 160 col. 2.

43. Stendahl speaks of "receiving a new and special calling in God's service" (*Paul Among Jews*, 7).

44. Ambrose, *Sacrament of Incarnation*, 244.

In 2 Corinthians 4:6 Paul says that "God ... shined in *our* (ἡμῶν) hearts to give the light (φωτισμόν)[45] *of* the knowledge *of* the glory [in other words, the light *that is* the knowledge, the glory][46] of God in the face of Christ." (RV) This shows that Paul experienced the action that God did with his glory. By this epexegetical relation of "light" and "glory," Paul is probably making reference to his Damascus Road experience. Jervell recognizes this when he interprets "light" (cf. Acts 9:3) and states, "Sie ist die Doxa des erhöhten Herrn (it [she] is the glory of the exalted Lord)."[47]

2 Corinthians 4:6 shows that God made his light and glory shine on Paul at the critical point of his transition to a new way of walking with God.[48] This is the saving action that the God of the new group accomplishes in the person who is moving toward that group. It is the divine action of the first stage of a transition to a new existence. God's action on Paul during the Damascus Road event has usually been construed without this focus on what a transition to a new life in antiquity looked like, and what its stages were.

Everts points out that "the traditional view of Paul's conversion ... sees it as an experience of being justified by faith" and "being freed by Christ" from "his struggle with the Law."[49] This view stresses the first stage of entry. This has been disputed.[50] Stuhlmacher, Kim and Westerholm are among the supporters of this traditional view, as Dunn notes.[51] In fact, Westerholm thinks that Paul recognizes (referring to Gal 2:16–17) that he and his fellow Jews were "sinners" before Jesus made them righteous.[52] Also Campbell notes a similar idea in Romans 3:20: "Paul stresses the equality of Jew and Gentile in

---

45. It means action: "illumination, bringing to light," cf. *ALGNT*, s.v. "φωτισμός."

46. The two genitives are epexegetical; a similar construction in Acts 22:11 with τῆς δόξης τοῦ φωτός, "of the glory of the light," see Lohfink, *Conversion of Paul*, 22.

47. Jervell, *Die Apostelgeschichte*, 280.

48. This is the "light" he was to bring to "his own and to the Gentiles" (Acts 26:18, 23; cf. Rom 1:3–4).

49. Everts, "Conversion and Call," 162 col. 2; Hansen: being freed from being "a zealot demanding adherence to the Jewish way of life" to "an apostle preaching salvation in Jesus" ("Paul's Conversion," 216).

50. Dunn, "Paul and Justification," 85.

51. Dunn, 85.

52. Westerholm, *Perspectives Old and New*, 371.

sin."⁵³ S. K. Stowers disputes the idea that the two groups are "equally sinful";⁵⁴ however he recognizes that "Paul certainly holds that his fellow Jews as a whole are under sin because of their unbelief in Christ and their failure to be a light to the Gentiles."⁵⁵ This view recognizes the first stage of transition for Paul; this study supports this view and brings new arguments associated with the wider idea of the first stage of entry and the divine action that it implies.

Alternatively, scholars argue that Paul's later doctrine of justification by faith should not be read back into the Damascus Road event. They effectively suggest that Paul was not a sinner who needed to be justified by God. This is Sanders' opinion when he says that Paul suffered no "guilt" of sin.⁵⁶ The same idea is adopted by Dunn and Suggate.⁵⁷ Before Sanders (the idea did not start with Sanders as Westerholm suggests),⁵⁸ Stendahl had already raised the issue. Rejecting the idea of "conversion" for Paul's change, the reason that Stendahl advances is that "during his time as a Pharisee" Paul did not experience "the anguish of a plagued conscience."⁵⁹ A similar idea had been expressed previously by Nygren in his view that "there is no trace of resentment" as Paul speaks of his pharisaic life (referring to Phil 3:4–9).⁶⁰ These conclusions show that due attention has not been given to what in first-century life a transition to a new religious way is, and to how the divine action that constitutes the first phase works. It is in connection with this that Paul sees himself as a person who needed grace (1 Cor 15:10; cf. 1 Tim 1:14)⁶¹ and saving action (1 Tim 1:15).

This section intends to examine how the first stage of entry (i.e. the divine action) applies to Paul's conversion. It is structured under two points. 1) As the second chapter describes, the idea of encounter with God is an important element of this first stage. Primarily, this idea of encounter in Paul's event is

---

53. Campbell, "Why Did Paul," 268–269.
54. Stowers, "Paul's Four Discourses," 118. He explains this by the idea that Paul "never charges [the Jews] with complete moral failure," 125.
55. Stowers, 125.
56. Sanders, *Paul and Palestinian Judaism*, 49.
57. Dunn and Suggate, *Justice of God*, 13.
58. Westerholm, *Perspectives Old and New*, xvii.
59. Stendahl, *Paul Among Jews*, 81.
60. Nygren, *Romans*, 13.
61. Also Rom 1:5; Gal 1:15; and in 1 Tim 1:13, 16.

given due attention. 2) Building on this, we consider what God's action on Paul's life is, and what sense it makes in relation to his movement into a new religious way of life. Both points will help us to understand his thinking on the Christian's transition from sin to God in Romans 5–6.

1) Initially we consider how Paul's encounter with God would be understood. T. Churchill considers that "given both the light and the presence of Jesus, it seems that Paul experienced something more than a *bat qol*."[62] This stresses the presence of Jesus. Generally, all scholars agree that something happened between Jesus and Paul, but in Paul's time such an encounter is more than scholars have sometimes described it. The person and the deity meet together and agreements are made, and this determines the seriousness of anything else that follows in the process. Dunn is not very sure that this is what happened to Paul when he states that "this one was *presumably* directly from heaven (referring to Acts 26:19; Gal 1:16)."[63] However Paul's experience is just such an encounter with God, one that fits the first-century cultural pattern. The religious reality of Paul's time shows that the first step of the process of entering into a new community of worship is a moment when the deity takes "pleasure" (as for Apuleius) to meet the person and "to reveal" his or her will (cf. ὅτε εὐδόκησεν ὁ θεὸς . . . ἀποκαλύψαι τὸν υἱὸν αὐτοῦ ἐν ἐμοί, "when God was pleased . . . to reveal his Son to me", Gal 1:15–16).

This has an effect on what Paul's encounter with God in the Damascus Road event really means. For example, as we will presently show, Paul's question "Τίς εἶ, κύριε; Who are you, Lord?" (Acts 9:5; 22:8; 26:15) is often interpreted as indicating that he is not sure who his interlocutor is. Given how entry to a new religious community works in Paul's time, we suggest that the question is asked for deeper knowledge about God and not because of doubt over the identity of Paul's interlocutor.

There are elements in Acts that are relevant to the issue of Paul's encounter with the Lord. These include the fact that "a light from heaven" (φῶς ἐκ τοῦ οὐρανοῦ) shone around Saul (Acts 9:3) and that a voice called his name twice

---

62. Churchill, *Divine Initiative*, 199 and 228. For meaning of *bat qol*, see 198–199. So also Camery-Hoggatt: "this can only be the work of God, ("Visions, Ecstatic Experience," 964). More on the definition of bat qol: "A Bat Qol (Literally 'daughter of a voice' in Hebrew) is a spirit-based kind that many . . . believe is a heavenly voice . . . ," see https://milhamah.com/bat-qol/, consulted on the 17th August 2022.

63. Dunn, *Christianity in Making*, 350 [italics mine].

(v. 4). Also important is Paul's address to the interlocutor as κύριε, "Lord" (9:5; 22:8; 26:15). From such elements, Haenchen, for example, concludes that Paul was in direct contact with God. Considering the fact that the other "men did not see anyone" (9:7), the idea of "seeing the Righteous One" (22:14), the expression "I saw a light" (26:13) and the words "a witness to what you have seen" (26:16), Haenchen's conclusion is that "Saul saw Jesus only inasmuch as he beheld this tremendous blaze of light."[64] Jervell has a similar view when he states, "Ob er in diesem Licht Jesus sieht, wird nicht direct gesagt, das kommt aber vv 7, 17 und 27 zum Ausdruck, vgl. auch 22,14 und 26,19 (It is not directly stated whether he sees Jesus in this light, but this is expressed in vv. 1, 17 and 27, cf. also 22:14 and 26:19)."[65] Keeping the same idea and drawing from other evidence, Dupont points out that Barnabas (Acts 9:27), Ananias (22:14–15), and Jesus himself (26:16, cf. v. 19) affirm that Paul has "seen" the Lord.[66]

This shows that Paul experiences a theophany, and it is better to interpret κύριε with this meaning. It is difficult to know exactly what Luke understood by "Τίς εἶ, κύριε" (Who are you, Lord?) and what Saul meant when he uttered it. However, there is enough evidence to suggest that by these words Luke considers seriously that an encounter with God is the first stage of Paul's transition to his new existence.

Some scholars interpret "Who are you, Lord?" as indicating Paul's doubt concerning the interlocutor that he is dealing with. For example, R. Peace's view is that this is "doubt . . . about the identity of the figure in the vision" and his opinion is that Paul may be thinking of an angel, a martyr, or God.[67] I. H. Marshall similarly suggests that "lord" is used in its sense of "sir" and that Paul uses it as a "reply to any heavenly figure."[68] Also Jervell speaks of "die Anwesenheit eines Kyrios" (the presence of a lord),[69] thus understanding that Paul thinks of being in the presence of any lord. In Jervell's view, "dass dieser Kyrios Jesus ist, Paulus weiss es nicht" (Paul does not know that this

---

64. Haenchen, *Acts*, 321–322.
65. Jervell, *Apostelgeschichte*, 280.
66. Dupont, *Nouvelles études*, 123.
67. Peace, *Conversion*, 80–81.
68. Marshall, *Acts*, 169; also Dunn, *Christianity in Making*, 350; and *Baptism in Spirit*, 73–74.
69. Jervell, *Apostelgeschichte*, 280.

Lord is Jesus).[70] This view rests especially on the idea that when Paul says κύριε he does not yet confess Jesus as Lord.[71]

Because of the theophanic elements, it is better to understand that Paul is in the presence of "the Lord" instead of "die Anwesenheit eines Kyrios" (the presence of any lord) as Jervell suggests. That is, Paul means to address God as Lord when he says κύριε, "Lord". Many recognize this, but without addressing the issue why κύριε, "Lord" is a reference to God despite the fact that it is part of "a question."[72] For example, Johnson states that "*kyrios* . . . should be taken at full value. Saul does not yet know it is *Jesus* who is Lord, but he recognizes that he is involved in a theophany!"[73] Also Bruce's view is that "he [Saul] probably recognized that the words were spoken with divine authority; κύριε (Lord) should therefore be treated as more than a mere courtesy title."[74] Parsons has a similar conclusion. Drawing from Israel's tradition, he notices that "the title Lord is usually reserved in Jewish thinking for Yahweh God."[75] In fact, from this Jewish tradition, Paul might have immediately thought this was an encounter with God. As Segal states (based on a survey of Old Testament, Second Temple and Rabbinic sources[76]), "Yahweh himself, the angel of God, and his Glory are peculiarly melded together, suggesting a deep secret about the ways God manifested himself to humanity."[77]

Thus, some maintain that Paul says "Lord" because he knows that he is speaking to God. However, what these scholars fail to show is why Paul's question cannot mean that he is just dubiously thinking that it may be a deceased saint, an angel or God. Paul's keen observance of the law is one thing that shows what his question is. Stendahl points out that Paul is proud that he has seriously observed God's law during his pharisaic career.[78] This is clear in Galatians 1:13–14 and Philippians 3:6 (cf. Acts 22:3–4; 26:4–5).

---

70. Jervell, 280.

71. So Dunn, *Christianity in Making*, 350; and *Baptism in Spirit*, 73–74; Marshall, *Acts*, 169.

72. Stressing this issue of a "question," e.g. Dunn, *Christianity in Making*, 350.

73. Johnson, *Acts*, 163.

74. Bruce, *Acts*, 235.

75. Parsons, *Acts*, 127; cf. also Segal, *Paul*, 7.

76. For this survey, Segal considers various texts including Exod 23:20–21; 33:18–23; Ezek 1:2; Dan 7:13; 12:3; *Asc. Isa.* 7:2–4; *Apoc. Zeph.* 6:1–15; *m. hag.* 2.1, see Segal, *Paul*, 39–58.

77. Segal, *Paul*, 42.

78. Dunn and Suggate, *Justice of God*, 14; Stendahl, *Paul Among Jews*, 8, 80.

From such devotedness, his question appears to be expressing his surprise, but also a desire to know who God really is and what his will is. That is, he appears to say, "God, I am zealous for your law, I am dealing seriously with those whose teaching is a threat to your law;[79] now you strike me! Who are you then and what is your will?" (cf. Τί ποιήσω, κύριε; "What should I do, Lord?" Acts 22:10). The questions "what should I do, Lord?" and "who are you, Lord?" (v. 8) are aspects of the same concern.

The substance of his question is not "may I know who I am dealing with?" Rather it is "may I have a better sense of who you are and what your will really is?" As the second chapter has shown, this deep apprehension of the deity is a feature of the stage of divine encounter. Such apprehension is necessary for a person who is about to belong to that deity and to serve him or her seriously. Exodus 3:13, which also occurs in a context of change to a new religious situation, illustrates how asking God his name is more than just asking about his identity. Like Paul, Moses is in a theophany. He asks what he should say if Israel asked what the name of God was (Exod 3:13). There is evidence that what Israel was going to ask was not something concerning identity *per se*. First, this verse shows that initially Moses would have told them, "the God of your fathers has sent me to you." Second, God's answer shows clearly that the interest is not just in identity, but in Yahweh's relationship with Israel on account of his covenant with the patriarchs, and by the virtue of this bond in the deliverance God intends to offer his people (cf. vv. 14–22).

The elements we have outlined are intended to show that divine encounter constitutes the first stage of Paul's move to a new religious life. Assuming that Luke is correctly reproducing Saul's question, "Who are you, Lord?", in this part the focus was on how these words should be understood in the context of Paul's transition. Now our focus is that this encounter implies salvation. In a context of change to a new religious way of life, the divine encounter must mean a saving action; it is more than just a theophany. What the initiand does in his or her transition (cf. stages two to four) is clarified if the significance of what God first does is understood. This next part considers what, in Saul's transition, God's action towards him means.

---

79. Similar idea when Peace contrasts Saul's self-appointed service and one appointed by Christ at his encounter with Saul (*Conversion*, 85).

2) As the second chapter outlines, the encounter with the deity is also the time when the person is delivered from the evil of his or her previous life. This section focuses on the idea of salvation for Saul and what this entails in relation to his transition to a new existence.

We have already touched upon the view of some scholars that Saul was not a sinner in need of salvation. This view is considered here in more detail, and the purpose is to show that, whether the pre-Christian Saul was conscious of sin or not, he met the risen Christ and had something done to him (stage one). Romans 5:12–6:23 shows the move of believers from being under sin to living in God's way. It is clear from Paul's "we" in this pericope (e.g. 6:2–4) that he too underwent this *passage* from sin to God. In order better to grasp the divine action of the first stage of entry in Romans 5:12–6:23, the focus in this section is on what this divine saving act from sin meant in Paul's own transition.

In 2 Corinthians 4:6, Paul says that God has shone his "*light* into *darkness*" and applies this to himself as well (ἡμῶν, "our"). The issue is what darkness is, and whether it concerns Paul's life as well. Elements of the answer are found in Acts, in Paul's letters and in the Old Testament.

In Acts 26:16–18, Paul's commission is "to open eyes and turn people from *darkness* to *light*, from the power of Satan to God" (v. 18). As Dupont shows, this means "les convertir des ténèbres à la lumière, de l'empire de Satan à Dieu, pour que par la foi (en Jésus), ils reçoivent le pardon des péchés"[80] (to convert them from darkness to light, from Satan's empire to God, so that by faith (in Jesus) they may receive the forgiveness of sins). The blind whose eyes need to be opened and who have not yet "a place among those who are sanctified by faith in Jesus" (v. 18) are the Gentiles and also the Jews (v. 17).[81] In 26:20 Paul shows clearly that this "repentance and conversion to God" (μετανοεῖν καὶ ἐπιστρέφειν ἐπὶ τὸν θεόν) is for the Jews and the Gentiles (cf. τοῖς ἐν Δαμασκῷ πρῶτόν τε καὶ Ἱεροσολύμοις, πᾶσάν τε τὴν χώραν τῆς Ἰουδαίας, καὶ τοῖς ἔθνεσιν, "first to those at Damascus and also at Jerusalem, and all the country of Judea, and to the Gentiles").[82] As Johnson points out, "children of Israel are not left behind in the mission"[83] (cf. 26:23). In fact,

---

80. Dupont, *Nouvelles études*, 450.
81. So Stendahl, *Paul Among Jews*, 81; also Haenchen, *Acts*, 688.
82. E.g. Dupont, *Nouvelles études*, 450.
83. Johnson, *Acts*, 165.

Paul "continues to preach to his fellow Jews until the very end of the story (28:23–28).''[84] There is evidence here that the Jews need the gospel. There is no reason to make Paul an exception.

Both Paul and Luke take seriously the fact that salvation in Jesus is needed also by the Jews. On this issue, there is strong agreement between Luke and Paul, as referred to earlier. Hence "weaving" ideas from them both is very helpful (*contra* Gaventa).[85] The idea that salvation is also for the Jews is a major theme in Romans (1:16; 3:9; 10:9–13). In 2 Corinthians 4:6, as mentioned earlier, Paul associates *light* (φωτισμός) with *knowledge* (γνῶσις, closely connected with the idea of "revelation")[86] and *glory* (δόξα). A similar cluster appears when Luke speaks of the Messiah: φῶς εἰς ἀποκάλυψιν ἐθνῶν καὶ δόξαν λαοῦ σου Ἰσραήλ, "a light for revelation to the Gentiles and for glory to your people Israel" (Luke 2:32). This is repeated in Acts 26:23: the Christ was to announce (καταγγέλλειν) the light "et au peuple et aux païens"[87] (τῷ τε λαῷ καὶ τοῖς ἔθνεσιν, "to the people and to the Gentiles"). Hence the idea that salvation is also for the Jews has value for Luke (as for Paul); and this shows why in Acts 26:17 Luke focuses on the fact that Paul also,[88] in his defence, speaks of God's light as being intended for both his people (λαοῦ) and the Gentiles (ἐθνῶν) [cf. Acts 9:15]. The Messianic saving mission to both Israel and the Gentiles has roots in Jewish tradition, for the words in Luke 2:32 are a quotation from Isaiah 42:6–8.[89] The idea is even clearer in Isaiah 49:5–6 (cf. also 9:1).

---

84. Johnson, 165.

85. Gaventa, *From Darkness*, 18.

86. Frequently Paul uses (esp. γινώσκω) as a result of being "revealed" something, e.g. in 1 Cor 2:10–12, "God has revealed to us (ἡμῖν ἀπεκάλυψεν) through the Spirit" (v. 10) "the things that he prepared for us" (v. 9), and this means we know since we have the Spirit (v. 12) who knows (ἔγνωκεν) these things (v. 11). And in Rom 7:7, knowing sin as a result of the fact that the law reveals it; see also 1 Cor 14:7, 9; cf. Matt 10:26; Luke 8:17. Also a sense of "revealing" is implied when γινώσκω (to know) is translated as to "discover" (e.g. 2 Cor 13:6) or "be evident" (e.g. Phil 4:5), see *GECNT*, s.v. "γινώσκω."

87. Carrez' attention to the force of τε and καὶ (*NTIGF*, Acts 26:23); for more on this, Dupont, *Nouvelles études*, 450–451.

88. This suggests Luke may have heard from Paul himself about his vision (*contra* Lohfink's doubt on this, see Lohfink, *Conversion*, 30).

89. Dunn (ref. to Knox, Stendahl, Räisänen) cites this text as showing "a calling rather than a conversion" ("Paul and Justification," 86–87). Conversion seems the sense because it shows that Paul also needed salvation and change.

These elements strongly show that Christ came to save the Jews (and Paul) just as he came to save the Gentiles. When in 2 Corinthians 4:6 Paul associates himself (ἡμῶν, "our") with the people on whom "God shone his light," he means that God saved him in the process of becoming a Christian.[90]

Such a divine saving action is a crucial aspect of a first-century view of transition to a new existence. Was Paul conscious that his way of life could be in conflict with God? Our intention here is not to go into the detail of the debate on whether Paul was conscious of sin. Although it is difficult to be conclusive on this issue, this study considers the possibility that Paul was indeed conscious of it. Religious life, which is our focus in this study, works with such ideas. As the second chapter shows, in first-century life the process of moving from one religious way to another depends on the consciousness that the old way was in conflict with the new. In Romans 6:19 Paul shows that this was true of his readers, and there is evidence that it is true for Paul himself as well.

The rescue from sin is evident as we consider how far from Jesus's way Saul was. As Parsons notes, "the use of the word 'persecute' is exclusively linked to the activities of Saul in the conversion accounts"[91] (cf. Acts 9:4–5; 22:4, 7–8; 26:11, 14–15). Hence, here a focus is given to Paul's crusade against Christ-followers. The expressions (διώκτης – a persecutor,[92] βλάσφημος – blasphemous,[93] ποιέω κακὰ τοῖς ἁγίοις – do[ing] evil to the saints)[94] that Luke and Paul use to depict Saul's life are important here. When Stendahl seeks to prove that Paul's experience was a "call," he asserts that "Serving the one and the same God, Paul receives a new and special calling in God's service."[95] This overlooks Paul's own declaration in Galatians 1:10 that he was "pleasing men" and that this was reversed (cf. ἔτι, "still") by his encounter with Christ.[96] As Kern points out, instead of being a servant, in reality Saul was

---

90. Also e.g. Eph 5:8 (if linked to v. 2), 1 Thess 5:5 (cf. Jas 1:17–18 – light and birth both by God).

91. Parsons, *Acts*, 127.

92. To Christ and the church, Acts 9:4, 13; 22:4–5; 26:9–11; 1 Cor 15:9; Gal 1:13; Phil 3:6; 1 Tim 1:13.

93. 1 Tim 1:13.

94. Acts 9:13.

95. Stendahl, *Paul Among Jews*, 7.

96. Cf. εἰ ἔτι ἀνθρώποις ἤρεσκον, Χριστοῦ δοῦλος οὐκ ἂν ἤμην, "If I were still pleasing men, I should not be a servant of Christ" (Gal 1:10).

an "ardent foe of Christ, who in inducing Christians to blaspheme himself commits blasphemy."[97] To force believers to renounce Christ was a serious sign of sin. As Conzelmann shows (drawing from Pliny),[98] similar acts were to urge believers to "offer sacrifices" and to "curse Christ, *maledicere Christo*"; these are things that "those who were really Christians" could only "be forced to perform."[99] In other words, Saul was an enemy of Christ and God, not a servant. As R. Peace states, "Paul was not, as he had assumed up to that point, walking in God's way and doing God's will."[100] By his encounter with Jesus, "Paul discovered that he was not working for God, as he had assumed, but against God."[101] As Gaventa notices, the account "is primarily a story about *the reversal of an enemy*."[102]

In fact, what kind of person does Paul discover he is, when God charges[103] him ἐκ τοῦ οὐρανοῦ, "from heaven" (9:3) with the words, τί με διώκεις; "why do you persecute me?" (9:4)? It is difficult to be conclusive that Paul's own hand exercised violence.[104] But the harshness of the crusade against believers is an essential element for understanding Paul's change. Gaventa suggests that "it seems probable that his persecution was verbal rather than violent."[105] I. H. Marshall similarly thinks that "perhaps the reference is . . . to what he would have liked to do to the Christians."[106] In this sense the imperfects (ἠνάγκαζον αὐτοὺς – I forced them, ἐδίωκον – I persecuted, cf. 26:11) are interpreted as conative. But, as Conzelmann recognizes, a literal description fits better the context,[107] and many agree that Saul's harassment was serious.[108] As Dunn

---

97. Kern, "Paul's Conversion," 70.

98. Cf. Pliny, *Letters and Panegyricus*, vol. 2, 10.96.5.

99. Conzelmann, *Acts*, 210.

100. Peace, *Conversion*, 41, 49.

101. Peace, 25.

102. Gaventa, *From Darkness*, 65.

103. Parsons: Paul is asked to "be accountable for his actions" (*Acts*, 127); Peace shows a different view: "there is no accusation or judgment" in God's words (*Conversion*, 53).

104. Although, as Dunn notes, Paul himself "refers to this pre-Christian past several times" and declares that he acted "in excessive measure to destroy it," see Dunn, "In Search," in Spitaler, *Celebrating Paul*, 19.

105. Gaventa, *From Darkness*, 26.

106. Marshall, *Acts*, 168.

107. Conzelman, *Acts*, 210.

108. Blomberg, *From Pentecost*, 40; Johnson finds a parallel to Apollonius in 4 Macc 4:1–14, cf. also 2 Macc 3:22–30 (*Acts*, 162); Peace shows how ardent violence it is and its roots

investigates "The Theology of Zeal" in the Jewish tradition and thinks of its link with Paul as a persecutor, he notes that zeal for Yahweh "involved violence and bloodshed, as necessitated"[109] and that what Paul was doing was "evidently as fierce as the tradition of zeal documented."[110] Ananias' fear serves as further evidence.[111] Although it not clear whether Paul himself exercised brutality, he was involved in a crusade that violently sought to destroy the new movement; he was in a serious "rejection" of Jesus.[112] This reveals how distant from God's will Paul was. More evidence from the Old Testament should be noted here.

It is important to note that the sense of διώκω (to persecute) in this context is "to pursue with malignity,"[113] because it is about inflicting "harm" (κακὰ, Acts 9:13) and "death" (θανάτου, 9:1; 22:4; 26:10) upon "the saints"[114] (26:10). Saul was well instructed in the law (22:3). Attention to the Old Testament is needed when discussing if the persecutor Saul was a "sinner" or not. Jesus drew an analogy of this issue with the Old Testament when he foretold the disciples that they were going to endure this kind of persecution (Matt 5:10–11) and death (John 16:1–2). He compared it with what the prophets had suffered (Matt 5:12). This reminded them of such events as when, instead of heeding the messengers of God, people mocked and scoffed them (2 Chr 36:15, 16), put them in prison or in a muddy cistern (Jer 37:15–38:13), and even worse stoned them (2 Chr 24:21) and slew them (1 Kgs 18:13; 19:10; Neh 9:26). Those who did these things were not acting in obedience to God. In fact these acts are clearly described as "wickedness" (e.g. it is said about what was done to Jeremiah: הֵרֵעוּ, "they acted wickedly," Jer 38:9).[115] It was wickedness not only because to harass people was morally wrong, but also

---

in Jewish tradition (*Conversion*, 38–43); on "I cast my vote" in Acts 26:10, Conzelman states, "the Jewish authorities had the *ius gladii*, the right to execute capital criminals" (*Acts*, 210).

109. Dunn, "In Search," 24.

110. Dunn, 24.

111. Lohfink, *Conversion of Paul*, 5.

112. e.g. Thompson, *Acts of the Risen Lord*, 61 fn. 112.

113. *ALGNT*, s.v. "διώκω;" "to harass someone (to death) because of belief," *GELNT-OECL*, s.v. "διώκω."

114. Marshall: this word is key for Paul, i.e. recurrent in his writings and "describing Christians as people who have been set apart for God's service and must show an appropriate character" (*Acts*, 171).

115. *NIV/IHEOT*.

because God had firmly prohibited "touching his anointed ones" and "harming his prophets" (μὴ ἅψησθε τῶν χριστῶν μου καὶ ἐν τοῖς προφήταις μου μὴ πονηρεύεσθε, "Touch not my anointed ones and do my prophets no harm," Ps. 104:15, LXX).[116]

As Kern recognizes, Saul like all the perpetrators of such things had no genuine relationship with God.[117] Saul's encounter with God and the following three days led him to an awareness that he was rather "an agent of the devil,"[118] someone seriously separated from God.[119] As Gaventa notices, Luke seems to stress this separation by the emphatic pronouns (i.e. ἐγώ – I, and σύ – you) in the sentence Ἐγώ εἰμι Ἰησοῦς ὃν σὺ διώκεις, "I am Jesus whom you are persecuting" (9:5; 22:8; 26:15).[120] In 1 Chronicles 24, the stoning of the prophets clearly is done by people who have "forsaken the Lord" (ἐγκατελίπετε τὸν κύριον, v. 20, LXX). In fact, Zedekiah and his men who were mistreating God's saints (vv. 15–16) are as good as heathen (they are people who have "trespassed very greatly after the abominations of Gentiles," ἐπλήθυναν τοῦ ἀθετῆσαι ἀθετήματα βδελυγμάτων ἐθνῶν, 2 Chr 36:14, LXX). Saul's situation was no different. He persecuted the saints because he was "in unbelief" (ἐν ἀπιστίᾳ) and lacked true knowledge[121] (ἀγνοῶν) of God and his will (1 Tim 1:13).[122] Ἀπιστία and ἀγνοῶν are in apposition, which emphasizes the problem that is expressed. It should be noted that this is about *erkennen* (knowing God personally with the idea of believing him).[123]

Thus, when Paul says that he persecuted God's saints (τῶν ἁγίων, Acts 26:10), he recognizes that he was not walking in God's plans. It is often understood that in Philippians 3 Paul speaks of his uprightness before God. Stendahl stresses that in this text Paul evaluates himself as a man who "went from glory to glory" and that his words "forgetting what is behind" (Phil 3:13)

---

116. In modern versions, Ps 105:15.
117. Kern, "Paul's Conversion," 78.
118. So Kern (drawing on S. Garrett), "Paul's Conversion," 76.
119. So Peace, *Conversion*, 80.
120. Gaventa: this emphasis "heightens the distance between Jesus and Saul and underscores the importance of this statement" (*From Darkness*, 58).
121. For an allusion to such a weakness, cf. John 16:3.
122. Dunn doubts if it is related to Paul's conversion ("Paul and Justification," 86).
123. E.g. Bibel/EÜ translates οὐκ ἔγνωσαν by *nicht erkannt haben* (have not recognised), thus using *erkennen*, "to understand, discern, recognize" so to "know personally," cf. *ITG*, vocab. "erkennen," and *CGD*, s.v. "erkennen."

concern "his achievements, not his shortcomings."[124] Blomberg's view is not different.[125] However, as Bultmann points out, the words of this verse are not a reason "to regard Paul as a hero of piety."[126] In fact, as outlined earlier, in the same text Paul shows clearly that he lived apart from God (Phil 3:7–8).

Paul's transition is very much in the pattern of the *passage* from one religious way of life to another. The first stage of his entry to the new religious community was being met by Jesus and being delivered by the Lord from the way of understanding God that was different from Jesus's way. To further illumine this point, we turn now to consider what God really did, and in what sense it locates Paul's entry within the first-century pattern of entry to new religious communities.

Paul says that he "received the gospel by revelation" (Gal 1:11–12), and this consisted of the fact that "God revealed his Son" to him (v. 16). What does this mean in his situation of a transition to a new way of life? Stendahl sees in this an idea of "assignment."[127] Serving the new system is certainly one element that has to be embraced in the transition to a new religious life (cf. stage four). What Stendahl asserts is a focus on this service and on the responsibility that Paul is taking during his transition. However, ἀποκαλύψαι τὸν υἱὸν αὐτοῦ ἐν ἐμοί, "to reveal his Son to me" (v. 16) draws attention primarily to the first stage, that is, to what God does to Saul. Gaventa hints at this when she recognizes that despite "the prophetic imagery in Gal 1:15–17" and the idea of a call that it conveys, in Galatians 1:11–17 Paul shows that it is more than just a "commissioning" that God communicates in the encounter.[128] What Ananias says in Acts 22:14 is noteworthy:

> God has chosen you (προεχειρίσατό σε) to know his will (γνῶναι τὸ θέλημα αὐτοῦ) and to see the Righteous One (ἰδεῖν τὸν δίκαιον) and to hear words of his mouth (ἀκοῦσαι φωνὴν ἐκ τοῦ στόματος αὐτοῦ).

---

124. Stendahl, *Paul Among Jews*, 13.

125. Speaking of the credentials in Gal 1:14 and Phil 3:4–6 (see *From Pentecost*, 41).

126. Bultmann, *Theology*, 190; for Kern, Luke does not "present Paul as pious" ("Paul's Conversion," 73).

127. Stendahl, *Paul Among Jews*, 7.

128. Gaventa, *From Darkness*, 28; for more on this prophetic imagery, see Stendahl, *Paul Among Jews*, 7–8.

To know, to see and to hear are Paul's actions (this will be examined in detail at stage two). Our focus here is on the things that are done by God which emerge in this verse. Not only is it God's "choice" (cf. God's pleasure, Gal 1:15) that allows Paul to enter the community of Jesus's followers, but this choice also consists of "making his Righteous One to be met" by Paul, and "making his will known" to Paul and doing this by "speaking" directly to him. These acts are really the key to Paul's move into a new existence.[129] They echo the divine actions that were described in chapter two. Earlier it was noted that Paul was separated from God. The One who is righteous and makes people righteous allows Paul to meet him. In addition, Paul's problem was an erroneous view of who God was and what his will is. He heard and learned the right view from God. This act of learning will be returned to when we speak of Paul's action in stage two. As Räisänen points out (referring to Gal 1:12), "the gospel was "taught" to him" by God himself.[130] Bruce concurs that Paul "had heard the claims for Jesus" made by the disciples that he was persecuting, but he was convinced when "he learned the truth by unmediated disclosure from heaven."[131]

We conclude that the divine saving act, that begins entry into a new religious system in antiquity, was a reality in Paul's experience. Thus, this idea is very characteristic in his writings, as Gaventa recognizes:

> For Paul, God's act in Christ reveals the sinful condition of all human beings and manifests God's grace for the overcoming of that condition (e.g. Rom 3:21–26). Thus, when Paul has reason to speak about the beginning of faith, he does so by reference to God's action rather than to human action: God calls (1 Cor 1:2, 9, 26; Gal 1:6), God purchases (1 Cor 6:20; 7:23), God grants grace (Rom 3:21–26), God liberates (Rom 6:17–18).[132]

Much of this statement is true, but Gaventa downplays the action of the believer involved in his or her entry into Christian life. In fact, as her idea develops, Gaventa recognizes that Paul speaks of the human role of "responding

---

129. God's act of making himself to be "seen" by Paul and "to teach" him is an important element. Luke picks it again in 9:27, clearly showing that this is the basis of Paul's change.
130. Räisänen, "Paul's Conversion," 406.
131. Bruce, *Epistle to Galatians*, 88.
132. Gaventa, *From Darkness to Light*, 44.

to God's action."¹³³ But by human response Gaventa means no more than "faith and/or confidence" in God's power manifested in Jesus.¹³⁴ Paul's action in the process of his entry into Christian life, as the pattern of transition to a new religious way of life dictates, is more than just confidence in God. This is what we attempt to demonstrate as we look at the next three stages (i.e. stages two to four).

3.4. Blind But Fasting and Praying (Stage Two)

The preceding section focused on what God did for Paul during his move into Christian life. In this section, our concern is with Paul's action. Was he just passive during the process of changing to the new community? As Gaventa considers Paul's use of ἐπιστρέφω and μετανοεω, her conclusion is that these words "most often connote the action of one who changes his or her convictions and thus turns to God (e.g. 1 Thess 1:9–10; 2 Cor 12:21). In this mindset, a person acts to rectify the relationship with God."¹³⁵ Is such action evident in Paul's own conversion?

The emphasis is on God's act and Saul is made inactive when the Damascus Road event is depicted as "the overthrow of an enemy"¹³⁶ or as "conquering an enemy."¹³⁷ The word κατελήμφθην¹³⁸ (Phil 3:12) is often understood in the sense that Saul was overpowered and no longer free to decide and to choose.¹³⁹ Corley points out that orthodox Christianity, following Augustine's legacy, has understood Paul's experience as "the vanquished will of a sinner" and "God's power over the human will."¹⁴⁰ A similar idea appears when Conzelmann

---

133. Gaventa, 44.
134. Gaventa, 44.
135. Gaventa, 44.
136. Gaventa, 97.
137. Kern, "Paul's Conversion," 71; also Conzelman speaks of "to put down the persecutor" (*Acts*, 73).
138. Its meanings include: win, seize (i.e. gain control of), understand (i.e. possess information), *GELNT-OECL*, s.v. "καταλαμβάνω."
139. Bruce speaks of "I was apprehended and constrained" (*Paul*, 74, also 75 fn. 4). This concerns also "it is no use to kick against the goads," which is understood by Bruce, for example, as "compulsion" (see *Paul*, 75). Rather it indicates the responsibility that Paul takes (see analysis of this expression at stage four).
140. Corley, "Interpreting Paul's Conversion," 5–9.

speaks of the "irresistibility of God's power."[141] Haenchen's view also is that the stress is on Christ's power.[142]

The idea of "vanquishing" was not a feature of the process of admission to a religious community in the first century. Likewise, Paul's transition shows that it was more than just being overthrown. Apart from God's act, there is evidence that Paul also acts in the process of this event. This is recognized by Gaventa when she states that Paul's prayer shows that "he moves beyond the stage of immobility"[143] (in contrast to Parsons' view of Paul's prayer and fasting as passivity).[144] Longenecker (referring to 2 Cor 11:24) thinks that "it was a new identity that Paul took on as a follower of Christ"[145] and that this was not an easy shift. In other words, it required Paul's choice and decision. As Gaventa puts it, the revelation of Christ caused "a radical disruption of his [Paul's] previous life; his previous *cosmos* had been crucified (cf. Gal 6:14)."[146]

As these examples show, some scholars recognize Paul's action in his transition, but often something requires further explanation. For example, reference has just been made to Gaventa's idea that one effect of the encounter was that Paul's "previous cosmos was crucified." The question is, who crucified it in this transition? Gaventa has Christ in mind, because she refers to Galatians 1:14, which speaks of Christ's action on the cross. However, because the Damascus Road event needs to be seen as part of a whole transition to a new religious life, the crucifixion of Paul's previous cosmos should be considered as Paul's personal action (cf. Gal 5:24).

In this section we focus on the action Paul takes during the time of his conversion. As mentioned earlier, Stendahl's view of Paul's experience as "a call to service" takes into account what Paul is to do and be after the event (stage four). Also, this idea of a "call" presupposes God's action, because God is the caller (stage one). The stages that Stendahl's idea leaves out of account are stages two and three. This comes to the fore when he rejects any idea of "giving up" in Paul's experience; speaking of Philippians 3:7–9, he states, "It

---

141. Conzelman, *Acts*, 211.
142. Haenchen, *Acts*, 322.
143. Gaventa, *From Darkness*, 61.
144. Parsons, *Acts*, 129, 132.
145. Longenecker, "Realized Hope," 27–28.
146. Gaventa, *From Darkness*, 28 [italics hers].

thus becomes clear that the usual conversion model of Paul the Jew who *gives up* his former faith to become a Christian is not the model of Paul but ours."[147]

However, there is certainly evidence that Paul gave up something of his former beliefs, as Peace recognizes.[148] Some scholars disagree with this idea of "giving up" in Philippians 3:7–8. For example, Campbell sees that Paul, as a Christ-follower, simply "re-evaluates all the previously listed privileges in the past"[149]; what Paul speaks of here is a "revision . . . rather than an *abandonment*."[150] The concern is that this idea of "giving up" suggests that Paul has abandoned his Jewish identity. Indeed, as Campbell (disagreeing with Gaventa) states, "becoming a Christ-follower" is not something that "requires the obliteration of previous 'worlds' and the relinquishment of previous identities."[151] Paul is clear that he never ceased to be a Hebrew, circumcised, of the people of Israel, of the tribe of Benjamin, a keen observer of God's law (Phil 3:4–5). To use Campbell's words, these can be "regarded as honourable, valuable, or at least profitable – the cherished things";[152] they remain cherished even at the time when Paul is in Christ.[153] But it appears that this is not the case with what goes on with the list in Phil 3:6; i.e. 1) the zeal of persecuting the Church, and 2) legalistic righteousness. These were "flesh" in action (cf. v. 2), and this idea of "flesh" in verse 2 applies to any person, including Jews (*contra* Nanos).[154] It makes sense if loss (v. 7–8) is a reference to these aspects of "flesh" in his past life.

---

147. Stendahl, *Paul Among Jews*, 9 [italics mine].
148. Peace, *Conversion*, 53 fn. 25.
149. Campbell, "I Rate All Things," 49.
150. Campbell, 50 [italics mine].
151. Campbell, 51.
152. Campbell, 51.

153. G. F. Hawthorne and R. P. Martin's view is that "Paul bundles up these many gains" and all for "an abandoning" (*Philippians*, 188–89). Our view is that things in vv. 4–5 are his national identity; things that he abandoned are those listed in v. 6.

154. On Phil 3:2, M. D. Nanos suggests that "Paul's language is probably intended to evoke a general negative stereotyping of options outside of Judaism," ("Paul's Reversal," 478–79), but "trusting in flesh" in verse 2 appears to apply to any person including the Jews, because the idea applies to Paul too (cf. v. 4). For a similar view, e.g. Campbell, "I Rate All Things," 55; Fowl, after his idea that *sarc* "has a wide range of meanings, ranging from the physical to 'human nature' to that realm opposed to God" (*Philippians*, 149). For a focus on Gentiles as the referent, see Grayston, "Opponents in Philippians 3," 170–72; and focusing more on Jews, e.g. Hawthorne and Martin, *Philippians*, 174.

Paul has "abandoned" these wrong convictions; this is stressed in Philippians 3:8. Paul affirms that in exchange for gaining Christ, he forfeited everything (τὰ πάντα ἐζημιώθην, "losing something, with implication of sustaining hardship"[155]) and considered it all "rubbish" (σκύβαλα). The word σκύβαλα itself presupposes action, i.e. an act of abandoning or throwing away (cf. "what is subject to disposal"[156]). As Bultmann puts it, Paul "surrendered his previous understanding of himself; i.e. he surrendered what had till then been the norm and meaning of his life, he sacrificed what had hitherto been his pride and joy."[157] This does not mean that he gave up everything connected with his Jewish identity and all his past life. As Dunn puts it, Paul was converted from "Judaism,"[158] but in the sense of "Judaea's determination not to be absorbed into a universal 'Hellenism' but to maintain its set-apartness, its holiness to Yhwh."[159] How did this exchange take place? Does the Damascus Road event reveal it?

Luke's account shows that rather than being passive, there are things that Paul had to do, ὅ τί σε δεῖ ποιεῖν, "what you are to do" (Acts 9:6; cf. also 22:10). Attention is now given to these words. They are not covered fully when Stendahl, for example, stresses simply the idea of commission or a call.[160] To understand the things that Paul "does" in his transition, stages two, three and four are examined.

The second stage as previously defined is the liminal step of initiation. It is a state of being between the old and the new. The person experiences a sort of death (i.e. death to his or her old way of life) and of non-identity (i.e. before taking the new identity with the new system). Thus, it is a kind of a vacuum. The vacuum is associated with things purposefully designed to stir up serious decision towards the system that the person is joining.

In Paul's case, this liminal state is seen particularly in the days he spends in blindness (9:8–9). The situation is as serious as the liminal phase of initiation

---

155. *GELNT-OECL*, s.v. "ζημία, ζημιόω."

156. *GELNT-OECL*, s.v. "σκύβαλον."; for more on this, see Fowl, *Philippians*, 153, esp. fn. 35.

157. Bultmann, *Theology* 188; as Dunn puts it, what Paul is saying in Phil 3:8 is "*on account of him* I have suffered the loss of everything" (*New Perspective on Paul*, 485 [italics his]).

158. Dunn, "In Search of Historical Paul," 25.

159. Dunn, 26.

160. Stendahl focuses on "action" but that of receiving the commission (*Paul Among Jews*, 9–10).

requires. As Lohfink notices, it is as if Saul is even going "deeper into the dark" as he is led into Damascus.[161] Not only is he blind; he also does not eat and drink. The picture is symbolic of non-existence and death. Thus for example Parsons makes an analogy between Paul's experience and "the three days Jesus spent in a dark tomb (cf. Luke 24:46)."[162] As Gaventa points out, this analogy is pressed too far when it is understood that "Saul is undergoing death and resurrection" like Christ.[163] Johnson also concludes that "there is not enough evidence for such allusion."[164] What is clear, and fits the reality of change to a new existence in antiquity, is the idea that Paul's situation "connotes his symbolic death."[165]

Paul's state is that of total vulnerability characteristic of liminality. Paul is helpless and only able to move by relying on his companions (9:8; 22:11). From great authority and power[166] he turns to dependency on others, and the restorer is the powerless Ananias who had just been one of Paul's potential victims (9:12). As Gaventa notes, the "scene" is really reversed.[167] Paul has become vulnerable.

However, this picture of total vulnerability does not mean that Paul is just passive. He is in this sort of dead state between the old and the new in order to judge between the two systems and, as a result, to embrace the new system decisively. Paul is making this action. As Peace states,

> In order for the turning to take place, there must be some sense of what one is turning from and an understanding of what one is turning to. Furthermore, there must be an awareness that what is turned away from is somehow wrong or inadequate and what is being turned to is right and better.[168]

---

161. Lohfink, *Conversion of Paul*, 4.
162. Parsons, *Acts*, 129.
163. Gaventa, *From Darkness*, 60.
164. Johnson, *Acts*, 164; for Gaventa, three days simply "refers to a short period of time" (*From Darkness*, 60).
165. Parsons, *Acts*, 128 (he notes a link between blindness and death in Jewish thinking, see 128–129).
166. Acts 9:1–2, 14; 22:4–5; 26:10.
167. Gaventa, *From Darkness*, 61.
168. Peace, *Conversion*, 37 (cf. p. 38, 49–50 for more on this).

This deep apprehension of how the new is better than the old lies at the heart of the Damascus three-day episode. This is clear when δεῖ ποιεῖν ("what is necessary to do") is considered (cf. 9:6). We suggest that this refers to what Paul is to do during this event that constitutes his transition to a new way of life. Marshall understands it as referring to Paul's task in the future; Paul is told "to get up and go to the city where he would be given fresh instructions about his future task."[169] Gaventa similarly suggests that "it is necessary (*dei*) . . . indicates that Saul will not only become a believer, but that he will have some particular role."[170] However, the idea primarily concerns what Paul does during this period of moving from one religious way to another.

Prayer is one of the things Paul does in this time. Besides the fact that Paul was blind, Luke says also that "he did not eat or drink" (Acts 9:9). This means fasting (as e.g. Jervell recognizes[171]) and prayer, as 9:11 also confirms it. The thing to consider is how important in the process of change to the new existence this act of prayer is. There are different views. Bruce understands Paul's prayer as just an effect of "shock" and that "there is no need to understand his abstinence as penance."[172] Marshall also maintains the idea of shock but thinks that penitence is a possibility.[173] The idea of penance is also Haenchen's view,[174] and Jervell states, "Denn es handelt sich um eine Bekehrung, wie das Fasten des Paulus als Akt der Busse zeigt (Then it is a question of conversion, as Paul's fasting as an act of repentance shows)."[175]

In the light of the first-century transition to a new religious existence, the three days (9:6–18) are more than just praying. As Johnson recognizes, "Paul is going through a holy period of transition, a stage of liminality."[176] Such a period is about action. Learning is a key element in one's transition to a new existence. As Johnson notes (drawing from OT and intertestamental sources), "Paul places himself in a position to receive further guidance from the Lord."[177]

---

169. Marshall, *Acts*, 170.
170. Gaventa, *From Darkness*, 59.
171. Jervell, *Apostelgeschichte*, 281, 282.
172. Bruce, *Acts*, 236; *contra* Conzelmann, *Acts*, 72.
173. Marshall, *Acts*, 170.
174. Haenchen, *Acts*, 323.
175. Jervell, *Apostelgeschichte*, 281.
176. Johnson, *Acts*, 164.
177. Johnson, 164.

As mentioned earlier, the event features God's action of teaching Paul. The counterpart of this is Paul's learning. In his writings, Paul speaks of the fact of "knowing" as part of his experience. He says this not only in 2 Corinthians 4:6, to which reference was made earlier, but also in Philippians 3:8 where he speaks of his experience of τὸ ὑπερέχον τῆς γνώσεως Χριστοῦ Ἰησοῦ, "the excellence of knowing Christ Jesus." Since both texts are connected with his conversion, it follows that in the three days Paul learned from God (cf. Gal 1:11–12, 16–17). As Longenecker points out (quoting J. S. Stewart), the three days were a "formative" time.[178]

Another action during the three days is the break with the old way of life. It is at this time that Paul dies personally to his old existence in which he lived separated from God. The apprehension of God and his will resulted in the action of abandoning what was, up till this time, Paul's way of life. This has a connection with the fact of learning from God during the three days. Earlier it was noted that Paul equates knowledge with light. Because of the illumination of God's revelation, Paul rejected all that had been "profit," κέρδη (Phil 3:7). The word he uses to describe his action is ἥγημαι (or ἡγέομαι). It means to "consider, count, esteem" with the purpose of "leading the way, ruling, governing."[179] "To consider" here implies seriously making up one's mind.[180] Thus the connotation is of deciding seriously. It is reasonable to understand that such a decision takes place in the three days. To link this act of "considering" just with "the appearance" of Christ outside Damascus (e.g. Longenecker)[181] is not enough. Stendahl's idea seems to allude to the moment outside Damascus when he recognizes that the "encounter with Christ . . . convinces and . . . creates faith."[182] Ἡγέομαι, "to consider" is used in a way that implies abandonment of a way of life, and this strong act is a result, we contend, of the three days with God that produced a deep comprehension of the value of the new way. As Peace states, "Conversion begins with insight into one's own condition" and as a result "a decision" is "made."[183] The three

---

178. Longenecker, "Realized Hope," 29; so also Bultmann, *Theology*, 187.

179. *ALGNT*, s.v. "ἡγέομαι"; "go before, command in war," *GEL*, s.v. "ἡγέομαι."

180. "to believe, hold," cf. *GEL*, s.v. "ἡγέομαι" "to think, to believe," cf. F. Büchsel, "ἡγέομαι," in *TDNT* vol. 2, s.v. "ἡγέομαι."

181. Longenecker, "Realized Hope," 25.

182. Stendahl, *Paul Among Jews*, 12.

183. Peace, *Conversion*, 54.

years in Arabia, referred to earlier, may be seen as an extension of this liminal time for Saul, but the three days in Damascus reveal the liminal, second stage of transition, which is about deciding for the new way of life.

The evidence that Paul has seriously made his choice is that this episode of prayer concludes with the fact that Paul "got up" and took the water ritual of baptism (9:18). This leads us to the third stage that examines the sense of the water ritual as part of the entry process of Paul.

3.5. Sealing Attachment to the New Way: Baptism (Stage Three)

As was shown in the second chapter, the third stage of entry consists of the ritual that seals attachment to the new way of existence. In Paul's conversion, baptism plays that role. This element of baptism is found only in the Acts accounts, and this is evidence of how important Acts is for understanding Paul's *passage* to Christianity. For example, when Longenecker examines Paul's conversion, he discerns seven elements that he describes as "the essential features of his [Paul's] conversion experience," but baptism is lacking because he chooses to work only from the letters.[184] Thus he covers stages one, two and four, but the third is overlooked. Our purpose in this part is to attempt to show how essential an aspect of Paul's *passage* to new existence baptism is. The point is also made that Paul's baptism means taking action.

In the light of the process of initiation or entry, undergoing baptism is an act by which Paul makes definite the choice and decision made in stage two. In other words, he embraces publicly the responsibility of attaching to the new system. Johnson expresses this thought when he states that "the baptism completes Paul's passage."[185] This study argues that the personal action of the candidate is involved in such a ritual that seals his or her entry. However, Paul's personal involvement is not the focus when the point that Johnson stresses is that baptism is the act by which Paul is "incorporated into the life of the community."[186] The idea that Paul takes action in his baptism is our focus here.

---

184. Longenecker, "Realized Hope," 25.
185. Johnson, *Acts*, 165.
186. Johnson, 165.

Dunn states that "we have no record whatsoever of Paul taking the decisive step *prior* to his baptism."[187] Luke simply says that "he got up and was baptized" (Acts 9:18). Our focus is on the action symbolised in "getting up". It shows a decision that comes as a result of the three days spent in learning and knowing God's right way. The deliberate choice and decision that was taken in the three days was affirmed through the act of taking baptism. As Turner states, "his conversional *commitment* was . . . to be formalised in baptism."[188] Paul formalises his decision. As outlined in chapter two, by taking this ritual he accepts fully the responsibility to live out the new way. Paul's personal choice and action is clear in what is happening here. In fact, Luke's sequence of events is intended to show this because Paul's baptism (v. 18) is followed by the fact that "at once (εὐθέως) he began to preach that Jesus is the Son of God" (v. 20).

There are elements in Acts 22:16 which confirm these points. Ananias says to Paul, τί μέλλεις; ἀναστὰς βάπτισαι (Why do you wait? Rise and be baptized, RSV). One possible sense here for τί μέλλεις; is "so, what do you intend to do now?"[189] Ananias "encourages" Paul.[190] The point of the exhortation is to take the last step and seal the attachment that he has already made. Luke's arrangement of events shows this. One of Christ's saints,[191] a person who should be hiding from the violent Saul if the situation had remained the same, comes to Saul calling him "brother" and is used by God for Saul's restoration (22:13). This is a powerful act that obviously must make Paul see the kind of difference the way of Jesus makes. But Paul had seen even more than this. Ananias reminds him of the grace that God has given him (Ὁ θεὸς προεχειρίσατό σε, "God has appointed you") to "see" the Righteous One and from him to learn and "know his will" (v. 14). Moreover, Ananias specifies that the witnessing work concerns "what you [Saul] have seen and heard" (v. 15b).

These elements show that Saul takes baptism after he has heard, seen and learned; and so he has fully chosen to attach himself to Jesus and the community that serves him (v. 16). Taking baptism stands as an act that winds up

---

187. Dunn, *Baptism in the Spirit*, 74 [italics his].

188. Turner, *Power from on High*, 375 [italics his].

189. One meaning of μέλλω is "to be going to do," cf. *GEL*, s.v. "μέλλω."

190. E.g. Dunn's view for τί μέλλεις; (*Baptism in the Spirit*, 74).

191. "Saints" is used by Paul (Acts 26:10) and Luke (9:13), contrasting the persecutor from Jesus's followers.

the process and endorses the commitment that has been taking place from the beginning of the event.

The act of "getting up" (ἀναστὰς, aor. act. ptcp. nom. sg. masc. – of ἀνίστημι) is Paul's personal act. This is Carrez's view when he translates it as *t'étant élevé* (having stood up).[192] It is his action, and the form of the verb is the same in 9:18 and 22:16. "Be baptized" also stresses Paul's personal act, although the action involves a third party. The third party is especially indicated in 9:18 by the passive ἐβαπτίσθη (aor. pass. ind. 3sg – of βαπτίζω). But in 22:16 the middle use, βάπτισαι (aor. mid. impr. 2sg – of βαπτίζω), should be noted. This has a reflexive sense, "make yourself to be baptized." Thus Carrez, for example, preserves the connotation when he translates it as "fais-toi baptiser" (literally: "make yourself to be baptized").[193] The translation "be baptized" is somewhat misleading.[194] Paul's baptism is an action that he takes personally. As Peace notices, by this act Paul "aligns himself with the church."[195]

What takes place during the process of entry has a connection with what becomes Paul's life. In other words, Paul aligns with the way his new community lives and serves the Lord. The next section focuses on how during the Damascus Road event Paul also takes action concerning what is going to be his Christian life.

3.6. The After-Entry Life Anticipated in the Entry Process (Stage Four)

As was outlined in the first chapter and explained with evidence in the second, the fourth stage of initiation consists of the life that the candidate is to live as a member of the new community. The idea is that it is another stage of initiation because this life is not something that follows initiation. Rather it begins in initiation and the proof is that during the process of initiation the candidate embraces it and takes the responsibility to live this new way. This section focuses on how this applies to Paul's transition.

---

192. Carrez in *NTIGF*, interlinear part; so also "Get up" (NIV); "lève-toi," (BFC).

193. Carrez, *NTIGF*, interlinear part; also "Reçois le baptême," literally: "receive baptism" (TOB).

194. E.g. NIV; so also "sois baptisé," BFC and SB/LS.

195. Peace, *Conversion*, 26.

What Paul is to be in the new system is mainly presented in terms of his mission (9:15; 22:15). Lohfink notices that Luke "emphasizes Paul's strict Jewish orthodoxy (Acts 22:3; 26:4f) and his zeal as persecutor of Christians (Acts 9:1f, 13f, 21; 22:4f, 19f; 26:9–11)."[196] From this, Lohfink's conclusion is that "Luke makes abundantly clear that Paul would never have undertaken his mission to the Gentiles on his own. It was the irresistible power of Christ alone that led him to it."[197] Peace has a similar view: "the Gentile mission must . . . derive from something apart from Paul and his background. It must derive from something outside the natural sphere."[198] This view shows that the mission is something that Paul just receives. However, this makes Paul passive. It was not "the irresistible power of Christ *alone*" that made Paul set out in mission as Lohfink suggests. This makes the mission something imposed by God. Such an idea overlooks Paul's deliberate decision about it in his conversion time.

Jesus states, "this is my instrument to carry my name," σκεῦος ἐκλογῆς ἐστίν μοι οὗτος τοῦ βαστάσαι τὸ ὄνομά μου (9:15). This clearly describes what Paul is going to be in his new existence. Ἐκλογῆς (elected) is parallel to Paul's statement that God "set him apart before he was born" (Gal 1:15). This does not mean that God just "hand-picked" Paul for the new service, as Stendahl suggests.[199] Acts describes a process in which Paul was thoroughly involved. The evidence suggests that what is going to be his new career is part of what goes on in his prayer time. Jesus's statement, "he is to carry my name" (Acts 9:15), is part of a unit which includes the episode of prayer and fasting (9:9–18). As explained earlier, this is Paul's time with God. As this leads him into knowing Jesus and his saving mission to both Jews and Gentiles, it is during this episode that Paul personally decides to embrace the call to preach the gospel.

This study has outlined how the Damascus Road event features both God's action (stage one) and Paul's action (stages two and three). The commission (stage four) is part of this paradigm of reciprocal action and agreement between God and Paul. Segal finds that "Only in Luke's third version

---

196. Lohfink, *Conversion of Paul*, 88.
197. Lohfink, 88.
198. Peace, *Conversion*, 19.
199. Stendahl, *Paul Among Jews*, 8.

(26:16–17) . . . is Paul's commissioning made part of the revelation itself."[200] From this, his idea is that the commission was not part of the event. Rather, it "was suggested by Paul's teachers of Christianity, symbolized by Ananias."[201] It is better to understand that the commission was one of the things learned about and fully embraced, when God teaches and Paul learns. In fact, to carry God's gospel was the Messiah's task, but in the event, Christ hands the baton and his task on to Paul. As Dupont notices (from his analysis of 26:16–23), it is clear in verse 23 that "le Christ devait 'annoncer (*katangellein*) la lumière'" (Christ was to "announce (*katangellein*) the light") and this "il fait pratiquement par le ministère de son témoin" (he does practically by the ministry of his witness).[202]

Paul is not just passive when Christ's task becomes his task. Dupont speaks of it as a "mission confiée au témoin" (a mission entrusted to a witness).[203] This is a commission from the Lord to his officer. What does it mean? Is this servant just passively receiving the task? When we considered speech-act theory in the first chapter, we gave the example of a similar commission from the Queen to a royal officer. It was shown that to accept such a mandate means to assume a serious responsibility and that one's will is fully engaged. In this transition to a different position, the officer is far from passive. However, in Paul's case, this active role is overlooked by Dupont when, in another place, he states,

> La place qui est faite aux témoins à l'intérieur même de l'événement du salut ne peut évidemment s'expliquer que par une *initiative divine*. Ils y avaient été destinés d'avance par Dieu . . ., le Seigneur Jésus les a choisis à cet effet . . . C'est le Ressuscité qui les a établis comme ses témoins . . ., lui qui leur a donné une part dans le ministère apostolique.[204]

---

200. Segal, *Paul the Convert*, 8.
201. Segal, 8.
202. Dupont, *Nouvelles études sur Actes*, 450.
203. Dupont, 451.
204. Dupont, 123–24 [italics his]. Translation: "The place given to witnesses within the very event of salvation can obviously only be explained by *divine initiative*. They had been destined there in advance by God . . ., the Lord Jesus chose them for this purpose . . . It was the Risen One who established them as his witnesses . . ., he who gave them a share in the apostolic ministry."

This shows how Dupont imagines what takes place during the time of change (cf. his citations related to the Damascus Road event, Acts 9:15; 22:14, 15; and 26:16). He focuses only on God's "initiative."

In Paul's transition, the mission is not just given to him. What makes the process special is the fact that in it, he personally adopts the mission for the rest of his life. This is the connotation of the words "it is hard for you to rebel[205] against the goads" (σκληρόν σοι πρὸς κέντρα λακτίζειν, 26:14). Earlier, it was shown that, for example, Bruce's view is that this refers to God's "compulsion."[206] Johnson's view is similar when he suggests that "the idea here is that God has been pushing Paul to become a Messianist and he has resisted."[207] This interpretation makes sense if the event means that God is stopping Paul and turning him by power. As mentioned earlier, exercising power is not the idea in entry. It is better to interpret this proverbial expression as linked to the aim (the ministry of the gospel) for which God wants Paul to change. What Jesus meant was that, in the event, Paul was going to know about the gospel, to value and love it, and the effect would be so strong that it would be impossible (cf. σκληρόν[208]) to rebel (cf. λακτίζειν[209]) against God's will again. Everts suggests this reading:

> It more probably refers to his future task and the cost of obeying the call he is about to receive. This phrase indicates that the call of Christ will constrain Paul and conform his whole life to the goal of making Christ known among the Gentiles.[210]

In other words, it is during the time of his conversion to Christianity that Paul is made aware of the responsibility that his new life entails. The aim is to adopt this mission and to attach to it seriously, before he embarks on his Christian life. One important purpose of initiation is to comprehend deeply the conduct that the new system requires, and then to attach to it.

---

205. Carrez' translation of λακτίζειν (*NTIGF*, Acts 26:14 interlinear part).
206. Bruce, *Paul*, 75.
207. Johnson, *Acts*, 435.
208. So σκληρός in the sense of "being difficult to the point of being impossible," *GELNT-OECL*, s.v. "σκληρός"; "costive, strong," *GEL*, s.v. "σκληρός."
209. Figuratively "unreasoning resistance," *GELNT-OECL*, s.v. "λακτίζω."
210. Everts, "Conversion and Call," 159 col. 2.

God himself spurs Paul on and "directs" (cf. κέντρα)²¹¹ him into embracing the right service. Undoubtedly, Paul grasps the worth of the mission and attaches himself to it.

Also in 26:16, Luke shows clearly that what Paul is going to be and do is anticipated in his Damascus Road experience. Paul is told that he is going to "serve" Christ (cf. ὑπηρέτην, "servant") and be his "witness" (cf. μάρτυρα). But it is clearly specified that this service and witness concern ὧν τε εἶδές με, "of things in which you have seen me". That is, in the three-day process Paul has "seen" what the service means. In 26:15–18, the risen Christ gives Paul an overview of what awaits him, once he embraces the call to "serve and testify" (v. 16). The same verb "to see" is also found in 9:12 in the section on prayer and fasting (9:9–18). This shows that what Paul saw – that which determined his ensuing career – is about God's teaching and Paul's personal decision that takes place during the three days with God.

3.7. Summary

This chapter has explored the episode of Paul's own move to Christianity, in the context of first-century religious transition. The four stages of action that characterize such a change in that time are evident in Paul's transition.

Paul's event shows divine action (stage one) and it is the very basis of every thing else that follows in the Damascus event. God encountered Saul. He delivered him from a wrong perception of God (which was not general to Judaism but his²¹² particular and wrong crusade) and instructed him, enabling him to grasp the greater value of the life that Christ brought about. All this is consistent with the pattern of first-century transition to a new religious group, as the second chapter shows.

In the Damascus Road event, Paul is more than just an immobilized or vanquished man. He takes action, as we have shown, in stages two, three and four. When for example Bruce uses "capitulation" to describe Paul's change,²¹³

---

211. The connotation of κέντρον as a goad for "directing, guiding," cf. Johnson, *Acts*, 435 (referring to Prov 26:3; *Ps of Sol* 16:4; Philo, *On the Decalogue* 87); also κέντρον as "spur, incentive," cf. *GEL*, s.v. "κέντρον."

212. Though such a zeal is not something of Paul only, but a philosophy of all the Zealots, see e.g. Hengel, *Zealots*, 301; Dunn, "In Search," 22.

213. Bruce, *Paul*, 75.

such language does not accord with how a first-century person would experience transition to a new religious community. Paul has an active role in this change, which in fact is his change. Elements from Acts and the letters show that Paul opened himself (cf. fasting and prayer) and learned from God. He gave up the zealous desire to promote his national values. As Marshall notes, Paul knew that this zeal "was for the cause of God" but "had turned into an attack on the God who raised Jesus."[214] Paul turned from a wrong zeal; and this change demanded serious choice and decision. It meant to die to a whole way of serving God, when he chose decisively to abandon his established pharisaic way of life and attached himself to Jesus's way. Paul did this in his Damascus Road event and the three following days. He took baptism as the final act and thus as a sign that by this ritual he fully intended to live out the choice and decision that were strongly made during this transition.

In the light of this, the next chapter examines whether there is evidence in Romans 5:12–6:23 that the four stages of entry are on Paul's mind when in this pericope he speaks of the *passage* from sin to God, and whether shared divine and human agency are a feature in his thinking.

---

214. Marshall, *Acts*, 170.

CHAPTER FOUR

The Four Stages and Action in Romans 5:12–6:23

4.1. Introduction

This fourth chapter will draw upon Romans 5:12–6:23 with a focus on the action involved in the believer's transition from sin to God. The second chapter focused on the social patterns involved in transition to new religious life in the first century. It was noted that in this socio-religious context of antiquity, initiation included the agency of both the deity and the initiand. The third chapter then explored whether the four stages, and what they show about the balance between the divine and human agency, are also present in Paul's own transition to Christianity. In the light of what we have seen, this fourth chapter examines whether the four stages of initiation, and the same balance between divine and human agency, are present in Paul's mind when in Romans 5:12–6:23 he speaks of the transition from sin to God.

Apart from Romans 6, many texts in the Pauline corpus are recognized to be about baptism. These include 1 Corinthians 6:11; 10:1–2; 12:3; 2 Corinthians 1:22; Galatians 3:27–28 (also in the pseudo-Paulines, cf. Ephesians 1:3; 4:30; 5:14, 26; Colossians 2:11–12; and Titus 3:5).[1] Paul's thinking on baptism in Romans 5–6 is the focus of this study for two reasons. First, as Fitzmyer notes on Romans 6, "verses 1–11 constitute the main discussion

---

1. E.g. Fitzmyer, *Romans*, 430.

of baptism by Paul in his letters."[2] Also, as outlined in our introductory chapter, this study considers that Romans 5:12–6:23 covers the whole idea of the Christian's transition from sin to God (of which baptism is a part). As the process of transition or initiation to new religious life is the working focus of this study, this pericope is a prime source for understanding what kind of balance Paul saw in initiation and baptism, between the agency of God and that of the initiand.

The literature survey illustrates how unclear the discussion of this point has been. For instance, Dunn states that "Christian conversion is nothing other than a being seized and overwhelmed by the love of God in the person of the Holy Spirit."[3] With a focus on Romans 5:12–6:23, this chapter intends to demonstrate that Paul shows that the move from sin to Christian life is more than just being seized and overwhelmed by God. As we will see, Paul speaks of a process that includes the person's agency. This human agency is also missing when Tannehill interprets Romans 6 and states, "If man *accepts* the cross as *God's act* of grace, he must give up his boast, for such acceptance means the recognition that his life is based upon God's gift, not on his own achievements."[4] It is clear that the *passage* from sin to Christian life is seen here as a time where human achievement has no role. A gap is placed between "God's gift" and human "achievement." As we will see, Paul's thinking about this transition emphasises God's action, but also serious action by the initiand.

Consistent with his approach, Tannehill further states: "It is not the grace which makes up for man's deficiencies and *helps* him along his way. Rather, it is the grace which *meets* man on his way and *turns him around*, for the whole direction of his life was wrong."[5] As we will see, Paul believes more than this. Making use of Tannehill's words (cf. italics), the purpose of this chapter is formulated as follows. The analysis of Romans 5:12–6:23 is intended to demonstrate that God's grace *meets* the person not just to *turn him around* without his or her agency. As we will see, Paul's idea is that, once touched by grace, and directly during their transition, believers take serious action

---

2. Fitzmyer, 430.
3. Dunn, *Baptism in Holy Spirit*, 139.
4. Tannehill, *Dying and Rising*, 125 [italics mine].
5. Tannehill, 125 [italics mine].

The Four Stages and Action in Romans 5:12–6:23

that amounts to taking serious responsibility for their new existence.[6] More than being *turned* around, they also personally *turn* around. To *help* them do this is exactly the aim of God's grace in *meeting* them. In other words, the Christian transition and baptism includes both divine and human agency. This interpretation accounts for believers' actions found in the pericope, such as to receive (5:17), to reign (5:17, 21), to die to sin (6:2, 11), and the act of undergoing the water ritual (cf. 6:3), as well as then "considering themselves" to be dead to sin and alive to God, their "members" reconstituted as "instruments of righteousness" (6:11, 13). To show this, in this chapter Romans 5:12–6:23 is considered in the light of the method used in chapters two and three; the focus is now on whether the four stages of entry to new existence, and the actions that they imply, are in this pericope that focuses upon the Christian's transition and baptism.

This chapter is divided into four sections. (1) In the first section, God's agency (stage one) is considered, with the focus on Romans 5:15. As was outlined in chapter one, death to sin (6:2) and undergoing the ritual (cf. 6:3) have been interpreted as focusing on God's action, but as this chapter will show, these focus on the baptizand's agency. Thus, a consideration of what God does in this transition is crucial; this enables us to distinguish where the stress is on God's agency, and where Paul implies the believer's role.

(2) The second section considers death to sin, and the focus is on 6:1–2. The purpose is to understand whether the initiand's death to his or her old way of life (stage two), as seen in chapters two and three, applies to what Paul says in 6:1–2. As we will see, there is evidence that by "death to sin" in 6:2, Paul is focusing not really on Christ's death itself, but on the break with a way of life that the believer makes in his or her transition to new life.

(3) The third section considers 6:3–4. With a focus on the expression ἐβαπτίσθημεν, this part seeks to understand what kind of agency is exercised by the initiand in this ritual that seals initiation (stage three).

(4) The last section considers the idea that to live the new life begins in the transition (stage four) and is also evidence of the initiand's agency. The focus here is on whether this is present in Romans 5:12–6:23. As we will see, this affects the reading of such expressions as βασιλεύσουσιν, "they will

---

6. Nygren: when "the gospel has exercised its power," an act of faith comes as "evidence" (*Romans*, 71).

reign" (5:17, cf. 21), δικαιοσύνη, "righteousness" (5:21), ἐν καινότητι ζωῆς περιπατήσωμεν, "we might walk in newness of life" (6:4) and the slave motif (6:6, 10–11, 13–23).

4.2. Divine Action at the First Stage: ἡ χάρις τοῦ θεοῦ καὶ ἡ δωρεὰ ἐν χάριτι... Ἰησοῦ Χριστοῦ εἰς τοὺς πολλοὺς ἐπερίσσευσεν (5:15)

This section focuses on whether the transition to new life about which Paul speaks in Romans 5:12–6:23 shows evidence of the first stage of initiation, i.e. the divine action which stands at the basis of the process of entry to new life. This is intended to enable us to see in the next sections the relationship between this divine deed, and what Paul then displays as acts of the initiand (cf. stages two, three and four of initiation).

L. Bouyer recognizes that the Christian initiation is first "la voie *de Dieu* vers l'homme" (God's way to man).[7] Whatever action Paul thinks of as taking place in the believer's transition, he sees it as linked with what God does first. This is evident when he states that to undergo baptism is an act "into Christ's death" (εἰς Χριστὸν Ἰησοῦν εἰς τὸν θάνατον αὐτοῦ, 6:3). As we will see, the pericope shows many actions of the believer. But the starting point in God's act of justification is heavily stressed when Paul begins to speak of the transition from sin and baptism. This section seeks to emphasise that, in Romans 5, Paul focuses on the experience of the grace of God reaching in and rescuing people. Then in Romans 6, when he comes to focus on the believer's response to God's grace, he naturally reminds the Romans of their experience of stages two, three and four.

The structure of Romans 5:12–6:23 makes it clear that Christ's saving work is the first stage of the person's change from sin's dominion to Christian life. As Ponsot notes, what the person does is "second."[8] Paul begins by stressing God's gift of salvation and makes it the basis for anything else that is done in the Christian transition and baptism. This emphasis arises from the preceding argument: Christ's work of justification has been the core of the first five

---

7. Bouyer, *Initiation chrétienne*, 51 [italics his].

8. Ponsot, *Romains*, 110; R. Gounelle: "Le baptême n'est pas premier (Baptism is not the first [act]) ; see Gounelle, "Le baptême," 182.

chapters.⁹ As Bultmann points out, 1:18–3:20 concerns the idea that all have sinned; 3:21–31 explains that "through the saving event in Christ, righteousness has been obtained"; and 4:1–15 is "the scriptural proof for this thesis."¹⁰ In 5:1–11 God's action is still the theme because stress is laid on reconciliation with God and its outcome.¹¹ Then in 5:12–21 (the first part of our pericope), justification continues to be the central idea.¹² The proof is that 5:12 reiterates (cf. 3:23) the idea that all sinned (πάντες ἥμαρτον), but¹³ God's salvation has broken in: ἡ χάρις τοῦ θεοῦ καὶ ἡ δωρεὰ ἐν χάριτι . . . Ἰησοῦ Χριστοῦ εἰς τοὺς πολλοὺς ἐπερίσσευσεν, "the grace of God and the gift in the grace . . . of Jesus Christ abounded for many" (5:15, cf. 18).

It should be noted here that this divine saving act underlies 6:3–4 (Christ's death), though the focus has moved there to the human agency in transition – the candidate's liminal death in stage two (v. 2) and the third stage act of undergoing the ritual that seals the move (v. 3–4). In chapter 6, the focus is on the stages of human agency; Christ's deed is repeated when giving the reason for these human acts. This will be clear in the next sections when these stages of human action are considered.

So, in Romans 5 (and before this), Paul stresses Christ's saving act and shows that it is the foundational stage in any person's change from the life of sin to the Christian life. As Moo observes, Paul emphasises that this transition is mainly due to "God's initiative" and "favour."¹⁴ But in Paul's thinking the agency of God does not displace that of the initiand as well.

Divine action is taken so that human action will be taken. In Romans 5:15–19 Paul appears to show this connection even when the divine action is still his focus. To maintain these connections appears to be a feature of Paul's style. Just as in Romans 6 his stress is on human agency, but he speaks again of Christ's act underlying it, so also in Romans 5 the focus is on God's

---

9. So Caragounis, "Romans 5:15–16," 143, and 146 fn. 4; Ponsot, *Romains*, 96.

10. Bultmann, "Adam and Christ," 143; Nygren, *Romans*, 30–31.

11. Cranfield, "On Some Problems," 325.

12. Cambier: "le centre d'intérêt de la péricope [5:12–21] est l'action rédemptrice du Christ" (The centre of interest of the pericope [i.e. 5:12–21] is the redemptive action of Christ), see "Péchés des hommes," 222, also 217–18; Godet: "l'apôtre est encore dans le sujet de la justification' (the apostle is still in the subject of justification), *Romains* I, 470, 474.

13. The force of ἀλλά, "but" in 5:15.

14. Moo, *Romans 1–8*, 350.

agency, but at the same time human agency is implied, assumed to be part of God's purpose in salvation.

Many have seen in Romans 5:15–19 the presence of both divine and human agency,[15] and views are guided by the debate about "synergism."[16] As was indicated earlier in our introductory chapter, the issue of "synergism" is not itself our focus.[17] Attention is on whether Paul's thinking shows that in this transition from sin to Christian life divine action is such that it is to be followed by human action.

For this, the expression ἐπερίσσευσεν εἰς, "abounded for" (5:15) is an element to consider. We argue that this expression shows that the purpose of God's action is that human response should follow, because we suggest that it is not just a rhetorical flourish emphasising greatness ("abound"[18]), but that it also entails the notion of its impact ("flowing over").[19] It is used in 5:15 with the idea of "spreading"[20] to reach many (cf. εἰς τοὺς πολλοὺς, "envers les plusieurs").[21] "Flowing over" suggests that grace prompts action first at the level of God himself, and it overflows to also prompt action on the level of people. Grace prompts God to save. As Dunn hints, in 5:15 grace is not just God's "gracious disposition" but his "gracious action."[22] Already Paul shows this in 5:6–8.[23] In other words, it is God's grace (i.e. his love)[24] that "prompts"[25]

---

15. Ponsot: "une fois que Dieu a accordé la réconciliation au monde, il reste à l'homme le devoir de se changer lui-même librement" (Once God has granted reconciliation to the world, it remains for man the duty to change himself freely), *Romains*, 97; Bultmann: "Christ brought for all the possibility (of life)" and " men face the decision" to take it ("Adam and Christ," 158); F.-J. Leenhardt: "on ne peut se taire sur ce qui concerne l'homme dans cette affaire" (we cannot be silent on what is the responsibility of man in this matter), *Romains*, 81; see also Cambier, "Péchés des hommes et péché d'Adam," 225; Godet, *Romains* I, 508.

16. E.g. Nygren, *Romans*, 70.

17. See chapter one of this study, fn. 3.

18. *ALGNT*, s.v. "ερισσεύω."

19. *GECNT*, s.v. "περισσός," "beyond"; for more, cf. the semantic group of this word in this source.

20. Cf. Carrez' use of "répandre" and not just "déborder," cf. *NTIGF*, Rom 5:15 interlinear part.

21. Godet, *Romains*, 508.

22. Dunn, *Romans 1–8*, 280; also Schreiner, *Romans*, 284; Moo, *Romans 1–8*, 350.

23. E.g. Nygren, *Romans*, 202.

24. Nygren, 202.

25. Barrett, *Romans*, 114; K. Haacker speaks of it as "the principle of salvation" (*Theology of Paul's Letter*, 29).

or "causes"[26] him to save sinners. As Sanday and Headlam think, grace (5:15) is Christ's "active favour towards humankind which moved Him to intervene for their salvation."[27]

When it overflows to believers, the aim is also to move people and "enable"[28] them to act (cf. Eph 2:8). Moo hints at this when he recognizes that grace overflows "with power to create life."[29] Also Schreiner thinks that "It overflows to such an extent that it conquers and subdues what Adam introduced into the world."[30] This study considers that the "overflowing" grace achieves this by enabling people to take action,[31] and Paul sees this happening also in connection with the Christian transition. This approach will impact our reading of key terms in Romans 5:16–21. For instance, in Romans 5:17, when people are acted upon by the grace of God, what follows is that they "reign". The human agency that is implied in this will be returned to later when we examine Paul's use of βασιλεύω. Also, as the analysis of δικαιοσύνη is expected to show, the idea in 5:19 is that when people receive Christ's righteousness, they act and live righteously. This is recognized for example by Nygren when he states that grace not only "restores all [that sin had] destroyed," but also it goes "beyond that to establish the righteousness of God among us."[32] Leenhardt also notes this idea and states, "l'obeissance du Christ . . . deviendra l'obeissance du croyant" (the obedience of Christ . . . will become the obedience of the believer)[33] And for Esler, "to enable righteousness" is the theme of Romans 5.[34]

In other places, Paul uses περισσεύω with this idea that what overflows entails action at its source and then also at its destination. In 2 Corinthians 4:15, grace overflows from believers to believers: grace "causes the act of giving thanks to abound" (εὐχαριστίαν περισσεύσῃ),[35] and it does so as it expands more and more (πλεονάσασα) amongst believers (through proclamation, v.

---

26. E.g. Hodge, *Romans*, 159.
27. Sanday and Headlam, *Romans*, 140.
28. Esler, *Conflict and Identity*, 201.
29. Moo, *Roman 1–8*, 350.
30. Schreiner, *Romans*, 285.
31. E.g. Jewett sees "piety" as outcome of what in 5:15 abounds (*Romans*, 381); a different view from Hodge: that δωρεὰ, vv. 15 & 17, "does not mean holiness" (*Romans*, 163).
32. Nygren, *Romans*, 220.
33. Leenhardt, *Romains*, 86.
34. Esler, *Conflict and Identity*, 195.
35. NIV translation.

13). In 2 Corinthians 1:5, περισσεύω (to abound) is used in connection with suffering. Suffering overflows from Christ to believers. Here also there is the idea that suffering is active in the life of believers, just as it was in Christ's life. A similar idea with περισσεύω (to abound) is found in 1 Thessalonians 3:12 and 2 Corinthians 9:8,[36] although χάρις (grace) is used in these passages with different nuances (cf. Dunn on this).[37] Paul's thinking shows very much that when the grace of God reaches out to people, their action is enabled and is expected to follow. This human agency is the focus in the next sections (stages two, three and four).

To sum up, in Romans 5 Paul emphasises that the believer's process from sin to God's realm begins with divine action. Paul's thinking appears to accord with the initiation patterns of his time. Christ's gracious act sets "free" the person (5:15; cf. also 6:18, 22). This enables the person to exercise his or her agency and take the action that his/her transition to new life requires. The next sections consider whether the initiatory stages we have identified fit the movement of thought in Romans 5:12–6:23.

Our case and argument will proceed as follows. As mentioned earlier, in Romans 5 Paul focuses on God's saving action and then in Romans 6, when he focuses on the human response to God's grace, he reminds the Romans of their experience of stages two, three and four. Paul's stress on this divine agency (stage one) has led some to downplay this human agency in the Christian transition. For example, Boring's view is that Paul presents Christ's work as a "unilateral act of God who conquers the realm of sin and death."[38] He concludes that Paul does not imply any "action of some human beings who decide to "transfer" from the rule of sin and death to that of righteousness and life."[39] Other scholars take a different view. For example Ponsot notes that the process of change from sin to Christian existence "demande le concours de l'homme . . .; celui-ci est appelé à s'établir dans ce Royaume de grâce, ou plutôt à l'accueillir" (asks for the participation of man . . .; he is called to settle in this Kingdom of grace, or rather to welcome it).[40] Also

---

36. A similar view from Dunn, *Romans 1–8*, 280.
37. Dunn, *Romans 1–8*, 280.
38. Boring, "Language of Universal Salvation," 284.
39. Boring, 284.
40. Ponsot, *Romains*, 96–97.

Moo thinks that this is not a situation "in which man is passive and only a receiver."[41] In line with Ponsot and Moo, the next sections focus on what the believer does in this transition by examining stages two, three and four, and arguing that these stages which are about the person's agency are emphasised in Romans 6:1-2 (stage two), 6:3-4 (stage three) and 6:4-6, 10-11, 13-23 with some elements in 5:17, 19 (stage four).

4.3. Second Stage Action: Death to the Old Way of Life (ἀπεθάνομεν τῇ ἁμαρτίᾳ, 6:1-2)

4.3.1. Stating the Issue

We may conveniently introduce the issue with reference to 6:11,[42] where Dunn comments on "count yourselves dead to sin" with these words: "whatever death the believer has died, he is not a merely passive object played upon and manipulated by transcendent forces."[43] This idea that the believer's death does not imply passivity is a vital insight. In Romans 6 Paul speaks of the believer's death and Christ's death together. The expression "with Christ" permeates his language (in συνετάφημεν αὐτῷ, "we were buried with him," v. 4; in σύμφυτοι, "the same plant," v. 5; in συνεσταυρώθη, "was crucified with," v. 6; in ἀπεθάνομεν σὺν Χριστῷ, "we died with Christ," v. 8, and in συζήσομεν αὐτῷ, "we will live with him," v. 8). Is Dunn right when he thinks that the believer's death in Romans 6 is not just a passive thing? Do we find stage two, the "liminal" in-between state of initiation, reflected in Paul's language here in Romans 6?

The second chapter outlined how, in Paul's cultural context, the crucial feature of a "liminal" stage in the process of entry to new existence is the initiand's personal act of breaking with (i.e. dying to) the status and life in which he or she was living.[44] Also our third chapter considered how this aspect was experienced by Paul himself during his Damascus Road transition. In the light of all this, it is natural to assume that this personal death in the "liminal" episode of initiation will also be present in Paul's mind in Romans

---

41. Moo, *Romans 1-8*, 350.
42. Both here in 6:11 and in v. 2, "death to sin" concerns the believer.
43. Dunn, *Romans 1 - 8*, 324.
44. So Carlson, "Role of Baptism," 257; and Wedderburn's idea about "the passage from [or better 'through'] a death event" (*Baptism and Resurrection*, 381-82), and speaking of how central was the concept of "stirb und werde" (see 360-363).

6:1–2 when he speaks of the Romans' transition to new life. As shown in the last section, in Romans 5 he focuses on God's agency (stage one). Then he reminds the Romans that they cannot go on with the life they used to live (6:1), because in their transition and baptism they personally took the responsibility to abandon that system of life. As 6:2–4 shows, in this process they took the liminal step of dying personally to sin (stage two) and then acted to undergo the ritual that seals this break with the life of sin (stage three). This part develops the idea that "death to sin" (6:2) is the Christian initiand's personal death in the liminal phase of his or her transition from sin to spiritual life.

As this section will show, very often scholars speak of "death to sin" (v. 2) as the same as the "death with Christ" that Paul spells out in verses 3–10. The section seeks to demonstrate that this distorts the meaning of death in 6:2 by making it Christ's death and act, not the believer's. For example, Moule sees in 6:2 the idea that "the death of Christ was thought of as the 'payment in full' [for] all that can be demanded" by sin.[45] Dunn also has Christ's act in mind in verse 2 when he writes that "what Paul had in mind is a death which puts the individual beyond the power of sin."[46] Many others agree with this line of thought.[47] But it makes better sense to read Paul's words as implying the baptizand's agency.

The expression ἀπεθάνομεν τῇ ἁμαρτίᾳ (we died to sin) shows two ideas: (1) that "something happens,"[48] and (2) it happens in the transitional process.[49] Basically Moo rejects these two points when he states that "the ultimate basis for Paul's appeal in this chapter is not what happened when we were baptized but what happened when Christ died and rose again. This death of His to sin is also our death to sin (vv. 2, 6, 9–10)."[50] But there is much consensus

---

45. Moule, *Essays*, 152–153.

46. Dunn, *Romans 1 – 8*, 307.

47. Just a few examples of this will suffice here, as more will be shown as we continue; e.g. it can only be Jesus's death as Ziesler thinks of "a complete separation" (*Romans*, 153); Edwards: "It is an objective reference to Christ's death" (*Romans*, 159); D. Seeley: "Jesus' death was a death to sin" and what is in 6:2 is just "to re-enact" it (*Noble Death*, 102).

48. See Beasley-Murray, *Baptism*, 140; also Dunn, *Romans 1– 8*, 307; Engberg-Pedersen, *Paul and Stoics*, 226.

49. Making hints at this but with a focus on the water ritual, e.g. Beasley-Murray, *Baptism*, 140; Wright, "Baptismal Community," 5; Käsemann, *Romans*, 165.

50. Moo, *Romans*, 371–372.

on the fact that Paul's concern is the entry process of the believer and what takes place therein. For example, Wedderburn's view is that the apostle is "speaking of the initiatory death [. . .]."[51] This is also the view of many others.[52] As Dunn himself recognizes, "The language has the same vivid quality and character which we would expect to find in a fundamental life-transforming experience or rite of passage."[53] In the first chapter, the idea that initiation is very much present in Paul's thinking in Romans 5:12–6:23 was illustrated. The question is, in this language of initiation, what could Paul's words mean to his readers when they are reminded (cf. ἀγνοεῖτε [you are ignorant][54] in 6:3) that they "died to sin" in their Christian *passage* to new life? Would they have thought of it as something they personally did as part of their entry process? In other words, the issue is whether in 6:2 Paul is speaking about the agency of Christ in the baptismal transition (stage one) or whether his focus is on the role of the candidate.

Some scholars opt for the believer's agency (which is the line of thought that this thesis follows), but often they lack clarity. For example, Reitzenstein notes four understandings of "we died to sin."[55] But, unhappy with these views, his own suggestion is that "the context requires first of all that the subject be seen not as a purely physical act of dying, nor a merely figurative one,

---

51. Wedderburn, *Baptism and Resurrection*, 389.

52. Often scholars link baptism to chap 6, e.g. O. Kuss entitles 6:1–11 as „In der Taufe sind wir mit Christus gestorben, um fortan in Neuheit des Lebens zu wandeln" (In baptism we died with Christ in order to walk in newness of life), *Der Römerbrief* 1, 294; same idea from P. Althaus on vv. 1–14 (*Der Brief*, 60); P. Stuhlmacher sees vv. 1–14 as „Der Herrschaftswechsel in der Taufe" (The change of rule in baptism), *Der Brief*, 83.

53. Dunn, *Romans 1 – 8*, 307.

54. A. D. Nock suggests that '"the phrase need not be more than a trick of style' style" ('("Early Gentile Christianity," " 115), but many see in ἀγνοεῖτε (you are ignorant) Paul's reminder of a doctrine they knew about baptism, so e.g. Wagner, *Pauline Baptism*, 284; Wedderburn, *Baptism and Resurrection*, 40–43; Barrett, *Romans*, 121. For Brandon: '"more likely . . . Paul . . . perceives a deeper significance in an existent custom' custom" (*History, Time and Deity*, 26 fn. 4).

55. (1) An "ethical" sense, i.e. "died to sin" with the idea of becoming "sinless" and "righteous in God's sight," (2) "actual, physical death" and thus to mean that "The person who has died is absolved because he has paid the penalty with his death," (3) that the person "is made free from sin" or that "through death in baptism satisfaction is achieved for the demands of law *for sin*," and (4) "that the deceased person, because he is no longer active, also is no longer sinning," see Reitzenstein, *Hellenistic Mystery-Religions*, 328. Number (1) is close to our line of thought because it shows that an act is done to sin. But to speak of something that makes sinless focuses on a divine deed. As we will see, Paul means the believer's action, and thus not something that renders the person sinless.

but above all a *voluntary* dying and surrendering oneself to death."[56] Here, Reitzenstein sees it as the act of the believer, but what he means is that "in the mystery [of dying][57] we have *assumed* Christ's person and *his lot*."[58] This study indeed considers that assuming Christ's person, which is to identify with him, is an important action. But as we will see, this is the third stage action that is implied in 6:3–4. This will be addressed when the meaning of the act of the water ritual itself will be considered. This section intends to consider how by death to sin, in 6:2, Paul implies more than just assuming the death and lot of Christ, and to show what the reading of Romans 6 is like when this death is understood as the believer's act in the "liminal" stage of initiation.

4.3.2. Death to Sin and the Initiatory Act of Breaking with the Old Way

Speaking of "death to sin" (6:2), G. Therrien states, "Dans l'union . . . du baptisé avec le Christ mort et ressuscité, le chrétien meurt au péché" (In the union . . . of the baptized with the Christ who died and was resurrected, the Christian dies to sin).[59] The death of the Christian in his or her transition is understood as our union with Jesus in his own death. Jesus's action (his death with and for the believer) on the cross, which is the divine saving act (stage one), is probably not the focus of Paul's meaning in 6:2. To demonstrate this, the following structure is adopted in this section: 1) attention is given to the fact that the real subject in the clause ἀπεθάνομεν τῇ ἁμαρτίᾳ (we died to sin) is the key issue; 2) with a focus on the believer, an attempt is made to show what the action "to die to sin" means.

1) First, we consider the real subject of "to die" in 6:2. Although the "we" of ἀπεθάνομεν is not a separate pronoun, this study argues that the importance of this subject has not been given due attention. When Paul says, ἀπεθάνομεν

---

56. Reitzenstein, *Hellenistic Mystery-Religions*, 328 [italics his].

57. What he means by "mystery" here appears to be that "As Christ surrendered voluntarily to death, so we also are to surrender voluntarily to death (of the old man). Then we are free from sin" (*Hellenistic Mystery-Religions*, 332 fn.12).

58. Reitzenstein, *Hellenistic Mystery-Religions*, 328–29 [italics mine]; also Wedderburn's view is of assuming what Christ did: "Paul is speaking of . . . the Christian acknowledging an experience already previously undergone by Christ on his behalf" (*Baptism and Resurrection*, 389); so also Seeley: this death is an "imaginative re-enactment" of Christ's death (*Noble Death*, 102).

59. Therrien, *Le discernement*, 268.

τῇ ἁμαρτίᾳ, "we died to sin" (6:2), is he referring to Christ's death and deed, or is it the action that the believer takes in his or her entry to new existence? Paul speaks of Christ's death both before and after 6:2. Based on what Paul says before 6:2, some have deduced that in 6:2 Paul's focus is on Christ's act. For example, Achtemeier suggests Paul's question to be, "who is dead?" and the answer to be, "You are, dear Christian readers!"[60] His opinion is that "this answer takes us back to the discussion of Christ and Adam" considering that Christ's obedience and death, that "undid" sin (referring to 5:8–10, 18–19),[61] is the death that Paul means in 6:2;[62] and so then "the Christian, in baptism, has shared in the death of Christ."[63] Other scholars make the same deduction from Christ's death mentioned after 6:2. For example, Cranfield does not see any distinction between verse 2 and the rest. He states that "verses 2–11 are all concerned with the Christian's death and resurrection *with* Christ."[64] So, in his view, death to sin in verse 2 also is implicit in "with Christ."

Often scholars think of Christ's death (with the believer represented in him) when they interpret 6:2. But, as we attempt to demonstrate now, Paul focuses on the agency of the believer. To demonstrate this, we consider Paul's overall argument in 6:1–11. Then, building on this, we consider how this act of the believer has been overlooked, and what sense Paul's argument makes if the "we" is the real actor in 6:2.

In Romans 6:1–11 as a whole, it is true that the death of Christ and the metaphorical death of the believer are juxtaposed in such a way that they can easily be considered as pointing to one and the same act – the death of Christ. In these verses, Paul speaks of the human act of death (stage two) and of its relationship with the divine act (stage one), and the two as such are interwoven. However, we must distinguish between these divine and human acts of death.

Paul says in verse 2 that believers die to sin (ἀπεθάνομεν τῇ ἁμαρτίᾳ), and he links this to baptism[65] through the clause ἀγνοεῖτε ὅτι ὅσοι ἐβαπτίσθημεν

---

60. Achtemeier, *Romans*, 103.
61. Achtemeier, *Romans*, 104.
62. It is a ref. to v. 2 when Achtemeier says, "Any serious discussion of human sin ... must include Christ's death" (*Romans*, 104).
63. Achtemeier, *Romans*, 104.
64. Cranfield, *Romans*, 296.
65. E.g. Barrett, *Romans*, 121.

(you are ignorant that all who were baptized), as explained earlier in the first chapter. The idea of death recurs in 6:3, still linking with baptism,[66] but there it is clearly the death of Christ[67] as Paul expresses the idea that one's baptism is "baptism to[68] Christ's death" (ἐβαπτίσθημεν εἰς Χριστὸν Ἰησοῦν εἰς τὸν θάνατον αὐτοῦ, "we were baptized into Christ Jesus, into his death"). So, 6:2–3 gives us two links between three elements (with the form 1 to 2, 2 to 3), and baptism (element 2) is in the middle. The three elements are linked together in this way: (1) the believer's death to (2) baptism, and (2) baptism to (3) Christ's death.

This leads to a question: as "the believer dies" to sin in "baptism" (1 and 2) and one's "baptism" is baptism *to* "Christ's death" (2 and 3), does this necessitate that the person's "death to sin" must refer to Christ's death, that is, the death he died with the believer represented in it? In other words, are the two deaths (death in v. 2 and death in v. 3) referring just to one action, the action of Christ on the cross? A chart helps to clarify how the idea of death recurs in Romans 6[69] but with three different referents:

	Death of	Action of	Location	Verses
1	Christ	Christ	Cross	vv. 3, 5, 9, 10
2	Believer	Believer	Transition process	vv. 2, 11
3	Believer with Christ	Christ	Cross	vv. 6, 8
			Cross (baptism as symbol)	v. 4 [buried with]

To note which death (Christ's, or the believer's, or the believer's together with Christ) Paul focuses on is very important for understanding his argument. So also is to note in which location the event happens. Paul's attention is on Christ's death and action in 6:3, 5, 9, 10 (no. 1 on chart). But in 6:2, 11 we suggest that he clearly focuses on the believer's act (no. 2). This is the

---

66. E.g. Schreiner, *Romans*, 309.

67. So Moo: "Paul's *syn* refers to . . . the cross," *Romans 1–8*, 381–82.

68. "into" for εἰς is the common translation (English versions in general; and the French "en" (in) e.g. SB/LS; also German "in," e.g. Bibel/NDUMLuthers) showing that the translator has already decided on the "entry" or "incorporation" sense. Instead, we choose "to," a translation that leaves the decision open; so also Schnackenburg, *Baptism*, 33; and some German translations with "auf" (to) instead of "in," e.g. Bibel/EÜ and Bibel/ES.

69. Attention is drawn to this e.g. by S. Sabou, *Between Horror*, 57.

believer's personal action, and it takes place in the transition process as Paul shows in 6:1–3 where he states that the believer cannot go on sinning (v. 1) because of what he or she has personally done to sin he or she has died to it (v. 2) – In his or her transition that includes baptism (v. 3). Verses 1 and 2 are such that the referents of death to sin (v. 2) are primarily believers.

But, in Paul's argument there is another believer's death. This is his or her death when he or she was represented in Christ on the cross (cf. no 3). This is the death that is "involved in that of Christ" as Tannehill describes it when he speaks of verses 5 and 8.[70] So, in the passage we have two kinds of death related to the believer, and there is a difference between the two acts. The idea in type 2 is clearly that the believer is doing something, but type 3 is Christ's action; the believer is only passively represented in it. As the chart shows, Paul focuses on this in 6:6, 8 and 4. In verses 6 and 8, the location is the cross, while in 6:4 the location can be the cross (with just a symbol in baptism)[71] or the location is the baptismal transition, as it is often understood especially focusing on immersion.[72] But there is a debate about whether immersion was a general method in the early church[73] and it is uncertain if the water ritual signified death (or burial).[74] This study considers that in verses 3–4 Paul focuses on the ritual of initiation and the fact that to undergo this (stage three) is to ratify one's death in the liminal, second stage (cf. v. 2). The next section of our argument below (4.4), where verses 3–4 become the focus, will expand this issue.

This chart helps us to see that in 6:1–11 Paul speaks of death but with a focus either on the believer or on Christ and that in 6:2 his concern is the believer's action taken in his or her *passage* to new existence. Here consideration is given to how a focus on the believer ("we") matters for us, so that we

---

70. Tannehill, *Dying and Rising*, 9.

71. E.g. this is Origen's idea: "'we have been buried with him' by his death," *Homily 14.1*, quoted by Finn, *Early Christian Baptism*, 202. Symbolic meaning is also M. Barth's view: "the burial of the believer in his baptism is a later confirmation of the finality, and irrevocability and recognition of his own death in the death of Jesus on the cross," cited by Beasley-Murray, *Baptism in NT*, 130.

72. Speaking of "buried with" Morris sees baptism as "interment" (*Romans*, 247–48 fn. 17); similar view with Stuhlmacher, *Romans*, 91; and Esler, *Conflict and Identity*, 211–213; Sanday and Headlam see immersion as death and submersion as burial (*Romans*, 153).

73. E.g. Fitzmyer's discussion of εἰς (*Romans*, 433).

74. E.g. Moo disputes the idea that baptism is a "symbol of dying" and burial (*Romans 1–8*, 371, cf. 378–80 for different views on this idea of "burial with Christ").

may clearly grasp that it is the candidate's death in the liminal, second stage of entry to new life that Paul expresses in 6:2.

When scholars deal with ἀπεθάνομεν τῇ ἁμαρτίᾳ, "we died to sin" (6:2), the tendency has been to think of Christ and his death instead of "we." For example, Sorin Sabou's study is devoted to "we died to sin." This idea is central to his study. He not only considers that "we died to sin" is the "thesis" that Paul develops in Romans 6:1–11,[75] but also states that "this basic affirmation is the core of our thesis."[76] Sabou seeks "to explain *who* 'dies' with *whom* and *to* what as necessary elements for arguing for a particular interpretation of Pauline metaphorical language of death."[77] To do this he ensures that "the areas of Christology, anthropology and cosmology, find their role" and thus he considers that "it is necessary to have full pictures of Christ, of man and salvation as necessary elements for a good interpretation of Paul's language."[78] About "we died to sin," instead of focusing on the believer, Christ is the focus when he states, "For understanding this language [i.e. of death to sin] Paul directs his readers' attention to *Christ's death*."[79] In fact, Sabou thinks that what matters is "a better understanding of 'dying with'"[80] He maintains consistency with this when he states, "Believers' 'death to sin' is to be defined *in the terms given by 6:3–7*"[81] (the section of the "with" language). This shows a shift of attention from "we" and their act of death (v. 2) to the death of Christ – and the believer, on the cross (cf. vv. 3–10).[82] From this, Sabou's conclusion shows that Christ's agency is what "we died to sin" implies when he states,

> Christ "died to sin" in the sense that . . . death itself was defeated and thus, sin was "ruined/abolished" as far as its effect is concerned – namely eschatological death. The believer is a mortal

---

75. Sabou, *Between Horror and Hope*, 57.
76. Sabou, 58.
77. Sabou, 43 [italics his].
78. Sabou, 43.
79. Sabou, 58 [italics his].
80. Sabou, 57.
81. Sabou, 140 [italics mine].
82. Dunn also states: Paul "goes on to clarify his meaning by spelling it out in terms of . . . Christ's death . . . and their participation therein" (*Romans 1–8*, 326); also Schnackenburg, *Baptism in Thought of Paul*, 33.

being (Rom 8:10), but eschatological death is no longer in view because Christ died to sin.[83]

The argument is solid, because at least it explains what the death of Christ (to sin) makes the situation of man to be, as far as Paul's argument is concerned. Sabou offers a clear idea of the relationship between Christ's death to sin (6:10) and the death to sin of the Christian (6:2) when he uses the word "coalescing"[84] to describe it, and this certainly fits the "with Christ" language by which Paul shapes his argument on Christ and the Christian in Romans 6. Sabou's idea is solid, as W. Campbell, for example, recognizes.[85] But this focus on Christ's act obscures the human agency that "we died to sin" implies.

Fitzmyer, to take another example, states that "the Christian is said to be "dead to sin" (6:11), associated *with* Christ precisely at the moment in which he [Christ] died."[86] Our focus is more on verse 2, but death in verse 11 clearly concerns the believer, just as in 6:2. Fitzmyer's idea that "death to sin" in both verses was *"with"* Christ in his death is the view of many; in this understanding, what Paul means in 6:2 is referred to as a "share" (or "participation") in Christ's act on the cross.[87]

However, we suggest that in 6:2, Paul does not have the "with Christ" concept in mind. As we mentioned earlier, the tendency has been to draw the "with" idea from the next verses (4–8). This is clear, for instance, as Engberg-Pedersen points out that "in baptism Christ-believers have altogether died to sin (6:2)," adding the explanation that "The 'old man' has been crucified with Christ . . . (*katargeisthai*, 6:6)."[88] Moo also relies on what follows 6:2 when he states that "That death of His to sin is also our death to sin (vv. 2, 6, 9–10)."[89] In this way, 6:2 is explained by means of the "with Christ" death,

---

83. Sabou, *Between Horror and Hope*, 140.

84. Sabou, 140.

85. W. S. Campbell draws upon Sabou when he states, "Christ's death to sin has a sharing possibility of 'dying with' because he died as the anointed Davidic king when he won a victory over sin and death by being raised from the dead. Those who belong to the anointed King of God share in his victory . . ." (Campbell, *Paul and Creation*, 154).

86. Fitzmyer, *Romans*, 434 [italics mine].

87. Moo, *Romans 1–8*, 371; Sabou, *Between Horror and Hope*, 93, 140; Dunn, *Romans 1–8*, 312; Flemington, *New Testament Doctrine*, 81, 109; Käsemann, *Romans*, 162; Schweitzer, *Mysticism of Paul*, 19; Stuhlmacher, *Romans*, 91.

88. Engberg-Pedersen, *Paul and Stoics*, 226.

89. Moo, *Romans 1–8*, 372.

which is Christ's act. As a result, "death to sin" (in v. 2) becomes Christ's act instead of being the believer's act (cf. our chart).

2) Having focused on the subject of the verb in 6:2, we now focus on the meaning of the believer's "death to sin" as a deliberate act of breaking with one's old way of life – dying to that life, just as in Paul's time the liminal and second stage of the transition to new existence required.

Very often reference is made to the four alternative meanings that Cranfield suggests for this clause.[90] The four senses are so important to our point that we use them as the framework for our discussion. They are as follows:

(i) The *juridical sense*: They [believers] died to sin *in the sight of God*, when Christ died on the cross for them. This is a matter of God's decision. His decision to take their sins upon Himself in the person of His dear Son . . .

(ii) The *baptismal sense*: They died to sin . . . in their baptism, which was at the same time both their ratification of their own acceptance of God's decision on their behalf (to regard Christ's death for their sins as their death . . . and God's bestowal of His seal and pledge of the fact that His decision really concerned them individually, personally).

(iii) The *moral sense*: They are called, and have been given the freedom, to die daily and hourly to sin by the mortification of their sinful natures and rise daily and hourly to newness of life in obedience to God.

(iv) The *eschatological sense*: They will die to sin finally and irreversibly when they actually die . . .[91]

How should we evaluate these alternatives? We may start with the last one. As Osborne notes, this fourth sense, reading it as a future "they will die," clearly "is not in the context."[92] He does not justify his opinion. But in our view he is right, because the questions of 6:1-2 show clearly that Paul is speaking of the believer's life now. This study considers that options (i), (ii) and (iii) are all possible in Romans 6, and building on these possibilities, suggests a different option that considers the person's liminal death.

---

90. E.g. Osborne, *Romans*, 148; Fitzmyer, *Romans*, 433.
91. Cranfield, *Romans 1-8*, 299-300.
92. Osborne, *Romans*, 149, footnote.

Because Cranfield (as mentioned earlier) understands death in 6:2 as the "with Christ" type (i.e. death on the cross), his own choice hovers between (i) and (ii), but he adopts (i) as he shows in these words:

> That Paul was already thinking particularly of baptism is possible, and some have argued that his use of the aorist points to this reference; but an aorist would be equally appropriate, if the reference were to the divine decision, and, on the whole, it seems rather more probable that the sense intended was sense (i).[93]

So, Cranfield's view is that "we died to sin" simply means our death when we were represented in Christ's act on the cross. In other words, "death to sin" (v. 2) refers to Christ's agency, not a different and personal act of the believer. Fitzmyer thinks that Paul speaks of the fact that "*Through Christ's death the ruling power of sin was broken.*"[94] But in fact options (ii) and (iii), that Cranfield rejects, seem to reflect better what the believer's death in relation to baptism means.

Osborne rejects (iii) suggesting that it makes "to live in sin" (vv. 1–2) refer to "individual sins rather than the principle or power of sin."[95] His judgment is that "the best is a combination of the first two: with the experience of

---

93. Cranfield, *Romans 1–8*, 300.
94. Fitzmyer, *Romans*, 433 [italics mine].
95. Osborne, *Romans*, 149, footnote. Sin as power or acts: there is dispute on which of these is the sense that Paul has in mind. This is important as this study is concerned with the movement from sin to God and also with the believer's action in this transition. For some sin is power in Romans 5–6 (e.g. Osborne, *Romans*, 149; Moo, *Romans*, 367; Ziesler, *Romans*, 153). But to die to sin is to break with sin both as power and as to actions. So it is better to think that Paul sees both dimensions of sin. The proof is that in Romans 5–6 Paul sees both dimensions alternatively. Sin is a power that entered the world (5:12), it rules (5:14, 17, 21; 6:12, 14), it enslaves (6:6), and it is a sphere of living (e.g. 6:1). But he also sees sin as actions, especially when he uses the verb ἁμαρτάνω (to sin), e.g. 5:12, 14, and expressions conveying the action of doing evil, such as "to obey sin's lusts" (ὑπακούειν ἐπιθυμίαις αὐτοῦ) in 6:12, "to offer the parts of the body as instruments of wickedness for [to the advantage of] sin" (παριστάνετε τὰ μέλη ὑμῶν ὅπλα ἀδικίας τῇ ἁμαρτίᾳ) in 6:13. In 6:12, Paul refers both to sin as power (βασιλευέτω ἡ ἁμαρτία, "let sin not reign") and speaks of doing evil, as the expression that we just mentioned shows, i.e. "to obey sin's lusts." Also significant is how Paul alternates the two senses of sin in 6:1 and 6:15. The two verses are parallel, as Esler notes: in vv. 1 and 15, Paul uses "the same device – a question that begins τί οὖν (what then), followed by the emphatic negative μὴ γένοιτο" (by no means!), Esler, *Conflict and Identity*, 203. Yet in v. 1 Paul refers to sin as sphere (or as a principle), whereas in v. 15 the verbal form connotes acts. He focuses on both in this pericope. Dunn recognizes this when he speaks of "power of sin," "its realm," "its authority" (*Romans*, 307) but also its act (cf. 287). Schreiner similarly suggests that it is "a mistake to separate sin as power from specific acts of sin" (*Romans*, 304).

justification at our conversion and with the pledge to live for him that seals our salvation contract at our baptism (see 1 Pet 3:21), "we die to sin and no longer live under its power."[96] But Osborne's words "at our baptism, we die to sin and no longer live under its power" show that he recognizes that Cranfield's (iii) [cf. obedience to God] is relevant as well. So, the sense (iii) cannot be ignored. It points to a life-long radical obedience strongly decided upon in the entry process[97] (cf. stage four of initiation).

In our view, what the candidate does in his or her transition to new life concerns options (ii) (reflecting stage two and three) and (iii) (stage four). Cranfield's first option is also clearly present in the pericope (cf. esp. 5:15), but that is not what the believer does; it is God's act (stage one) and constitutes the basis of what the believer does in his or her entry event. More consideration of this will follow in the next sections of this chapter.

Concerning (ii) and (iii), while (ii) is clearly in relation to baptism, (iii) requires clarification. In fact, what Cranfield does not do (which we intend to do in the section that deals with how stage four works together with baptism) is to explain why, in relation with "we died to sin", he finds it possible to use such words as "daily and hourly" – words that correspond to stage four because they point to the continuing, after-initiation life. Though attention to stage four is still to come, these aspects are considered here as they help us to explain "death to sin" as an act of the liminal phase.

It is true that "daily and hourly" apply to ἀπεθάνομεν τῇ ἁμαρτίᾳ (we died to sin), but this requires explanation, because their use tends to give the aorist ἀπεθάνομεν (we died) a sense of timeless action (making it "gnomic"), and yet this verb appears to state just that something important happened (so a constative or historical aorist) as some scholars point out.[98] But this aorist is not just used constatively; it also includes a timeless sense. Cranfield's hint at this calls for elucidation. Insofar as Paul is thinking of the initiatory process (cf. our first chapter), ἀπεθάνομεν τῇ ἁμαρτίᾳ (we died to sin) must combine the constative and the timeless connotations. The constative meaning is that the break from sin or death to sin is decided and takes place during stage

---

96. Osborne, *Romans*, 149, footnote.

97. E.g. Beasley-Murray speaks of "the crucifixion of old nature" and that "dying and rising begin in the baptismal event" (*Baptism*, 132).

98. So e.g. Barrett, *Romans*, 121; Morris, *Romans*, 245; Käsemann, *Romans*, 165.

two of the initiatory process. There is a hint of this in Cranfield's sense (ii). But the idea of dying is also unbound in time, because – though a radical decision against sin takes place in the entry process – sin is still a threat, as Edwards notes.[99] This is clear in the question of 6:1, and 6:4b–8 presumes the real possibility of sinning and is the ground of all the parenesis of vv. 11–23. In other words, the decision is made but the reality of this act is such that it has to be re-actualised continuously. As Osborne notes, Christians die to sin (vv. 2, 11), but "this does not mean that sin no longer affects the believer," it is still "a force tempting us."[100] Morris' comment on συνεσταυρώθη, "was crucified with" (another aorist, v. 6) is in the same line of thought.[101] The gnomic sense reflects the fourth stage (or feature) of entry. This will be clearer when stage four is considered. As we argued above, the fourth stage is part of the initiatory process because it is implicit in the decisions taken in stages two and three; and therefore a "gnomic" reading of "we died to sin" is necessary, as well as a "constative."

So far we have been examining the view that "death to sin" in 6:2 is just to be linked with what happened on the cross. We can now turn to consider the fact that some scholars recognize that "death to sin" does indeed refer to something that happens in the initiatory process, but do not make a clear distinction between this entry action and the "with Christ" idea that starts in verse 3. As a result, the believer's agency in the liminal stage is less accounted for. Earlier, reference was made to Ziesler's idea that "death to sin" implies such strong actions as "release" and "complete separation" from sin.[102] In a reflexive sense, the believer could be the subject, releasing himself or herself after being enabled by receiving God's grace in stage one. But Ziesler has in mind the "liberating" death of Christ.[103]

Often this is because a distinction of stages between death to sin in 6:2 (stage two) and the ritual of baptism itself in 6:3 (stage three) is not made clear. For example, Käsemann states, "Christ died for all [he refers to 2 Cor

---

99. Edwards remarks that, "Rather than releasing its grip at conversion, sin usually tightens it, as Paul well knew," *Romans*, 159.

100. Osborne, *Romans*, 149.

101. Morris states: "There is a sense in which a death has taken place once and for all in the believer, but there is another in which he dies every day" (*Romans*, 251).

102. Ziesler, *Romans*, 153.

103. Ziesler, 153–54 [italics mine].

5:14] and, as the context [of Rom 6] shows, he has caught up Christians into his death; this took place in baptism."[104] Here Käsemann sees death to sin (v. 2) in baptism (v. 3) and all in connection with "dying with Christ," because he actually rejects the interpretation of *dying with Christ* "as though the general baptism took place on Golgotha and we have died already on the cross with Christ."[105] He conflates stages two and three and finds them both in 6:2, but insists that our death in baptism is distinct from our death with Christ on the cross. Also K. Barth says, "In baptism He [Christ] says to the candidate that He also for him and *with him* is dead and risen . . ."[106] Death to sin (v. 2) is seen in baptism (v. 3), and in consequence instead of the believer's agency, Christ's agency is emphasised because the death stressed in verse 3 is Christ's. As Christ died then "we died to sin" is seen as "reception of his act" [i.e. his death] through baptism.[107] As we will see in the next section, the ritual of baptism referred to in 6:3–4 stands for a different phase of initiation (stage three). It implies the believer's agency in making a pledge. As indicated earlier, Christ's saving death (cf. stage one) is referred to in 6:3–4 to explain the ritual.

Some scholars, while also not making a distinction between the second stage of initiation in 6:2 and third in 6:3, have preserved a focus on the human agency involved in "we died to sin."[108] For example, in their paraphrase of 6:2, Sanday and Headlam state, "When we took the decisive step and became Christians we may be said to have died to sin."[109] So "to die to sin" is viewed as "to take a decisive step." On the relationship between this and the "with Christ" idea in 6:3–4, Sanday and Headlam are cautious. Speaking of 6:4 they state, "When we descended into the baptismal water, that meant that we died – to sin. When the water closed over our heads, that meant we lay buried with Him, in proof that our death to sin, like His death, was real."[110] In this, "we" is clearly the agent. The dative "with him" is understood not in

---

104. Käsemann, *Romans*, 165.
105. Kasemann, 165.
106. Barth, *Teaching of Church*, 29 [italics mine].
107. Käsemann, *Romans*, 166. Some emphasise "receiving" and tend to reduce "we died to sin" to this sense, e.g. Sanders, *Paul and Palestinian Judaism*, 452; Edwards speaks of "baptism [as] an act of faith wherein God communicates the effects of Christ's death . . . to the *receptive* heart" (*Romans*, 160); and Dakin, "Christian Baptism," 41, 42.
108. E.g. Sanday and Headlam, *Romans*, 154; Morris, *Romans*, 245–47.
109. Sanday and Headlam, *Romans*, 154.
110. Sanday and Headlam, 154.

a quasi-literal sense of sharing Christ's grave, but in the sense of imitating his action (i.e. a burial in the form of his). And about the death itself, they put a stress on the person's act (i.e. to descend into water). In addition, the words "our real death" and "his real death" show their intention to distinguish these two referents.

But as the next section shows, the ritual of water (cf. 6:3–4) means a different stage and action which follows and seals the second stage act of dying to the way of life that is being abandoned. As Sanday and Headlam do not distinguish the death of the liminal and second stage (cf. 6:2) from the ritual that seals initiation (cf. 6:3–4), the ritual of baptism is described as just "*expressing symbolically a series of acts corresponding to the redeeming acts of Christ.*"[111] What initiation entails is overlooked when it is understood that Christ's death and the believer's death are both connected to baptism just because baptism "expresses symbolically" the believer's death and how it relates to Christ's saving act. In 6:3–4, the water ritual, as a stage of initiation, means more than this. More than expressing what God has done, the ritual implies the person's vow of consecration to this God for salvation. More on this is given in the next section when εἰς τὸν θάνατον αὐτοῦ, "to his death" (6:3) is considered.

By way of conclusion, regarding the meaning of "we died to sin" the main points are as follows. Paul is "speaking of the initiatory death," as Wedderburn recognizes.[112] But this initiatory death means more than Wedderburn's view that the baptizand, in his death to sin, is "acknowledging an experience already previously undergone by Christ on his behalf."[113] Paul does not speak of a physical death, but of a personal death. This is his point in 6:2. Wedderburn misses this when he states that "Paul is . . . speaking not so much of the baptized person dying himself."[114] In 6:2 Paul implies the initiand's death in the liminal phase (stage two) – the candidate's personal act of breaking with the way of life that is being abandoned. This is what this section has tried to prove. Romans 6:1–2 shows that Paul reminds the Romans of this act of serious responsibility that they have personally taken.

---

111. Sanday and Headlam, 153 [italics theirs]; just as "representation," cf. Rawlinson, "Corpus Christi," 233.

112. Wedderburn, *Baptism and Resurrection*, 389.

113. Wedderburn, 389.

114. Wedderburn, 389.

Our contention is that Paul's thought on the transition from sin to God is very structured. After a focus in Romans 5 on the divine agency and salvation (stage one), in Romans 6 Paul focuses on what actions, in response to this divine act, the Christian initiand takes in transition. In 6:1–2 he speaks of the candidate's act of dying to the old way of life (stage two). In 6:3–4, Paul reminds his readers of the third stage of their *passage* to new life – the water ritual that they underwent. The next section now considers these verses in order to understand the agency of the believer at this stage and the responsibility that is taken.

4.4. Third Stage Action: The Ritual of Baptism, Sealing the Rejection of the Old and the Bond with the New (6:3–4)

The idea that the baptizand is not the one actually doing the dying (i.e. that Paul speaks of death in or with Christ on the cross, so envisaging a passive act of being released by Christ's deed) has been very common in scholarship on Romans 6, as the previous part has attempted to show. This derives from the fact that "we died to sin" (v. 2) is followed immediately by the idea of baptism being εἰς τὸν θάνατον αὐτοῦ, "into his death" (v. 3), and from the fact that "death with Christ" dominates the following passage. For this reason, in the next section we consider the water ritual of baptism itself (stage three). In this section we ask what this ritual means for the balance of divine and human action in initiation. How does Paul think that the stage of undergoing the water ritual (stage three) relates to the preceding stage(s)? Is the agency of the believer also present in this ritual, and what is its connection with the saving agency of God (Christ and his death) of the stage one that Paul recapitulates here after a focus on it in Romans 5?

Kuss states: "die in der Taufe ‚im Namen' oder ‚auf den Namen Jesu' begründete Beziehung des Getauften zu Jesus Christus wird bei Paulus in hohem Masse verstärkt und verinnerlicht" (the relationship of the baptized to Jesus Christ, which is found in baptism "in the name" or "in the name of Jesus," is to a great extent strengthened and internalised in Paul).[115] This idea that to undergo the ritual of baptism "establishes relation" is the focus in this section,

---

115. Kuss, *Römerbrief* 1, 308 (specifically about 6:3, 296–97).

and particularly whether this shows that the believer has any agency. Strong states that "Baptism symbolizes the previous entrance of the believer into the communion of Christ's death and resurrection."[116] Though Strong recognizes that the ritual is not the first stage, the issue arises, as Moo points out, because Strong shows merely that "baptism *pictures* what has taken place . . . through conversion."[117] We examine Romans 6 (especially verses 3–4) and try to prove that baptism, like other first-century rituals of sealing entry, meant more than just a picture of the salvation (i.e. of the divine action) that preceded it. In the light of what was noted of initiation in first-century culture (cf. chapter 2) and in Paul's experience (chapter 3), this section seeks to show that in 6:3–4 Paul shows that by the water ritual the Christian initiand pledges to belong to God. To pledge and to belong to God are key ideas in ἐβαπτίσθημεν εἰς Χριστὸν εἰς τὸν θάνατον αὐτοῦ, "we were baptized into Christ, into his death" (v. 3) and show the serious agency of the initiand.

Paul says that Christians cannot go on living in sin (6:2) because they should "remember"[118] that they were "baptized to[119] Christ, to his death," ἐβαπτίσθημεν εἰς Χριστὸν εἰς τὸν θάνατον αὐτοῦ (v. 3). As T. George notes, this shows that in Paul's time baptism is "an act of radical obedience in which a specific renunciation is made and a specific promise is given."[120] This is also Vermes' view when he understands that Paul thinks of baptism as a rite that "binds the Christian to the New Covenant."[121] This act of binding is very personal. Similarly this emphasis on personal agency in baptism appears

---

116. Strong, *Systematic Theology*, 940.

117. Moo, *Romans 1–8*, 378 [italics mine].

118. Fogleman notes that ἢ ἀγνοεῖτεν; (6:3) can be "or do you forget," see "Romans 6:3–14," 296; also *GECNT*, s.v. "γινώσκω"; Jas 5:20, for "remember" as a possible sense.

119. Εἰς (into, to, in) was earlier referred to when we just showed how it is translated. Here we look at its impact on the meaning. There are various uses of εἰς (see *VGT*, s.v. "εἰς"). Because baptism seals the initiation to Christ and means to belong to him, there is idea of "motion to" (so Dunn, *Romans 1–8*, 311) and "advantage." Εἰς as "to" preserves better both ideas. See Kuss: "auf den Namen Jesu" (to the name of Jesus) as a possibility (*Römerbrief*, vol. 1, 308); Schnackenburg: "to Christ" (*Baptism*, 24, 111); Origen speaks of "buried unto Christ through baptism" (from von Balthasar, *Origen: Spirit and Fire*, 340, section 948); Godet: "*en rapport avec* la personne ou le fait indiqué comme regime du εἰς" (in relation to the person or the fact indicated as the regime of εἰς), *Romains*, II, 17.

120. George, "Reformed Doctrine of Believers' Baptism," 243.

121. Vermes, "Baptism and Jewish Exegesis," 308.

with the use of ἐπερώτημα (pledge[122]) in 1 Peter 3:21. The word ἐπερώτημα (pledge) is not used in Romans 6, but as Achtemeier recognizes, Peter's idea is such that "the comparison with Paul's view is inevitable."[123] Focusing on this word, Selwyn notes that "baptism was a seal of contract" and that this shows why this ritual was linked with "*sacramentum*, 'military oath.'"[124] This military oath is a serious recognition of responsibility. A "religious oath" was even more "powerful" according to W. W. Fowler.[125] The ritual that sealed the move from one way of life to another was an oath in which the person concerned had taken the responsibility of "belonging" to the new system.

It makes sense that this is what Paul implies by βαπτισθῆναι εἰς Χριστὸν (to be baptized to Christ), when it is considered that Paul speaks of the ritual that seals entry (stage three), coming next to the liminal and second stage where the initiand dies to (or rejects) sin, a break with sin which itself has happened in response to God's grace and salvation (stage one). To show this, some views are considered from which the structure of our argument in this section will derive.

Ἐβαπτίσθημεν εἰς Χριστὸν εἰς τὸν θάνατον αὐτοῦ, "we were baptized to Christ to his death" (v. 3) has been understood in various ways. Interpreting εἰς as "with reference to," Hartman's view is that βαπτισθῆναι εἰς Χριστὸν (to be baptized to Christ) "was primarily used to qualify the rite and distinguish it from other rites."[126] He thinks (drawing on Thyen) that the idea "distinguishes" Christian baptism from another baptism (i.e. John's baptism).[127] Moo

---

122. *ALGNT*, s.v. "ἐπερώτημα." As to ἅπαξ in the NT, the meaning of this word is under dispute. As Greeven notes, in classical Greek and the LXX the meaning is "request, question, appeal" and in later use (i.e. second-century AD), it took a "diplomatic" sense of "judgement" or "decision" as the verb ἐπερωτάω also became "a technical diplomatic term" with the sense of "to accept the terms of a treaty, to ratify" (Greeven, "ἐρωτάω," in *TDNT*, vol. 2, 687, 688). Thus some have opted for "prayer" and "appeal" as the sense in 1 Pet 3:21 (as shown in the discussion of this word by e.g. Kelly, *Commentary on Peter and Jude*, 162–63; and K. H. Jobes, *1 Peter*, 255). But Greeven's view is that if "prayer" to God is the sense in 1 Pet 3:21, it must have a "legal" connotation, expressing the idea of making a "covenant" with God (Greeven, "ἐρωτάω," 688–689). Following this line, many have opted for the sense of a "pledge" (e.g. Achtemeier, *1 Peter*, 270–271; Jobes, *1 Peter*, 255; Kelly, *Peter and Jude*, 162).

123. Achtemeier, *1 Peter*, 267.

124. Selwyn, *First Epistle of Peter*, 205 [italics his].

125. Fowler, *Religious Experience*, 358.

126. Hartman, "Into the Name," 440.

127. Hartman, 440.

also thinks of this "designating" function,[128] as does Cranfield.[129] But what does "to Christ" in fact mean? When Hartman chooses the "distinguishing" meaning, he resists those who suggest that εἰς Χριστὸν (to Christ) means union and belonging to Christ.[130] He is also resisting Delling's view that in this formula "'the name of Jesus Christ' stands for the salvation accomplished by Jesus Christ and/or the message of that salvation"; and the conclusion is that to "baptize into the name of Jesus Christ" means "to endow someone with the blessed consequences of the salvation brought about by Jesus Christ."[131] But in 6:1–3 Paul is not so much referring to a blessing as reminding of a responsibility that his readers have personally endorsed.

Belonging to Christ has also been considered as a meaning. As Schnackenburg shows, this derives from the fact that βαπτισθῆναι εἰς Χριστὸν (to be baptized to Christ) was connected with the idea that "The naming of a person had the meaning of attaching the baptized to this person so that the baptized belonged to him."[132] Thus Beasley-Murray thinks the ritual was "baptism 'for the sake of' the Lord,"[133] and this meant "appropriation by Him."[134] Many recognize this sense.[135] Sometimes this idea of being Christ's is pushed to the point of seeing εἰς as indicating "union" with him.[136] For

---

128. Moo, *Romans 1–8*, 377.
129. Cranfield, *Romans 1–8*, 301.
130. Hartman, "Into the Name," 440.
131. Delling, cited by Hartman, "Into the Name," 434.
132. Schnackenburg, ref. to 1 Cor 1:12, 13b; 3:23, cf. *Baptism in Thought*, 20, also page 23 concerning εἰς τὸν Μωϋσῆν ἐβαπτίσαντο (1 Cor 10:2).
133. Beasley-Murray, *Baptism*, 102, cf. 100.
134. Beasley-Murray, 102.
135. E.g. Furnish, *Theology and Ethics*, 176–180; Schreiner, *Romans*, 307–308; Bultmann, *Theology of New Testament*, vol. 1, 312; Sanders, *Paul and Palestinian Judaism*, 468; Ridderbos, *Paul*, 403; Kuss, *Römerbrief 1*, 307; Schlier, *Römer*, 192; Leenhardt, *Romains*, 88; Kaylor, *Paul's Covenant Community*, 127, and 124; Dunn, *Romans 1–8*, 311; Wedderburn, *Baptism and Resurrection*, 57–58; Westerholm, *Perspectives Old and New*, 278; G. Barth, *Die Taufe in frühchristlicher Zeit*, 99; Walsh, *Sacraments of Initiation*, 79; Barrett, *Romans*, 122; Moo, *Romans*, 377.
136. It was made more prominent since Heitmüller's idea that "in the name of" was a Hellenistic banking formula led to interpreting εἰς by the locative "into" (cf. W. Heitmüller, cited by Tannehill, *Dying and Rising*, 22 (referring to Heitmüller, *Taufe und Abendmahl*, 9) and εἰς Χριστὸν as meaning "to enter on Christ's account" (cf. Heitmüller, his detailed idea, in Hartman, "Into the Name," 432–433; also in Edwards, *Romans*, 160; Schnackenburg, *Baptism*, 19–20). Many have adopted this view, e.g. Tannehill, *Dying and Rising*, 22; Badke, "Baptized into Moses," 26 (in fact the entire article, 23–29), especially 29 for Rom 6:3; Légasse, "Etre baptisé," 553; Sanday and Headlam, *Romans*, 154.

example, Calvin defines baptism as "notre entrée . . . en lui" and this has the effect of "être faits un avec lui."[137] We do not intend to consider the question of any difference in sense between "belonging" and "union."[138] This study focuses on the idea of being Christ's by baptism, in which the two strands appear woven together.

In the second and third chapters, it was noted that belonging to the new system is the meaning of the ritual that seals entry. Does Paul's thinking on baptism in 6:3–4 as the third stage of entry show this? This section focuses on this first aspect. Also, it was stated earlier that a consideration of 6:3–4 in relation to verses 1–2 suggests that Paul speaks of baptism not so much as signifying a blessing as recalling a responsibility that the Romans have personally endorsed by undergoing this ritual. Is this agency and act of the believer present in what Paul says in 6:3–4 concerning the water ritual (i.e. stage three)? This section will focus on this agency of the initiand.

1) First, we consider whether in the context of transition to a new existence βαπτισθῆναι εἰς Χριστὸν, "to be baptized to Christ" (6:3) means "to become Christ's" just as the ritual of sealing entry means, as our second chapter has shown. The context is of transition to new existence. Origen applies to 6:2–4 Israel's crossing through Moab (Num 21:19–31).[139] Paul's conviction that his readers' baptism to Christ should have ended their relationship with sin shows that the change from one lordship to another (which is the main idea from 5:12) is still Paul's point in 6:3, as some scholars recogize.[140] This aspect is noteworthy. In the second chapter, we showed that by the ritual that forms the entry "climax" (a meaning for baptism too as Dunn recognizes),[141] a first-century person took full responsibility for belonging to the new way of life to which he or she was moving. There is evidence that "to belong to" is also the significance of undergoing the ritual of baptism in this pericope, as it concerns the *passage* from sin to live the Christian way.

---

137. Calvin, *Romains*, 136–137.

138. For more, cf. Barrett, *Romans*, 122; Schreiner, *Romans*, 307; Moo, *Romans*, 377.

139. Balthasar, *Origen: Spirit and Fire*, 300, passage 842.

140. E.g. Tannehill, *Dying and Rising*, 18, also 8, 41–42; Bultmann: "Baptism brings man under the dominion of the Lord," *Theology*, 312; Seeley, *Noble Death*, 108; Moo, *Romans 1–8*, 368–69; Furnish, *Theology and Ethics*, 174; Sanders, *Paul and Palestinian Judaism*, 468; Schreiner, *Romans*, 307.

141. Dunn, *Baptism in Spirit*, 146.

But when εἰς Χριστὸν, "to Christ" (6:3) is explained as meaning "to belong to," an important aspect of a first-century ritual that seals entry needs to be taken into account – namely, that the ritual occupies the third stage of the initiation process and that at this stage the focus is more on the candidate's action than on divine action. This aspect is overlooked when the εἰς (to/into) phrases (v. 3) are seen as one and the same thing as the σύν (with) phrases (vv. 4–8). For example, Tannehill suggests both unity and "belonging to."[142] To justify this, he suggests that baptism εἰς Χριστὸν εἰς τὸν θάνατον αὐτοῦ (that is, baptism to Christ, to his death) "must be understood in the same way" as buried σύν, "with" (v. 4) and united together (cf. σύμφυτοι, v. 5).[143] Also Schreiner (on the phrase εἰς τὸ ὄνομα Χριστοῦ, "to/into the name of Christ")[144] suggests that "those who are baptized belong to Christ and are united with him."[145] To account for this, he points to the fact that "'with (σύν) Christ' expressions permeate verses 4–8."[146] Likewise Kaylor considers that "all the prepositional phrases by which Paul expresses relationship between Christ and the believer [he refers to 'in,' 'into,' 'with,' 'according to,' and 'through'] . . . are equivalent to 'belonging to' Christ."[147]

Though these words show relationship with Christ, in Romans 6:3–10 Paul uses εἰς (to, into) and σύν (with) with nuance. As baptism is the ritual of entry, βαπτίζεσθαι εἰς Χριστὸν εἰς τὸν θάνατον αὐτοῦ, "to be baptized to Christ, to his death" (v. 3) is best seen as referring to the third stage of initiation; thus the focus rests on the candidate. The "σύν Christ" (with Christ) language points primarily to divine action (as we showed earlier with "death to sin"). Verses 2 and 3 make one cluster and 6–10 another. The difference is that verse 3 (in line with v. 2) focuses on the baptizand's act of submitting to the initatory

---

142. This is the idea when Tannehill sees "baptism into Christ" as to "enter Christ" and "to share in Christ," cf. *Dying and Rising*, 22.

143. Tannehill, *Dying and Rising*, 22.

144. There is dispute over its equivalence with εἰς Χριστρὸν, "to/into Christ" (for more on this, Wedderburn, *Baptism and Resurrection*, 57; Dunn, *Romans 1–8*, 311). E.g. Dunn sees a difference (cf. Dunn's idea in our literature survey). But as Wilckens shows, many consider these phrases to be synonymous (cf. *Der Brief an die Römer 6–11*, 48). We treat them as synonymous in this study.

145. Schreiner, *Romans*, 307.

146. Schreiner, 307.

147. Kaylor, *Paul's Covenant Community*, 127.

ritual, an act of taking full responsibility for belonging to Christ's way of life.[148] But the "with Christ" verses (6–8) focus on what Christ has done. Verses 4–5 are a junction between the two clusters because, as we want to show, these two verses describe "death" as the key factor of moving to the new existence, a factor which Christ and the believer share (for this reason the sign 4/5 is used in the explanation that follows). For clarity, this chart is proposed [On the chart we deliberately leave out verses 1 and 11, though the idea of death spans verses 1 to 11. These two verses are left out simply because death is first expressed as such in verse 2 – not in 1 – and 11 recapitulates verse 2].

A-B (2–4/5): DEATH AND MOVE TO NEW REALM
(Focus: on the Believer)[149]

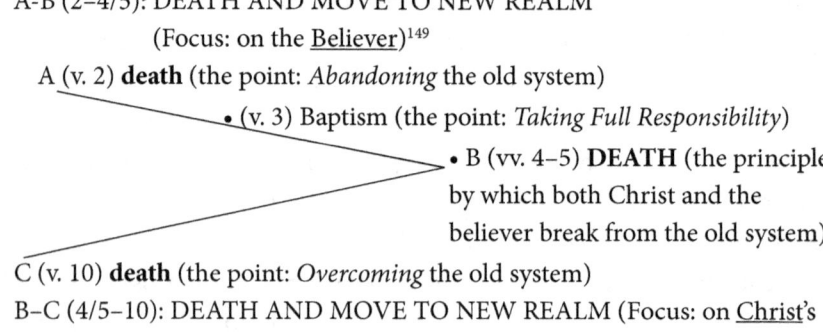

A (v. 2) **death** (the point: *Abandoning* the old system)
• (v. 3) Baptism (the point: *Taking Full Responsibility*)
• B (vv. 4–5) **DEATH** (the principle by which both Christ and the believer break from the old system)
C (v. 10) **death** (the point: *Overcoming* the old system)
B–C (4/5–10): DEATH AND MOVE TO NEW REALM (Focus: on Christ's action)[150]

---

148. The Liddell-Scott-Jones Greek-English Lexicon shows that, among various meanings of εἰς, this preposition can sometimes "express relation," including the relation "of a dedication," see LSJ 1940, s.v. "εἰς or ἐς", https://outils.biblissima.fr/en/eulexis-web/index.php, accessed on 15 July 2021. In line with our argumentation, the sense of a personal dedication is good option. That is, by undergoing baptism εἰς Χριστὸν (to Christ), the candidate decides personally to belong to Christ. In the same way some scholars have also understood εἰς as it stands in Rom 6:3. Examples (though their purpose was not primarily to show how in εἰς Χριστὸν lies the baptizand's own decision) include Schnackenburg who, commenting on Rom 6:3, thinks that "The naming of a person had the meaning of attaching the baptized to this person [Christ] so that the baptized belonged to him" (Schnackenburg, *Baptism in Thought*, 20). Similarly, Beasley-Murray states, "Baptism in the name of the Lord Jesus . . . was in the earliest time a baptism 'for the sake of' the Lord" (see his *Baptism in New Testament*, 102, also 100); in other words, the person is "sealed as the Lord's in baptism" (*Baptism in New Testament*, 96). For the same interpretation, see also Leenhardt, *L'épître aux Romains*, 88; Kaylor, *Paul's Covenant Community*, 127, also 124; Dunn, *Romans 1–8*, 311; Wedderburn, *Baptism and Resurrection*, 57–58; and Schreiner, *Romans*, 307–308.

149. Cf. Leenhardt, *Romains*, 92.
150. Leenhardt, *Romains*, 92.

What this chart shows fits into the framework of stages one to three of initiation. The believer's action in the transition process is the focus in verses 2–4/5 (A–B). Bultmann hints at this when he says that the believer's initiation is related to "the salvation-occurrence" but "special reference is to him [the baptized]."[151] We focus first on verses 2 and 3 (4/5 is considered separately because of its link with both clusters). Death to sin (v. 2) refers to the fact that change to the new existence involves the person's death to the old way (stage 2). As our analysis of "death to sin" has shown, this "death" is the radical choice "when we took the decisive step and became Christians."[152] This strong choice occurs during the transition "before" baptism (cf. Tertullian),[153] when the person is between the two existences (cf. *Didache*).[154] But the transition process culminates in the ritual by which the person shows a serious choice and decision, taking full responsibility to belong to the new way (stage 3). Baptism (v. 3) refers to that ceremony.[155] Thus verses 2–3 focus on the believer, and what the believer is doing in the process of changing to new life.

The beginning of the transition process is due to divine action (stage one). As T. George notes, what we have just said of verses 2–3 is part of the entry, but follows as "a response to what God has done."[156] That is, as Bultmann points out, all that the transition implies is based on "Christ's death" and the fact that his act "is the means of release from the powers of this age."[157] This shows why to "declare" full attachment to the liberator is part of the process, and the rite constitutes just such a step.[158] Paul focuses on this saving act of

---

151. Bultmann, *Theology of New Testament*, 312.

152. Sanday and Headlam, *Romans*, 154.

153. Tertullian: "We are not baptized so that we may cease committing sin but because we have ceased, since we are already clean of heart," cf. *On Penance* 6; also Ridderbos: the "choice of faith that attends and precedes it [baptism]," *Paul*, 411.

154. Referred to earlier in chapter 2.

155. E.g. Morris, *Romans*, 246; Moo, *Romans 1–8*, 376, also 371; Godet, *Romains* II, 17; Dunn interprets baptism here as that of the Spirit rather than of water ("Birth of Metaphor," 174), but the context of initiation suggests a physical event.

156. George, "Reformed Doctrine," 243.

157. Bultmann, *Theology of New Testament*, 99–100.

158. Badke: baptism is to "declare allegiance," cf. "Baptized into Moses," 25, 28–29.

Christ in 6:4/5–10.[159] In this part he is explaining that the believer is "able"[160] to abandon the life of sin (v. 2) and declare full attachment to Christ (v. 3) because Christ's act which *overcomes* sin (v. 10) [C] guarantees freedom (v. 6, 18). Paul has already spoken of this saving action in 5:12–21; but he returns to it because "death" is the gateway for both Christ (cf. v. 10)[161] and the believer in their *passage* to new existence.[162] It is a principle they share.

This sharing of the same principle is what B (vv. 4/5) is about.[163] As we want to show, the thing shared is "a death," that is, "la notion de mort" (the concept of death)[164] or, as Leenhart states, "une similitude de sa mort, i.e. une mort semblable à la sienne" (a similitude of his death, i.e. a death similar to his)[165] (cf. 6:5, τῷ ὁμοιώματι τοῦ θανάτου αὐτοῦ, "in a death like his," RSV[166]). Stuhlmacher speaks of this share in a different way when he states that "baptism in the name of Christ Jesus . . . gives one a share in Jesus' death 'for our sins,' in his burial . . ."[167] Though this is a popular idea,[168] the sharing in Christ's acts "precedes" baptism.[169] Christ's death and resurrection are divine acts by which people are saved (5:6, 8–9, 18; esp. 3:24–25, cf. 6:13, 18), and Christians share in them at salvation,[170] that is, when God's grace overflows to us and saves us (as we showed earlier, cf. stage one). In 6:4–5 what is shared is the idea and experience of dying to a system, an idea and experience that the believer (A–B) and Christ (B–C) have in common (cf. also v. 7).

---

159. So Viard (on v. 6 instead of vv. 4–5), *Romains*, 144; and Feuillet, "Le plan salvifique," 364 fn. 2.

160. Edwards, *Romans*, 164; and Byrne: that 6:14 reminds of this "capacity" offered by grace in Christ, cf. Byrne, "Living out Righteousness," 564.

161. In fact, v. 10 shows that Paul sees Christ also going through a liminal stage and the act of dying as its feature and then moving to belonging to God, a feature of the third stage.

162. So Calvin, *Romains*, 139.

163. Cf. Esler, *Conflict and Identity*, 213.

164. Godet, *Romains* II, 19.

165. Leenhardt, *Romains*, 92.

166. Also Chrysostom, *Baptismal Instruction* 10.10, Trans. from Bray, *Romans*, 152.

167. Stuhlmacher, *Romans*, 91.

168. Some using "participation," e.g. Schweitzer, *Mysticism of Paul*, 117; Sanders, *Paul and Palestinian Judaism*, 467–68; Beasley-Murray, *Baptism*, 130, 144, 287; Kaylor, *Paul's Covenant*, 124.

169. Cranfield, *Romans 1–8*, 303; McRay, *Paul, His Life*, 407; Godet, *Romains* II, 18; Kreitzer, "Baptism in Pauline Epistles," 78.

170. Cf. Strong's view noted earlier; also Flemington, *New Testament Doctrine*, 109; Beasley-Murray, *Baptism*, 140.

As some scholars have noted, "death" (cf. A, B, C) is the key idea in verses 1–10.[171] Paul's main point is that death, as the gate to the new existence, concerns both Christ and the believer, and this is centred in 6:4–5 which forms a bridge between A–B and B–C. The sharing in death consists of two aspects. First, the believer's radical *rejection* of sin (A) is "a death" (v. 2) just as Christ's decisive act against sin (C) is his own death (vv. 6, 10).[172] The second aspect is the purpose. By this personal act of death to the old way (A) believers pass into belonging to Christ, who died to save them (v. 3) and this leads into living for God (v. 4). Also by a death, his own death, Christ (C) passed into a new state (vv. 7, 9–10). From "the sphere over which sin exercises its tyranny"[173] and from the life of scorn and shame, he changed into glory (6:4; cf. Phil 2:7–11).[174] So, there is an idea of "identification" with Christ, as Haacker suggests, but not (contra Haacker) an identification which rests simply on the fact of "having taken part in" his death.[175] What Paul implies is more than having been spiritually with him in his death. As Godet states, the identification consists in the fact that our death is "cette mort à laquelle nous a conduits la foi en sa mort" (that death to which faith in his death has led us).[176] In other words, "La mort au péché a bien lieu . . . à la ressemblance et sur le modèle de la mort de la croix" (Death to sin does take place . . . in the likeness and model of the death on the cross).[177]

This idea of identification intertwines with "belonging" to Christ. To die to sin entails turning to God and belonging fully to him (6:1–2, 6–7, 10–13, 18–19). This appears especially in the expression ζάω τῷ θεῷ (to live for God) and applies to both Christ (v. 10) and the believer (vv. 11, and 4). We will touch on this more in the next section, where we consider the idea that the new way of life is embraced within the initiation process.

2) The second point as referred to earlier is whether the agency and act of the believer is present in what Paul says in 6:3–4 concerning the water

---

171. Of vv. 1–11: e.g. Edwards, *Romans*, 58; Sabou, *Horror and Hope*, 1, 57; of vv. 1–13: e.g. Morris, *Romans*, 247.

172. For this comparison, Furnsish, *Theology and Ethics*, 172.

173. Westerholm, *Understanding Paul*, 108.

174. A common idea in the apostolic kerygma, cf. Luke 24:26; Heb 12:2; 1 Pet 1:11.

175. Haacker, *Theology of Romans*, 64–65.

176. Godet, *Romains* II, 18–19.

177. Godet, 26.

ritual (i.e. stage three). The last section has sought to explore how the idea of belonging to Christ is connected with undergoing the ritual of baptism. Does "to belong to" give a sense that to undergo the water ritual is to take a responsibility, as far as what Paul says in 6:3–4 is concerned?

We note that when baptism εἰς Χριστὸν (to Christ) is referred to in scholarly discussion, the terms used tend to suggest a passive state. For example, the word "transfer" denotes this. As Hartman shows, the connection of εἰς Χριστὸν (to Christ) with bank accounts "led to the interpretation that . . . the baptized person was transferred"[178]; or was "entered upon Christ's account," as Edwards puts it.[179] This suggests passivity, and this idea that the water ritual expresses such a "transfer" is adopted by many.[180] Clearly the agency of the baptizand is not the focus when Bultmann states that in baptism "the individual is taken into the 'body of Christ.'"[181] Likewise the agency of the initiand is not apparent when Godet states that by baptism "ils ont été consacrés à Christ" (they were consectrated to Christ).[182] Here the baptizand is acted upon, rather than acting.

Though the passive verbs ἐβαπτίσθημεν, "we were baptized" (v. 3) and συνετάφημεν, "we were buried with" (v. 4) point to the role of God (or his minister),[183] divine action is less Paul's focus in 6:3. The focus on what God does (stage one) precedes the ritual (stage three). For example, Tertullian shows this to his catechumens when he tells them that having "been in contact with the Lord" is their "first baptism" which "cleans the heart" and allows them to take the rite with "perfect fear."[184] In line with Tertullian's emphasis, we suggest that the action of the believer appears to be more what the ritual of baptism in 6:3–4 is about.

---

178. Hartman, "Into the Name," 432.

179. Edwards, *Romans*, 160.

180. Sanders, *Paul and Palestinian Judaism*, 468; Käsemann, *Romans*, 165; Tannehill, *Dying and Rising*, 18.

181. Bultmann, *Theology of New Testament*, 311.

182. Godet, *Romains* II, 17; for similar passive ideas, Schnackenburg e.g. speaks of "attaching the baptized to" (cf. *Baptism in Thought of Paul*, 20); and Beasley-Murray states that the person "is sealed as the Lord's" (cf. *Baptism in New Testament*, 96).

183. Attention on God and his minister, e.g. Ambrose of Milan, *On the Sacraments* 1.6, cited by Finn, *Early Christian Baptism: Italy*, 63.

184. Tertullian, *On Penance* 6.

Cranfield is among those who recognize this when he states that baptism εἰς τὸν θάνατον αὐτοῦ (to his death) means "a pledge on the believer's side."[185] What he does not spell out is how this applies to Romans 6:3. Similarly, Sanday and Headlam hint at an active baptizand when they comment (on 6:3) that the Christian "enters into a relation to Him [Christ]."[186] Vermes uses similar words when he states that "the Christian, by means of baptism, entered into the New Covenant."[187] But they all move on without evidence on how such action truly appears in 6:3.

As the second chapter has outlined, in the culture of Paul's time, by undergoing the ritual that sealed entry, the initiand was pledging to a new community and its god, and was fully assuming the responsibility of belonging to this group and this deity and their system. If Paul was influenced by contemporary initiatory patterns (cf. our first chapter), then he will instinctively have thought that the water ritual is about such a pledge, about making a serious commitment to belonging to Christ and his system. He appears to show this.

However, as mentioned earlier, Paul does not use a word that specifically means "pledge." Here one might have expected to see for instance ἐπερνώτημα as in Peter. Paul does not use it. But his line of thought in verses 1–3 suggests that he has in mind just the kind of responsibility[188] that this word implies. By an emphatic "never" (μὴ γένοιτο) Paul reminds the Romans of the serious incompatibility of living in sin, because not only did they die to it in one stage of their initiatory move, but also they underwent the ritual. There is a strong sense that there was something they personally did in this ritual, something which was seriously binding upon them. Paul does not specify it, but the contemporary initiatory process makes it clear that the pledge made before God and the church is in his mind.

Ἀγνοεῖτε, "you are ignorant" (v. 3) seems important to consider in relation to this. Ἀγνοέω simply means "to be ignorant of" or "uninformed about,"[189] just the fact of being unaware of something (as Paul uses it in Romans 1:13). This is the meaning when Abimelech claims innocence of "not knowing"

---

185. Cranfield, *Romans*, 303.
186. Sanday and Headlam, *Romans*, 154.
187. Vermes, "Baptism and Jewish Exegesis," 319.
188. Giving attention to this, e.g. Morris, *Romans*, 246.
189. *GELNT-OECL*, s.v. "ἀγνοέω."

that Sarah was Abraham's sister (using the same verb, Gen 20:4, LXX). But it can mean "to forget" what is known,[190] i.e. to disregard (e.g. τῶν ἠγνοημένων, "things ignorantly done," in 2 Macc 11:31, LXX). One example in the Old Testament is when Israel acts "in ignorance unwillingly" (ἀγνοήσῃ ἀκουσίως) but actually doing what they already know to be something forbidden by the Lord, καὶ ποιήσωσι μίαν ἀπὸ πασῶν τῶν ἐντολῶν Κυρίου, ἣ οὐ ποιηθήσεται, "and should they do one thing forbidden of any of the commads of the Lord, which ought not to be done" (Lev 4:13, LXX; cf. Sir 28:7). Also ἠγνοήσαμεν, "we were ignorant," is used (Num 12:11, LXX) where in fact the sin of Aaron and Miriam is deliberate jealousy towards Moses's position and clear xenophobia against the Ethiopian woman (vv. 1–2).[191] These instances point towards a kind of "deliberate forgetting". Such a connotation is not absent in Paul. In fact, used with οὐ, "not" (e.g. 2 Cor 2:11), it means to "know very well" or to "be well aware."[192] This is why ἀγνοέω (to be ignorant) can be associated with "foolishness."[193]

To forget what is well known is very likely the idea in 6:3 (though used without οὐ).[194] There are two possible reasons. First, the radical negative answer (v. 2) indicates that they are forgetting something they should not (cf. also Rom 7:1). Second, in fact such inattention to things that must not be ignored is what ἀγνοέω stands for, as Bultmann shows:

> As in γινώσκειν (to know) . . . the practical element in this knowledge can be more or less strongly emphasised, Romans 10:3 making it plain that ignorance is also disobedience. In the OT sense such ἀγνοεῖν (to be ignorant) is not merely "lack of information," which is excusable, but a "misunderstanding" which stands under the ὀργή (anger) of God . . .[195]

---

190. *GEL*, s.v. "ἀγνοέω." cf. association of "forgetfulness" and "ignorance," λήθης καὶ ἀγνοίας οὐ δεσπόζει; "is it not master of forgetfulness and ignorance?" (4 Macc 1:5; 2:24).

191. Comp. Wis 14:22.

192. *GEL*, s.v. "ἀγνοέω"; *GELNT-OECL*, s.v. "ἀγνοέω."

193. 1 Sam 26:21, LXX: μεματαίωμαι καὶ ἠγνόηκα πολλὰ σφόδρα, "I have been foolish and have erred exceedingly." Cf. also Wis 13:1 (RSV).

194. Bultmann: "the οὐ form corresponding to the ἢ οὐκ οἴδατε . . . and (ἢ) ἀγνοεῖτε." Cf. ἀγνοέω, ἀγνόημα, ἄγνοια, ἀγνωσία, ἄγνωστος, *TDNT* vol. 1, 116.

195. Bultmann, "ἀγνοέω," 116.

There is something serious related to their baptism which does not sanction any involvement with sin again. As Luther notes, what Paul means is "vous ne devez pas ignorer."[196] This serious thing is the responsibility when they pledged to belong to Christ's way (v. 3). As Badke also thinks, by the question "ἀγνοεῖτε;" (are you ignorant?), Paul's point is: "Are you unaware that . . . you declared yourselves loyal servants of Christ by baptism . . ."[197] This declaration is present in 6:1–3 even though Paul uses no word that shows it directly.

To sum up our argument, the rite of baptism means belonging to Christ. Considering this against the background of first-century initiation assumptions, Paul will have thought of this dimension of baptism as primarily being an action of the baptizand. This study argues that in Romans 6:3 Paul focuses on the believer and sees the person who undergoes this ritual as taking the responsibility of belonging to God. By this Paul's idea of belonging to Christ is important, because the believer belongs to God not only by Christ's act (stage one) but also by personally and publicly declaring him or herself so to belong, through the ritual (stage three). In other words, this status of belonging to God incorporates both divine and human agency. Believers are, in the first place, brought to God by Christ's death and in the moment when by his grace they encounter him and are reconciled with God (5:1–2, 10–11).[198] People belong to God by this divine act, the moment of encounter in the first stage of the Christian's transition.[199] When Paul's focus is still on God's saving action (stage one), he shows that people become children of Abraham when they believe (Rom 4:16–17) and receive the life given by God (v. 18; comp. 5:12–21). This first idea of belonging to God rests on Christ's act.[200]

But the fact of belonging to God is repeated by baptism, and there the believer undertakes the action as this section has shown. Godet speaks of the idea that to belong to God is by Christ's death, and then about baptism he

---

196. Luther, *MLO* vol. 11, 86.

197. Badke, "Baptized into Moses," 29.

198. The idea that Christ's death wins believers to God is recurrent in Paul (cf. 1 Cor 1:13; 3:16, 23; 6:19–20; also Rom 14:7–9; 2 Cor 5:15, 18; Eph 1:5, 10, 14).

199. *Contra* Basil's idea that it is baptism which makes to be "children of God," cf. Basil, *Baptism*, cited by Ferguson, *Baptism in Early Church*, 585; also Cyril of Alexandria, cited by Finn, *Early Christian Baptism: Italy*, 224.

200. Focusing on this, e.g. Godet, *Romains* II, 17; also Dunn, "Birth of Metaphor," 174.

states "c'est là ce que constate le baptême."[201] This means that baptism is just a symbol that reflects what happens before it, as in Strong's idea to which we referred earlier.[202] For Paul baptism makes concrete this idea of being God's. The water ritual is the stage whereby to belong to God is a responsibility personally taken.[203] This is the nature of a ritual that seals entry in Paul's time. This agency of the initiand in baptism is downplayed by Ridderbos when he states that "baptism according to its nature is an activity of God and on the part of God."[204]

This section has rested its focus on whether the third stage of initiation – the ritual that seals initiation and the initiand's pledge that it expresses – is present in Romans 5–6. The fourth stage of initiation, as referred to in chapter 1, concerns the fact that the new life that the person is going to live, as a member of a new community, is embraced during initiation. The next section focuses on whether this too is present in Paul's thinking, and especially whether this also shows evidence that the Christian transition encompasses both divine and human agency.

4.5. Fourth Stage: The After-Entry Life Embraced in the Transition Process

N. T. Wright notes a link between baptism and the new life when he understands "passing through the water of baptism as the sign of and means of leaving behind the old life and beginning the new."[205] This expresses that action is taken. However, Wright does not explain what this action really means. This section intends to argue that the new life of the Christian is embraced in the transition process, instead of being something that follows as a consequence after baptism.

---

201. Godet, *Romains* II, 17, translation: "that is what baptism confirms"; and Käsemann uses the word "projection," *Romans*, 163.

202. So also Cuvillier, "Baptême chrétien," 167.

203. E.g. Schlatter: "it demanded a definite act," *Church in New Testament*, 26; also Kaylor, *Paul's Covenant*, 123–24; Beasley-Murray, *Baptism*, 100–101, 286–287; Dunn, *Baptism in Spirit*, 145; *Theology of Paul*, 447.

204. Ridderbos, *Paul*, 412.

205. Wright, *Surprised by Hope*, 240.

In the previous sections, consideration has been given to how much Paul's thinking in Romans 5–6 shows the agency of God in the first stage of the transition from sin to God (cf. Romans 5) and the agency of the Christian initiand in the liminal death of the second stage (cf. 6:1–2) and in the water ritual or the third stage when commitment was sealed (cf. 6:3–4). The next section considers whether the idea that the new life begins in initiation is also present in Romans 6, and whether this also shows human agency responding to God's act.

Our contention is that the fourth stage ideas are found in Romans 6, but some are also drawn from Romans 5. Four aspects are considered in this section. (1) The idea that the believer is to "reign" (cf. 5:17) is considered in this study as one aspect of the new life of the person concerned by the move from sin to God. The intention is to show that from the initiatory presuppositions of Paul's context, he will have understood this as a responsibility that the Christian takes and starts to fulfil since their transition process. Hence as we will see, it is not eschatological future that Paul has in mind, in βασιλεύσουσιν and in other future verbs in Romans 5:12–6:23. The initiatory future that was referred to in the second chapter appears here also. (2) We also focus on Paul's idea that "righteousness" is the means for the reign of grace (cf. 5:21). The purpose is to show that, if Paul is thinking in line with the contemporary initiatory pattern, this has to be the righteous living of stage four, i.e. an act of the believer that comes as a response to the saving act of God (stage one). It should be noted that "righteousness" is connected with "reign" which (point (1) above) is considered as focusing on the believer's action. (3) The ideas of "walking in newness of life" (cf. 6:4) and (4) the slave motif (cf. 6:6, 10–11, 13–23) are also considered, to see whether they express aspects of the new life, conceived as a responsibility taken during initiation and in response to the act of God.

4.5.1. βασιλεύσουσιν (5:17) and Initiatory Future in Romans 5:12–6:23

Paul speaks of the transition from sin to God and says clearly that those who believe are to "reign" (βασιλεύσουσιν, 5:17). Our intention is to understand whether Paul speaks of an aspect of the new life into which the transition leads. This section seeks to show that from the initiatory presuppositions of Paul's background, in all likelihood he would have considered this as a responsibility taken by the believer and initiated during the process of transition (stage four). In other words, one aspect of this section is to understand whether it fits better to see this as eschatological future. Hence two elements are considered in this section: 1) Attention is given to evidence that "to reign" (5:17) entails a responsible act performed by the believer in their transition. To reign is part of the way of life that the believer endorses during initiation, not later on. 2) building on this, we consider the nature of the future tense in βασιλεύσουσιν (with other future verbs in 5:12–6:23). In the light of what we have discovered so far, we would expect Paul to emphasise the real change in people's lives right now, not (just) some eschatological transformation.

The first aspect is to ask whether Paul has in mind the agency of the Christian in their transition. Sometimes βασιλεύσουσιν (they will reign) has been interpreted without attention to any link with the action that takes place during the transitional process from sin to God. Effectively this makes "reign" God's act. But Paul focuses on believers (cf. οἱ . . . λαμβάνοντες, "those who receive [grace]"). In other words, what Paul sees as a human act of the fourth stage has typically been seen as a divine act.

In Romans 5:15–17, Paul speaks of divine action (stage one) and then moves to speak of "reign" as one aspect of the life the Christian starts to live from initiation onwards. Paul says that God has given his grace abundantly (5:15) and that people who receive it "reign in life" (οἱ . . . λαμβάνοντες ἐν ζωῇ βασιλεύσουσιν, "those who receive [it] will reign in life," 5:17). The future βασιλεύσουσιν (they will reign), which will be considered in the next point, has led many to project into an eschatological future any idea of reign for the believer. As a consequence the "reigning" action is linked with God. For example, Wilckens recognizes that Paul speaks of Christians in 5:17 when he states, "die λαμβάνοντες sind also die Christen, 'wir' (the λαμβάνοντες [those who receive grace] are therefore the Christians, 'we' [referring to v. 10 for the 'we'])."[206] But then he states, "Aber *die Christen* sehen ihrer eigenen vollendeten Teilhabe an dieser Herrschaft als ihrer Zukunft entgegen." (But Christians look to their own perfect participation in this reign as their future.)[207] For Wilkens the reign of believers – "their part" – is still in the future. But Paul says that the transition from sin to grace is such that grace reigns (5:21). Who

---

206. Wilckens, *Römer 1–5*, 325.
207. Wilckens, 325 [italics his].

is involved in this reign? As the second chapter has shown, in initiation the initiand embraces the new way of life. As Paul is speaking of a transition to new life, the initiation assumptions of contemporary culture will have inclined him towards thinking that what is embraced in initiation is a contemporary way of life, not an eschatological hope.

There are elements which show that Paul indeed thinks of "to reign" as an aspect of the new life of the believer, and that Paul sees its beginning in initiation as an immediate result and response to the saving act of God. A consideration of the connection between βασιλεύσουσιν, "they will reign" (v. 17) and βασιλεύσῃ, "it might reign" (v. 21) is illuminating on this point. Scholars stress a difference of subjects,[208] and of epochs.[209] This is the believer's act in both verses, although grammatically believers play the role in 5:17 and grace does it in 5:21. The reason is that for Paul the believer's reign is also the reign of grace, and *vice versa*. What is said of believers in 5:17 is actually the act of grace. As Wilckens recognizes, it is "Der Herrschaftsantritt *der Gnade*" (The coming to power *of grace*).[210] Those who reign are οἱ τὴν περισσείαν τῆς χάριτος λαμβάνοντες, i.e. those who have accepted (Godet, "qui prennent," "who take")[211] God's grace. As B. Dickson puts it, this is a reign of "les graciés" (the pardoned).[212]

This illustrates the direct, consequential relationship between God's action and the initiand's action, as this study has continued to show. In 5:16 and 18 the repeated preposition εἰς (to, into) appears to express this sense of consequence. Εἰς here means "to become, to result in";[213] it shows the idea of passing from one state to another. As Segond translates, the free gift of Christ "deviant," "becomes", (εἰς) justification.[214] This is clarified in verse 18. The sequence is such that from a state of death in which the person is met by

---

208. Believers in v. 17 and grace in v. 21, e.g. Viard, *Romains*, 140; Dunn, *Romans 1–8*, 287; Murray, *Romans*, 209.

209. As eschatological future in v. 17 but present future in v. 21 or vice versa, e.g. Stuhlmacher, *Romans*, 87, 88; Viard, *Romains*, 138, 140.

210. Wilckens, *Römer 1–5*, 325 [italics his].

211. Godet, *Romains*, 467; similar to "to take in the hand, to take on one's self," cf. *ALGNT*, s.v. "λαμβάνω."

212. Dickson, *Romains*, 123, chart and fn.14 (though less academic work).

213. *ALGNT*, s.v. "εἰς."

214. Translation of SB/LS, Rom 5:16.

God, Christ's justification *"donne","*makes", (εἰς) to live.²¹⁵ The act of reigning (v. 17) is in line with this notion of "resulting in" that we find in verses 16 and 18. As Jewett points out, "Christ's event brought an overwhelming victory of grace [. . .]."²¹⁶ Also as Sabou states "if the king is victorious his people is free";²¹⁷ they pass into the state of reigning. The point here is that in Paul's thinking, βασιλεύσουσιν (they will reign) refers to the present life that the Christian initiate lives, the life which began within and from the time of transition from sin to God.

This leads us to our second point, which is to ask whether Paul could have thought of using βασιλεύσουσιν (they will reign) here (and other future verbs in our pericope)²¹⁸ as expressing an eschatological future.²¹⁹ As mentioned earlier, if Paul is thinking in the initiation patterns of first-century religious life, we would expect that he will have seen this reign of the Christian initiand at least as beginning in their present life. As chapter 2 has shown, the new life begins in initiation and goes on after it; it does not await another time.

Among the scholars who consider this as the reign of the believer, there are at least two lines of interpretation in relation to whether it means a present or an eschatological future. One strand are those who see βασιλεύσουσιν, "they will reign" (v. 17) as eschatological and βασιλεύσῃ "it might reign" (v. 21) as present future or *vice versa*. For example, Stuhlmacher thinks that βασιλεύσουσιν points to the time when "the promise from Daniel 7:18, pronounced by Jesus to his disciples (in Lk. 12:32; 22:28–30), will be fulfilled for them in that they will judge the world with the Son of Man, Jesus Christ, and share in his reign (cf. 1 Cor 6:2; 15:23; Rev 20:4)."²²⁰ This view is adopted by others.²²¹ On the other hand, when he turns to βασιλεύσῃ, "it might reign"

---

215. Translation of SB/LS, Rom 5:18.

216. Jewett, *Romans*, 389.

217. Sabou, *Between Horror and Hope*, 140. The idea is noted in 6:7–10; cf. also Dunn, *Romans 1–8*, 287–288.

218. Other future verbs are κατασταθήσονται, "they will be made" (5:19), ἐσόμεθα, "we will be" (6:5), συζήσομεν, "we will live with" (6:8), οὐ κυριεύσει, "it will not have dominion" (6:14).

219. This is often the view, and reference is made to texts where "to reign" is clearly eschatological, such as, Pauline: 1 Cor 6:2; 15:23–58; Johannine: Rev 20:4–15; and Lukan: Luke 12:32; 22:28–30; cf. Viard, *Romains*, 138; Stuhlmacher, *Romans*, 87.

220. Stuhlmacher, *Romans*, 87.

221. Schlatter: "The future tense of *basileusousin* points to what will take place in the revelation of Christ" (cf. *Romans*, 131); Dunn: Christians "are receiving grace, but they are not

(v. 21), Stuhlmacher thinks of the present time as he states that "Christians who believe in Jesus as their reconciler and Lord have received reconciliation and stand under the reign of the grace of God."[222] Stuhlmacher does not explain how this difference of epochs applies for a person who is moving from sin's rule to a new system, an idea that he recognizes to be on Paul's mind.[223] Viard handles these verbs in a similar way.[224]

A second strand recognize this reign to mean the present life both for βασιλεύσουσιν, "they will reign" (v. 17) and βασιλεύσῃ, "it might reign" (v. 21). For example, Käsemann's view is that, since God granted righteousness, "the rule of God has dawned for "the many" as the new world."[225] This is also Wilckens' idea when, on 5:17, he says "Der Herrschaftsantritt *der Gnade* ist erfolgt" (The taking on of power by grace is successful),[226] although in the next instance he thinks the actor is God, as mentioned earlier. Jewett also lays stress on a present future. Drawing on Brandenburger,[227] on 5:21 he states, "Since it was the Christ's event that brought the overwhelming victory of grace, the reign of sin ended there and the new reign of grace began."[228] Jewett grants that βασιλεύσουσιν, "they will reign" (v. 17) is widely understood as pointing to the eschaton, but maintains "the reference to 'life'" that is connected with this verb "might imply its force in the immediate future as well."[229] Others who strongly recognize the present in this use of the future include Osborne,[230] Esler,[231] Murray[232] and Ziesler.[233] While all concur with the idea that in Romans 5–6 Paul speaks of the transition from the rule of sin to the rule of God, less focus has rested on how the notion of passing from one

---

reigning" and Paul speaks "of a still future inheritance of the kingdom" (cf. *Romans 1–8*, 282. Dunn lists other supporters of this view).

222. Stuhlmacher, *Romans*, 88.
223. When he speaks of "baptism as a change in lordship," Stuhlmacher, *Romans*, 100.
224. Viard, *Romains*, 138, 140.
225. Käsemann, *Romans*, 157–58.
226. Wilckens, *Römer 1–5*, 325 [italics his].
227. Ref. to Brandenburger, *Adam und Christus*, 254.
228. Jewett, *Romans*, 389.
229. Jewett, 384.
230. Osborne, *Romans*, 143–44.
231. Esler, *Conflict and Identity*, 202.
232. Murray, *Romans*, 198.
233. Ziesler, *Romans*, 150.

religious existence to another might affect our choice of a present or eschatological future for this act of reigning. Against the initiatory background of his time, one would certainly expect that Paul would mean the present time.

The change from one system of life to another leads the candidate directly into the new way, as our second chapter has shown. Does Paul's thinking in Romans 5–6 fit in this? In 5:21 Paul says that the new system of existence has already taken place. As Viard notes, the reign of grace is already "*inauguré par la révélation de justice de Dieu en Jésus Christ et la justification présente des croyants*" (*inaugurated* by the revelation of God's righteousness in Jesus Christ and the *present* justification of believers).[234] Sin's rule has ended (cf. the aorist ἐβασίλευσεν ἡ ἁμαρτία, "sin reigned"). Grace has taken over; its reign is a present reality. Similarly βασιλεύσουσιν (they will reign) should be seen as predictive but starting with the present, that is, this action of "reigning" is one that will continue in the future, but it has already started at the moment that Paul is writing.[235] It falls in the "progressive" category that Wallace mentions.[236] As we noted earlier with Käsemann and Wilckens, from the time God's grace offered righteousness, the rule of God has started and will continue.[237] In fact, it will continue for ever[238] (cf. 1 Cor 15:24–25 about its everlastingness). Paul's idea is shaped by the patterns of initiation. As the second chapter outlined, in initiation the candidate embraces what the new life is about, begins to live it while still undergoing the process, but will live it much more in the future as a full member. Osborne summarises this when he states, "life reigns from the moment one becomes a follower of Christ and will be consummated at the eschaton."[239]

It appears that Paul uses the future not because he speaks of something still to come, but because of the continuity[240] of this reign (it is εἰς ζωὴν αἰώνιον, "to eternal life," 5:21; cf. also 6:22, 23). The idea of the present also

---

234. Viard, *Romains*, 140 [italics mine].

235. As Porter suggests, this is a case where "absolute tense conception" barely works; cf. *IGNT*, 25–26.

236. Wallace, *GGBB*, 567 fn. 1.

237. Dunn hints at this continuity when he describes δικαιοσύνη (the means by which grace reigns, v. 21) as having an "ongoing and future dimension," cf. Dunn, *Romans 1–8*, 287.

238. Murray, *Romans*, 198.

239. Osborne, *Romans*, 144.

240. Dunn: "in contrast to the epoch which ends in death the epoch of grace is life unbounded," *Romans 1–8*, 287–88.

emerges when we focus on the word "life" which is associated with reign (ἡ χάρις βασιλεύσῃ ... εἰς ζωήν, "grace will reign to life," 5:21; also ἐν ζωῇ βασιλεύσουσιν, "they will reign in life," 5:17). In 5:18, Paul describes Christ's act of justification as δικαίωσιν ζωῆς, "justification of life," that is to say, justification *that is* life. Here ζωῆς (of life) is best seen as an epexegetical genitive, though other meanings are also possible.[241] This is because in 5:15–18, God's justification of the person involved in this transition (stage one) is synonymous with an offer of life, just as the condemnation inherited from Adam is synonymous with death. The parallelism of these ideas is such that, just as Christ's grace and justification are already a reality (cf. aorist ἐπερίσσευσεν, "abounded," v. 15) for believers, the life (in which they walk, cf. 6:4) is also to be taken as already a fact in the present experience of the Christian. Life appears to be a key concept in this pericope (5:17, 18, 21; 6:2, 4, 8, 10 [twice], 11, 13, 22, 23), and links with Christ's work which is also already a reality (cf. 5:15–18). Thus, it makes sense to understand that in all these instances Paul speaks of a reality that is already present, but which extends to eternity (cf. αἰώνιον, 5:21; 6:22, 23). Viard, for instance, perceives "life" and "eternal life" as appositive expressions.[242]

In the light of these elements, our conclusion is that Paul speaks of the life of the baptized using a future that has a present sense. This use of the future, labelled in this study as an *initiatory* future, is a feature of initiation as outlined in chapter two. We consider that this fits Paul's thinking in Romans 5–6 where he is concerned with the *passage* from one way of religious life to another.

To sum up, this section has sought to consider what Paul means in 5:17 when he says that those who receive the grace of God (οἱ ... λαμβάνοντες) are to reign (βασιλεύσουσιν). Focusing on "to reign," the aim has been to show how in the initiation patterns of his time we expect to see Paul showing that

---

241. Δικαίωσιν (justification) and ζωῆς (of life) are appositive to each other; "life" identifies "justification" more specifically: i.e. justification *which is* life. This epexegetical sense is recognized by the translation "justification (acquittal) *and* life" (e.g. RSV, NRSV, NAB). However, this is not really exclusive but complementary to the other main interpretation, which is to consider ζωῆς (of life) as a genitive of purpose. Thus, e.g. NIV translates it as "justification *that brings* life" (same for TOB and SB/LS with the translation "la justification *qui donne* la vie" (the justification *that gives* life) and "die Leben *gibt*" (that *gives* life) as in Bibel/ES; also "die Rechtfertigung *zum* Leben" (the justification *for* life) in Bibel/NDUMLuthers [italics mine]).

242. As shown by the description "cette vie, qui est la vie éternelle" (this life which is eternal life), cf. Viard, *Romains*, 138.

this is an aspect of the new life that the initiand endorses and starts to live from the time of initiation (stage four). This has an impact on the reading of Romans 5–6. Hence one aspect of this section has been to show how a focus on the initiatory *passage* to new existence delivers exegetical gain, and helps us to make new and clear sense of the future used in this pericope in connection with the believer's life.

For a better understanding of what Paul says about the after-initiation life that begins in initiation, there is more worth considering. The next section focuses on "righteousness" as the means by which the "reigning" works.

4.5.2. Διὰ δικαιοσύνης (5:21): Forensic, or the Initiate's Righteous Life?

In this section we consider διὰ δικαιοσύνης, "through righteousness" (v. 21), the means by which the reign of grace takes place. Ziesler considers that "righteousness" in Romans 5:12–21 "is neither simply forensic, nor simply ethical, but both together. It is relational, but it is also to do with actions in relationship."[243] A contribution to clarifying the meaning of this term can be expected from examining the pericope from the perspective of what a transition to a new life implies, for this perspective provides us with a framework within which we can ask whether Paul is just speaking of stage one (i.e. the righteousness that saves) or whether his thinking moves to focus also on the moral righteousness, namely, another element of the initiand's life stemming from the transition from sin to God (stage 4).

A glance at the structure of Paul's thought is illuminating. As the last section has shown, the transition from sin to God is such that the grace of Christ saves people (stage one) then reigns (5:21), or as 5:17 shows more precisely, people receive it and start to live its reign (stage four). Then Paul adds that this act of reigning is διὰ δικαιοσύνης, "through righteousness" (5:21). It is obvious that there is a connection between this idea of righteousness and the act of reigning which itself is a focus on the believer's life in and after theirtransition, as we suggested in the last section. Focusing on the idea that Paul's thinking in Romans 5–6 is shaped by the initiation patterns of first-century religious

---

243. Ziesler, *Meaning of Righteousness*, 198; for an expanded discussion of this idea in 5:12–21: 197–200.

experience, this section expects to show that "righteousness" forms another element of the life of the believer that stems from the process of initiation.

Three elements contribute to showing this and are considered in this section: the first is the relationship of "reign" and "righteousness" in Paul's argument; the second is the observation that δικαιοσύνη (righteousness), in our pericope, consistently concerns Christian living; and the third is how much "to be made righteous" (5:19) appears to confirm our working assumption that by "righteousness" Paul speaks of the believer's life that starts in his or her initiation.

First, we consider that in the words διὰ δικαιοσύνης, "through righteousness" (v. 21), as in his use of βασιλεύω (to reign), Paul is more concerned with the believer's moral life that stems from the transition from sin to the Christian way than with a forensic sense.[244] One element that appears to show this is the parallel construction of 5:17 and 21. In both verses "reign" and "righteousness" are connected. Thus Hodge, for example, links διὰ δικαιοσύνης (through righteousness) to believers' living when he speaks of grace being actually "displayed" so that "Christ is to be admired in his saints."[245] But then, because of διὰ Ἰησοῦ Χριστοῦ, "through Jesus Christ" (v. 21), he asserts, "so the triumph of grace is through *the righteousness of Christ*."[246] This is not different from what he sees in verse 17 to be "*the righteousness of Christ* by which we are justified."[247] Romans 5:15–17 clearly speaks of the righteousness of justification, the one that is a "gift." But the stages of transition appear in these verses. Paul's idea progresses from a stress on God's saving righteousness (stage one) to what this divine action brings about for the believer in the transition, that is to say, the believer's righteous life (stage four). The parallel construction of verses 17 and 21 shows this.

Paul uses δικαιοσύνη (righteousness) in association with "grace" and "reign" not only in 5:21 (ἡ χάρις βασιλεύσῃ διὰ δικαιοσύνης [. . .] διὰ Ἰησοῦ Χριστοῦ, "grace might reign through righteousness [. . .] through Jesus Christ), but also in v. 17 (οἱ τὴν περισσείαν τῆς χάριτος καὶ τῆς δωρεᾶς τῆς δικαιοσύνης λαμβάνοντες βασιλεύσουσιν διὰ . . . Ἰησοῦ Χριστοῦ, "those who receive the

---

244. So Schreiner, *Romans*, 296–97.

245. Hodge, *Romans*, 174.

246. *Romans*, 174 [italics mine]; for similar ideas, Osborne, *Romans*, 146; Stuhlmacher, *Romans*, 88.

247. Hodge, *Romans*, 163 [italics mine].

abundance of *grace* and of the gift of *righteousness* will reign through . . . Jesus Christ"). A chart makes clearer what he means:

V. 17 A   <u>τῆς χάριτος</u> (grace)
       B   <u>καὶ δικαιοσύνης</u> (and righteousness) } λαμβάνοντες (receivers of)
       C   βασιλεύσουσιν (will reign)
       D   διὰ Ἰησοῦ Χριστοῦ (through Jesus Christ)

V. 21 A' <u>ἡ χάρις</u> (grace)
       C' βασιλεύσῃ (might reign)
       B'   διὰ δικαιοσύνης (through righteousness)
       D'   διὰ Ἰησοῦ Χριστοῦ (through Jesus Christ)

In both verses, the words grace, reign and righteousness are Paul's key terms, and at the end he mentions Christ as he shows that all depends on Jesus.[248] The elements in italics (A, C and D) keep their position, and they are: the grace (which is a composite idea[249]), the act of reigning, and διὰ Χριστοῦ (through Christ) as the ground of it all. The issue is whether δικαιοσύνη (righteousness) in 5:17 and 21 is referring to (just) the justifying righteousness (cf 5:1, 9) or (also) to the moral righteousness which then issues from grace in the believer's life (cf. 6:13) when he or she encounters God's grace. A focus on what is underlined, namely, the A, A' elements, is illuminating. Both in 5:17 and 21, "A" is about grace and this shows that Paul takes seriously the fact that God's grace is the origin and the basis of the reign that he speaks about. However, as to the agent who reigns, Paul's focus is primarily on believers, not on God *per se*. As the underlined elements show, when he speaks of grace his reference is not just to God but to a composite reality in which the believer, too, is the centre as A and B at verse 17 show. God's active grace and justifying righteousness are the origin of the whole, but Paul describes God's action in a composite way that includes the person whom God's grace

---

248. E.g. Carrez, about διὰ Ἰησοῦ Χριστοῦ (through Jesus Christ), he translates διὰ (through) as "de par" thus with a sense of "ground" or "cause," thus "à cause du Christ" (because of Christ), cf. *NTIGF*, s.v. Rom 5: 17, the BFC part.

249. It encompasses righteousness and the believer, cf. A, B in v. 17.

encountered (stage one) and then moved to live (stage four) as a follower and representative of Christ, "a saint"[250] just as it was noted of Paul also.[251]

We argue that this notion of "sainthood" – noticed in 5:21 by Hodge as mentioned earlier – appears in 5:17 as well, and that in verse 17 the term righteousness includes a reference to the character and life of the followers of Christ, even though Paul describes it there as an abundant gift of grace and righteousness (5:15-17). The transition process requires more than this divine gift. Verse 19 makes even more clear that those who receive this gift (cf. οἱ λαμβάνοντες) become righteous in character and life, as we will see shortly. As a result, they reign, that is, they manifest God's reign, through their righteous living. That διὰ δικαιοσύνης (through righteousness) is about the believer's life is also confirmed by the wider use of this term in the pericope. The next point focuses on this use.

In Romans 5:12-6:23, consistently Paul uses δικαιοσύνη (righteousness) with the sense of righteous acts and life. This is particularly evident in 6:13-19 where Paul speaks of offering oneself as an instrument of righteousness. It is clear that he means righteous life when he urges his readers "not to present themselves to be tools of unrighteousness" (μηδὲ παριστάνετε τὰ μέλη ὑμῶν ὅπλα ἀδικίας, 6:13). Then Paul not only repeatedly mentions righteousness (or its opposite) in 16, 18, 19, and 20, but along with that, repeats "present yourselves slaves/ tools" (παριστάνετε ἑαυτοὺς δούλους, vv. 16, 19). The passage has literary devices which support this practical emphasis in "righteousness." In verse 16, the parallel, δούλους εἰς ὑπακοήν (slaves for obedience), ὑπακοῆς εἰς δικαιοσύνην (of obedience for righteousness), suggests that the focal idea is "slaves for/of righteousness." This is confirmed by verse 19, which is similar to verse 13. In other words, 6:13-19 concentrates on this idea of serving righteousness, and this service should be understood as righteous life. In fact, in 6:18, 19 and 20, clearly Paul speaks of the practical service of righteousness (instead of sin). This strongly suggests that the δικαιοσύνη (the righteousness) through which grace manifests its reign (5:21) is a reference

---

250. So Baulès when he associates righteousness with the receiver's life: "Cette justice est la qualité d'être justifié à vivre, c'est la justice de vie" (This justice is the quality of being justified for living, it is the justice for life), cf. L'Evangile, 180 [italics mine].

251. In Acts 9:13-15, as noted in chapter 3, Paul in his transition becomes ἅγιος (saint), or a σκεῦος ἐκλογῆς (a chosen instrument).

to the righteous life of believers,²⁵² and this righteousness (and what is said about it in 6:13–19) begins with the transition (stage four). It is not a result that follows later after initiation. 5:17 and 21 connect this righteous life and God's act in a way totally appropriate within the initiation process. Δίκαιος (a righteous) (5:19) gives more evidence in support of this, and our third point takes us to this verse.

Δίκαιοι κατασταθήσονται (will be made righteous, 5:19) is also an expression that supports the idea that in our pericope righteousness is very much about life and deeds, and particularly that Paul's focus is on the life that is embraced in the process of transition (stage four). There is a connection between this expression and the use of δικαιοσύνη, "righteousness" (vv. 17, 21) that has just been considered. Δίκαιοι, "the righteous" (5:19) is considered separately with more attention because of its connection here with the idea of "making," which appears to support our assumption that in Paul's thinking the life of the Christian starts with his or her initiation.

Three views concerning κατασταθήσονται (they will be made) and δίκαιοι (righteous) are found: a "forensic" view, a "practical" view, and one which wavers between these two. The "forensic" view emphasises the passive κατασταθήσονται and interprets the whole phrase as indicating God's forensic act of declaring people to be righteous before him, thus of imparting a status. For instance, Murray's view is that "'constituted righteous' has the same forensic character as justification."²⁵³ Many have interpreted it in this way.²⁵⁴ Hodge thinks of status when he comments (on v. 19a):

> The word made in the clause the many were made sinners strictly means that they were set down in the rank or category of sinners. In the New Testament, the Greek word translated here as made means "to make" in the sense of effecting or causing a person or thing to be in its character or nature other than it was before. This clause does not mean "to make one sinful,"

---

252. E.g. Dunn on 5:21, that righteousness here refers to "an ongoing status, living relationship," cf. *Jesus, Paul and Law*, 207.

253. Murray, *Romans*, 205.

254. Jewett: to "be *accounted* righteous," cf. *Romans*, 387 [italics mine]; Mounce: "righteous by account and acceptance," *ALGNT*, s.v. "δίκαιος"; Stuhlmacher: to be "righteous *before God* through the obedience of Christ," cf. *Romans*, 88 [italics mine].

but to set him down as such, to regard or appoint him to be in that category.²⁵⁵

Thus, Hodge thinks that Paul's point in 5:19a is not that people became doers of sin as a result of Adam's act; rather his disobedience set them in a "category" of sinners. From this, his conclusion is that δίκαιοι κατασταθήσονται (they will be made righteous) "can only mean that the obedience of Christ was the basis on which the many are to be placed in the category of the righteous – that is, will be regarded and treated as righteous."²⁵⁶ This is a forensic view.

Our approach, however, opens the possibility of a close connection between the forensic act of God (stage one) in 5:15–18 and an emphasis in verses 17, 19 and 21 on people's life and acts as they embrace the new realm (stage four). Ziesler, to name one who holds this line of thought, recognizes this when, about δίκαιοι (righteous), he states:

> Some think we should take "righteous" (*dikaioi*) in a strictly forensic or relational sense, to mean "justified, accepted, acquitted", not least because throughout the passage there is a stress on justification and the absence of condemnation. Yet "righteous" is in parallel with "sinners", and the latter really are sinners who do wrong things, not just those who have the status of sinners. It seems likely, therefore, that in this verse we have a complete reversal: the many will find a whole new life, not just a new status, a new life that reverses the spread of sin, cf. v. 12.²⁵⁷

Ziesler recognizes that δίκαιοι (righteous) concerns "practical" life.²⁵⁸ What he does not consider is how this links with the person's process of transition from sin to God, especially whether this presumes human agency in such process.

A third attitude toward δίκαιοι (righteous) considers how uneasy the expression δίκαιοι κατασταθήσονται (they will be made righteous) is. Osborne, for example, allows the possibility here for δίκαιοι (righteous) to mean the

---

255. Hodge, *Romans*, 169 [bold his; italics his].
256. Hodge, *Romans*, 169.
257. Ziesler, *Romans*, 152.
258. His other statement is that "something more than forensic is in v. 19," cf. Ziesler, *Meaning of Righteousness*, 199.

"ethical result of righteous living" (ref. to Rom 1:17; 3:10; 5:7),²⁵⁹ but he then says that what he finds "best" is the forensic sense.²⁶⁰

A legal sense is mainly derived from the fact that the forensic act of justification is stated in 5:18. For instance, speaking of 5:18–19, Haacker asserts, "Das *solus Christus* und das im Kontext wiederholt klargestellte *sola gratia* sind dem *sola fide* anscheinend übergeordnet" (The *solus Christ* and the *sola gratia*, repeatedly clarified in the context, are apparently superior to the *sola fide*).²⁶¹ Indeed in verse 18, δικαίωμα, "justification" (and its genitive) means "making right or justified."²⁶² This seems clearly forensic. But as Godet notes, the fact that Paul leaves the δικαίωμα/ δικαίωσις (justification) terminology in verse 18 and returns in verse 19 to the δίκαιος /δικαιοσύνη (righteous/ righteousness) type (of v. 17) suggests that he moves back towards οἱ λαμβάνοντες (those who receive [grace]) and their life that righteously manifests God's reign.²⁶³

It seems evident that Paul takes steps in what he says. Verse 18 recollects the forensic work of God (stage one) already expressed in verses 15–17. In verse 19, the δίκαιοι (the righteous) are the product²⁶⁴ of what God has done, people who in their transition from sin to God respond to God's salvation by embracing the new life and living it (stage four).²⁶⁵

This appears to emerge from the interplay which Paul develops around the notion of "making" in verses 18 and 19. The idea of "making" appears in verse 18 with δικαιόω, "to make or render right."²⁶⁶ In verse 19, Paul speaks

---

259. Osborne, *Romans*, 145.

260. Osborne, 145.

261. Haacker, *Römer*, 121.

262. Cf. *ALGNT*, s.v. "δικαίωσις"; cf. also the meaning of words of its group: δικαιόω (to make right), δικαίωμα (justification).

263. Godet, *Romains*, 468.

264. So NIV as it begins v. 19 by translating ὥσπερ as "consequently"; and Utley: "Jesus' one act of obedience, Calvary, *resulted in* (1) a new age, (2) *a new people*, and (3) a new covenant," see Utley, *Romans*, 96 [italics mine]; Schreiner: "Those who are in Adam and those who are in Christ actually become sinners and righteous, respectively," *Romans*, 288; Viard: "l'oeuvre accomplie par le Christ . . . *permet* . . . d'obtenir dès maintenant la vie" (The work accomplished by Christ . . . allows . . . to obtain life now), *Romains*, 138–39 [italics mine]; Schlater: God's gift "grants power to reign," *Romans*, 130; and Osborne, *Romans*, 143.

265. *Contra* Carrez' trans. of δίκαιοι as "justifés" (the justified), *NTIGF*, 697, interlinear section.

266. *ALGNT*, s.v. "δικαιόω."

The Four Stages and Action in Romans 5:12–6:23

again of "to make" but this time uses καθίστημι, "to make, render."[267] The shared aspect is that the two are pointing to where the believer's new life begins (καταστᾰθήσονται, "will be made," as present future, that is, this taking effect within initiation and after, cf. our previous section). But there is also a difference, consisting in the fact that the first emphasises a forensic "making" and the second points more to taking a responsibility. Καθίστημι (to make) implies this responsibility, as considered below.

The word καθίστημι (to make) is much debated, as Schreiner shows.[268] In 5:19, it is variously translated as "be constituted,"[269] "be rendered"[270] and "be made."[271] All this suggests God's act of placing people into a class or a category (as noted earlier from Hodge and Osborne). But the word also means "to cause to be" [and to do, we should add].[272] The idea is "to cause" a person "to be" something, in fact to play a certain role. Though it is a ἅπαξ in Paul's writings (only found again in the post-Pauline of Titus 1:5), in the New Testament it occurs many times. In nearly all places the idea is action and responsibility instead of a mere status.[273] For example, Matthew uses it four times with the idea of becoming a steward or manager (24:45, 47; 25:21, 23; cf. Luke 12:44). Other examples are to become a judge (Luke 12:14),[274] to take a responsibility (Acts 6:3; cf. Titus 1:5), to become ruler (Acts 7:10, 27, 35), and in 2 Peter 1:8 it is about effectiveness and being productive.[275] The focus is clearly on the person's active life and responsibility. These elements suggest that δίκαιοι κατασταθήσονται (they will be made righteous) could be understood as focusing on the active, righteous life. Moreover, as the last

---

267. *ALGNT*, s.v. "καθίστημι."

268. Schreiner, *Romans*, 287–88.

269. E.g. *NTIGF*, 697; Viard, *Romains*, 139.

270. E.g. TOB; BFC; this is the idea when the Bibel/EÜ puts it as "Gerechten versetzt warden" (the righteous are the shifted).

271. This trans. is adopted by the majority, e.g. NIV, RV, NRSV, NJB, NEB; also it is this idea when the Bibel/ES says "zu Gerechten gemacht warden" (to be made righteous).

272. *ALGNT*, s.v. "καθίστημι."

273. For the range of its use in NT, cf. *GECNT*, s.v. "καθίστημι."

274. Other e.g.: "appointed" as elders (Titus 1:5) and as high priest (Heb 7:28), "appointed" to represent people (Heb 5:1) or to offer sacrifices (Heb 8:3).

275. 2 Pet 1:8 is an example in which Mounce finds that the meaning can be "make, render, or cause to be," thus suggesting καθίστημι to be rendered as "to make or to render" with the connotation of "to cause to be"; *ALGNT*, s.v. "καθίστημι."

paragraph shows, Paul's thinking in verses 18 and 19 is such that he has in mind the responsibility of a life that stems from the Christian transition.

To sum up, this section on διὰ δικαιοσύνης (through righteousness) has illustrated that, when in 5:21 Paul speaks of righteousness as the means of the reign of grace, he means the believer's life and action; a life embraced by the Christian during the transition from sin to God. Dunn recognizes that "the sense should not be forcibly confined to the sense 'status of righteousness.'"[276] Also what δικαιοσύνη (righteousness) means here is more than Stuhlmacher's idea of a "faith" just in the sense of consent.[277] Paul considers the responsibility that the *passage* to the new existence entails, the righteous "walk" which bears a testimony to the fact that God is reigning through believers.[278] By righteousness as the means of the reign of grace, he means to "walk" in the new way of God (6:4). The next section examines whether to "walk in new life" fits into Paul's argument as another element of the life that is endorsed in the *passage* from sin to God (stage four).

4.5.3. Walking in the New Existence (ἐν καινότητι ζωῆς περιπατήσωμεν, 6:4–5)

Speaking of baptism and τῆς ἀναστάσεως ἐσόμεθα, "we shall be in a resurrection" (6:5), Jagger states, "We will take possession of our new life at the final resurrection . . . Paul is clear that we do not yet share in Christ's resurrection the way we share in his death."[279] When does the baptizand take this new life? From the beginning of Romans, Paul stresses the life appropriate to the believer (cf. ὑπακοὴν πίστεως, "the obedience of faith," 1:5). Thus, some understand this life to be the "main purpose of Romans."[280] We would naturally expect Paul to emphasise the Christian life even more in a pericope about the *passage* from one existence to another, because attaching oneself

---

276. Dunn, *Romans 1–8*, 287; for a similar idea, cf. Ziesler, *Romans*, 150.

277. Stuhlmacher speaks of "righteousness of faith" (*Romans*, 87), and "faith" seems to be consent, 88.

278. So Schreiner, *Romans*, 296–297, also 286; Viard: God's aim is that his glory "manifestée en Jésus-Christ, 'le Seigneur de gloire,' brille désormais, grâce au *rayonnement* de l'Évangile et de la gloire du Christ" (manifested in Jesus Christ, the Lord of glory, might *shine* from now on, thanks to *the radiance* of the Gospel and of the glory of Christ), cf. *Romains*, 100 [italics mine]; also Schlatter, *Romans*, 130, 132.

279. Jagger, *Christian Initiation 1552–1969*, 104.

280. Garlington, "Obedience of Faith," 201; also Wright, "Messiah and People," iii.

to a new way of life is the very reason for undergoing initiation. Paul speaks of this new life by means of two things:

First, he shows that the purpose of baptism (or of the transition as a whole) is the new life (διὰ τοῦ βαπτίσματος ... ἵνα ... ἐν καινότητι ζωῆς περιπατήσωμεν, "by baptism ... so that ... we may walk in newness of life," v. 4). As Campbell recognizes, baptism is seen by Paul as "a raising to walk in newness of life."[281] The living of a new life is strongly emphasised here [282]and Paul's conviction is clearly (we suggest) that the new life has begun in the transition. This emerges not only through the connection with the third stage act of undergoing water baptism (cf. διὰ τοῦ βαπτίσματος), but also through the use of the aorist tense (συνετάφημεν, "we were buried"), showing that he reminds the readers of their transition and baptism. That the new way of life has been embraced as the very purpose of initiation denotes the baptizand's agency in the process of moving from sin to God.

Second, in 6:4–5 Paul describes the new life through the resurrection analogy between Christ and the believer. We again note a progression between the stages of initiation. As discussed earlier, in 6:1–2 Paul reminds the Romans of the death they experienced in the liminal and second stage. In 6:3 Paul appears to speak of the third stage – the ritual and pledge that seal the person's entry. As the new life takes over when one dies to the old way and pledges attachment to the new, one would expect that "life" in 6:4–5 is referring to the fourth stage – the life that the person endorses in the process of initiation and starts to live while still in initiation. Does this expectation cohere with a closer examination of Romans 6:4–5?

To test this, 6:4–5 is considered. These verses show parallel clauses (i.e. A, A' and B, B' B") which produce the following chart:

---

281. Campbell, *Paul and Creation*, 163.

282. There is deliberate repetition of ideas through using both ζωη (life) and περιπατέω (to walk), which itself means "to live" or "to conduct the walk of life" – a sense which is "especially common in the LXX," cf. Seesemann and Bertram, "πατέω," in *TDNT*, vol. 5, 941. Seesemann and Bertram also point out that, in the LXX, it is "frequently used" religiously "to express man's religious and ethical walk" and that it is as "the walk of life, more ... in the moral sense" that Paul also uses it, cf. Seesemann and Bertram, "πατέω," 942, 944.

A   συνετάφημεν οὖν αὐτῷ διὰ τοῦ βαπτίσματος εἰς τὸν θάνατον, ἵνα   v. 4
(We were buried therefore with him by baptism into death), so that)
    B   ὥσπερ ἠγέρθη Χριστὸς ἐκ νεκρῶν διὰ τῆς δόξης τοῦ πατρός,
    (as Christ was raised from the dead by the glory of the Father)
    B'   οὕτως καὶ ἡμεῖς ἐν καινότητι ζωῆς περιπατήσωμεν
    (we too might walk in newness of life)
A'   Εἰ γὰρ σύμφυτοι γεγόναμεν τῷ ὁμοιώματι τοῦ θανάτου αὐτοῦ,   v. 5
(For if we have been united in the likeness of his death)
    B"   ἀλλὰ καὶ τῆς ἀναστάσεως ἐσόμεθα
    (but also we shall be [in the likeness of his] resurrection)

Cuvillier sees a "tension" between B' (which he concludes is about the present life) and B" which is about the future.[283] Earlier this issue was considered, and our argument was that if Paul was thinking within the initiation assumptions of his time, he will not have meant (just) eschatological life when he speaks of the life of a person who is in transition from sin to God.[284] B" is widely interpreted as referring to future (the final) resurrection.[285] However the idea is also interpreted by many as a present future, the new state and life of the believer.[286] The perfect γεγόναμεν, "we have become" (v. 5) fits better

---

283. Cuvillier, "Baptême chrétien," 166; also for the present (v. 4) and future life (v. 5), cf. Edwards, *Romans*, 161–62; Barrett, *Romans*, 123; Morris, *Romans*, 250.

284. We hear a hint at this also when on 6:4 Dunn recognizes that in Paul life "is part of the 'already' as well as the 'not yet,'" cf. *New Perspective on Paul*, 76 fn. 313.

285. So Matera, *Romans*, 151; Keck, *Romans*, 162; Dunn, *Romans 1–8*, 318, Tannehill, *Dying and Rising*, 10–11; Bultmann, *Theology of New Testament*, 140; Schreiner, *Romans*, 312; Bornkamm, "Baptism and New Life," 78; Thüsing, *Per Christum in Deum*, 70; Siber, *Mit Christus leben*, 242–243; Käsemann, *Romans*, 166, 169; Barth, *Taufe in frühchristlicher*, 96; Moo, *Romans 1–8*, 388; Edwards, *Romans*, 162. Schreiner notes that it is the view of many, see *Romans*, 312, so also Dunn, *Romans 1–8*, 318.

286. So Hodge, *Romans*, 180; Beasley-Murray, *Baptism in New Testament*, 139–40; and "Dying and Rising," in *DPL*, 220 col. 1–2; Esler, *Conflict and Identity*, 213–214; Calvin, *Romains*, 139; Godet, *Romains* II, 25; H. Frankemölle, *Das Taufverständnis des Paulus*, 51, 71–73; Thyen, *Studien zur Sündenvergebung*, 206–08; Fitzmyer, *Romans*, 345; Cranfield, *Romans 1–8*, 308; Schreider, "ὅμοιος," 195; Schnackenburg, *Baptism in Thought*, 38; Leenhardt, *Romains*, 93; Cramer, *Baptism and Change*, 46–47; Ambrose of Milan, *On Sacraments* 1.4, Trans. of Finn, *Early Christian Baptism*, 63; MacDonald, *Pauline Churches*, 142; McRay, *Paul*, 407. Oepke, 'ἀνίστημι' in *TDNT*, vol. 1, 370.

with the latter view. It "emphasizes the present state" (intensive perfect).²⁸⁷ For more on these two strands, Wedderburn, for example, has much material.²⁸⁸

Since the issue of the future reference here need not be discussed again at length, we can focus on considering whether it makes sense to see Romans 6:4–5 as describing the life that the Christian embraces in stages three and four of his or her transition. To argue for this, some new grammatical and syntactical analysis is offered.

Attention has to be given to the relationship between the clauses in which Paul speaks of life. As the chart shows, B, B' and B" are parallel. Indeed, this does not mean they have to refer to the same thing, but some "synonymy" emerges between the concepts in these lines.²⁸⁹ The same idea of rising to life spans the three clauses. This is shown by the position of ἐγείρω (to rise up) at the beginning of the structure. This is significant in Semitic parallelism and indicates that this verb controls the whole sequence.²⁹⁰

The idea of resurrection (rising to life) is clearly stated in B and B", but not in B'. In fact, Viard points to B' as different because in it, "ressusciter" (to rise from the dead) is not used.²⁹¹ This change of words however is not really a change in thought; rather it is parallelism with change of words.²⁹² The analogy that links B and B' sufficiently suggests that the notion of rising to life appears in both clauses. Also, the comparison of B and B' may work the other way round by prompting us to ask if "new life" (B') is already echoed in B. In this respect, ἐκ νεκρῶν (from the dead) is noteworthy. As such, to be "out of the dead" is to be alive²⁹³ (a connotation much exploited by Paul),²⁹⁴ also ἐγείρω ἐκ νεκρῶν (to rise from the dead) and to live and serve are two concepts which he often connects (e.g. Rom 6:9; 7:4; 8:11; 1 Thess 1:10).²⁹⁵

---

287. Cf. *GGBB*, 574.
288. Wedderburn, *Baptism and Resurrection*, 39, 43–44.
289. Synonymy is also reinforced by the similarity expressed by ὥσπερ . . . οὕτως καὶ . . .
290. So Beasley-Murray, "Romans 1:3f," 147.
291. Viard, *Romains*, 143.
292. Cf. *IBI*, 288.
293. Ἐγείρω (to rise up) has the connotation of "being well and whole," cf. Oepke, "ἐγείρω," 334. As *GECNT* (s.v. ἐγείρω) shows, ἐγείρω (to rise up) is linked with γρηγορέω "to be awake" and διαγρηγορέω "to be thoroughly awake"; also *ALGNT*, s.v. γρηγορέω and διαγρηγορέω.
294. E.g. Rom 4:25 (raised to life, cf. NIV); Rom 10:9; 1 Cor 15:12, 15–16, 32 (νεκροὶ ἐγείρονται, "the dead are raised"); Gal 1:1; cf. Matt 14:2; 28:7.
295. Cf. John 5:21; 12:1; Acts 3:15; 1 Pet 1:21.

Thus the idea of B is picked up in B'. As Godet notes, in B' Paul expresses "un fait" (a fact) by its "conséquence" (consequence).[296] What he uses is "specification, concretization," a device that Alter discerns from biblical parallelism.[297]

B and B' are synonymous not only with each other, but with B" as well. This is shown by their relation to A and A'. B–B' are a conclusion to the premise A, and B" is a conclusion to A'. The premises (A, A') are not only parallel but identical in meaning. Paul's idea in A and A' is that believers become "co-naturalisés" (co-naturalised) with Christ[298] when they too undergo a death that is "en conformité à sa mort" (in accordance with his death).[299] This correspondence of the premises (A and A') makes it possible that Paul means the same thing also in the conclusions (B–B' and B").[300] That is, when one dies to sin and breaks with it as a system of life, the new way of life takes over, and this applies to both Christ and the believer. Paul's thinking rests on the patterns of interconnection between stages two, three and four of initiation.

Does this show that in Paul's thinking the transition from sin to God encompasses both divine and human agency? Theodore of Mopsuestia recognizes that Paul speaks of the present life when he states that Christians are "already risen."[301] Here Theodore thinks of the "glorified" life,[302] and this may not favour the idea of human agency as the cause of it. It is Christ's agency that is at the fore. Schweitzer expresses a similar view: "Because Christ had passed into the resurrection mode of existence, and because Christians share

---

296. Godet, *Romans* II, 22.

297. Alter, cited in *IBI*, 285.

298. Leenhardt, *Romans*, 92; Davies speaks of "new creation," cf. *Paul and Rabbinic Judaism*, 120; Viard: to be "une même nature" (the same nature) with Christ, cf. *Romans*, 14; so also Cuvillier, "Baptême chrétien," 166; Fitzmyer: to be "the same" as Christ, cf. *According to Paul*, 74; Cyril of Jerusalem: to be "christs" by the virtue of becoming "likenesses of Christ," cited by Finn, *Early Christian Baptism: Syria*, 50.

299. Cuvillier, "Baptême chrétien," 166; Hodge, *Romans*, 180.

300. Bruce hints at this when he handles 6:3–5 together and considers the idea as "to rise with him in the likeness of his resurrection and so 'walk in newness of life,'" cf. *Paul*, 433; also Flemington, *New Testament*, 81.

301. Theodore of Mopsuestia, cited by Finn, *Early Christian Baptism: Syria*, 86.

302. As the life that begins in the transition is our focus, this study follows the view that 6:4bc refers to the believer's present life. That "glorified" life is not the idea, so also e.g. Barrett: the Christian is still "marked by sin," cf. *Romans*, 122; and many recognize Romans 6 as an ethical section, e.g. Haacker, *Theology of Romans*, 64–65. For Byrne, this concerns Rom 6:1–8:13, cf. "Living out the Righteousness," 557. When Paul deals with ethics, it should be noted that in his tradition "this life was key [. . .], life and death all related to this life primarily," cf. Osborne, "Resurrection," 673, col. 2.

in His corporeity, the latter had also died and risen with Christ into the life of the resurrection."[303] As Käsemann argues, "the idea of mystical union with Christ" may favour a present future in 6:5,[304] but makes it difficult to allow for an initiatory human role in the new life that is linked with such a transition.

However, in the light of these structural observations, and especially in line with our idea that Paul is reflecting the staged pattern of the life that the individual embraces personally in initiation, it appears that Paul means more than just that Christians were risen "in Christ"[305] in his resurrection event. Paul's interest is on "rising in him" now in the present, taking full responsibility to live like Christ.[306] As Byrne states, the idea is to "allow Christ to live out in them his total submission to God."[307] In other words, as Westerholm puts it, this is to "share with Christ a new life in God's service."[308] It is to take responsibility, and this echoes first-century socio-religious patterns of attaching to a new group. The idea reflects what Malina describes as "sharing a common fate" by the members of the kin group following the group's "central personage."[309]

A phrase that also shows that this life encompasses divine and human agency is the expression διὰ τῆς δόξης τοῦ πατρός, "by the glory of the Father" (v. 4). This also shows how Paul's thinking was guided by initiatory assumptions. It appears to be the διά "of efficient cause"[310] and is much used by Paul.[311] God's glory causes the rising to life (cf. stage one), but the human agency also adopts it as a responsibility (cf. stage four). Note that God is not just the cause;

---

303. Schweitzer, cited by Davies, *Paul and Rabbinic Judaism*, 98; for more on this idea, cf. Schweitzer, *Mysticism of Paul*, 117.

304. Käsemann, *Romans*, 167.

305. Focus on rising in him, e.g. Beasley-Murray, "Dying and Rising," 220, col. 1.

306. So Edwards, *Romans*, 161. This appears to be the idea when in Col 2:12 people rise in him (ἐν ᾧ) when they believe in his resurrection (διὰ τῆς πίστεως τῆς ἐνεργείας τοῦ θεοῦ τοῦ ἐγείραντος αὐτόν, "through faith in the working of God, who raised him"); drawing attention to this, e.g. Ambrose of Milan, *On Sacraments* 2.20, Translation of Finn, *Early Christian Baptism: Italy*, 71.

307. Byrne, "Living out Righteousness," 563. The idea is "to share in his risen life" (cf. Fitzmyer, *According to Paul*, 15, 74; also Schnackenburg, *Baptism in Thought*, 172) but in the sense that the transition implies that the person takes Christ's will as a responsibility to live up to.

308. Westerholm, *Understanding Paul*, 108; so also Godet, *Romains* II, 21.

309. Malina, "Let Him Deny Himself," 115.

310. *GELNT-OECL*, s.v. "διά"; Fitzmyer, *According to Paul*, 74.

311. E.g. references in *GELNT-OECL*, s.v. "διά," cf. 224 col. 2.

his glory is also the goal (cf. Rom 5:2; 11:36; Phil 1:11). As Cramer points out, it is to be "alive with a life which looks towards God"[312] (cf. vv. 10–11: ζῆ τῷ θεῷ, "live for God"). In 6:4b (cf. A on the next chart) Paul does not make God's glory the direct reason for which Jesus is raised (he would have used διά + accusative),[313] but that idea is implied (as we want to show), and service to God is clearly the goal in 6:6 (cf. τοῦ μηκέτι δουλεύειν ἡμᾶς τῇ ἁμαρτίᾳ, "we might no longer be enslaved to sin"). God's glory as the goal in 6:4 emerges as we compare 6:4b (A) and 6:4c (B). The structure makes $a\ b\ c\ /\ a'\ d$:

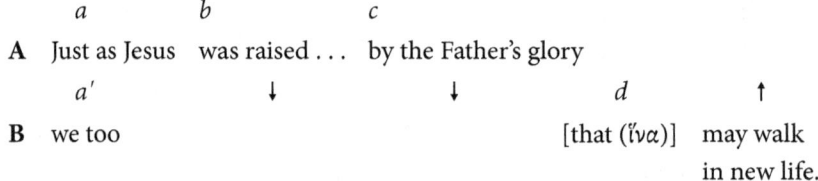

As mentioned earlier, Paul uses a parallelism with each *Stich* displaying elements unparalleled but assumed in the other *Stich*.[314] As the chart shows, assumed in anticipation in 6:4b (A) is "may walk in new life," and unparalled but assumed in 6:4c (B) are the elements "to be raised"[315] and the glory of God as the causal factor. This parallel construction shows that God's glory and to walk in new life are related[316] (cf. 2 Cor 3:18b). The new life is caused by God, and is given in the pattern of a commission as referred to earlier in relation to speech-act theory. The person who is given this life from God is to receive it as a responsibility and live it now for his glory (6:6, 11–14, 22). This is a common idea in Paul.[317]

To sum up, in Romans 6:4–5 Paul speaks of the Christian's resurrection and life, but the present life of the Christian (the life which is embraced and starts in initiation) is his theme. Paul focuses on the transition from sin to God and on the new life that is the purpose of such a process. The idea of

---

312. Cramer, *Baptism and Change*, 47.
313. E.g. *GELNT-OECL*, s.v. "διά," point B.
314. Cf. *IBI*, 287–88, chart on Ps 50:4.
315. So Tannehill, *Dying and Rising*, 10.
316. So Cyril of Jerusalem, cited by Finn, *Early Christian Baptism: West and East Syria*, 49; Godet, *Romains* II, 22.
317. E.g. Rom 1:21–23; 3:23; 4:20; 9:23b; 1 Cor 10:31; 2 Cor 3:18a; 4:15; Phil 2:11.

the "new state" to which the believer moves is in mind when he uses the word resurrection[318] (cf. 6:9; but also pointing to the future, see also 1 Cor 15:42–44, 51–52). Paul's thinking on newness of life is consistent with the initiation assumptions of his time. The evidence is that in 6:4–5, this idea of a new life to walk in (stage four) is linked with the fact that it emanates from God's glory (stage one), requires a death like Christ's (stage two), and is ratified and confirmed in baptism (stage three).

4.5.4. Serving the New Existence: The Slave Motif (6:6, 13–22)

The previous section focused on rising to new life and walking in it. One aspect of this, namely "to serve" the new system to which the person moves, is emphasised in our pericope, and it deserves focus here. In the second chapter we noted that to serve the new system was a key feature of initiation. It is also stressed by Paul when he speaks of the Christian transition. Paul reminds his readers that sin is no longer their master (5:21, 6:17–18) and that their service of sin must stop (6:1–2, 6, 12–14). Badke thinks that service is implied in 6:2–3.[319] Antithetically to serving sin, Paul speaks of offering oneself to God (6:13, 19) and this includes sacrifice and service.[320] Serving emerges also in Paul's prominent use of δουλεύω (to be a slave or servant) and its cognates δοῦλος (slave, servant) and δουλόω, "to enslave" (cf. 6:6, 16–20, 22).

What does Paul mean by this? He is speaking of the transition from existence under sin to God; we would the use of this word-group to refer to the responsibility of serving which stems from the process of this transition (stage four). In this section, we ask whether this is truly Paul's point, and examine whether with this Paul shows that the initiand takes an active part in their *passage* to new existence.

First, therefore, we ask whether Paul's use of the "serving" concept involves the initiand in taking hold of the notion of service in their transition.[321] Paul's

---

318. J. Kremer notes a similar use in Eph 5:14, cf. Kremer, "ἀνάστασις," in *EDNT*, vol. 1, 91 col. 1.

319. So Badke, "Baptized into Moses," 29.

320. R. J. Daly, "New Testament Concept," 99–107.

321. Several scholars hint at this, e.g. Garlington thinks that Paul implies the believer's "service now," cf. "Obedience of Faith," 88; and Barrett, "baptism is the gateway not to heaven . . . but to a life which is related . . . to the present age," cf. *Romans*, 122; Hill finds that one's entry (baptism) meant a commitment to serve, cf. Hill, "On Suffering and Baptism," 189.

emphasis on service is correlated with the idea of a change of existence. His idea is that the Romans were to show that they have moved from serving ἀκαθαρσία (uncleanness) and ἀνομία (lawlessness) to serving δικαιοσύνη, "righteousness" (6:19). In 6:6 (and 6:22; cf. 5:21), Paul juxtaposes service (δουλεύω) of God and the fact that to serve sin must now stop (cf. καταργηθῇ – as we will see). It appears that initiation presumptions are probably in Paul's mind, and that service was a key feature at the heart of such a process. This is reflected by Malina when he notices that for any first-century Mediterranean "coalition," service was part of the "virtue" required for "the honour" of the group and its founder.[322] For Paul and contemporary Christians, changing "to a new 'order of being' means a new way of life in service to a new master."[323]

It influences our sense of the meaning of Romans 5–6, to suggest that Paul thinks here of initiation, and of how a change of service from one master to another takes place. It is relevant to ask how Paul would have understood the status of sin as the system of life that is left by the initiand. Important here is the verb καταργέω (to render useless)[324] (cf. ἵνα καταργηθῇ τὸ σῶμα τῆς ἁμαρτίας, "the sinful body be rendered powerless" 6:6), whose sense is disputed. Did Paul see this word as meaning "destroyed"[325] or "made inoperative"?[326] This is important because understanding what Paul thought of the servitude left behind τὸ σῶμα τῆς ἁμαρτίας (sinful body)[327] will help us to appreciate the action that this change of masters implies.

Paul is often understood as meaning in Romans 5–6 that sin is destroyed and dead. For instance, Chrysostom's view was that God has "killed our

---

322. Malina, "Let Him Deny Himself," 115–116.

323. Tannehill, *Dying and Rising*, 8.

324. In secular use καταργέω is "to render inactive, to condemn to inactivity, to put out of use"; the LXX uses it with the sense "to destroy," cf. G. Delling, "ἀργός, ἀργέω, καταργέω," in *TDNT*, vol. 1, 452.

325. As understood by e.g. Murray, *Romans*, 221; Schreiner, *Romans*, 316; Jewett, *Romans* 403, 404; Tannehill, *Dying and Rising*, 24; Seeley, *Noble Death*, 99; Esler, *Conflict and Identity*, 213. cf. also Watson, *Paul, Judaism, and Gentiles*, 279.

326. So e.g. Engberg-Pedersen, *Paul and Stoics*, 225–26, 228–29, 231–32; Bruce, *Romans*, 138.

327. τὸ σῶμα τῆς ἁμαρτίας, "sinful body," (6:6) has raised various connotations, but all concur with sin. E.g. Jewett sees in it sin as "a collective entity," cf. *Romans*, 403; same view with Dunn, *Romans 1–8*, 332; Bruce, *Romans*, 139; Tannehill, *Dying and Rising*, 24. Cranfield speaks of the "whole man as controlled by sin," *Romans*, 309; and Mohrlang sees it as "the sinful drives of the physical body," *Romans*, 100.

former evils" and that "sin itself is dead."[328] Also Cranfield speaks of sin as "dead."[329] Sanday and Headlam offer a similar interpretation when they describe the baptized as a person who has "ceased from all contact with sin."[330] This view is also the core of the "Exchanged Life" theology.[331] However, Delling's view is that it is "in the religious sense" that Paul uses this word "almost exclusively," and that here in Romans 6 the meaning is "to make completely inoperative."[332] And if Paul's thinking is shaped by initiation presumptions, this will suggest that he will not have seen sin as a way of life that is dead, at least not in this pericope. His emphasis on the serious commitment implied by the challenge to die to one system (stage two), to pledge full attachment to the new system (stage three) and turn to serve the new system (stage four) suggests strongly that the old system is still able to have the person back. A look at καταργηθῇ (rendered useless) indeed shows that this is Paul's view of sin as a way of life.

Through initiation a person moves to a new existence, but the former way of life does not die out.[333] As Dunn recognizes, "Conversion is a *decisive* event . . . But this does not mean that the believer's old nature (attitudes, values, desires, etc.) are dead."[334] Paul's thinking in his use of καταργηθῇ (rendered useless) appears to be that sin is "overcome," as Mohrlang puts it.[335] As Delling thinks, the idea is possibly "rendered insignificant" in the sense "be deprived of significance in the judgment" of the believer.[336] This implies a

---

328. Chrysostom, *Homilies on Romans*, 164 (on 6:18), also 148 (on 6:2).

329. Cranfield, *Romans 1–8*, 310.

330. Sanday and Headlam, *Romans*, 153; also Theodore of Mopsuestia, *Early Christian Baptism: West and East Syria*, 84.

331. For more on this theology, e.g. Pyne and Blackmon, "Critique of 'Exchanged Life,'" 131–57, cf. esp. 143–44.

332. Delling, 'ἀργός,' 453.

333. As Cyril of Jerusalem thinks, baptism implies that sin is "overthrown," cf. *Catechesis* 3, Trans. of Finn, *Early Christian Baptism: West and East Syria*, 50–51.

334. Dunn, *Jesus and Spirit*, 335 [italics his].

335. E.g. Mohrlang, *Romans*, 100. A similar sense is "made impotent," cf. Morris, *Romans*, 252, fn. 38; or made "paralyzed," cf. Dunn, *Romans 1–8*, 319.

336. Delling, "ἀργός," 453.

responsibility to keep.³³⁷ Having moved to Christ and his system, believers are to see sin as unnecessary, lest the system of sin should still affect them.

Sin survives initiation, as verse 7 seems to show. After καταργηθῇ (rendered useless) in 6:6, verse 7 shows that the one who dies in this transition from sin to God is the believer. Sin itself as a way of life continues, even if during initiation the person seriously rejects its way. Its ability to enslave remains. Many Church Fathers understand this to be the idea in 6:1–2 and in the verses where the δουλ- word-group features (vv.6, 16–22),³³⁸ and this view is widely held by modern scholarship.³³⁹ Speaking of 6:6, Dunn, for example, draws attention to the fact that "The very formulation, with the μηκέτι and the present tense, implies that the possibility of the believer's *continuing* to serve sin is very real."³⁴⁰ Paul's thinking appears to be guided by the reality that an initiate may leave their old way of life but the system itself is not dead. In their new existence, the initiate must be very much on their guard.

Second, we explore how much Paul sees the agency of the believer involved when, in initiation, the choice between serving sin and serving God is made. Does this idea of the persistence of the abandoned master make the believer's agency even stronger? To understand this further, closer attention is now given to the use of the δουλ - word-group in Romans 6.

The idea that the old way of life continues after initiation, and is still able to influence the baptized to serve it, shows that the δοῦλος (slave), as far as Romans 6 is concerned, is a person who is able to choose.³⁴¹ As mentioned earlier, in 6:19 the word seems to imply an act of choice where one way of life is rejected and another is embraced. The picture is of what the initiand does

---

337. Delling misses this point when he sees "rendered insignificant in one's judgment" as meaning that sin "is robbed of its power to affect the religious and moral attitude . . . of man," cf. "ἀργός," 453.

338. As shown by their views on e.g. 6:6, 16, 18; cf. translations in Bray, *Romans*, 152–54, 162–64.

339. Moo, *Romans 1–8*, 369; Cranfield, *Romans 1–8*, 298–99; Achtemeier, *Romans*, 110; Edwards, *Romans*, 162 (on 6:6); also Gaventa, *From Darkness to Light*, 45.

340. Dunn, *Romans 1–8*, 320; also *Jesus and the Spirit*, 335. A similar view when Moo suggests that in 6:6 instead of "we are no longer servants of sin" the idea is "we should no longer serve sin," cf. Moo, *Romans 1–8*, 394, 415.

341. Link's idea on δοῦλος (slave) and its word-group: "when used figuratively, they can . . . lose the sense of compulsion . . . Here . . . dependence can be seen, not as an enforced loss of one's self, but also as an independent self-realization," cf. Link, "Slave, Servant, Captive," 589; cf. especially Christ as a slave (597), and δοῦλος (slave) with the sense of διακονος, "a servant" (596).

in initiation (stage four). Hodge for example sees this word in its ordinary sense of a person who is under "coercion."[342] Slavery did not always mean deprivation of power and choice.[343] So in Romans 6, the δοῦλος (slave) is more than the powerless slave who acts by order.

Lyall, for example, considers that "the slave . . . did not even have power over himself," and sees this as the key idea in this pericope.[344] The fact that in antiquity "slaves are in the *potestas*, 'the power', of their masters,"[345] leads him to conclude that "it is in the detail of this power that the fullness of Paul's analogy is to be seen."[346] But the initiatory patterns that appear to form the background of Paul's thinking would suggest another sense. A person who undergoes initiation is not like a slave deprived of any power and choice. Paul thinks of persons who freely choose their master and their way to live. What is reflected here seems to be Bartchy's idea that "self-sale into slavery is the most likely context for understanding Paul."[347] It is noteworthy that in the Septuagint, δοῦλος (slave) is "sometimes *voluntary*" service,[348] done by "*voluntary* decision" though "in favour of the powerful claim of another."[349] One would expect Paul to have this idea in mind when he speaks of the Christian

---

342. Hodge, *Romans*, 181, 190.

343. E.g. Lightfoot: some owners treated their slaves with humanity, cf. *Colossians and Philemon*, 319, fn. 5; see also Bartchy, "Slavery (Greco-Roman)," 68 col. 2–69 col. 1. Moreover, it has been recognized that in Jewish-Christian circles "slaves are considered responsible human beings," Abraham showing the model in Gen 15:2–3 (cf. Parsons, "Slavery and New Testament," 91; also Harrill, "Slavery," 300 col. 1, 302 col. 1–303 col. 1); and some believe that Paul uses δοῦλος (slave) in this sense (cf. Lightfoot, *Colossians and Philemon*, 318; Longenecker, *New Testanebt Social Ethics*, 54). In fact, as in Paul the idea δοῦλος τοῦ θεοῦ is used in Philo and the *Septuagint* (for more on this, e.g. Rengstorf, "δοῦλος," 264, 267). Even outside Jewish-Christian circles, "slavery . . . often wore the mask of civility" (Longenecker, *New Testament Social Ethics*, 54) as "others found themselves in relatively good circumstances" (Dandamayev, "Slavery (ANE)," 60 col. 2–61 col. 1; also Harrill, "Slavery," 301 col. 1; more in Meeks, *First Urban Christians*, 20). This characterized not only the ANE period (cf. Dandamayev, "Slavery (ANE)," 60 col. 2–61 col. 1; Harrill, "Slavery," 299, col. 2) but also the Greco-Roman era (e.g. Bartchy, "Slavery (Greco-Roman)," 69 col. 2; Harrill, "Slavery," 305, col. 1). As Paul speaks of the free transition from one religious life to another, one may understand that he uses δοῦλος (slave) in this positive sense.

344. Lyall, "Roman Law," 76.

345. Lyall, 75.

346. Lyall, 75.

347. Bartchy, "Slavery (Greco-Roman)," 67 col. 2; cf. also Jewett, *Romans*, 416; a similar idea by the Stoics (also adopted by Philo) was that "no one is originally a δοῦλος (slave) but a man makes himself a δοῦλος," cf. detail on Stoics and Philo in Rengstorf, "δοῦλος," 264.

348. Rengstorf, 266 [italics mine].

349. Rengstorf, 267 [italics mine].

who, at the heart of the transition, rejects the service of sin and turns to live for and serve Christ. As we noted in chapter 2, the language of slavery is frequently applied to religious transition to new life (e.g. with Lucius in *The Golden Ass*), and in such contexts the word simply denotes service to the new community and their god, a service personally taken up by the initiand.

There is internal evidence to support this in Romans 6. When Paul speaks of believers and their service, he means service which is freely offered (6:12–13, 19). This is recognized by Shulam who maintains that the idea in 6:17, 20 is that "one cannot serve two masters simultaneously."[350] Ziesler thinks that 6:16 conveys the same idea.[351] Also Jewett points out that ἤτοι . . . ἤ (6:16) can mean "either . . . or" and that this indicates a serious "choice."[352] What is not noted by these commentators is that Paul is concerned not just with a choice that believers need to keep exercising, but also with the serious and responsible choice they already made in their transition (cf. aor. παρεστήσατε /παραστήσατε, "you yielded/yield" (6:19).

We argue that initiation assumptions form the background to Paul's thinking when he uses "service" language in Romans 6. As in the initiation process, the core of Paul's thinking is the serious responsibility of choosing between two masters (God and sin). A person moves from the life of sin but as *The Shepherd of Hermas* shows, after baptism "the devil . . . is always contriving something against the *servants* of God, and maliciously lays snares for them."[353] To illustrate this situation, the slavery image serves well for Paul. Slave masters (including bad ones) are always waiting in the market. Thus, slaves who are enjoying gracious slavery[354] must keep their commitment to avoid being sold. This means showing outstanding service as proof of the seriousness of their pledged attachment to the master and to his system of life. This is familiar to Paul, who is aware of how Israel's unfaithful service and attachment resulted

---

350. Shulam, *Jewish Roots of Romans*, 224–25; as also in Josh 24:14–15; Matt 6:24.

351. Ziesler, *Romans*, 167 (on v. 16).

352. Jewett, *Romans*, 416.

353. Shepherd of Hermas, *His Commands* 4.3, 235 [italics mine]; so also John Chrysostom, cited by Finn, *Early Baptism: West and East Syria*, 80.

354. As Harrill notes, Paul distinguishes the "good slavery" with God (cf. Rom 12:11; 13:4; 14:4, 18; 1 Cor 7:22–23; Gal 5:13) and "bad slavery" (cf. Rom 7:14), cf. Harrill, "Slavery," 306 col. 2.

in their being handed over to unhappy bondage (Jer 34:8–22; Ezek 39:23). Like Israel, the baptized is also warned (cf. also 1 Cor 10:1–12).[355]

Simply put, Paul reminds his baptized readers of the renunciation which they certainly experienced and know well, because in all religions, renunciation functions as the key to transition.[356] At the heart of Paul's emphasis is the whole contract idea of people who encounter God and his saving action (stage one) and their responsive consecration to him (stages two, three and four). When Paul's readers renounced their old way of life, they made an "alliance"[357] with God; the "covenant" concept applies here between God and the Christians as in the Old Testament, as Sherman notes.[358] Paul seeks to awaken the Christians in Rome to this agreement. The basis of making such an alliance is the serious conviction that the old master is a tyrant to "overthrow,"[359] and that there is a continuing need to keep "immune from [his] tricks."[360] Only God has the "armour"[361] and God has already dealt with the bad master (stage one). As Chrysostom states, the believer must take the responsibility to "show great vigilance in guarding what has been given to [him or her]."[362] So the centre of it all is the fact that sin seeks to re-conscript the believer in an unhappy situation. As *The Shepherd of Hermas* recognizes, all that this alliance demands of believers is for their own "profit"[363] (cf. καρπός, 6:21, 22).

---

355. For more on this, see e.g. Bultmann, *Theology of New Testament*, vol. 1, 312.

356. For more on this, in addition to what was given in chapter 2, see: for Christians' entry as recognized by Fathers, e.g. Gounelle, "Le baptême aux temps patristiques," 185–186; Finn, *Early Christian Baptism: West and East Syria*, 7; and 83–84 (on Theodore of Mopsuestia's *Homilies*), 98–101 (the "Ordo of Constantinople"); Hill, "On Suffering," 187–188; for initiation into Jewish faith, e.g. Heron, "Theology of Baptism," 39; for the Qumran covenanters, cf. 1QS v.6, 8–10; for renunciation at the centre of the OT covenant, e.g. Exod 20:2–6; cf. Sklba, "Call to New Beginnings," 67–68; for entry to mysteries, e.g. Reitzenstein, *Hellenistic Mystery-Religions*, 28.

357. So Chrysostom, *Early Baptism: West and East Syria*, 80.

358. Sherman, "Getting in," 111.

359. So Cyril of Jerusalem, *Catechesis* 3, *Early Baptism: West and East Syria*, 51.

360. So Chrysostom, *Early Baptism: West and East Syria*, 80.

361. Cf. Cyril, *Catechesis* 3, *Early Baptism: West and East Syria*, 51.

362. Chrysostom, *Early Baptism: West and East Syria*, 80.

363. The Shepherd of Hermas, *His Commands* 4.3, in Burton, *Apostolic Fathers*, vol. 1, 235.

4.6. Summary

This chapter has provided an analysis of Romans 5:12–6:23, seeking to understand whether the four stages of initiation, and the divine and human agency that they imply, are present in this pericope where Paul speaks of the transition from sin to God. We have suggested that initiatory language can be found in Paul's rhetoric on baptism. In the initiatory patterns of Paul's time, the transition to new religious life involves not only the action of the deity but that of the initiand as well. Our argument has sought to show that Paul has this in mind in Romans 5–6. Paul shows that God's saving action is the basis of it all (stage one). He emphasises this divine act in Romans 5:15–19 and refers to it further in 6:3–10 when he shows its relationship with the initiand's (baptizand's) action.

The initiand's agency is stressed in Romans 6, though anticipated in Romans 5. In 6:1–2 Paul focuses on the initiand's death to (i.e. breaking from) the old way of life (stage two). Bearing in mind the initiatory assumptions of Paul, "we died to sin" is more than (just) referring to Christ's act against sin on the cross; the focus is more on the initiand's death in the liminal stage. In the third and fourth stages there are more elements of the initiand's agency. The pledge of belonging to the new system, which is linked to the ritual that seals initiation (stage three), is seen in 6:3–4. We have also looked at different aspects of the actions linked to the new life embraced in the transition (stage four): these have included reigning (5:17, 21), living righteously (5:21, also 19), walking in newness of life (6:4–5) and the servant life (6:6, 13–22). New elements of meaning emerge as these aspects of the believer's life are considered in connection with first-century initiation assumptions. As was noted, these are actions taken within the transition process, not after it. In relation to this, the future tense of some of the verbs with which these actions are linked is primarily an initiatory (present) future, although an eschatological future sense may also be implied.

CHAPTER FIVE

Conclusion

This chapter draws the threads of our argument together. The focus of this study has been the idea that baptism is about taking action. Paul's utterances "we died to sin" (Rom 6:2) and "we were baptized" (v. 3) entail action rather than passivity. To prove this, the study has attempted to show how, in antiquity, the process of change from one religious existence to another consisted of four stages of action. With a focus on this religious background, the study has endeavoured to show that, according to Paul's view in Romans 5:12–6:23, both God and the believer take decisive action during the transition from the realm of sin to the realm of God. One of these actions is to die to one's old way of life. When Paul speaks of dying to sin in Romans 6:2, he sees an action by the believer. In the pericope, Paul also writes of Christ's deeds. But in Romans 6:2 he is not thinking of the death of Christ on behalf of people. His concern is with the believer's personal act of breaking with the old way of life. And so we have argued that "we were baptized" is not just an allusion to undergoing the water ritual. More than this, "baptism" encompasses and expresses stages of actions, of which dying to one's old way of life is one. To understand whether baptism means action or passivity, this study has considered the idea of baptism in Romans 6 in connection with these stages of a transition from one way of existence to another and the action implied by each stage.

To draw a conclusion to our argument, we undertake three things in this chapter: 1) a summary of our findings, 2) some suggestions for further research, and 3) a summary of what was achieved.

5.1 Summary of Findings

The first chapter was introductory. This summary focuses on the findings arising from the second chapter (the exploration of the process of entry from one existence to another in Paul's time) and from the third chapter (the study of Paul's own transition to Christianity). Then we will focus on the findings arising from Paul's view on baptism in Romans 5:12–6:23 (cf. chapter 4).

5.1.1. The Rite that Seals Entry, a Time for Action: Chapters Two and Three

In the course of understanding baptism in Romans 5–6, the second chapter has explored initiation in the religious life of Paul's time; what this chapter has showed concerning the ceremony that marks the entry is summarised here. The ritual that sealed the person's initiation was a time of action, not passivity. It is true that the religious settings explored in this study (mysteries, Jewish religious life, and state religion) show with emphasis that in first-century religious life the deity takes an active role in initiation. In the initiation process, the deity saves the person from the wrong things connected to his or her previous life (cf. mysteries and Judaism) or imparts favours such as protection (cf. state religion). Also it is the deity that enrols the candidate into the new community and the new holy service. Physically this role is assumed by religion officials,[1] but they were acting on behalf of the deity, who in fact was supposed to be present. Thus, there is a stress on the role and the presence of the deity, and this is evidence that there is a theological dimension linked to initiation.

However, religious life in antiquity shows that people undergoing initiation were not just passive. The ritual that sealed initiation was more than just having things done to the initiand by the gods or the officials. At various stages of initiation, the candidate took serious responsibility in relation to the new existence. This was especially true of the ritual sealing the entry. It emphasised the personal choice and decision to undergo such ceremonies. This was evident with entry in the mysteries (e.g. Lucius' account), in Judaism (cf. the stress on the choice of the proselyte) and in state religions. Action is also seen in the fact that undergoing such a ritual was a personal oath to the watching men and gods that the new life will be abided in. The rite meant a

---

1. As mentioned earlier, this study has not gone into detail on this role of officials.

public declaration to the new community and its deity of personal acceptance of belonging to them, thus taking a binding responsibility to live for them. To make such a pledge and taking such a responsibility are not passive.

The third chapter focused on Paul's own *passage* from his life as a Pharisee to the Christian life. There is a similarity between what the second chapter shows and what is noted about Paul's transition. Paul's *passage* to new life puts emphasis on God's role, but without nullifying Paul's own agency. God delivered him from a wrong perception of Israel's God and his will for mankind. The Damascus Road event emphasises this divine intervention. However, Paul was more than a "vanquished" man during the three days of his transition. His prayer and fasting (cf. stage two) implied a time of learning from God and agreeing with God. This is not passivity. And his baptism, which is the focus here, was a time of action. Ananias' conversation with Paul shows that it was Paul's own choice and decision to "get up" for baptism. Also, even if the word pledge (or oath) is not used in the Acts accounts, the aspect of "pledge" is linked to Paul's baptism. As chapter 2 has shown, the rite that seals entry is a pledge to the gods and the community; both are assumed to be present when the candidate undergoes this ceremony. Paul's baptism was also a pledge to God; God's presence permeates the whole episode. What is not evident is the presence of the community of believers. But the presence of Ananias covers this aspect. As a minister of Jesus, he represents sufficiently his church. In this sense, the responsibility that Saul takes in the presence of this minister of the Church is serious and binding. Like any first-century rite of sealing the transition from one religious existence to another, Paul's baptism implied action. It meant to take responsibility.

This leads us now to a summary of what a focus on baptism in Romans 5–6 reveals concerning the divine and human agency in the believer's transition and baptism.

5.1.2. Baptism in Romans 6: A Time for Action

In our endeavour to show that in Romans 5:12–6:23 there is a focus on the acts of responsibility that the baptizand takes during their transition to new life, in the first chapter two elements were considered very important. (1) Baptism (i.e. the water ritual) is a part of the process of initiation or entry to new life. When Paul says "we were baptized," he is referring not just to the water ceremony that his readers have undergone; Paul is reminding them what their whole transition from sin to God was about. We proposed that we will achieve a better understanding of the action which baptism implies, if the four stages of such a transition, and the action that they imply, are considered. (2) We argued that the whole of Romans 5:12–6:23 is occupied with this entry by believers into their new existence. What Paul says concerning this transition, and particularly the action that it entails, is better grasped if what he says in 6:1–4 is understood in relation to the wider unit of Romans 5:12–6:23. This first section (5.1) is a summary of these two elements of our argument. The purpose of this summary is to provide a more concise picture of the contribution of this study.

a. "We Were Baptized" Meaning More than Taking the Water Ritual

To show that in Romans 6 baptism means action, one key idea in this study is that "we were baptized" is a reference not only to the water ceremony but also to the entire process of the believer's transition from sin to God. Paul has in mind the action that takes place at different stages of this transition, including the stage of the water ceremony. A summary of this is as follows:

First, in Romans 6 Paul certainly focuses his thought on the water ceremony of baptism and the action that is taken at this stage of the person's transition from sin to God. When he reminds his readers of their baptism, he first means this ritual. As was shown in this study (especially in the first and fourth chapters), there is evidence that by βαπτίζειν, "to baptize" (6:3–4) Paul refers to this public ceremony. His focus rests on the fact that to undergo such a ceremony is to attach to a system. It was explained in chapter 4 how this closely links with Paul's questions in 6:1–2. His baptized readers cannot go on sinning because they underwent the water ceremony (v. 3), by which they publicly declared their attachment to Christ's community and its life. Paul sees baptism as a serious action, because agreeing to undergo this ritual is to take the responsibility of not returning to one's old way of life. This study aimed to demonstrate that this sense of action rests on the idea of the public pledge that such initiation ceremonies as baptism meant for Paul and first-century Christians. In antiquity, to undergo such a public ritual during one's *passage* to a new religious way of life was to make a pledge to the members of the new community and to their deity. In this sense, the person was by no means passive when undergoing this church ritual.

Second, however, Paul means more than just the water ceremony when he says to his readers that they "were baptized." These words encapsulate what their whole transition from sin to God meant. In other words, Paul uses a *synecdoche*.[2] His concern is to remind his readers not just of the pledge that they made by taking the public ritual; he is drawing their attention to all the acts of responsibility that they made during their transition from sin to living in God's way. Scholarly interpretation of "we were baptized" in Romans 6:2–4 has not given sufficient attention to this aspect of the expression – the way in which it serves as a *synecdoche*. The readers of Romans, as people who have been baptized, are shown in 6:1–2 the significant responsibility that they have personally taken. This responsibility was not only taken by undergoing the water ritual. As this study has described, their initiation encompassed a staged sequence of personal acts of commitment.

Apart from the pledge that is meant by undergoing the water ritual (stage three), another personal act in this process of change was their death to sin (6:2). Examining the process of transition to a new religious life in antiquity, which is the focus of this work, has led us to affirm that "death to sin" in 6:2 is the act of the believer, not of Christ, as scholarship has often held. This new view is summarized here. Generally, the interpretation of death in 6:2 has depended on what the water of baptism is understood to symbolize. Some have linked the connection between death and baptism with the idea that water symbolizes threat and death.[3] Thus the immersion of believers under water is thought of as giving them a sense of dying. Other scholars have stressed that the water of baptism symbolized cleansing,[4] rather than a threat of death. Each of these views produces a different understanding of what death in Romans 6:2 means; for example, Dunn maintains that the death of the readers of Romans 6 is "their being baptized to share in Jesus' death."[5] This is also Moule's opinion when he suggests that Romans 6:2 and 3 are about "accepting his [Christ's] death in oneself" and "being swamped in

---

2. *Synecdoche* is the figure of speech "by which the whole could stand for the part, or a part for the whole," cf. Kaiser, "My Heart Is Stirred," 148; and Klein, *Introduction to Biblical Interpretation*, 313–314.

3. E.g. Barth, *Teaching of the Church*, 9, 11; Morris, *Romans*, 246; Fiddes, "Baptism and Creation," 54 (for more, pp. 53–55); Haymes, "Baptism as Political Act," 72.

4. E.g. Dunn, *Romans 1–8*, 312; Moule, *Birth of New Testament*, 38.

5. Dunn, *Romans 1–8*, 312; so also Cullmann, *Baptism in New Testament*, 19–20.

it."[6] In the fourth chapter of this study, we argued that what Paul means in 6:2 is more than the believers' share in Christ's death on the cross. In connection with the responsibility that the apostle expresses in 6:1–2, death to sin is the personal act of the believers against sin. Paul is speaking of the act of dying to one's old way of existence (stage two).

Besides breaking with their old way of life, in their transition Paul's readers have begun walking in their new existence (stage four). To live the new existence is not something that comes after initiation. Rather, to start walking in the new way is part of the believer's transition (6:4–5). As we suggested in the fourth chapter, "we shall live" is the logical future of an action that continues into the future, but which has begun already. The baptized of Rome are reminded that they have already undertaken the responsibility to serve the new way (cf. 6:6, 13, 16–22). The aorist ἐδουλώθητε (e.g. v. 18) shows that Paul leads them to think of what happened at a specific time in the past. This time, according to the context, is that of their transition from sin to God. In this they acted personally: they offered themselves to God (6:13). This is another element which shows that Paul points to different acts of responsibility when he says "you were baptized." These words encompass more than just the pledge of taking the water ritual.

This section has focused on the action of the believer implied by "you were baptized." However, more than this, these words also connote the divine action that takes place during the believer's transition from sin to God. But because this expression encompasses both divine action and the action of the believer, usually no distinction has been made and as a result "to die to sin" (6:2) has been interpreted as a reference to the act of Christ on the cross. Seeing Romans 5:12–6:23 as the relevant pericope has been crucial for our argument in making this distinction between divine and human action. In other words, a consideration of this whole pericope shows how "you were baptized" embraces both God's and the believer's agency in the transition. A summary on this is given in this next section.

---

6. Moule, *Birth of New Testament*, 38.

b. Romans 5:12–6:23: God and the Baptizand in Connection with Baptism

This study has focused on the believer's acts of taking responsibility during their baptismal transition. One aspect of this has been to consider how this act of the believer fits together with the action of God, which of course Paul also affirms in Romans 6 in connection with baptism. We have given attention to Romans 5:12–6:23 (instead of 6:1–11/14), because this pericope helps us to see how the actions of God and the believer fit together during the transition from sin to the Christian life. This present section summarises the contribution made by considering this pericope. Our focus here is especially on what Paul sees as the relationship between God and baptism as an element of transition from one existence to another.

As Moisés Silva recognizes, the task of the interpreter of the epistles is not only "to inquire into their historical context" but also to enquire into "the theological meaning."[7] Käsemann concurs: any "attempt to interpret the New Testament" should be "comprehensive, historical and theological."[8] In this study also, history and theology have been combined.

The historical aspect has consisted in asking and considering what, in Paul's *Sitz im Leben*, the believer as an initiand was expected to undergo during the process of their transition to new existence. The action expected included dying to the life of sin or breaking with it (second stage), publicly taking an oath of commitment to the Christian way through the water ritual (third stage), and embracing the new life and beginning to live it during these initiation episodes (stage four). In connection with these elements, the study has addressed Paul's theological understanding of baptism as entry to a new religious life and its relationship to God. Here we summarise the theological ideas that Paul develops about the believer's transition and baptism in Romans 5–6.

Repeating the relationship with the divine that has been expressed at each stage is not our intention here. The focus now is on the comprehensive idea that covers the different phases. Paul says, ὅσοι ἐβαπτίσθημεν εἰς Χριστὸν Ἰησοῦν εἰς τὸν θάνατον αὐτοῦ ἐβαπτίσθημεν, "we all who were baptized to Christ Jesus, to his death we have been baptized" (6:3). These words show a

---

7. Silva, "How to Read," 184.
8. Käsemann's approach in his "later theological work" as noticed by Way, *Lordship of Christ*, 4.

connection between Christ's deed (his death) and baptism. In other words, one can speak of a theology of baptism. Our intention here is to ask how this theology is impacted if we focus on the stages of the transition from sin to God and on the action that they imply.

The words of 6:3 quoted above show an intricate connection between two ideas: one about God and another that concerns the believer. The words ὅσοι ἐβαπτίσθημεν εἰς Χριστὸν Ἰησοῦν εἰς τὸν θάνατον αὐτοῦ ἐβαπτίσθημεν (we all who were baptized to Christ Jesus, to his death we have been baptized) are both about Christ and about believers. They show clearly that baptism concerns Christ and his death, but they also communicate something about the believer. As explained in the fourth chapter, they convey the idea that believers ("we") undertake an act in baptism. As Beasley-Murray recognizes, there is in this a connotation that baptism involves an "act of man" as well as an "act of God."[9]

This study has shown that the theological idea that Paul is making rests on these twin ideas in 6:3. When "being baptized in Christ" (6:3) was analyzed in the fourth chapter of this study, we argued that belonging to God is the key notion expressed in these words. The connection of this idea of belonging to God with the whole baptismal process is the core element in the theology that Paul constructs out of the believer's transition and the action implied by this event. Belonging to God has a link with all the different phases of the transition and the action that is taken by both God and the believer. The believer has belonged to God since the first stage when God saved the believer from the slavery of sin (cf. Rom 5:12–18). The believer was passive in this phase. But at the other phases (stages two, three and four) the believer takes action to express their decision to attach to God's realm and to belong to it as the rule of their life. As Mcvann notes, this was a serious act for believers, as it meant "renouncing their status as members" of their original community, resulting in "making themselves marginal."[10] The seriousness of the act taken is especially implied by the water ceremony.[11] As the explanation of stage

---

9. Beasley-Murray, *Baptism in New Testament*, 100–101, 103.

10. M. Mcvann, "Baptism, Miracles," 151; even more serious for Jewish believers as they could be excommunicated, so e.g. Schneiders, "Reflections on Commitment," 41.

11. For a hint at this idea, cf. e.g. Auque, "La re-con-naissance," 64. The difference is that Auque speaks of the baptism of the child and in this case the choice to belong to God is made not by the initiand but by the parents and the priest.

three has shown, by this public ritual of initiation believers pledge to Christ and to their fellow members that they belong to Christ and his church.

The believer's action as an element of this theological idea of Paul is overlooked if the water ceremony is understood as a stage where the action is solely divine. Cranfield, for example, understands the water ceremony as the place where God makes "a pledge that the benefits of Christ's death . . . apply" to the baptizand.[12] The water ceremony is rather the place for the candidate's pledge. It is the place where the candidate personally unites with Christ, when by undergoing the ritual the believer makes an oath that they belong to Christ and his system, and to live accordingly. God's act of uniting with the believer happens at the first stage. But in the water ceremony the baptizand personally makes belonging to Christ their responsibility by the pledge made before the community and God.

Thus, the four stages of initiation show what baptism is in Paul's theology. Dunn wonders if we should try to specify Paul's theology of baptism. The intricacy mentioned above is noted by Dunn when he speaks of the life of a Christian as something that is "a complex whole."[13] This complexity leads to his suggestion that "it may be less important to give a precise *location or function for baptism within Paul's theology* than to recognize that it was part of the complex whole and filled an *important role* within the complex whole."[14]

The four stages of initiation help us to specify the location and the role of the water ceremony within the complex of ideas in 5:12—6:23. Paul's theological conviction about entry to new existence is connected with the stages that this transition implies. The first stage of the move to God's realm is the encounter with God and his saving action. By this divine act the person enters into unity with God and becomes his. This divine encounter leads to other stages which focus on the responsive action of the person concerned. This transition process as a whole shows a theology of baptism whose key features can be summarised as follows:

---

12. Cranfield, *Romans 1–8*, 303.

13. Dunn thinks of a whole that consists of "justification by faith, participation in Christ, and the gift of the Spirit," *Theology of Paul*, 455.

14. Dunn, 455 [italics mine].

1. God's *double* action – his work in Christ on the cross, and then his encounter with the individual that constitutes stage one in that person's move from sin to God's realm.
2. Baptism expresses belonging to Christ – spiritual connection. This appears in the idea that the person undergoes the water ritual in the presence of Christ and that the pledge, entailed by this ritual, is made to Christ himself.
3. It expresses belonging to the church – social connection. The pledge of commitment is made not only to Christ but also to his community.
4. Points 1–3 imply synergy – God's work and our response are equally vital to the initiation process. Grace does not overwhelm human freedom. This fourth point, especially the idea of synergy, raises a question: What would be the position of someone who had a real, genuine encounter with God but then backed out during stage two and never proceeded to stage three? We will return to this in the section of issues for further study, when we suggest a tentative answer to this question and propose it to be another issue for further reflection.
5. Baptism expresses "new life" – the ethical commitment to obey the whole new "way" to which we commit ourselves in the water.

5.2. Suggestions for Further Research

Our study suggests areas for further research arising out of the distinctive interpretation of elements of Romans 5:12–6:23 that it has proposed. At the same time, we seek to identify ways in which the argument of this study needs further work before it can be regarded as fully established. We have undertaken an exegetical study based on just one passage in Paul, albeit a central one for his thought about baptism. But we cannot therefore claim to have explored exhaustively all the issues relevant to the clarification of Paul's theology of initiation. Just as Romans 5:12–6:23 is just a section within the wider argument of Romans and of Paul's writings, so our discussion reaches out into wider issues relevant to understanding Paul's theology, on which we have not touched. We will conclude the study by touching on some of these areas in outline.

1) *Further work on the mysteries.* This study touches upon the issue of the difference between the mysteries and Christian ideas, especially regarding initiation. Ferguson's view is that "There were no true parallels to baptism in the mysteries."[15] In this study, it was shown that as far as baptism is concerned, this transition of the Christian has much in common with non-Christian religions of Paul's world. Also referring to what Paul says in Romans 6:2–4, Edwards states that "Whereas the mysteries stressed the initiates' experience, Paul stresses God's decisive act on behalf of believers that is both signified and assured by baptism."[16] As this study has shown, the idea that Paul's stress is on God's action overlooks the fact that the candidate's action comes to the fore in Romans 5:12–6:23.

It is important to clarify the difference between Paul and the mysteries. It is not who acts, the deity or the initiand, that constitutes the point of difference. As this study has shown, in both the mysteries and in Paul initiation consists of divine action combined with the action of the initiand. So, the question is what aspect we should focus on to understand the point of contrast between Christian initiation and initiation into the mysteries. Our tentative suggestion would be that stage one of the initiation process should be explored for discovering the key difference. In other words, the action of the deity during the transition is the aspect to focus on.

Earlier in this study it was mentioned that, in first-century life, people chose to leave state religion and mysteries and entered Christianity, even knowing that such a choice could cost their lives. The key to understanding this is to become aware of what the Christian God was seen to offer, and how more fulfilling were the conditions of entry. For instance, one needs to understand how Jesus would have been heard when he states, "Come to me, take my yoke, for my yoke is easy and my burden is light" (Matt 11:28–30). What meaning might these words have had to Jews (and other people) who read Matthew in the world of early Christianity? Clearly these words are sectarian, party-making. They show that there is something different on the other side. They should be understood in relation to what entry to a new religious group involved in first-century society.

---

15. Ferguson, *Backgrounds of Early Christianity*, 239.
16. Edwards, *Romans*, 160.

2) *Further reflection on "baptism saves."* Is baptism a necessary element in the believer's *ordo salutis*? Kaylor, for example, hints at this when he asks whether Paul "requires baptism as a necessary rite" since Paul's gospel is a "radical gospel of grace and faith."[17] Another way of formulating this is to ask in which sense Peter's claim that "baptism saves" is made (1 Pet 3:21).[18] Paul does not say in a direct way that baptism saves, but this idea is very much echoed when he connects baptism with the idea of becoming children of God (Gal 3:26–28).

So, is baptism a necessary step? Earlier, we mentioned that the "synergy" aspect of the theological idea that Paul is making on baptism was raising this question: What would be the position of someone who had a real, genuine encounter with God but then backed out during stage two and never proceeded to stage three? In light of the argument of this study, our tentative answer is that, in this specific case, initiation is not completed, and so this individual does not belong either to God or to the church. However, this requires further explanation. The whole issue here touches upon the debate over the question "once saved, always saved?" A connection between this debate and the ideas offered in this study requires further discussion.

In this study, the socio-religious approach to baptism as a rite of initiation has shown that believers are children of God by his grace in Christ. However, in the process of their transition, they personally take action over this status. They exercise their will and choice of seriously breaking with sin and attaching with God and his family. As Kaylor states, what they do is "a conscious self-determination."[19] The situation is comparable to that of a child born in a family. The child is born in a family and belongs to it without the child's decision. As H. Auque recognizes, "notre naissance est dépendante du désir de nos géniteurs"[20] and by virtue of this we are in "une proximité de possession" to them.[21] Later, through initiation, the young person belongs to this

---

17. Kaylor, *Paul's Covenant Community*, 126.

18. On this text, Brooks speaks seriously of baptism as "That is the convert's salvation!"; cf. *Drama of Decision*, 157.

19. Kaylor, *Paul's Covenant Community*, 123; Beasley-Murray, *Baptism in New Testament*, 143.

20. Auque, "La re-con-naissance," 62. Translation : "our birth depends on the desire of our begetters".

21. Auque, 64. Translation : "a proximity of possession".

family in such a way as to take all the rights and obligations that such a status implies. The young person takes action to confirm the status of belonging to the family. The idea that baptism "saves" could be understood in this sense, expressing what such a transition adds to the status of belonging to God. That this could mean "salvation" is an aspect that needs to be studied and expounded in more detail.

3) *Further reflection on the relationship between circumcision and baptism.* From this study, the comparison between circumcision and baptism is another area for further study. As Christianity is an off shoot of Judaism, the relationship between circumcision and baptism is worth exploring. This is especially an issue when the religious life of God's people is considered. Dunn recognizes that the two practices assume the same role when he states, "it is true, speaking sociologically, that Christian baptism . . . formed as effective a group boundary as circumcision."[22] The difference, according to Dunn's view, lies in the fact that the thing that constitutes "the newness of Christianity," and which takes the place of circumcision, is "the reality of grace through faith" not baptism.[23] It is not clear whether water baptism as a rite of entry directly replaced circumcision as a ritual that played the same initiatory role in Judaism. In fact, as Davies recognizes, in Judaism the proselytes underwent both baptism and circumcision.[24] But in the light of the focus of this study, Dunn's opinion that what takes the place of circumcision in the church is not baptism is something to explore. The following idea is suggested as a start.

A focus on the action taken in the Christian's transition from sin to living as a member of the church of God reveals a difference between circumcision and baptism. Further study could make this clearer. Davies for example recognizes that baptism was different from circumcision because "baptism assumed a growing importance."[25] What he does not show is why baptism grew in importance. A reason is advanced by Fiddes, for example, but his is a doctrinal reflection, not a biblical study. Fiddes suggests that "baptism actually fits better than circumcision into the network of concepts concerning

---

22. Dunn, *Theology of Paul*, 455; also Gisel, *Pourquoi baptiser*, 45.
23. Dunn, 454–455.
24. Davies, *Paul and Rabbinic Judaism*, 121.
25. Davies, 121.

leaving and entering phases of life."²⁶ As this study has shown, such verbs as "to leave" and "to enter" are personal actions. Thus, the pattern of the change, comparing circumcision and baptism (as also Burkert notices from Greek religion), is such that from an "ancestral custom" that is a rather "collective ritual" a move is made to a ritual that puts a stress on "the autonomy of the individual" and "on one's own responsibility,"²⁷ but as a member of the group.

This appears to be the pattern of comparison that distinguishes circumcision and baptism. However, a full biblical study of this has still to be explored. Among things that such a study would be interested in is the fact that circumcision served as a "bodily sign of covenant,"²⁸ and that the future covenantal sign, as the Bible shows, was to concern mind and heart (e.g. Jer 31:33; cf. Col 2:11: "a circumcision which is not of hands"). As this study has shown, a transition to new religious life is an event of entry that focuses more on the action of heart and mind than on that of hands.

Another thing to consider is that baptism had a tremendous impact on the dynamics of gender within the community, especially when it is compared to circumcision, which was only participated in by the men.²⁹ The option of participation for female initiands in baptism and its social, religious and cultural implications could make for a worthwhile study. Jesus created a new community that came with new social rules. One important innovation brought by this community is that the rite of entering applies undiscriminately to men and women as well. How did this affect the social life of women for the Jews and also for the Gentiles? And how could that contribute to the ongoing gender debate today?

4) *The relation between our Graeco-Roman social approach and the social approaches that are distinctively "Christian" methods.* We touched on the relationship between circumcision and baptism as an issue for further research, because in this study we have given attention to baptism, not to circumcision. Similarly, further reflection might be conducted about the relation between

---

26. Fiddes, "Baptism and Creation," 56.
27. Burkert, *Greek Religion*, 278.
28. E.g. Cramer, *Baptism and Change*, 47.
29. This has been noted in first and second century rabbinic Judaïsm with regards to proselytes' entry. As Furgusson points out, a discussion arose among the rabbis: "Since women were immersed but not circumcised," some Rabbis (e.g. Rabbi Joshua b. Hananiah) thought that "one bathed but not circumcised, as was the case with women, was a proper proselyte." (Fergusson, *Baptism in Early Church*, 80)

the social approach used here and social methods not adopted. The method we have used is to read baptism in Paul against the Greco-Roman background; it was a Greco-Roman socio-religious reading. There are social methods for examining baptism which are distinctively "Christian" and theological, especially approaches that emphasise the Old Testament background to baptism, and the background in the ministries of Jesus and John the Baptist. This study has not sought to explore what these other approaches could show about the idea of the four stages and action. It might be important to see how the socio-religious reading of baptism that we adopted might relate to or fit in with these more theological approaches.

5) *How much βαπτίζειν applies as synecdoche in the New Testament*. Further study could be done of the idea that βαπτίζειν (to baptize) is used in Romans 6 to encapsulate not just the water ritual but the whole process of transition including God's saving action and the acts of commitment of the baptizand. This study has only focused on showing this is the idea in Romans 5 and 6. The idea may be explored by examining all the New Testament passages where βαπτίζειν (to baptize) is used. For example, Colossians 2:9–13 is a baptismal text which features different stages of initiation: it speaks of forgiveness (v. 13) which echoes the stage of God's action (stage 1), washing (v. 12) which echoes the stage of separation from and rejection of the old life (stage 2), and circumcision (v. 11) which echoes the idea of integration and the ritual that seals this integration (stage 3). These various stages are also present in other baptismal texts such as 1 Corinthians 6:9–11; 10:1–12; Galatians 3:26–28 and 2 Timothy 2:18.

Such an investigation would need to reflect on the importance of the action of God and the baptizand in these various texts. For example, this might give new insight into the analogy that Jesus makes between his death and baptism in Luke 12:50. Speaking of this text, Moule's view is that baptism here is used in a metaphorical sense, though he does not suggest precisely which metaphorical sense Luke has in mind.[30] Cullmann also thinks of it as a metaphor. His view is that in this passage βαπτίζεσθαι (to be baptized) is "just to die."[31] However, the sense might be more than this. As this study has

---

30. Moule, *Birth of New Testament*, 38.
31. Cullmann, *Baptism in New Testament*, 19; Dunn, *Parting of Ways*, 72; and *Unity and Diversity*, 159.

shown, βαπτίζεσθαι (to be baptized) can stand for the whole transition from one realm to another, from sin to a life which is according to God's will. So, there is a possibility that Jesus is using it to mean his transition from his earthly life to his glorified state. A focus on all action taken in such a transition might show that he is thinking of the action of God (cf. Rom 6:4) and of his own action during this move,[32] whatever it all means.

5. 3. Achievement

This section summarises what we see as the achievement in examining, in this study, whether the clauses ἀπεθάνομεν τῇ ἁμαρτίᾳ, "we died to sin" (Rom 6:2) and ἐβαπτίσθημεν, "we were baptized" (v. 3) are a reference to action in baptism, or just to passivity. The scholars' views on these verses make it evident to us that due attention is not given to whether, by these words, baptism appears to mean a time for action. This focus on what the commentators say was the first motivation for us to consider how Paul sees baptism. The second motivation came from personal, field experience. A lack of understanding that baptism might imply taking a serious responsibility was noted in the Congo. This has been clear when, in the Congo, many church members, who through baptism have made their *passage* to the Christian existence, have participated in killing innocent people during the recent tribal conflicts of 1998–2003. Clearly, Christians have not understood that baptism should not be undertaken lightly.

All of this find an answer in this study, when it makes clear how in these utterances mentioned above, Paul stresses the agency of the person during his or her transition and baptism. The study has given evidence that these clauses show the baptizand's actions of breaking personally with the sinful way of life (v. 2) and undergoing publicly the ritual that ratifies this move (v. 3), and that it all amounts to the serious action of taking the responsibility of never again ἐπιμένειν τῇ ἁμαρτίᾳ, "continue in sin" (Rom 6:1–2).

By expounding on this, the study makes a significant contribution to some of the current debates. As a whole, this study offers a contribution to the debates over "synergism" and over "once saved, always saved." Though the intention was not to consider either of these debates in detail, the content

---

32. Cf. Jesus's words, "I lay my life down, no one takes it from me" (John 10:18).

of this study is such that it offers new arguments to these areas of discussion. The study has given evidence that there is an important role assumed by the person in the transition from sin to God, and that it is not only God who is active in this move. The study also offered new arguments touching on the debate of "once saved, always saved." The study makes it clear that belonging to God is not completed when God is encountered and operates the initial, divine action over the person. To become a child of God is something that occurs in stages, and some of these stages imply the action of the individual.

Bibliography

1. Books and Articles

Achtemeier, Paul J. *1 Peter: A Commentary on First Peter*. Minneapolis: Fortress, 1996.

———. *Romans*. Louisville: John Knox Press, 1985.

Alexander, Philip S. "Rules." In *Encyclopedia of the Dead Sea Scrolls*, vol. 2, edited by L. H. Schiffman and J. C. VanderKam, 799–803. Oxford: Oxford University Press, 2000.

Althaus, Paul. *Der Brief an die Römer*, NTD 6. Göttingen: Vandenhoeck & Ruprecht, 1970.

Ariel, Yaakov. "Proselyte." In *The Oxford Dictionary of the Jewish Religion*, edited by R. J. Z. Werblowsky and G. Wigoder, 550–51. New York: Oxford University Press, 1997.

Auque, Hubert. "La re-connaissance." *Etudes théologiques et religieuses* 77, no. 1 (2002): 61–68.

Austin, J. L. *How to Do Things with Words*. Oxford: Clarendon, 1962.

———. *Philosophical Papers*. 3rd edition. Oxford: Oxford University Press, 1979.

Badia, Leonard F. *The Qumran Baptism and John Baptist's Baptism*. Lanham: University Press of America, 1980.

Badke, William B. "Baptized into Moses – Baptized into Christ: A Study in Doctrinal Development." *Evangelical Quarterly* 60 (January 1988): 23–29.

Barrett, C. K. *A Commentary on the Epistle to the Romans*. London: Black, 1962.

———, ed. *The New Testament Background: Selected Documents*. London: SPCK, 1958.

Bartchy, S. Scott. "Slavery (Greco-Roman)." In *The Anchor Bible Dictionary*, vol. 6, 65–73.

Barth, G. *Die Taufe in frühchristlicher Zeit*. Neukirchen: Neukirchener Verlag, 1981.

Barth, Karl. *The Epistle to the Romans*. 6th edition, trans. by Edwyn C. Hoskyns. Oxford: Oxford University Press, 1933 (Original: *Der Romerbrief*).

———. *The Teaching of the Church Regarding Baptism*, trans. Ernest A. Payne. London: SCM, 1948.

Barton, Stephen C. "Social-Scientific Approaches to Paul." In *Dictionary of Paul and His Letters*, edited by G. F. Hawthorne and R. P. Martin, 892–900. Downers Grove: InterVarsity Press, 1993.

Batulukisi, Niangi. "Ngindi and Mukanda Initiation Rites: Forces of Social Cohesion among the Holo." In *Chokwe!: Art and Initiation Among Chokwe and Related Peoples*, edited by Manuel Jordan, 85–91. Munich: Prestel, 1998.

Baulès, Robert. *L'évangile, puissance de Dieu: Commentaire de l'épître aux Romains*, LD 53. Paris: Cerf, 1968.

Beall, Todd S. *Josephus' Description of the Essenes Illustrated by the Dead Sea Scrolls*. Cambridge: Cambridge University Press, 1988.

Beasley-Murray, G. R. *Baptism in the New Testament*. Grand Rapids: Eerdmans, 1973.

———. "Dying and Rising with Christ." In *Dictionary of Paul and His Letters*, edited by G. F. Hawthorne and R. P. Martin, 218–22. Downers Grove: InterVarsity Press, 1993.

Beasley-Murray, Paul. "Romans 1:3f: An Early Confession of Faith in the Lordship of Jesus." *Tyndale Bulletin* 31 (1980): 147–54.

Betz, Hans Dieter. "Transferring a Ritual: Paul's Interpretation of Baptism in Romans 6." In *Paul in His Hellenistic Context*, edited by Troels Engberg-Pedersen, 84–118. Edinburgh: T. T. Clark, 1994.

Beyer, Hermann W., and Paul Althaus. "Der Brief an die Galater." In *Die Kleineren Briefe des Apostels Paulus*, NTD 8, übersetzt und erklärt von Hermann W. Beyer, et al., 1–55. Göttingen: Vandenhoeck & Ruprecht, 1962.

Black, Matthew. *Romans*. London: Marshall, Morgan & Scott, 1973.

———. *The Scrolls and Christian Origins: Studies in the Jewish Background of the New Testament*. London: Nelson, 1961.

Blomberg, Craig L. *From Pentecost to Patmos: Acts to Revelation*. Nottingham: Apollos, 2006.

Boer, Martinus C. de. "Apocalyptic as God's Eschatological Activity in Paul's Theology." In *Paul and the Apocalyptic Imagination*, edited by Ben C. Blackwell, John K. Goodrich, and Jason Maston. Minneapolis: Fortress Press, 2016 (Kindle edition).

Borgen, Peder. "Philo of Alexandria." In *Jewish Writings of the Second Temple Period*, edited by Michael E. Stone, CRJNT/ 2: LJPPSTT, vol. 2, 233–82. Assen: Van Gorcum; Philadelphia: Fortress Press, 1984.

Boring, M. Eugene. "The Language of Universal Salvation in Paul." *Journal of Biblical Literature* 105 (1986): 269–92.

Bornkamm, G. "Baptism and the New Life in Paul: Romans 6." In *Early Christian Experience*. London: SCM, 1969.

———. "μυστήριον, μυέω." In *Theological Dictionary of the New Testament*, edited by Gerhard Kittel, vol. 4., 802–28. Translated and edited by G. W. B. Bromiley. Grand Rapids: Eerdmans, 1967.

Bott, Elizabeth. "Psychoanalysis and Ceremony." In *The Interpretation of Ritual: Essays in Honour of A. I. Richards*, edited by J. S. La Fontaine 205–37, London: Tavistock, 1972.

Bouyer, Louis. *Initiation chrétienne*. Paris: Librairie Plon, 1958.

Brändle, Rudolf, and Ekkehard W. Stegemann. "The Formation of the First 'Christian Congregations' in Rome in the Context of the Jewish Community.'" In *Judaism and Christianity in First-Century Rome*, edited by Karl P. Donfried and Peter Richardson, 117–27. Grand Rapids: Eerdmans, 1998.

Brandon, S. G. F. *History, Time and Deity*. Manchester: Manchester University Press, 1965.

Bray, Gerald, ed. *Romans*. ACCS/NT 6, general editor Thomas C. Oden. Downers Grove: InterVarsity Press, 1998.

Briggs, Richard S. *Words in Action: Speech Act Theory and Biblical Interpretation: Toward a Hermeneutic of Self-Involvement*. Edinburgh: T&T Clark, 2001.

Broneer, Oscar. "Paul and the Pagan Cults at Isthmia." *Harvard Theological Review* 64 (1971): 169–87.

Brooke, George J. *The Dead Sea Scrolls and the New Testament*. London: SPCK, 2005.

Brooks, Oscar S. *The Drama of Decision: Baptism in the New Testament*. Peabody: Hendrickson, 1987.

Bruce, F. F. *The Acts of the Apostles: The Greek Text with Introduction and Commentary*, 3rd ed. rev. and enlarged. Grand Rapids: Eerdmans, 1990.

———. *The Epistle of Paul to the Romans: An Introduction and Commentary*. TNTC. Leicester: Inter-Varsity Press, 1977 reprint (1st ed. 1963).

———. *The Epistle to the Galatians: A Commentary on the Greek Text*. NIGTC. Grand Rapids: Eerdmans, 1982.

———. *Paul: Apostle of the Heart Set Free*. Grand Rapids: Eerdmans, 2000.

Büchsel, Friedrich. "ἡγέομαι, ἐξηγέομαι, προηγέομαι, διήγησις." In *Theological Dictionary of the New Testament*, edited by Gerhard Kittel, vol. 2, translated and edited by G. W. B. Bromiley, 907–909. Grand Rapids: Eerdmans, 1964.

Bultmann, Rudolf. "Adam and Christ according to Romans 5." In *Current Issues in New Testament Interpretation*, edited by W. Klassen and G. F. Snyder, 143–65. London: SCM, 1962.

———. "ἀγνοέω, ἀγνόημα, ἄγνοια, ἀγνωσία, ἄγνωστος." In *Theological Dictionary of the New Testament*, vol. 1, edited by Gerhard Kittel, translated and edited by G. W. B. Bromiley, 115–21. Grand Rapids: Eerdmans, 1964.

———. *Theology of the New Testament*, vol. 1. Translated by Kendrick Grobel. London: SCM, 1952.
Burkert, Walter. *Greek Religion*. Translated by John Raffan. Cambridge, MA: Harvard University Press, 1985 (originally: *Griechische Religion der archaischen und klassischen Epoche*, 1977).
Burton, Edward. *The Apostolic Fathers: The Epistles of SS. Clement of Rome and Barnabas and the Shepherd of Hermas, with the History of the Christian Church in the First Century*. Vol. 1. Edinburgh: John Grant, 1909.
Burton, Ernest de Witt. *A Critical and Exegetical Commentary on the Epistle to the Galatians*, ICC. Edinburgh: T&T Clark, 1921.
Byrne, Brendan. "Living out the Righteousness of God: The Contribution of Rom 6:1–8:13 to an Understanding of Paul's Ethical Presuppositions." *Catholic Biblical Quarterly* 43 (1981): 557–81.
Calvin, John. *Commentaires de J. Calvin sur le Nouveau Testament, Vol. 4 : Epître aux Romains*. Edited by Jules-Marcel Nicole. Genève: Labor et Fides, 1960.
———. *Institutes of the Christian Religion*, vol. 2, LCC 21. Edited by John T. McNeill, Translated by Ford L. Battles. Philadelphia: Westminster, 1960.
Cambier, Jean. "Péchés des hommes et péché d'Adam en Romains 5:12." *New Testament Studies* 11 (1964–65): 217–55.
Camery-Hoggatt, Jerry A. "Visions, Ecstatic Experience." In *Dictionary of Paul and His Letters*, eds. G. F. Hawthorne and R. P. Martin, 963–965. Downers Grove, IL: InterVarsity Press, 1993.
Campbell, Douglas A. "Apocalyptic Epistemology: The Sine Qua Non of Valid Pauline Interpretation." In *Paul and the Apocalyptic Imagination*, edited by Ben C. Blackwell, John K. Goodrich, and Jason Maston, 1343–1747 (Kindle edition). Minneapolis: Fortress Press, 2016.
Campbell, William S. "The Addressees of Paul's Letter to the Romans: Assemblies of God in House Churches and Synagogues?" In *Between Gospel and Election: Explorations in the Interpretation of Romans 9–11*, edited by F. W. Wilk and J. R. Wagner, 22 pages [conference version]. Tubingen: Mohr, 2010.
———. "'I Rate All Things as Loss': Paul's Puzzling Accounting System. Judaism as Loss or the Re-evaluation of All Things in Christ?" In *Celebrating Paul: Festschrift in Honor of Jerome Murphy-O'Connor, O. P. and Joseph A. Fitzmyer, S. J.*, edited by Peter Spitaler, 39–61. CBQ/MS 48, Washington: The Catholic Biblical Association of America, 2011.
———. *Paul and the Creation of Christian Identity*. LNTS 322. New York: T&T Clark, 2006.
———. "Why Did Paul Write Romans?" *Expository Times* 85 (October 1973–September 1974): 264–69.
Caragounis, C. C. "Romans 5:15–16 in the Context of 5: 12–21: Contrast or Comparison?" *New Testament Studies* 31 (1985): 142–48.

Carlson, Richard P. "The Role of Baptism in Paul's Thought." *Interpretation* 47 (July 1993): 255–66.
Carrington, Philip. *The Early Christian Church, Vol. 1: The First Christian Century.* Cambridge: Cambridge University Press, 1957.
Charlesworth, James H., et al., eds. *The Dead Sea Scrolls: Hebrew, Aramaic, and Greek Texts with English Translations, Vol. 1: Rules of the Community and Related Documents.* Tübingen: Mohr; Louisville: Westminster John Knox, 1994.
———. "John the Baptizer and the Dead Sea Scrolls." In *The Bible and the Dead Sea Scrolls*, vol. 3, edited by James H. Charlesworth, 1–35. PSJCO 2. Waco, TX: Baylor University Press, 2006.
———. "Community Organization in the Rule of the Community." In *Encyclopedia of the Dead Sea Scrolls*, vol. 1, edited by L. H. Schiffman and J. C. Vanderkam, 133–36. Oxford: Oxford University Press, 2000.
Charlesworth, James H., and Carsten Claussen. "Halakah A: 4Q251." In *The Dead Scrolls: Hebrew, Aramaic, and Greek Texts with English Translations*, vol. 3, edited by James H. Charlesworth and Henry W. M. Rietz, 271–85. Tübingen: Mohr; Louisville: Westminster John Knox, 2006.
Churchill, Timothy W. R. "Divine Initiative and the Christology of the Damascus Road Encounter." PhD thesis, Brunel University, 2008.
Clarke, Andrew D. "Jew and Greek, Slave and Free, Male and Female: Paul's Theology of Ethnic, Social and Gender Inclusiveness in Romans 16." In *Rome in the Bible and the Early Church*, edited by Peter Oakes, 103–25. Grand Rapids: Baker Academic, 2002.
Cohen, Shaye J. D. *From the Maccabees to the Mishnah.* Philadelphia: Westminster Press, 1987.
———. "Crossing the Boundary and Becoming a Jew." *Harvard Theological Review* 82, no. 1 (1989): 13–33.
Conzelman, Hans. *Acts of the Apostles.* Hermeneia. Translated by J. Limburg et al. Philadelphia: Fortress Press, 1987 (original: *Die Apostelgeschichte*, 1972).
Corley, Bruce. "Interpreting Paul's Conversion – Then and Now." In *The Road from Damascus: The Impact of Paul's Conversion on His Life, Thought, and Ministry*, edited by Richard N. Longenecker, 1–17. MNTS. Grand Rapids: Eerdmans, 1997.
Cramer, Peter. *Baptism and Change in the Early Middle Ages, c. 200–c.1150.* Cambridge: Cambridge University Press, 1993.
Cranfield, C. E. B. *A Critical and Exegetical Commentary on the Epistle to the Romans, Vol. 1: 1–8*, ICC. Edinburgh: T&T Clark, 1975.
———. "On Some Problems in the Interpretation of Romans 5:12." *Scottish Journal of Theology* 22 (1969): 324–41.
Cullmann, Oscar. *Baptism in the New Testament.* London: SCM, 1950.

Cuvillier, Elian. "Le baptême chrétien dans le Nouveau Testament: éléments de réflexion." *Etudes théologiques et religieuses* 70, no. 2 (1995): 161–77.

———. "Evangile et traditions chez Paul: lecture de Romains 6:1–14." *Hokhma* 45 (1990): 3–16.

Dakin, Arthur. "Christian Baptism and John's Baptism Contrasted: Baptism a Sign of the Endowment of Personality." In *Concerning Believers Baptism*, edited by F. C. Bryan, 39–44. London: Kingsgate Press, 1943.

Daly, Robert J. "The New Testament Concept of Christian Sacrificial Activity." *Biblical Theology Bulletin* 8 (1978): 99–107.

Dandamayev, Muhammad A. "Slavery (ANE)." In *The Anchor Bible Dictionary*, vol. 6, edited by David N. Freedman, 58–62. New York: Doubleday, 1992.

Das, A. Andrew. *Solving the Romans Debate*. Minneapolis: Fortress Press, 2007.

Davies, J. P. "Paul among the Apocalypses? An Evaluation of the 'Apocalyptic Paul' in the Context of Jewish and Christian Apocalyptic Literature." PhD thesis, St. Andrews University, 2015. https://research-repository.st-andrews.ac.uk/bitstream/handle/10023/6945/JamesDaviesPhDThesis.pdf?sequence=6&isAllowed=y.

Davies, W. D. *Paul and Rabbinic Judaism: Some Rabbinic Elements in Pauline Theology*. 4th ed. London: SPCK; Philadelphia: Fortress Press, 1981.

Deasley, Alex R. G. *The Shape of Qumran Theology*. Carlisle: Paternoster, 2000.

De Boer, Martinus C. "Apocalyptic as God's Eschatological Activity in Paul's Theology." In *Paul and the Apocalyptic Imagination*, edited by B. C. Blackwell, J. K. Goodrich, and J. Maston, 875–1336 (Kindle edition). Minneapolis: Fortress Press, 2016.

Delling, Gerhard. "ἀργός, ἀργέω, καταργέω." In *Theological Dictionary of the New Testament*, vol. 1, edited by Gerhard Kittel, translated and edited by G. W. B. Bromiley, 452–54. Grand Rapids: Eerdmans, 1964.

Dickson, B. *Romains*. La Bégude de Mazenc: Ed. Clé, 2005.

Driver, G. R. *The Judaean Scrolls: The Problem and a Solution*. Oxford: Blackwell, 1965.

Dunn, James D. G. *Baptism in the Holy Spirit: A Re-examination of the New Testament Teaching on the Gift of the Spirit in Relation to Pentecostalism Today*. London: SCM, 1970.

———. "The Birth of a Metaphor: Baptized in the Spirit." *Expository Times* 89 (1977–78): 134–38, 173–175.

———. *Christianity in the Making, Vol. 2: Beginning from Jerusalem*. Grand Rapids: Eerdmans, 2009.

———. *Christology in the Making: A New Testament Inquiry into the Origins of the Doctrine of the Incarnation*. 2nd ed. London: SCM, 1989.

———. "In Search of the Historical Paul." In *Celebrating Paul: Festschrift in Honor of Jerome Murphy-O'Connor, O. P. and Joseph A. Fitzmyer, S. J.*, edtied by Peter

Spitaler, CBQ/MS 48, 15–38. Washington: The Catholic Biblical Association of America, 2011.

———. *Jesus and the Spirit*. London: SCM, 1975.

———. *Jesus, Paul and the Law: Studies in Mark and Galatians*. London: SPCK, 1990.

———. "Mystery." In *The New Interpreter's Dictionary of the Bible*, vol. 4, edited by Katherine D. Sakenfeld, 185–87. Nashville: Abingdon, 2009.

———. *The New Perspective on Paul*, Rev. ed. Grand Rapids: Eerdmans, 2005.

———. *The Parting of the Ways: Between Christianity and Judaism and Their Significance for the Character of Christianity*. 2nd ed. London: SCM, 2006.

———. "Paul and Justification by Faith." In *The Road from Damascus: The Impact of Paul's Conversion on His Life, Thought, and Ministry*, MNTS, edited by Richard N. Longenecker, 85–101. Grand Rapids: Eerdmans, 1997.

———. *Romans 1–8*. WBC 38a. Nashville: Nelson, 1988.

———. *The Theology of Paul the Apostle*. Edinburgh: T&T Clark, 1998.

———. *Unity and Diversity in the New Testament: An Inquiry into the Character of Earliest Christianity*. London: SCM, 1977.

Dunn, James D .G. and A. M. Suggate. *The Justice of God: A Fresh Look at the Old Doctrine of Justification by Faith*. Carlisle, UK: Paternoster, 1993.

Dupont, Jacques. *Nouvelles études sur les Actes des Apôtres*, LD 118. Paris: Cerf, 1984.

Du Toit, Philip La Grange, "Was Paul a Christian?" *Neotestamentica* 53, no. 1 (2019): 1–29.

Edmundson, G. *The Church in Rome in the First Century*, BL. London: Longmans, Green, 1913.

Edwards, James R. *Romans*. NIBC 6. Peabody: Hendrickson, 1992.

Eliade, Mircea. *Rites and Symbols of Initiation: The Mysteries of Birth and Rebirth*. Translated by W. R. Trask. New York: Harper & Row, 1975.

Ellis, E. Earle. *Paul and His Recent Interpreters*. Grand Rapids: Eerdmans, 1961.

Elsas, Christoph, and Balthasar Fischer. "Initiation Rites." In *The Encyclopedia of Christianity*, vol. 2, edited by Geoffrey W. Bromiley et al., 703–6. Grand Rapids: Eerdmans; Leiden: Brill, 2001.

Engberg-Pedersen, Troels. *Paul and the Stoics*. Edinburgh: T&T Clark, 2000.

Esler, Philip F. *Conflict and Identity in Romans: The Social Setting of Paul's Letter*. Minneapolis: Fortress Press, 2003.

Evans, Donald D. *The Logic of Self-Involvement: A Philosophical Study of Everyday Language with Special Reference to the Christian Use of Language about God as Creator*. London: SCM, 1963.

Everts, Janet M. "Conversion and Call of Paul." In *Dictionary of Paul and His Letters*, edited by G. F. Hawthorne and R. P. Martin, 156–63. Downers Grove: InterVarsity Press, 1993.

Fee, Gordon D. "Paul's Conversion as Key to His Understanding of the Spirit." In *The Road from Damascus: The Impact of Paul's Conversion on His Life, Thought, and Ministry*, MNTS, edited by Richard N. Longenecker, 166–83. Grand Rapids: Eerdmans, 1997.

Feldmann, Louis H. *Jew and Gentile in the Ancient World: Attitudes and Interactions from Alexander to Justinian*. Princeton: Princeton University Press, 1993.

———. "Jewish Proselytism." In *Eusebius, Christianity, Judaism*, SPB 42, edited by H. W. Attridge and G. Hata, 372–408. Leiden: Brill, 1992.

Ferguson, Everett. *Backgrounds of Early Christianity*. Grand Rapids: Eerdmans, 1987.

———. *Baptism in the Early Church: History, Theology, and Liturgy in the First Five Centuries*. Grand Rapids: Eerdmans, 2009.

Ferguson, John. *The Religions of the Roman Empire*, AGRL. London: Thames and Hudson, 1970.

Fiddes, Paul S. "Baptism and Creation." In *Reflections on the Water: Understanding God and the World through the Baptism of Believers*, edited by Paul S. Fiddes, with a response by Christopher Rowland, RSG 4, 47–67. Oxford: Regent's Park College; Macon: Smyth & Helwys, 1996.

Finn, Thomas M. *Early Christian Baptism and the Catechumenate: Italy, North Africa, and Egypt*, MFC 6. Collegeville: Liturgical Press, 1992.

———. *Early Christian Baptism and the Catechumenate: West and East Syria*. MFC 5. Collegeville: Liturgical Press, 1992.

Fisher, J. D. C. *Christian Initiation: Baptism in the Medieval West: A Study in the Disintegration of the Primitive Rite of Initiation*, AC 47. London: SPCK, 1965.

Fitzmyer, Joseph A. *According to Paul: Studies in the Theology of the Apostle*. New York: Paulist Press, 1993.

———. *The Dead Sea Scrolls and Christian Origins*. Grand Rapids: Eerdmans, 2000.

———. *Romans: A New Translation with Introduction and Commentary*, AB 33. New York: Doubleday, 1993.

Flemington, W. F. *The New Testament Doctrine of Baptism*. London: SPCK, 1957.

Fogleman, William J. "Romans 6:3–14." *Interpretation* 47 (July 1993): 294–98.

Fowl, S. E. *Philippians*. Grand Rapids: Eerdmans, 2005.

Fowler, W. Warde. *The Religious Experience of the Roman People: From the Earliest Times to the Age of Augustus*. GL/EU 1909–10. London: Macmillan, 1911.

Frankemölle, H. *Das Taufverständnis des Paulus: Taufe, Tod und Auferstehung nach Röm 6*, SBS 47. Stuttgart: KBW, 1970.

Furnish, Victor P. *Theology and Ethics in Paul*. Nashville: Abingdon, 1968.

Garlington, D. B. "The Obedience of Faith in the Letter to the Romans, I: The Meaning of ὑπακοὴ πίστεως (Rom 1:5; 16:26)." *Westminster Theological Journal* 52 (1990): 201–24.

———. "The Obedience of Faith in the Letter to the Romans, III: The Obedience of Christ and the Obedience of the Christian." *Westminster Theological Journal* 55 (1993): 87–112; 281–297.

Gaventa, Beverly R. *From Darkness to Light*. Philadelphia: Fortress Press, 1986.

George, Timothy. "The Reformed Doctrine of Believers' Baptism." *Interpretation* 47 (July 1993): 242–54.

Gennep, Arnold Van. *The Rites of Passage*. Translated by Monika B. Vizedom and Gabrielle L. Caffee, AE. London and New York: Routledge, 1960.

Gisel, Pierre. *Pourquoi baptiser: mystère chrétien et rite de passage*, EL 32. Genève: Labor et Fides, 1994.

Godet, Frédéric. *Commentaire sur l'épître aux Romains*. Genève: Labor et Fides, 1968 (original ed. 1879).

Gorman, Michael J. *Reading Paul*. CCo. Eugene: Cascade, 2008.

Gounelle, Rémi. "Le Baptême aux temps patristiques: le cas de la *Tradition apostolique*." *Etudes théologiques et religieuses* 70, no. 2 (1955): 179–89.

Grayston, Kenneth. *The Epistle to the Romans*. Peterborough: Epworth Press, 1997.

———. "The Opponents in Philippians 3." *Expository Times* 97 (October 1985-September 1986): 170–72.

Greeven, Heinrich. "ἐρωτάω, ἐπερωτάω, ἐπερώτημα." In *Theological Dictionary of the New Testament*, edited by Gerhard Kittel, vol. 2, 685–89. Translated and edited by G. W. B. Bromiley. Grand Rapids: Eerdmans, 1964.

Gundry, Robert H. "Faith, Works and Staying Saved in Paul." *Biblica* 66 (1985): 1–38.

Gunther, John J. *St Paul's Opponents and Their Background: A Study of Apocalyptic and Jewish Sectarian Teachings*. SNT 35. Leiden: Brill, 1973.

Haacker, Klaus. *Der Brief des Paulus an die Römer*. THNT 6. Leipzig: Evangelische Verlagsanstalt, 1999.

———. *The Theology of Paul's Letter to the Romans*. NTT. Cambridge: Cambridge University Press, 2003.

Haenchen, Ernest. *The Acts of the Apostles: A Commentary*. Oxford: Blackwell, 1971.

Hamman, Adalbert, Ernest Dassmann, and Russell J. de Simone. "Baptême." In *Dictionnaire encyclopédique du christianisme ancient*, vol. 1, edited by Angelo di Berardino, 332–38. Translated and edited by F. Vial. Paris: Cerf, 1990 (originally: *Dizionario patristico e di antichità cristiane*, Genova, 1983).

Hansen, G. Walter. "Paul's Conversion and His Ethic of Freedom in Galatians." In *The Road from Damascus: The Impact of Paul's Conversion on His Life,*

Thought, and Ministry, MNTS, edited by Richard N. Longenecker, 213–37. Grand Rapids: Eerdmans, 1997.

Harrill, J. Albert. "Coming of Age and Putting on Christ: The *Toga Virilis* Ceremony, Its Paraenesis, and Paul's Interpretation of Baptism in Galatians." *Novum Testamentum* 44, no. 3 (2002): 252–77.

———. "Slavery." In *The New Interpreter's Dictionary of the Bible*, vol. 5, edited by Katheline D. Sakenfeld et al., 299–307. Nashville: Abingdon, 2009.

Hartman, Lars. "Into the Name of Jesus: A Suggestion Concerning the Earliest Meaning of the Phrase." *New Testament Studies* 20 (1973–74): 432–40.

Hatch, Edwin. *The Influence of Greek Ideas and Usages upon the Christian Church*, HL 1888. London: Williams and Norgate, 1891.

Haymes, Brian. "Baptism as a Political Act." In *Reflections on the Water: Understanding God and the World through the Baptism of Believers*, edited by Paul S. Fiddes, with a response by Christopher Rowland, RSG, 469–83. Oxford: Regent's Park College; Macon: Smyth & Helwys, 1996.

Hawthorne, Gerald F., and Ralph H. Martin. *Philippians*. Revised and expanded. Nashville: Nelson, 2004.

Heald, Suzette. "Rites of Passage." In *The Social Science Encyclopedia*, edited by Adam Kuper and Jessica Kuper, 747–49. London: Routledge, 1996.

Helm, P. "Will." In *New Dictionary of Theology*, edited by Sinclair B. Ferguson and David F. Wright, 722–23. Downers Grove: InterVarsity Press, 1988.

Hendriksen, William. *Romans, Vol. 1: 1–8*. NTCom. Edinburgh: Banner of Truth Trust, 1980.

Hengel, Martin. *The Zealots: Investigations into the Jewish Freedom Movement in the Period from Herod I until 70 A. D.* Translated by David Smith. Edinburgh: T&T Clark, 1989 (Original: *Die Zeloten*, 2nd ed., 1976).

Heron, John. "The Theology of Baptism." *Scottish Journal of Theology* 8 (1955): 36–52.

Highet, Gilbert, and Andrew W. Lintott. "Clubs, Roman." In *Oxford Classical Dictionary*, 3rd ed., edited by S. Hornblower and A. Spawforth, 352–53. Oxford: Oxford University Press, 1999.

Hill, David. "On Suffering and Baptism in 1 Peter." *Novum Testamentum* 18 (1976): 181–89.

Hirsch, Emil G. "Proselyte." In *The Jewish Encyclopeda: A Descriptive Record of the History, Religion, Literature, and Customs of the Jewish People from the Earliest Times*, vol. 10, edited by Isidore Singer, 220–24. New York: KTAV, 1901.

Hodge, Charles. *Romans*. CCC. Wheaton: Crossway, 1993.

Hultgren, Arland J. *Paul's Letter to the Romans: A Commentary*. Grand Rapids: Eerdmans, 2011.

Hunsinger, George. "The Dimension of Depth: Thomas F. Torrance on the Sacraments of Baptism and the Lord's Supper." *Scottish Journal of Theology* 54, no. 2 (2001): 155–76.

Ingham, R. *A Handbook on Christian Baptism*. London: Simpkin, Marshall & Co, 1865.

Jaeger, Werner. *Paideia: The Ideals of Greek Culture*. 3 volumes, translated by G. Highet. Oxford: Blackwell, 1939, 1944, 1945.

Jagger, Peter J. *Christian Initiation 1552–1969: Rites of Baptism and Confirmation since the Reformation Period*, AC 52. London: SPCK, 1970.

Jeffers, James S. *The Greco-Roman World of the New Testament Era: Exploring the Background of Early Christianity*. Downers Grove: InterVarsity Press, 1999.

Jervell, Jacob. *Die Apostelgeschichte*. KEKNT. Göttingen: Vandenhoeck & Ruprecht, 1998.

Jewett, Robert. *Romans: A Commentary*. Hmn. Minneapolis: Fortress Press, 2007.

Jobes, Karen H. *1 Peter*. BECNT. Grand Rapids: Baker Academic, 2005.

Johnson, Luke T. *The Acts of the Apostles*, SPS 5, edited by Daniel J. Harrington. Collegeville: Liturgical Press, 1992.

Kaiser, Walter C. "My Heart Is Stirred by a Nobel Theme: The Meaning of Poetry and Wisdom.'" In *Introduction to Biblical Hermeneutics*, edited by W. C. Kaiser and M. Silva, 139–54. Grand Rapids: Zondervan, 2007.

Karecki, Madge. "Discovering the Roots of Ritual." *Missionalia* 25 (August 1997): 169–77.

Käsemann, Ernest. *Commentary on Romans*. Translated by G. W. Bromiley: Grand Rapids: Eerdmans, 1980.

Kaylor, R. David. *Paul's Covenant Community: Jews and Gentiles in Romans*. Atlanta: John Knox, 1988.

Keck, Leander E. *Romans*. ANTC. Nashville: Abingdon, 2005.

Kelly, J. N. D. *A Commentary on the Epistles of Peter and of Jude*. BNTC. London: Black, 1969.

Kern, Philip H. "Paul's Conversion and Luke's Portrayal of Character in Acts 8–10." *Tyndale Bulletin* 54 (2003): 63–80.

Kim, Seyoon. *The Origin of Paul's Gospel*. Tübingen: Mohr, 1981.

———. *Paul and the New Perspective: Second Thoughts on the Origin of Paul's Gospel*. Grand Rapids: Eerdmans, 2002.

Knibb, Michael A. "Community Organization in the Damascus Document [*plus*] in Other Texts." In *Encyclopedia[sic] of the Dead Sea Scrolls*, vol. 1, edited by L. H. Schiffman and J. C. Vanderkam, 136–40. Oxford: Oxford University Press, 2000.

———. "Rule of the Community." In *Encyclopedia of the Dead Sea Scrolls*, vol. 2, edited by L. H. Schiffman and J. C. Vanderkam, 793–97. Oxford: Oxford University Press, 2000.

Kreider, Alan. "Worship and Evangelicalism in Pre-Christendom." *VE* 24 (1994): 7–38.

Kreitzer, L. Joseph. "Baptism in the Pauline Epistles: with Special Reference to the Corinthian Letters." *Baptist Quarterly* 34, no. 2 (April 1991): 67–78.

Kremer, J. "ἀνάστασις, ἀνίστημι, ἐξανάστασις, ἐξανίστημι." In *Exegetical Dictionary of the New Testament*, vol. 1, edited by H. Balz and G. Schneider, 88–92. Grand Rapids: Eerdmans, 1990.

Kuen, Alfred. *Le baptême hier et aujourd'hui*. Saint-Légier: Emmaüs, 1995.

Kümmel, W. G. *Introduction to the New Testament*, NTL, rev. ed. London: SCM, 1975 (original *Einleitung in das Neue Testament*, 1973).

Kuss, Otto. *Der Römerbrief* 1. Regensburg: Verlag Friedrich Pustet, 1963.

Lampe, Peter. "The Roman Christians of Romans 16." In *The Romans Debate*, revised and expanded edition, edited by Karl P. Donfried, 216–30. Edinburgh: T&T Clark, 1991.

Leenhardt, Franz J. *L'Epître de saint Paul aux Romains*, 2nd ed. Genève: Labor et Fides, 1981 (1st ed. 1957).

Légasse, Simon. "Etre baptisé dans la mort du Christ: étude de Romains 6:1–14." *Revue biblique* 98 (October 1991): 544–59.

Lembezat, Bertrand. *Les populations païennes du Nord-Cameroun et de l'Adamaoua*, MEA. Paris: Presses Universitaires de France, 1961.

Levison, Nahum. "The Proselyte in Biblical and Early Post-biblical Times." *Scottish Journal of Theology* 10 (1957): 45–56.

Lewis, Gilbert. "Magic, Religion and the Rationality of Belief." In *Companion Encyclopedia of Anthropology*, edited by Tom Ingold, 563–90. London: Routledge, 1994.

Lightfoot, J. B. *Saint Paul's Epistles to the Colossians and to Philemon*. 9th ed. New York: Macmillan, 1890.

Link, Hans-Georg, R. Tuente, and G. T. D. Angel. "Slave, Servant, Captive, Prisoner, Freedman." In *The New International Dictionary of New Testament Theology*, vol. 3, edited by Collin Exeter Brown, 589–99. Carlisle: Paternoster, 1978 (Original: *Theologisches Begriffslexikon zum Neuen Testament*, 1971).

Lohfink, Gerhard. *The Conversion of St. Paul: Narrative and History in Acts*. Translated and edited by Bruce J. Malina. Chicago: Franciscan Herald Press, 1976 (original: *Paulus vor Damascus*, 1967).

Lohse, Eduard. *Colossians and Philemon*, Hmn. Edited by H. Koester, translated by W. R. Poehlmann and R. J. Karris. Philadelphia: Fortress, 1971.

Loi, Vincenzo, Ernest Dassmann, et al. "Paul." In *Dictionnaire encyclopédique du christianisme ancient*, vol. 2, edited by Angelo di Berardino, 1937–944. Translated and edited by F. Vial. Paris: Cerf, 1990 (originally: *Dizionario patristico e di antichità cristiane*, Genova, 1983).

Longenecker, Richard N. *New Testament Social Ethics for Today*. Grand Rapids: Eerdmans, 1984.

———. "A Realized Hope, a New Commitment, and a Developed Proclamation: Paul and Jesus." In *The Road from Damascus: The Impact of Paul's Conversion on His Life, Thought, and Ministry*, MNTS, edited by Richard N. Longenecker, 18–42. Grand Rapids: Eerdmans, 1997.

Luther, Martin, *Martin Luther: Oeuvres XI: Commentaires de l'épître aux Romains*, Vol. 1. Genève: Labor et Fides, 1983.

Lyall, F. "Roman Law in the Writings of Paul – the Slave and the Freedman." *New Testament Studies* 17 (1970–71): 73–79.

Maccoby, Hyam. *Paul and Hellenism*. London: SCM Press, 1991.

MacDonald, Margaret Y. *The Pauline Churches*. Cambridge: Cambridge University Press, 1988.

Mahieu, Wauthier de. *Structures et symboles* (Pers Leuven: Institut Africain International, s.d.

Malina, Bruce J. *Christian Origins and Cultural Anthropology: Practical Models for Biblical Interpretation*. Atlanta: John Knox, 1986.

———. "Let Him Deny Himself (Mark 8:34 & par): A Social Psychological Model of Self-Denial." *Biblical Theology Bulletin* 24 (1994): 106–19.

Marshall, I. Howard. *The Acts of the Apostles: An Introduction and Commentary*, TNTC. Leicester: Inter-Varsity Press, 1980.

———. "A New Understanding of the Present and the Future: Paul and Eschatology." In *The Road from Damascus: The Impact of Paul's Conversion on His Life, Thought, and Ministry*, MNTS, edited by Richard N. Longenecker, 43–61. Grand Rapids: Eerdmans, 1997,

Martinez, Florentino G. "The Dead Sea Scrolls." In *The People of the Dead Sea Scrolls*, edited by F. G. Martinez and J. T. Barrera, 3–16. Leiden: Brill, 1995 (Originally: *Los Hombres de Qumran*, 1993).

———. "The Men of the Dead Sea." In *The People of the Dead Sea Scrolls*, edited by F. G. Martinez and J. T. Barrera, 31–48. Leiden: Brill, 1995 (Originally: *Los Hombres de Qumran*, 1993).

Matera, Frank J. *Romans*, PCNT. Grand Rapids: Baker Academic, 2010.

McKnight, Scot. "Proselytism and Godfearers." In *Dictionary of New Testament Background*, edited by C. A. Evans and S. E. Porter, 835–47. Downers Grove: InterVarsity Press, 2000.

McRay, John. *Paul, His Life and Teaching*. Grand Rapids: Baker Academic, 2003.

Mcvann, Mark. "Baptism, Miracles, and Boundary Jumping in Mark." *Biblical Theology Bulletin* 21, no. 3 (1991): 151–57.

Mead, James K. *Biblical Theology: Issues, Methods, and Themes*. Louisville: Westminster John Knox Press, 2007.

Meeks, Wayne A. *The First Urban Christians: The Social World of the Apostle Paul.* New Haven: Yale University Press, 1983.

Meyer, Marvin W., ed. *The Ancient Mysteries, A Sourcebook: Sacred Texts of the Mystery Religions of the Ancient Mediterranean World.* San Francisco: Harper & Row, 1987.

———. "Mysteries." In *Dictionary of New Testament Background*, edited by C. A. Evans and S. E. Porter, 720–25. Downers Grove: InterVarsity Press, 2000.

Moo, Douglas J. *Romans 1–8*, WEC. Chicago: Moody Press, 1991.

Morris, Leon. *The Epistle to the Romans.* Grand Rapids: Eerdmans; Leicester: Inter-Varsity Press, 1988.

Moule, Charles F. D. *The Birth of the New Testament*, BNTC, 3rd ed. rev. and rewritten. London: Black, 1981.

———. *Essays in New Testament Interpretation.* Cambridge: Cambridge University Press, 1982.

Murray, John. *The Epistle to the Romans.* Grand Rapids: Eerdmans, 1968.

Nanos, Mark D. "The Jewish Context of the Gentile Audience Addressed in Paul's Letter to the Romans." *The Catholic Biblical Quarterly* 61 (1999): 283–304.

———. "Paul and the Jewish Tradition: The Ideology of the *Shema*." In *Celebrating Paul: Festschrift in Honor of Jerome Murphy-O'Connor, O. P. and Joseph A. Fitzmyer, S. J.*, edited by Peter Spitaler, 62–80. CBQ/MS 48. Washington: The Catholic Biblical Association of America, 2011.

———. "Paul's Reversal of Jews Calling Gentiles 'Dogs' (Philippians 3:2): 1600 Years of an Ideological Tale Wagging an Exegetical Dog?" *Biblical Interpretation* 17, no. 4 (2009): 448–82.

———. *Romans: To the Churches of the Synagogue of Rome*, www.marknanos.com/Romans-synagogues-8-31-10.pdf.

Nash, Ronald H. *Christianity and the Hellenistic World.* Grand Rapids: Zondervan, 1984.

Neuner, Peter. "Synergism." In *The Encyclopedia of Christianity*, edited by Geoffrey W. Bromiley et al., 271–73. Grand Rapids: Eerdmans; Boston: Brill, 2001.

Neusner, Jacob. "The Conversion of Adiabene to Judaism." *Journal of Biblical Literature* 83 (1964): 60–66.

Nickelsburg, George W. E. "Stories of Biblical and Early Post-Biblical Times." In *Jewish Writings of the Second Temple Period*, edited by Michael E. Stone, CRJNT/2: LJPPSTT, Vol. 2, 33–87. Assen: Van Gorcum; Philadelphia: Fortress Press, 1984.

Nock, Arthur D. *Conversion: The Old and the New in Religion from Alexander the Great to Augustine of Hippo.* Oxford: Clarendon, 1933.

———. "Early Gentile Christianity and Its Hellenistic Background." In *Essays on the Trinity and the Incarnation*, edited by A. E. J. Rawlinson, 51–156. London: Longmans, Green, 1928.

Nygren, Anders. *Commentary on Romans*. Translated by Carl C. Rasmussen. London: SCM Press, 1952 (originally: *Romarbrevet*, 1944).

Obelitala, Alphonse. *L'initiation en Afrique noire et en Grèce: confrontation de quelques rites de passage*. Brazzaville and Heidelberg: Ed. Bantoues, 1982.

Oepke, Albrecht. "ἀνίστημι, ἐξανίστημι, ἀνάστασις, ἐξανάστασις." In *Theological Dictionary of the New Testament*, vol. 1, edited by Gerhard Kittel, 368–72. Grand Rapids: Eerdmans, 1964.

———. "ἐγείρω, ἔγερσις, ἐξεγείρω, γρηγορέω (ἀγρυπνέω)." In *Theological Dictionary of the New Testament*, vol. 2, edited by Gerhard Kittel, 333–39. Grand Rapids: Eerdmans, 1964.

Osborne, Grant R. "Resurrection." In *Dictionary of Jesus and the Gospels*, edited by J. B. Green, 673–88. Downers Grove: InterVarsity Press, 1992.

———. *Romans*. IVPNTS. Edited by Grant R. Osborne. Downers Grove: InterVarsity Press, 2004.

Parsons, Mikeal C. *Acts*, PCNT. Grand Rapids: Baker Academic, 2008.

———. "Slavery and the New Testament: Equality and Submissiveness." *Vox Evangelica* 18 (1988): 89–96.

Peace, Richard V. *Conversion in the New Testament: Paul and the Twelve*. Grand Rapids: Eerdmans, 1999.

Pellegrino, Michelle C. "Culture classique et Christianisme." In *Dictionnaire encyclopédique du christianisme ancient*, vol. 1, edited by Angelo di Berardino, Translated and edited by F. Vial, 597–602. Paris: Cerf, 1990 (originally: *Dizionario patristico e di antichità cristiane*, Genova, 1983).

Ponsot, Hervé. *Une introduction à la lettre aux Romains*. Paris: Cerf, 1988.

Porter, Stanley E. *The Paul of Acts: Essays in Literary Criticism, Rhetoric and Theology*, WUNT 115. Tubingen: Mohr Siebeck, 1999.

Pyne, Robert A., and Matthew L. Blackmon. "A Critique of the 'Exchanged Life.'" *Bibliotheca Sacra* 163 (April–June 2006): 131–57.

Quesnel, Michel. *Petite bible du baptmême*. 4th ed. Montrouge: Nouvelle cite, 1987.

Rahner, Hugo. *Greek Myths and Christian Mystery*. Translated by Brian Battershaw. New York: Harper & Row, 1963 (Originally: *Griechische Mythen in christlicher Deutung*, 1957).

Räisänen, H. "Paul's Conversion and the Development of His View of the Law." *New Testament Studies* 33 (1987): 404–19.

Rawlinson, Alfred E. J. "Corpus Christi." In *Mysterium Christi*, edited by G. K. A. Bell and D. A. Deissmann, 225–44. London: Longmans, Green, 1930.

Reitzenstein, Richard. *Hellenistic Mystery-Religions: Their Basic Ideas and Significance*. Translated by J. S. Steely. PTMS 15, edited by D. Y. Hadidian. Pittsburgh: Pickwick Press, 1978 (original: *Die hellenistischen Mysterienreligionen*).

Rengstorf, Karl H. "δοῦλος, σύνδουλος, δούλη, δουλεύω, δουλεία, δουλόω, καταδουλόω, δουλαγωγέω, ὀφθαλμοδουλία." In *Theological Dictionary of the New Testament*, vol. 2, edited by Gerhard Kittel, translated and edited by G. W. B. Bromiley, 261–80. Grand Rapids: Eerdmans, 1964.

Ridderbos, Herman. *Paul: An Outline of His Theology*. Translated by J. R. De Witt. Grand Rapids: Eerdmans, 1975.

Rose, H. J. *Ancient Roman Religion*, HUL 27. New York: Hutchinson's University Library, 1948.

Sabou, Sorin. *Between Horror and Hope: Paul's Metaphorical Language of Death in Romans 6:1–11*. Milton Keynes: Paternoster, 2005.

Salmon, Edward Togo. "Apuleius." In *The Oxford Classical Dictionary*, edited by M. Cary, M. et al, 73–74. Oxford: Clarendon, 1964 reprint (original ed., 1949).

Sanday, William, and Arthur C. Headlam. *A Critical and Exegetical Commentary on the Epistle to the Romans*. 5th ed., ICC. Edinburgh: T&T Clark, 1902.

Sanders, E. P. *Judaism: Practice and Belief, 63 B.C.E. – 66 C.E.* London: SCM, 1992.

———. *Paul and Palestinian Judaism: A Comparison of Patterns of Religion*. London: SCM Press, 1977.

Schiffman, Lawrence H. "Oaths and Vows." In *Encyclopedia of the Dead Sea Scrolls*, vol. 2, edited by L. H. Schiffman and J. C. Vanderkam, 621–23. Oxford: Oxford University Press, 2000.

Schlatter, Adolf. *Romans: The Righteousness of God*. Translated by S. S. Schatzmann. Peabody: Hendrickson, 1995 (Original: *Gottes Gerechtigkeit: Ein Kommentar zum Römerbrief*, 1935).

———. *The Church in New Testament Period*. Translated by Paul P. Levertoff. London: SPCK, 1955 (Originally: *Die Geschichte der ersten Christenheit*).

Schlier, Heinrich. *Der Römerbrief*. Freiburg, Basel and Wien: Herder, 1977.

Schnackenburg, Rudolf. *Baptism in the Thought of St. Paul: A Study in Pauline Theology*. Translated by G. R. Beasley-Murray. Oxford: Blackwell, 1964 (rev. new ed. of original dissertation of K. Zink, *Das Heilsgeschehen bei der Taufe nach dem Apostel Paulus*, 1950).

Schneiders, Sandra M. "Reflections on Commitment in the Gospel According to John." *Biblical Theology Bulletin* 8, no. 1 (1978): 40–48.

Schreider, Johannes. "ὅμοιος, ὁμοιότης, ὁμοιόω, ὁμοίωσις, ὁμοίωμα, ὀφομοιόω, παρόμοιος, παρομοιάζω." In *Theological Dictionary of the New Testament*, vol. 5, edited by Gerhard Kittel, translated and edited by G. W. B. Bromiley, 186–99. Grand Rapids: Eerdmans, 1967.

Schreiner, Thomas R. *Romans*, BECNT. Grand Rapids: Baker, 1998.

Schweitzer, Albert. *The Mysticism of Paul the Apostle*. 2nd ed. London: Black, 1967 (Originally: *Die Mystik des Apostel Paulus*, 1953, 2nd ed.).

———. *Paul and His Interpreters: A Critical History*. Translated by W. Montgomery. London: Black, 1912.

Schweizer, Eduard. "Dying and Rising with Christ." *New Testament Studies* 14 (1967–68): 1–14.

Searle, John R. *Speech Acts: An Essay in the Philosophy of Language.* Cambridge: Cambridge University Press, 1969.

Seeley, David. *The Noble Death: Graeco-Roaman Martyrology and Paul's Concept of Salvation.* Sheffield: Sheffield Academic Press, 1990.

Seesemann, Heinrich, and Georg Bertram. "πατέω, καταπατέω, περιπατέω, ἐμπεριπατέω." In *Theological Dictionary of the New Testament*, vol. 5, edited by Gerhard Kittel, 940–945. Translated and edited by G. W. B. Bromiley. Grand Rapids: Eerdmans, 1967.

Segal, Alan F. *Paul the Convert: The Apostolate and Apostasy of Saul the Pharisee.* New Haven: Yale University Press, 1990.

Selwyn, Edward G. *The First Epistle of St. Peter: The Greek Text with Introduction, Notes, and Essays.* Grand Rapids: Baker Books, 1983 reprint.

Shaw, David A. "'Then I Proceeded to Where Things Were Chaotic' (1 Enoch 21:1): Mapping the Apocalyptic Landscape." In *Paul and the Apocalyptic Imagination*, edited by B. C. Blackwell, J. K. Goodrich, and J. Maston, 465–870 (Kindle edition). Minneapolis: Fortress Press, 2016.

Sherman, Hazel. "Getting in and Staying in: Unexpected Connections between E. P. Sanders on Paul and Expectations of Baptism Today." In *Dimensions of Baptism*, BTS 234, edited by Stanley E. Porter and Antony R. Cross, 111–19. New York: Sheffield Academic Press, 2002.

Shulam, Joseph. *A Commentary on the Jewish Roots of Romans.* Baltimore: Messianic Jewish Publishers, 1998.

Siber, P. *Mit Christus leben: Eine Studie zur paulinischen Auferstehungshoffnung.* Zürich: TVZ, 1971.

Silva, Moisés. "How to Read a Letter: The Meaning of the Epistles." In *Introduction to Biblical Hermeneutics*, edited by Walter C. Kaiser and Moisés Silva, 173–88. Revised and expanded edition. Grand Rapids: Zondervan, 2007.

Simon, Marcel. *Jewish Sects at the Time of Jesus.* Translated by James H. Farley. Philadelphia: Fortress Press, 1967 (originally: *Les sectes juives au temps de Jésus*, 1960).

Skemp, J. B. *The Greeks and the Gospel.* London: Carey Kingsgate Press, 1964.

Sklba, Richard J. "The Call to New Beginnings: A Biblical Theology of Conversion." *Biblical Theology Bulletin* 11 (1981): 67–73.

Sorel, Reynal. "Mystères d'Eleusis." In *Dictionnaire de l'antiquité*, edited by Jean Leclant, 1485–1488. Paris: Presses universitaires de France, 2005.

Sourvinou-Inwood, Christiane. "Further Aspects of *Polis* Religion." In *Oxford Readings in Greek Religion*, edited by Richard Buxton, 38–55. Oxford: Oxford University Press, 2000.

———. "What is *Polis* Religion?" In *Oxford Readings in Greek Religion*, edited by Richard Buxton, 13–37. Oxford: Oxford University Press, 2000.

Stacey, David. *Groundwork of Biblical Studies*. London: Epworth, 1979.

Stendahl, Krister. *Meanings: The Bible as Document and as Guide*. Philadelphia: Fortress Press, 1984.

———. *Paul among the Jews and the Gentiles, and Other Essays*. London: Fortress Press, 1976.

Stone, Michael E. *Scriptures, Sects and Visions: A Profile of Judaism from Ezra to the Jewish Revolts*. Oxford: Blackwell, 1980.

Stowers, Stanley K. "Paul's Four Discourses about Sin." In *Celebrating Paul: Festschrift in Honor of Jerome Murphy-O'Connor, O. P. and Joseph A. Fitzmyer, S. J.*, CBQ/MS 48, edited by Peter Spitaler, 100–27. Washington: The Catholic Biblical Association of America, 2011.

Strong, Augustus H. *Systematic Theology*. London: Pickering & Inglis, 1956 reprint (originally 1907).

Stuckenbruck, Loren T. "Some Reflections on Apocalyptic Thought and Time in Literature from the Second Temple Period." In *Paul and the Apocalyptic Imagination*, edited by B. C. Blackwell, J. K. Goodrich, and J. Maston, 2595–2950 (Kindle edition). Minneapolis: Fortress Press, 2016.

Stuhlmacher, Peter. *Der Brief an die Römer*, NTD 6. Göttingen: Vandenhoeck & Ruprecht, 1989.

———. *Paul's Letter to the Romans: A Commentary*. Translated by S. J. Hafemann. Edinburgh: T&T Clark, 1994 (Original: *Der Brief an die Römer*, 1989).

Tannehill, Robert C. *Dying and Rising with Christ: A Study in Pauline Theology*. Berlin: Alfred Töpelmann, 1967.

Therrien, Gérard. *Le discernement dans les écrits pauliniens*, EB. Paris: J. Gabalda et Cie, 1973.

Thiering, B. E. "Qumran Initiation and New Testament Baptism." *New Testament Studies* 27 (1981): 615–31.

Thompson, A. J. *The Acts of the Risen Lord Jesus*, NSBT 27. Nottingham: Apollos; Downers Grove: InterVarsity Press, 2011.

Thüsing, W. *Per Christum in Deum: Das Verhältnis der Christozentrik zur Theozentrik*, 3rd ed. Münster: Aschendorff, 1986.

Thyen, H. *Studien zur Sündenvergebung im Neuen Testament und seinem alttestamentlichen und jüdischen Voraussetzungen*, FRLANT 96. Göttingen: Vandenhoeck & Ruprecht, 1970.

Tidball, Derek J. "Social Setting of Mission Churches." In *Dictionary of Paul and His Letters*, edited by G. F. Hawthorne and R. P. Martin, 883–92. Downers Grove: InterVarsity Press, 1993.

Tod, Marcus N., and Simon Hornblower. "Clubs, Greek." In *Oxford Classical Dictionary*, 3rd ed., edited by S. Hornblower and A. Spawforth, 351–52. Oxford: Oxford University Press, 1999.

Torrance, Thomas F. "The Origins of Baptism." *SJT* 11 (1958): 158–71.

———. "Proselyte Baptism." *NTS* 1 (1954–55): 150–54.

———. *Theology in Reconciliation: Essays Towards Evangelical and Catholic Unity in East and West*. London: Geoffrey Chapman, 1975.

Turner, Max. *Power from on High: The Spirit in Israel's Restoration and Witness in Luke-Acts*. Sheffield: Sheffield Academic Press, 1996.

Turner, Victor W. *The Forest of Symbols: Aspects of Ndembu Rituals*. Ithaca, NY: Cornell University Press, 1969.

Utley, Bob. *The Gospel According to Paul: Romans*. ibiblio.org/ freebiblecommentary/ pdf/EN/VOL05.pdf, 27 June 1996.

VanderKam, James C. "Covenant." In *Encyclopedia of the Dead Sea Scrolls*, vol. 1, edited by L. H. Schiffman and J. C. Vanderkam, 151–55. Oxford: Oxford University Press, 2000.

Vanhoozer, Kevin J. *Is There a Meaning in This Text?: The Bible, the Reader and the Morality of Literary Knowledge*. Leicester: Apollos, 1998.

Vermes, G. "Baptism and Jewish Exegesis: New Light from Ancient Sources." *New Testament Studies* 4 (1957–58): 308–19.

Viard, André. *Saint Paul: épître aux Romains*. SBib, Paris: Gabalda, 1975.

Wagner, Günter. *Pauline Baptism and the Pagan Mysteries: The Problem of the Pauline Doctrine of Baptism in Romans 6. 1–11, in the Light of its Religion-Historical "Parallel."* Translated by J. P. Smith. Edinburgh and London: Oliver & Boyd, 1967 (Originally: *Das religionsgeschichtliche Problem von Römer 6, 1–11*, 1962).

Walsh, Liam G. *The Sacraments of Initiation: Baptism, Confirmation, Eucharist*. London: Geoffrey Chapman, 1988.

Watson, Francis. *Paul, Judaism, and the Gentiles: Beyond the New Perspective*. Rev. and expanded editions. Grand Rapids: Eerdmans, 2007.

———. "The Two Roman Congregations: Romans 14:1–15:13." In *The Romans Debate*, rev. and expanded, edited by Karl P. Donfried, 204–15. Edinburgh: T&T Clark, 1991.

Way, David. *The Lordship of Christ: Ernest Käsemann's Interpretation of Paul's Theology*. Oxford: Clarendon Press, 1991.

Wedderburn, A. J. M. *Baptism and Resurrection: Studies in Pauline Theology against Its Greco-Roman Background*, WUNT 44. Tübingen: Mohr, 1987.

———. "The Soteriology of the Mysteries and Pauline Baptismal Theology." *Novum Testamentum* 29 (1987): 53–72.

Wei, Ebele. *Le paradis tabou: autopsie d'une culture assassinée*. Douala: CERAC, 1999.

Weinfeld, Moshe. *The Organizational Pattern and the Penal Code of the Qumran Sect: A Comparison with Guilds and Religious Associations of the Hellenistic-Roman Period*, NTOA 2. Fribourg: Editions Univeristaires and Göttingen: Vandenhoeck & Ruprecht, 1986.

Wenham, David. "Acts and the Pauline Corpus II: The Evidence of Parallels." In *The Book of Acts in its Ancient Literary Setting*, edited by Bruce W. Winter and Andrew D. Clarke, 215–58. Carlisle: Paternoster, 1993.

Westerholm, Stephen. *Perspectives Old and New on Paul: The "Lutheran" Paul and His Critics*. Grand Rapids: Eerdmans, 2004.

———. *Preface to the Study of Paul*. Grand Rapids: Eerdmans, 1997.

———. *Understanding Paul: The Early Christian Worldview of the Letter to the Romans*. 2nd ed. Grand Rapids: Baker Academic, 2004.

White, R. E. O. *The Biblical Doctrine of Initiation*. London: Hodder and Stoughton, 1960.

Wiefel, Wolfgang. "The Jewish Community in Ancient Rome and the Origins of Roman Christianity." In *The Romans Debate*, rev. and expanded edition, edited by Karl P. Donfried, 85–101. Edinburgh: T&T Clark, 1991.

Wilckens, Ulrich. *Der Brief an die Römer 1–5*, EKKNT 6/1. Zürich: Benziger Verlag and Neukirchen-Vluyn: Neukirchener Verlag, 1978.

———. *Der Brief an die Römer 6–11*, EKKNT 6/2. Zürich: Benziger Verlag and Neukirchen-Vluyn: Neukirchener Verlag, 1980.

Wright, David F. "The Baptismal Community." *Bibliotheca Sacra* 160 (January–March 2003): 3–12.

Wright, G. Ernest. *God Who Acts: Biblical Theology as Recital*, SBT 8. London: SCM, 1952.

Wright, Nicholas T. "Apocalyptic and the Sudden Fulfillment of Divine Promise." In *Paul and the Apocalyptic Imagination*, edited by B. C. Blackwell, J. K. Goodrich, and J. Maston, 2428–2433 (Kindle edition). Minneapolis: Fortress Press, 2016.

———. *Christian Origins and the Question of God, Vol.1: The New Testament and the People of God*. London: SPCK, 1992.

———. "The Messiah and the People of God." DPhil thesis, Oxford University, 1980.

———. *Surprised by Hope*. London: SPCK, 2007.

Zahniser, A. H. Mathias. *Symbols and Ceremony: Making Disciples across Cultures*, IM. Monrovia, CA: MARC, 1997.

Zempléni, Andràs. "Initiation." In *Dictionnaire de l'ethnologie et de l'anthropologie*, 2nd ed., edited by Pierre Pierre and M. Izard, 375–78. Paris: Presses Universitaires de France, 1992.

Ziesler, John A. *The Meaning of Righteousness in Paul: A Linguistic and Theological Enquiry*, SNTSMS 20. Cambridge: Cambridge University Press, 1972.

———. *Paul's Letter to the Romans*, TPINTC. London: SCM; Philadelphia: Trinity Press International, 1989.

2. Intertestamental, Greco-Roman, Rabbinic and Early Christian Writings

Ambrose (Saint). *The Sacrament of the Incarnation of our Lord* 64. Translation from Roy J. Deferrari, *Saint Ambrose: Theological and Dogmatic Works*, FC/NT 44. Washington: The Catholic University of America Press, 1963.

Ambrose of Milan. *On the Sacraments* 1.4, 12; 2.20. Translation from Thomas M. Finn, *Early Christian Baptism and the Catechumenate: Italy, North Africa, and Egypt*; MFC 6. Collegeville: Liturgical Press, 1992.

Apuleius. *The Golden Ass* xi. Translation from The Loeb Classical Library, Apuleius, *The Golden Ass: Being the Metamorphoses of Lucius Apuleius*, Trans. by W. Addlington. Cambridge: Harvard University Press; London: Heinemann, 1977.

Aristotle. *Nicomachean Ethics* iii.1.17. Translation from The Loeb Classical Library, *Aristotle, Vol. 19: The Nicomachean Ethics*. Trans. by H. Rackham. Cambridge: Harvard University Press; London: Heinemann, 1982.

———. *Art of Rhetoric* ii.24.2. Translation from the Loeb Classical Library, *Aristotle, Vol. 22: The Art of Rhetoric*. Trans. by J. H. Freese. Cambridge: Harvard University Press; London: Heinemann, 1975.

Chrysostom. *Baptismal Instruction* 10.10. Translation from Gerald Bray (ed.), *Romans*, ACCS/NT 6, gen. ed. Thomas C. Oden. Downers Grove: InterVarsity Press, 1998.

Chrysostom. *Homilies on Romans*, II. Translation from Gerald Bray (ed.), *Romans*, ACCS/NT 6, gen. ed. Thomas C. Oden. Downers Grove: InterVarsity Press, 1998.

Cyril of Jerusalem. *Catechesis* 3. Translation from Thomas M. Finn, *Early Christian Baptism and the Catechumenate: West and East Syria*, MFC 5. Collegeville: Liturgical Press, 1992.

Demosthenes. *De Corona* 259. Translation from The Loeb Classical Library, Demosthenes, *De Corona*, vol. 2, trans. by C. A. Vine and J. H. Vine. Cambridge: Harvard University Press, 1992.

The Didachè, I–VII. Translation from Philip Schaff, *The Teaching of the Twelve Apostles (DIDAXH TWN DWDEKA APOSTOLWN) or the Oldest Church Manual*, 3rd ed., rev. and enlarged. New York: Funk & Wagnalis, 1889.

Dio Chrysostom. *Discourses* 17.5. Translation from The Loeb Classical Library, *Dio Chrysostom*, vol. 2, trans. by J. W. Cohoon. Cambridge: Harvard University Press; London: Heinemann, 1977.

Epictetus. *Discourses* iii.13–17, 21. Translation from The Loeb Classical Library, *Epictetus: The Discourses as Reported by Arrian, the Manual, and Fragments*, vol. 2. Trans. by W. A. Oldfather. Cambridge: Harvard University Press; London: Heinemann, 1978.

Josephus, Flavius. *Against Apion* ii.283. Translation from The Loeb Classical Library, *Josephus I: The Life* and *Against Apion*, trans. by J. Thackeray. London: Heinemann; Cambridge: Harvard University Press, 1966.

———. *Life* 10. Translation from The Loeb Classical Library, *Josephus I: The Life* and *Against Apion*, LCL, trans. by J. Thackeray. London: Heinemann; Cambridge: Harvard University Press, 1966.

———. *Jewish Antiquities* xviii.117, xx.38–41. Translation from The Loeb Classical Library, *Josephus IX: Jewish Antiquities xviii–xx*, trans. By L. H. Feldman. London: Heinemann; Cambridge: Harvard University Press, 1969.

———. *Jewish War* ii.137–142, 145. Translation from The Loeb Classical Library, *Josephus II: The Jewish War i–iii*, trans. by J. Thackeray. London: Heinemann; Cambridge: Harvard University Press, 1967.

———. *Jewish War* vii.45. Translation from The Loeb Classical Library, *Josephus III: The Jewish War iv–vii*, trans. by J. Thackeray. London: Heinemann; Cambridge,: Harvard University Press, 1968 reprint.

Joseph and Aseneth. Translation from C. Burchard, "Joseph and Aseneth." In *The Old Testament Pseudepigrapha*, edited by J. H. Charlesworth, vol. 2, 177–247. London: Darton, Longman & Todd, 1985.

———. Translation from D. Cook, "Joseph and Aseneth." In *The Apocryphal Old Testament*, edited by H. F. D. Sparks, 465–503. Oxford: Clarendon, 1984.

Judith 14:10. From *The Septuagint with Apocrypha: Greek and English*. Peabody: Hendrickson, 2009.

Lucian. *Hermotimus or Concerning the Sects* 4. Translation from The Loeb Classical Library, *Lucian*, vol. 6, trans. by K. Kilburn. Cambridge: Harvard University Press; London: Heinemann, 1968.

Lycophron. *Alexandra* 1325–29; Translation from The Loeb Classical Library, Lycophron, *Callimachus, Lycophron, Aratus*, trans. by A. W. Mair and G. R. Mair. Cambridge: Harvard University Press; London: Heinemann, 1977.

The Mishna, *Eduyoth* 5.2. Translation from Philip Blackman, "Eduyoth." *Mishnayoth, Vol. 4: Nezikin*, 2nd ed. Gateshead: Judaica Press, 1977.

———. *Mikevaoth* 1.7. Translation from Philip Blackman, "Mikevaoth." *Mishnayoth, Vol. 6: Taharoth*, 2nd ed. Gateshead: Judaica Press, 1977.

———. *Miqvaot* 7:7. Translation from J. Neusner. *The Mishnah: A New Translation*. New Haven: Yale University Press, 1988.

———. *Pesachim* 8.8. Translation from Philip Blackman, *Mishnayoth, Vol. 2: Moed*, 2nd ed. Gateshead: Judaica Press, 1977.

Origen. *Homily 14.1*. Translation from T. M. Finn, *Early Christian Baptism and the Catechumenate*, MFC 6. Collegeville: Liturgical Press, 1992.

Origen. *Spirit and Fire*. Translation from Balthasar, Hans Urs von (ed.), *Origen: Spirit and Fire: A Thematic Anthology of His Writings*. Trans. by R. J. Daly. Edinburgh: T&T Clark, 2001 reprint (Originally: *Origenes GEIST UND FEUER: Ein Aufbau aus seinen Schriften*, 1938).

Philo. *Decalogue* 85–86. Translation from The Loeb Classical Library, *Philo*, Vol. 7. Trans. by F. H. Colson. London: Heinemann; Cambridge: Harvard University Press, 1958.

———. *On the Virtues* 102, 178, 219. Translation from The Loeb Classical Library, *Philo*, vol. 8. Trans. by F. H. Colson. London: Heinemann; Cambridge: Harvard University Press, 1968.

———. *On the Giants (De Gigantibus)* 14–15. Translation from The Loeb Classical Library, *Philo*, vol. 2. Trans. by F. H. Colson and G. H. Whitaker. London: Heinemann; Cambridge: Harvard University Press, 1968.

———. Quaest. Exod. ii.51. Translation from The Loeb Classical Library, Philo, *Supplement, Vol. 2: Questions and Answers on Exodus*. Trans. by R. Marcus. Cambridge: Harvard University Press; London: Heinemann, 1970.

———. Quaest. Gen. iv.8. Translation from The Loeb Classical Library, Philo, *Supplement, Vol. 1: Questions and Answers on Genesis*. Trans. by R. Marcus. Cambridge: Harvard University Press; London: Heinemann, 1979.

Plato. *Gorgias* 497c. Translation from the Loeb Classical Library, Plato, *Lysis, Symposium, Gorgias*. Trans. by W. R. M. Lamb. Cambridge: Harvard University Press, 1925.

———. *Phaedrus* 249b–d. Translation from The Loeb Classical Library, Plato, *Euthyphro, Apology, Crito, Phaedo, Phaedrus*, Vol. 1. Trans. by H. N. Fowler. Cambridge: Harvard University Press; London: Heinemann, 1977.

———. *Symposium* 210a. Translation from the Loeb Classical Library, Plato, *Lysis, Symposium, Gorgias*. Trans. by W. R. M. Lamb. Cambridge: Harvard University Press, 1925.

Pliny. *Letters* x. 96.5. Translation from The Loeb Classical Library, Pliny, *Letters and Panegyricus, Vol. 2: Books viii–x and Panegyricus*. Trans. by Betty Radice. Cambridge: Harvard University Press; London: Heinemann, 1975.

Plutarch. *On Exile* 604c. Translation from the Loeb Classical Library, *Plutarch's Moralia*, Vol. 7. Trans. by P. H. De Lacy and B. Einarson. Cambridge: Harvard University Press; London: Heinemann, 1968.

———. *Table-Talk* i.4.621.c. Translation from the Loeb Classical Library, *Plutarch's Moralia*, Vol. 8. Trans. by P. A. Clement and H. B. Hoffleit. Cambridge: Harvard University Press; London: Heinemann, 1969.

———. *Obsolescence of Oracles* 417a, 417b. Translation from The Loeb Classical Library, *Plutarch's Moralia*, Vol. 5. Trans. by F. C. Babbitt. Cambridge: Harvard University Press; London: Heinemann, 1984.

———. *A Letter to Apollonius* 107e. Translation from The Loeb Classical Library, *Plutarch's Moralia*, Vol. 2. Trans. by F. C. Babbitt. Cambridge: Harvard University Press; London: Heinemann, 1971.

———. *On the Malice of Herodotus* 857c. Translation from The Loeb Classical Library, *Plutarch's Moralia*, Vol. 9. Trans. by L. Pearson and F. H. Sandbach. Cambridge: Harvard University Press; London: Heinemann, 1970.

The Shepherd of Hermas. *His Commands* 4.3. Translation from E. Burton. *Apostolic Fathers*, Vol. 1. Edinburgh: John Grant, 1909.

The Talmud (Babylonian), *Abodah Zarah* 57a. Translation from A. Mishcon and A. Cohen, "Abodah Zarah." *b. Seder Nezkin*, Vol. 4. Edited by Isidore Epstein. London: Soncino Press, 1935.

———. *Bekoroth* 47a. Translation from L. Miller and Maurice Simon, "Bekoroth." *b. Seder Kodashim*, Vol. 3. Edited by I. Epstein. London: Soncino Press, 1948.

———. *Kerithoth* 8b–9a. Translated from I. Porusch, "Kerithoth." *b. Seder Kodashim*, Vol. 3. Edited by I. Epstein. London: Soncino Press, 1948.

———. *Kiddushin* 62a–b. Translated from H. Freedman. "Keddushin." *b. Seder Nashim*, Vol. 4. Edited by I. Epstein. London: Soncino Press, 1936.

———. *Pesahim* 92a. Translated from H. Freedman. "Pesahim." *b. Seder Mo'ed*, Vol. 2. Edited by I. Epstein. London: Soncino Press, 1938.

———. *Sanhedrin* 56a–58b. Translated from J. Schachter and H. Freedman. "Sanhedrin." *b. Seder Nezikin*, Vol. 3. Edited by I. Epstein. London: Soncino Press, 1935.

———. *Yebamoth* 22a; 47a–b; 48b; 62a. Translated from Israel W. Slotki. "Yebamoth." *b. Seder Nashim*, Vol. 1. Edited by Isidore Epstein. London: Soncino Press, 1936.

Tertullian. *On Penance* 6. Translation from William P. Le Saint. Tertullian, *Treatises on Penance: On Penance and on Purity*, ACW 28. Westminster: Newman Press; London: Longmans, Green, 1959.

Tosefta, *Pisha* 7.14. Translation from Jacob Neusner, "Pisha (Pesahim)." *The Tosefta: Moed*. New York: KTAV, 1981.

Wisdom of Solomon 14:22. Translation from *The Septuagint with Apocrypha: Greek and English*. Peabody: Hendrickson, 2009.

3. Reference Books

Balz, Horst, and G. Schneider, eds. *Exegetical Dictionary of the New Testament*. 3 vols. Grand Rapids: Eerdmans, 1990.

Bullinger, E. W. *A Critical Lexicon and Concordance to the English and Greek New Testament*. Grand Rapids, MI: Kregel, 1999 (originally 1908).

Carrez, Maurice. *Nouveau Testament interlinéaire grec/français*. Swindon: British and Foreign Bible Society, 1993.

Collins German Dictionary, siebte Auflage. 2007.

A Concordance to the Apocrypha/Deuterocanonical Books of the Revised Standard Version. Grand Rapids: Eerdmans; London: Collins Liturgical Publications, 1983.

Danker, F. William, ed. *A Greek-English Lexicon of the New Testament and other Early Christian Literature*, 3rd ed. Chicago: University of Chicago Press, 2000.

Green, Jay, ed. *The Interlinear Hebrew/Greek English Bible, Vol. 1: Genesis – Ruth*. Wilmington: Associated Publishers and Authors, 1976.

Hatch, Edwin, and H. A. Redpath, eds. *Concordance to the Septuagint and the other Greek Versions of the Old Testament (Including the Apocryphal Books)*, 2nd ed. Grand Rapids, MI: Baker Books, 1998.

Hornblower, S., and A. Spawforth, eds. *Oxford Classical Dictionary*, 3rd ed. Oxford: Oxford University Press, 1999; and the ed. of 1949.

Kaiser, Walter C., and Moisés Silva. *Introduction to Biblical Hermeneutics: The Search for Meanings*, rev. and expanded ed. Grand Rapids: Zondervan, 2007.

Klein, William W., Craig L. Blomberg, and Robert L. Hubbard. *Introduction to Biblical Interpretation*, rev. and updated. Nashville: Nelson, 2004.

Kohlenberger III, John R., ed. *NIV Interlinear Hebrew-English Old Testament*, 4 Vols. Grand Rapids: Zondervan, 1987.

Kohlenberger III, John R., E. W. Goodrick, and J. A. Swanson. *The Greek English Concordance to the New Testament*. Grand Rapids, MI: Zondervan, 1997.

Lampe, G. W. H., ed. *A Patristic Greek Lexicon*. Oxford: Clarendon, 1961.

Liddell, Henry G., and R. Scott, eds. *A Greek-English Lexicon*, new ed. Oxford: Clarendon, 1940. Electronic version: LSJ 1940, s.v. "εἰς or ἐς", at https://outils.biblissima.fr/en/eulexis-web/index.php.

Louw, Johannes P., and Eugene A. Nida, ed. *Greek-English Lexicon of the New Testament:* Based on Semantic Domains, vol. 1. New York: United Bible Societies, 1988.

Manton, J. D. *Introduction to Theological German*. Grand Rapids: Eerdmans; Eugene, OR: Wipf & Stock, 2004.

Martinez, Florentino Garcia. *The Dead Sea Scrolls Translated: The Qumran Texts in English*, 2nd ed. Trans. Wilfred G. E. Watson. Leiden: Brill; Grand Rapids: Eerdmans, 1996.

Morrish, George. *A Concordance of the Septuagint*. Grand Rapids: Regency, 1976 reprint (originally: S. Bagster and Sons, 1887).

Moulton, James H., and George Milligan. *The Vocabulary of the Greek Testament: Illustrated from the Papyri and Other Non-Literary Sources*. Grand Rapids: Eerdmans, 1974 reprint (ed. 1930).

Mounce, William D. *The Analytical Lexicon to the Greek New Testament*. Grand Rapids, MI: Zondervan, 1993.

Porter, Stanley E. *Idioms of the Greek New Testament*, BLG 2. Sheffield: JSOT Press, 1992.

The Septuagint with Apocrypha: Greek and English. Peabody: Hendrickson, 2009.

Slotki, Judah J. *Index Volume to the Soncino Talmud*. The Babylonian Talmud, edited by Isidore Epstein. London: The Soncino Press, 1952.

Taylor, Bernard A. *Analytical Lexicon to the Septuagint*, expanded ed., with word definitions by J. Lust, E. Eynikel, and K. Hauspie. Peabody: Hendrickson, 2009.

Vermes, Geza. *The Complete Dead Sea Scrolls in English*, rev. ed. London: Penguin Books, 2004.

Wallace, Daniel B. *Greek Grammar Beyond the Basics: An Exegetical Syntax of the New Testament with Scripture*. Grand Rapids: Zondervan, 1996.

Langham Literature, with its publishing work, is a ministry of Langham Partnership.

Langham Partnership is a global fellowship working in pursuit of the vision God entrusted to its founder John Stott –

> **to facilitate the growth of the church in maturity and Christ-likeness through raising the standards of biblical preaching and teaching.**

Our vision is to see churches in the Majority World equipped for mission and growing to maturity in Christ through the ministry of pastors and leaders who believe, teach and live by the word of God.

Our mission is to strengthen the ministry of the word of God through:
- nurturing national movements for biblical preaching
- fostering the creation and distribution of evangelical literature
- enhancing evangelical theological education

especially in countries where churches are under-resourced.

Our ministry

Langham Preaching partners with national leaders to nurture indigenous biblical preaching movements for pastors and lay preachers all around the world. With the support of a team of trainers from many countries, a multi-level programme of seminars provides practical training, and is followed by a programme for training local facilitators. Local preachers' groups and national and regional networks ensure continuity and ongoing development, seeking to build vigorous movements committed to Bible exposition.

Langham Literature provides Majority World preachers, scholars and seminary libraries with evangelical books and electronic resources through publishing and distribution, grants and discounts. The programme also fosters the creation of indigenous evangelical books in many languages, through writer's grants, strengthening local evangelical publishing houses, and investment in major regional literature projects, such as one volume Bible commentaries like the *Africa Bible Commentary* and the *South Asia Bible Commentary*.

Langham Scholars provides financial support for evangelical doctoral students from the Majority World so that, when they return home, they may train pastors and other Christian leaders with sound, biblical and theological teaching. This programme equips those who equip others. Langham Scholars also works in partnership with Majority World seminaries in strengthening evangelical theological education. A growing number of Langham Scholars study in high quality doctoral programmes in the Majority World itself. As well as teaching the next generation of pastors, graduated Langham Scholars exercise significant influence through their writing and leadership.

To learn more about Langham Partnership and the work we do visit **langham.org**

www.ingramcontent.com/pod-product-compliance
Lightning Source LLC
Chambersburg PA
CBHW051538230426
43669CB00015B/2643

Pontien Batibuka shows us how far we are removed today from the early church when one's baptism was understood as the most important and maybe the most frightening experience of one's life. Most Christians today are baptized in infancy. Many of those who are baptized as adults come from Christian families and have grown up in the Christian faith. This means that baptism is simply a practice they are used to since childhood. In this way, baptism has become more of a ritual than what the apostle Paul meant it to be when writing Romans 6.

For the Christians of the first century to whom Paul addresses his letter, baptism was a radical event. As an act of initiation to a new world, it was understood as a radical decision to renounce allegiance to all other authorities in the empire and to oneself, and to surrender one's life to Christ alone as Lord. This submission required the deliberate and daily effort of the baptized to please the Lord Jesus and to build the new community of believers.

This book should be carefully read, discussed and contextualized by African theologians to help the church recapture what it has lost: the true meaning of baptism.

Bungishabaku Katho, PhD
Dean, Graduate School at Shalom University of Bunia,
Senior Researcher,
Centre de Recherche Multidisciplinaire pour le Développement de Bunia,
Democratic Republic of the Congo

In this fascinating study, Dr. Pontien Batibuka analyses Romans 5:12-6:23 as a multi-faceted account of Christian initiation. By comparing this with ancient Graeco-Roman and Jewish initiation processes, and with Paul's own experience, Batibuka very effectively brings out four stages of Christian initiation: encounter with God, death to the old self, identification with Christ in baptism, and the move into the new, committed life. In mapping this pattern onto Romans 5:12-6:23, Batibuka particularly argues for the active role of the believer in responding to God's gracious action. This study offers enlightening food for thought, both for those interpreting Romans and for those considering the pattern of initiation in churches today.

Peter Oakes PhD
Rylands Professor of Biblical Criticism and Exegesis,
University of Manchester, UK

Pontien Batibuka adds a significant element to the debate about Christian baptism. He addresses the instrumentality of baptism in the context of a process which concludes with the initiatory claims of Christ in regard to baptism as a spiritual transition from death to life. But it is the ongoing address of the reality of baptism, as an active rather than passive process, which pertains to the believer that gets much needed attention in this study and allows for a rethinking of its place within the *ordo salutis*. These two elements come together with the necessary emphasis upon the grace of our Lord Jesus Christ, which allows for the once for all Christian initiation and the ongoing testimony of a secure reality contextually explored within the pericope of Romans 5:12–6:23.

Raymond Potgieter, PhD
Senior Research Professor, Systematic Theology and Apologetics,
North West University, South Africa

Paul's understanding of baptism is much debated, including whether baptism is divine or human action. Dr. Batibuka offers a fresh approach to the question through a fourfold model of initiation drawn from the ancient world: an encounter with the divine, a break with the old way of life and attachment to the new, a public ceremony of transfer, and a commitment to a new way of life. The application of this model to Paul's own conversion and to Romans 5–6 is thoughtful and engaging, drawing on a wide range of scholarship. It is particularly good to see Francophone scholarship well represented. Dr. Batikbuka argues cogently that both divine initiative and responsive human dimensions of baptism are indispensable. To be baptized entails: a life-changing encounter with God-in-Christ; a change of allegiance to Christ; a public, ceremonial expression of that change in water; and a commitment to a new life with Christ as Lord. This thoughtful study deserves a wide readership.

Steve Walton, PhD
Professor of New Testament,
Trinity College, Bristol, UK